The Reality of the Resurrection

The Reality of the Resurrection
The New Testament Witness

Stefan Alkier

Leroy A. Huizenga

TRANSLATOR

BAYLOR UNIVERSITY PRESS

The Reality of the Resurrection was originally published in German as *Die Realität der Auferweckung in, nach und mit den Schriften des Neuen Testaments* © 2009 Narr Francke Attempto Verlag GmbH + Co. KG. English translation by Leroy A. Huizenga, with David Moffitt.

Library of Congress Cataloging-in-Publication Data

Alkier, Stefan.
    [Realität der Auferweckung in, nach und mit den Schriften des Neuen Testaments. English]
    The reality of the resurrection : the New Testament witness / Stefan Alkier ; Translated by Leroy A. Huizenga ; Foreword by Richard B. Hays.
    351 pages cm
    "The Reality of the Resurrection was originally published in German as Die Realität der Auferweckung in, nach und mit den Schriften des Neuen Testaments © 2009 Narr Francke Attempto Verlag GmbH + Co. KG. English translation by Leroy A. Huizenga, with David Moffitt."
    Includes bibliographical references and index.
    ISBN 978-1-60258-977-3 (pbk. : alk. paper)
    1. Resurrection—Biblical teaching. 2. Jesus Christ—Resurrection. 3. Bible. N.T.—Criticism, interpretation, etc. I. Title.
    BS2545.R47A4513 2013
    232'.5—dc23
                                    2013008945

Printed in the United States of America on acid-free paper with a minimum of 30% post-consumer waste recycled content.

For my father

Friedrich Anton Alkier

(1930–2005)

The reality of things consists in their persistent forcing themselves
upon our recognition.

—Charles Sanders Peirce
(1893 paper on "Fallibilism, Continuity, and Evolution"; CP 1.175)

Thus I stand here, then, with my comfort and my hope alone in the Word of
Scripture, modest and yet so rich, "It doth not yet appear what we shall be,
but we know that when he appears we shall be like him, for we shall see him
as he is" [1 John 3:2], and in the powerful prayer of the Lord: "Father, I would
that where I am, they also may be whom Thou hast given me" [John 17:24].

—Friedrich D. E. Schleiermacher, on the occasion of the burial
of his son Nathanael on November 1, 1829
(translated in *This Incomplete One*)

What God has promised, he is also able to do.

—Paul, Romans 4:21b

Table of Contents

Foreword to the English Edition

Readers in the English-speaking world should welcome this translation of Stefan Alkier's book *Die Realität der Auferweckung in, nach und mit den Schriften des Neuen Testaments*. This is a thought-provoking work that not only makes a significant contribution to theological debates about the resurrection but also offers fresh perspectives on the relation between biblical studies and theology.

Alkier shows that the NT's understanding of the resurrection of Jesus is inextricably bound together with its discourse about the general eschatological resurrection of the dead. For the New Testament authors, Jesus' resurrection is not an isolated miracle, but a crucial revelatory disclosure concerning the nature of reality, the identity of God, and the destiny of human beings. For that reason, the interpretation of the resurrection necessarily entails not only historical but also theological and existential dimensions. Alkier's study insists on keeping these dimensions in play together, as components of a complex interpretative conversation.

The structure of Alkier's book is threefold. The first, and lengthiest, section offers a thorough descriptive exegetical survey of "Die Rede von der Auferweckung in den Schriften des Neuen Testaments" ("Resurrection Discourse in the Scriptures of the New Testament: Exegetical Investigations"). For the purposes of this analysis, he divides the NT literature into five subsections: the Pauline epistolary literature, the Letter to the

Hebrews, the Synoptic Gospels and Acts, the Johannine writings (including the Apocalypse), and the Catholic Epistles. This ordering of the material might suggest an attempt to produce something like a developmental history of early Christian teaching on the resurrection, with the early Pauline material placed first and organized in chronological order of composition (1 Thessalonians, Galatians, 1 Corinthians, 2 Corinthians, Romans, Philippians, and Philemon, followed by the Deutero-Pauline and Pastoral Letters) rather than in canonical order. But this would be in fact a slightly misleading impression, for the chief aim of Alkier's exposition is not to reconstruct a historical line of development, but rather to portray the way in which each of the NT writings proclaims the resurrection of the Crucified One within its own distinctive narrative/theological symbolic world.

As Alkier formulates the question, "Wie wird die Rede von der Auferweckung in den Schriften des Neuen Testaments gestaltet und wodurch erhält sie dort ihre Plausibilität?" ("How is resurrection discourse in the New Testament formulated, and how does it maintain its plausibility?") His consistent attention to this issue gives his descriptive survey a much broader and more balanced perspective than one finds in most strictly historical treatments of the resurrection in the NT; such treatments have tended to focus narrowly on a few passages such as 1 Corinthians 15, 1 Thessalonians 4:13-18, and the resurrection narratives in the Gospels, considered in isolation from the narrative or discursive context in which they occur. By contrast, Alkier offers skillful literary readings of each NT writing that show how the resurrection is woven into the fabric of the entire work. For example, his handling of the material in Luke and Acts demonstrates that in these texts the resurrection is both the decisive fulfillment of Israel's scriptures and "der Grundgedanke, den das Lukasevangelium und dann auch die Apostelgeschichte narrativ gestalten" ("the fundamental idea undergirding the narrative form of both the Gospel of Luke and the Acts of the Apostles").

One possible criticism of Alkier's organization of the material would concern his decision to treat the Apocalypse as part of the Johannine writings. While this grouping of material has a certain traditional justification, almost surely the Apocalypse is not the product of the author of the Gospel of John or the author(s) of the Johannine Epistles; furthermore, its whole theological/symbolic world differs materially from that of the other Johannine writings. Particularly with regard to the resurrection, the Apocalypse is much more strongly stamped by Jewish apocalyptic thought. For all these reasons, it really deserves to be categorized separately from the Gospel and Epistles. But this is a minor criticism that concerns only the organization of the material. With regard to matters of substance, Alkier's exposition of the role of resurrection in the Apocalypse is clear, accurate, and powerful—particularly his understanding of "Die kosmische Macht des auferweckten Gekreutzigten als Grund des Hoffens und Ausharrens in der Nachfolge der Zeugenschaft Jesu Christi" ("The Cosmic Power of the Resurrected Crucified One as the Ground of Hope and Perseverance in Discipleship after the Witness of Jesus Christ").

In the second major section of the book, Alkier addresses the systematic theological interpretation of the NT's discourse about resurrection. Here the governing question is "Wie kann nach der Wahrnehmung der neutestamentlichen Rede von der Auferweckung die Auferweckung Jesu Christi und die Auferweckung der Toten heute gedacht werden?" ("How can one think of the resurrection of Jesus Christ and the resurrection of the dead according to the perception of resurrection discourse in the New Testament?"). Alkier develops his response to this challenging question with the aid of "Das Realitätskonzept kategorialer Semiotik" ("the reality-concept of categorical semiotics"), a theoretical framework heavily indebted to the work of the American philosopher Charles Sanders Peirce. It is this part of the book that is most hermeneutically innovative, and therefore likely to produce the most controversy among readers and reviewers. Peirce's categories of "firstness," "secondness," and "thirdness" (Peirce's own original coinages) provide the analytical framework for Alkier's hermeneutical deliberations. In this brief introduction I cannot hope to do justice to the conceptual sophistication of Alkier's discussion. Let it suffice to say that his semiotic method allows him to affirm the reality of the resurrection without falling into either a fundamentalist literalism or a modernist reductionism. Instead, in Alkier's interpretation the resurrection actually leads us to develop a new epistemology and a new understanding of reality, in which the resurrection of the Crucified One is a sign (*Zeichen*) of the living, merciful, and just creator God who desires to redeem and restore all creation. Alkier's use of Peirce enables him to transcend the dichotomy between myth and history that has dominated biblical interpretation since the Enlightenment, and especially since Bultmann. This is one of the chief reasons that Alkier's book needs to be read and discussed in the English-speaking world.

In the third and final part of the book, Alkier sketches briefly the way in which his interpretation of the resurrection might impact the praxis of churches and schools. He gives particular attention to the teaching of religion in schools and to the church's practices of funeral services and the Lord's Supper. This last section, though it is brief, is a particularly unusual and important feature of the book. Typically, NT scholarship confines itself to narrowly conceived *wissenschaftlichen* accounts of past historical texts and events. Even where NT scholarship has dared to move beyond historical description to engage issues of hermeneutics, it is rare to find a scholarly work of this quality that ventures specific proposals about the church's practices in our time. Alkier is to be applauded for moving the discussion to this level of concretely embodied communal action. In the United States, there has recently been quite a lot of interest in "practices" as a focal point for theology and ministry; however, this movement has been driven, to a large extent, either by American pragmatism or, in its more sophisticated versions, by an Aristotelian stream of thought mediated by the work of Alasdair MacIntyre and Stanley Hauerwas. But rarely has this interest in praxis been informed by or contributed to careful engagement with biblical hermeneutics. Alkier's final section offers a fascinating illustration of how his semiotic model can enable the scriptural texts to be "cashed out" in the living praxis of Christians today, in a way that has hermeneutical integrity.

In order to understand the contribution of *The Reality of the Resurrection*, it may be helpful to situate Alkier's contribution in relation to other recent works in the realm of English scholarship. I identify three general approaches that have been influential.

The first is a view of the resurrection as a mythical fiction developed in early Christianity. In some cases, advocates of this position regard belief in the resurrection as a naive precritical error (similar to the position of Gerd Lüdemann); in other cases, the category of myth is treated more sympathetically as a sort of poetic construct that can be embraced by theology (e.g., Marcus Borg, John Shelby Spong). The second approach is the comparative historical approach of N. T. Wright. In his book *The Resurrection of the Son of God*, Wright sifts the NT evidence carefully, compares it to other ancient ideas about death and afterlife, and argues robustly in favor of the historical factuality of the resurrection of Jesus. But this eight-hundred-page opus does not focus primarily on hermeneutical issues. (Wright's later popular book, *Surprised by Hope*, does address the pastoral and practical implications of his understanding of resurrection.) The third major approach is that of Dale Allison, whose book *Resurrecting Jesus* seeks to interpret the NT's resurrection accounts on the analogy of comparative social psychology and various anecdotal reports of communication with the dead.

Against the background of these studies, Alkier's book will prove provocative because it does not fit into any of these boxes. Rather than attempting to fit resurrection into modernity's conceptual categories, whether positively or negatively, Alkier insists on an intellectual revolution, a transformation of the mind brought about by the resurrection as a real event—that is, by the power of God. In this respect, the book is more deeply theological than are the other positions described above, while at the same time offering the prospect of doing justice to the NT documents on their own terms. One of the merits of Alkier's study is that he firmly binds the message of the resurrection to the word of the cross; he never allows the reader to forget that the resurrection proclaimed in the NT is the resurrection of the Crucified One—and consequently that this event can be only an act of God and a disclosure of God's love and power.

In its English-language form, *The Reality of the Resurrection* will no doubt provoke much debate and discussion about questions that stand at the heart of the New Testament's message. Readers of these pages will be brought into a deeper encounter with a proclamation that the Apostle Paul describes as a matter of "first importance"—not only for the early Christian communities but also for the shaping of our communities today.

Richard B. Hays
Durham, N.C.
November 11, 2012

Foreword to the German Edition

While the study at hand is indeed a monograph, many have contributed to the generation of the idea of writing a book about resurrection discourse in the New Testament, but thanking all those with whom I have discussed the concept and constituent parts by name would go beyond the scope of a foreword. Therefore I would thank all my conversation partners of recent years, above all those Frankfurt students in the Department of Protestant Theology and also those students of the university of the third *Lebensalter* (post-60). Their questions have prompted me to write the third part of the book. In addition, numerous lectures given in congregational, academic, and continuing educational contexts on the topic of resurrection have also made a contribution, from which I have learned how very much the question of one's own death and the possibility of life after death continues to engage people existentially even today.

I thank our children Max, Florian, and Julian. Their thoughts and questions on the occasion of the deaths of their grandparents Dieter Karweick, Emmi Karweick, and Friedrich Anton Alkier inside the space of a single year were decisive in my reworking of the present academic project in an existentially grounded direction.

A seminar on the topic of resurrection I offered with Hermann Deuser, my teacher and colleague, made it clear to me that the book needed a systematic section that would set forth a conception of reality that is conceivable today, and with which the biblical witness to the reality of the resurrection of Jesus Christ and the hope in the resurrection of the dead can be interpreted for the present day. I owe him a special debt of gratitude, for he accompanied the evolution of the book in all its phases and, with his clear and creative thinking, considerably furthered it.

Finally I thank all my colleagues who have provided me with the opportunity to present my exegetical investigations of resurrection discourse in the New Testament, and to assess it through their expertise, in the context of the Frankfurt Society for the New Testament and through invitations to give guest lectures. Here I offer my special thanks to Andrea Bencsik, Kristina Dronsch, Richard B. Hays, Werner Kahl, Eckart Reinmuth, Guntram Schindel, Michael Schneider, and Heiko Schulz, who, like Hermann Deuser, furthered the evolution of the book from start to finish with their insights and inquiries.

I thank the deanery of the Department of Protestant Theology and the presidium of Goethe University for the approval of a research semester, which permitted me to lay the cornerstone of the present monograph.

I thank Friedrich W. Horn, Oda Wischmeyer, and Hanna Zapp for accepting the book for publication in the series that they publish, *Neutestamentliche Entwürfe zur Theologie*. I thank François Vouga for his encouragement to conceive a monograph on the topic of resurrection for this series. I thank Michael Schneider and Katrin Krüger for the technical production of the manuscript. To them as well as to Kristina Dronsch and Sylvia Usener thanks are due for their efforts in proofreading.

I thank Francke Verlag for over ten years of fruitful collaboration, especially editor Susanne Fischer, who also oversees the *Zeitschrift für Neues Testament* with her usual competence and amiability. I also thank the publisher Günter Narr, who through his academic, cultural, and human concerns not only makes possible the publication of the successful *ZNT* but also tackles theological book projects again and again.

Above all I thank my wife, Stefanie E. Alkier-Karweick, who in multifold ways aided in the generation of the present monograph: as a theological conversation partner, as a pastor with experience in theological praxis in school and at the deathbed in nursing homes, as an interested and critical reader of manuscripts, and as a caring life partner even in situations in which the desire for academic work and teaching was often supplanted through the burden of the many time-intensive demands of university administration. I am pleased that with the publication of this monograph my research project concerning "the reality of the resurrection" has come to a conclusion for the time being. I thank you, dear reader, as your reading of this monograph frees it from the narrow limits of the monologue and returns it to the dialogue from which it came.

Stefan Alkier
Frankfurt/Bochum
Advent 2008

The Problem, the Concern, and the Structure of the Investigation

The belief about the resurrection of the crucified Jesus of Nazareth determines the textual collection of the New Testament to a decisive degree. Discourse concerning the resurrection of the dead is bound up with it. The present investigation approaches the question of the reality of the resurrection in three steps: (1) How is resurrection discourse in the New Testament formulated, and how does it maintain its plausibility? (2) How can one think of the resurrection of Jesus Christ and the resurrection of the dead according to the perception of resurrection discourse in the New Testament? (3) How can one speak of resurrection with regard to praxis in contemporary educational and ecclesial contexts in a manner commensurate with the fact of the canonical connection between the scriptures of the Old Testament and the scriptures of the New Testament?

Having laid out the investigation in this way, I would like to counteract the double narrowing of the location of the question within New Testament studies. One narrowing consists in the extensive reduction of the discussion to two historical questions: (1) Was Jesus' tomb empty after Easter, or not? (2) Were the appearances of the resurrected Crucified One recounted in 1 Corinthians 15 subjective visions, and thus hallucinations to be explained psychologically, or objective visions, which permitted something to be seen that is not dissolved into individual or sociopsychological explanations? Both questions lie along the lines of attempts at historico-empirical reconstruction, and for many today these questions appear to decide the question of the reality of the resurrection. For some, the acceptance of a body in the tomb is tantamount to the end of the truth of Christianity. For others, the acceptance of an empty tomb is tantamount to a biblicism that enables the maintaining of a closed-minded ignorance of the significance of the natural sciences for understanding the world. Indeed, both groups come together to the extent that the question of the empirical condition of the tomb after Easter must be answered if one wants to say something about the reality of the resurrection. But is that the perspective of the New Testament scriptures? Does their understanding of reality rest on the same level of argumentation as that of the historical questions concerning the empty tomb and the nature of visions?

Even if the New Testament scriptures argue in ways other than the assumptions about reality familiar to us, the historico-empirical questions must find their place in the present investigation, for historico-empirical reality is an ineluctable realm of the reality we experience. The investigation of historico-empirical reality as a partial realm of the comprehensive reality in which we live, and thus also the analysis that both questions prompt, remain necessary. They lead to theological and philosophical blind alleys, however, if the question of the resurrection is (or should be) answered implicitly or explicitly with them alone.

The second narrowing consists in the reduction of the investigation to the consideration of a limited number of passages, a situation produced by both of the above-named lines of inquiry. The question concerning the visions investigates as a rule only 1 Corinthians 15 and at best mostly classifies them as legendary appearance stories taken from the canonical Gospels. The question concerning the empty tomb considers only the few passages from the Gospels that concern it. Isolating these excerpts from their contexts, however, conceals that which the present investigation principally seeks: the assumptions about reality and the plausibility strategies of the New Testament texts on whose basis discourse about the resurrection, the empty tomb, and the appearances of the Resurrected One can reveal its sense. The New Testament texts must be read as whole compositions in order to perceive their view of things.

But reconstructing resurrection discourse in the New Testament Scriptures answers neither the contemporary question about the resurrection of the crucified Jesus of Nazareth nor the question about the resurrection of the dead. Perhaps the assumptions about reality with which the New Testament metaphors of the resurrection ("Auferweckung bzw. Auferstehung") are bound up the outdated worldviews, such that—even if it is with an attitude of regret—we must admit that they have irretrievably lost the possibility of being plausibly conceived. The Catholic exegete and student of the history of religion Dieter Zeller has recently stated the point in all candor:

It could also necessarily be the case that the symbolism of resurrection is "dead." Thus does R. C. Neville name symbols that do not (any longer) engage interpreters with that to which they refer. That is due neither to the wishes nor to the skill of the interpreter, however, but rather to the historical contingency of the symbol "resurrection." It is chiefly burdened by its origins in the crisis situation of the embattled people of Israel, who could not realize its expectations on this earth. Therefore it is also indissolubly involved with apocalyptic cosmological scenarios which we today can no longer comprehend.[1]

As a matter of fact, the theologian, philosopher, and religious scholar Robert Cummings Neville does not regard the symbol of resurrection as "dead" at all. Indeed, the debate between Robert Neville and Hans Kessler, with an introduction by Hermann Deuser, in the volume of *Zeitschrift für Neues Testament* dedicated to the topic of resurrection (*ZNT* 19, 2007), in which one finds the above-cited article from Zeller too, shows that if one wishes to interpret the early Christian resurrection message properly, with due justice to its content, it is precisely the pressing cosmological, ontological, and theological problems of the present that may no longer be excluded from the exegetical debate concerning the resurrection of the dead. One ought readily to agree with Zeller that the early Jewish and early Christian theology of resurrection could be made plausible only on the basis of fundamental cosmological principles. But along with the works of Deuser, Neville, and Kessler, the present investigation comes to a different conclusion, from this fact: resurrection theology can be plausibly formulated today as well, but only if one conceives of a comprehensive conception of reality that can articulate afresh the cosmological and ontological implications of the biblical theology of resurrection. Thus, the historicist constriction of the discipline of the New Testament is here rejected in favor of an explicitly theologically argued semiotic conception of the discipline of the New Testament. Mere historical research is in no position to deal adequately with the substance of the exegetical and theological problems of the New Testament's message of resurrection, and, incidentally, this inability is often to the detriment of its historical investigation. Whoever wishes to be only a historian ceases to be a theologian.

This in no way means, however, that the historical problems should play no further role in a semiotic investigation (that is to say, a paradigm oriented to a categorical theory of sign processes)[2] of resurrection texts. Again, that would lead only to an inappropriate reduction of the problem to either the level of subjective faith or the level of a truncated constructivist conception of meaning. Rather, reality, by which life, feeling, and thinking are determined, encompasses all three dimensions of experience: the first level of emotional, precritical perception; the second level of empirical-historical facts; and the third level of interpretation constitutive of meaning, which opens up connections. Faith, which is more than regarding empirical-historical (that is to say, quasi-historical) facts as true, is that which shapes the emotional basis for all relevant life decisions. Such faith stands, however, in danger of devolving into biblicist narrow-mindedness or even fundamentalist aggression when it denies both of the other levels of reality: the level of empirical-historical facts and the level of meaning-constituting, critical interpretation. Therefore, part II of this investigation will engage in the interpretation of New Testament resurrection discourse with the help of semiotic-categorical differentiation in the service of grounding an appropriate manner of speaking according to the scriptures of the New Testament.

The third part of this study will show how a modern faith (that is, a faith that is pluralistic, informed, and critical, as well as capable of making distinctions) can speak of the resurrection of Jesus Christ and of the resurrection of the dead along with the biblical writings in the contexts of present ecclesial and educational praxis.

With the following investigation I hope not only to stimulate academic discussion that can open up for us the reality in which we live, but also to further such discussion with the help of Protestant theological reflection concerning the resurrection of the dead, and to make known the cosmological and ontological relevance of this issue in order to generate interdisciplinary discourse about it. Because, however, I also have educational and ecclesial praxis in mind, I am ultimately much more concerned with making a contribution that can help Protestants to speak about the resurrection of Jesus Christ and the hope in the resurrection of the dead in a way that can be lived, thought, taught, and learned today.

PART I

Resurrection and the New Testament
Exegetical Investigations

Chapter 1

The Pauline Literature

The letters of the Apostle Paul are not only the oldest writings of the New Testament; they are also the oldest Christian writings of any kind that have come down to us. But not all the letters that name Paul as the sender were authored by him. Stylistic and material differences from those letters more certainly formulated by Paul lead one to distinguish between Proto-Pauline and Deutero-Pauline letters. First Thessalonians, Galatians, 1 and 2 Corinthians, Romans, Philippians, and Philemon are unanimously assigned to the Proto-Pauline letters. With the Letters to the Colossians and the Ephesians, however, one finds substantial differences regarding the resurrection over and against the Proto-Pauline letters. But one can also make out clear shifts of emphasis that point to a later time of composition and a different author in 2 Thessalonians and the so-called Pastoral Letters.

The Letter to the Hebrews, which does not claim Paul as the sender, was assigned in the early Church to the Corpus Paulinum as well. While the letters designated here as Deutero-Pauline exhibit a substantive closeness to the Proto-Pauline letters in spite of their serious differences, and while these also intended and, indeed, therefore employed the name of Paul in order to fashion a "Pauline" theology for their own respective situations with his authority, the Letter to the Hebrews, with its priestly approach, presents such a discrete theology that it will receive its own chapter and will not be ranked here with the Deutero-Pauline letters.

The Letters of the Apostle Paul

"If there is no resurrection of the dead, then Christ has not been raised; and if Christ has not been raised, then our proclamation has been in vain and your faith has been in vain" (1 Cor 15:13-14). The significance of the resurrection of Jesus Christ, which these verses from 1 Corinthians 15 discuss and which can hardly be overestimated, matters not only for the strategy of the argument of this chapter, but also for 1 Corinthians as an entire letter. In fact, Paul's *theologia crucis*,[1] his "word of the cross" as the speech of the eschatological, powerful, and salvific action of the merciful and just creator God,[2] emerges from it.

Richard B. Hays,[3] Ben Witherington III,[4] Eckart Reinmuth,[5] and finally Ian Scott[6] have convincingly demonstrated that the framework of Pauline discourse exhibits a narrative substructure, and that the word of the cross as the story of the death and resurrection of Jesus Christ in this God- and world-interpreting narrative has been given a decisive role. This role fundamentally transforms the great story in which Paul, the persecutor of the church, lived.

In connection with Hays and others, Scott represents the thesis that the theological knowledge of Paul is structured by a great, coherent narrative that extends from the creation of the world to the new creation at the end of the world. This great story forms for Paul the hermeneutical framework for the interpretation of the world, the interpretation of history, and every single event in past history as well as present and future. Pauline rationality is thus not a Greek logic rationality but rather a hermeneutical-narrative one, whose criterion constitutes the coherence of the great narrative.

Ethical knowledge is included in this narrative theology as well. Believers are located *in* this story. Concrete ethical problems or instructions are, therefore, formulated in view of how one should play one's role in the story well—that is, action must correspond to the role. The reflective unfolding of this story, as it is found in the Proto-Pauline letters, helps one understand both how to live and what consequences to expect, if one gives oneself over to this story as a true story. The indispensable Spirit of God, however, necessarily effects the leap, the decision for the truth of the story. If this leap has taken place through the work of the spirit of the story of Jesus Christ, then an experience-saturated, faithful relationship to God and to Jesus Christ develops for believers. The relationship is to God through giving him the worship due him alone. It is to Jesus Christ through imitating his life in the community with him as the Kyrios. In this way the narrative of the cross and resurrection forms the center of its own action and self-understanding. Believers live in the great story in the assurance that through their sharing in Jesus' fate of death they will be raised at the end of the ages and will receive eternal life in order to live with him in eternal communion. I shall explore the individual letters of Paul in order to make this thesis concrete with a view to Pauline discourse about the resurrection of Jesus Christ and the resurrection of the dead.

1 Thessalonians

1 Thessalonians is regarded as Paul's oldest extant letter and thus also as the oldest extant written record of Christian faith. It is directed to a community that Paul founded shortly before the composition of the letter.[7] The concern of the letter is to strengthen the community on the way of faith marked out for it in the face of pressures, and thus to contribute to its sanctification. Taking account of their election,[8] they should expect the coming (παρουσία) of the Lord. From that point on, they will be together with him forever (cf. 4:17; 5:23). "Their perspective on the immediate *parousia* shapes the theology of 1 Thessalonians from its organization to its ethical directives. . . . Thus a closed theological conception arises: In faith in Jesus Christ, risen from the dead, in the presence of the Spirit sent by God (cf. 1 Thess 4:8; 5:19), the community expects the coming of the Son from heaven who will save them from the wrath to come."[9] This theological conception and the fundamental concern of the letter that comes with it are born of the certainty that the crucified Jesus did not remain dead, but rather was raised by God and is now the living Kyrios of the community (cf. 1:1b).[10]

The Resurrection of Jesus Christ as the Fundamental Narrative of the Pauline Gospel

At the beginning of the letter Paul praises the young congregation for carrying on with the gospel, for remembering how they came to hear it from Paul, and for how this message of the gospel was effective among them: "[H]ow you turned to God from idols, to serve a living and true God, and to wait for his Son from heaven, whom he raised from the dead—Jesus, who rescues us from the wrath that is coming" (1 Thess 1:9b-10).

The gospel Paul announced effected their turning from idols and their turning to the living and true God. In this way the vitality and truth of idols are denied. They are illusions that are powerless to effect anything.

In this section, however, the vitality and truth of God are not only maintained propositionally, they are also presented in a narrative manner, a narrative constituted by God's act of resurrection and his coming wrath. In both ways is God's immeasurable power shown.

The resurrection of Jesus is introduced as a unique and exceptional[11] event that has happened in the past. "V. 10 speaks of the expected 'Son' of God and in identifying him gives his name as 'Jesus'—this is the one risen from the dead who saves believers from the coming wrath. This verse does not concern the expectation of an unknown, undetermined heavenly existence, but rather speaks of Jesus who was raised from the dead, whose story is represented in these succinct phrases."[12] The readers learn nothing about the precise circumstances of the resurrection. They are informed, however, about the location of the Resurrected One. He is in heaven, for his return is expected from heaven. His coming again has as its first function the salvation of believers from the coming wrath of God.

Verses 1:9b-10 provide further insight into the narrative substructure of the gospel Paul announced in Thessalonica: the Day of the Lord, on which God's wrath is poured out on all sinners, stands immediately at hand (cf. 5:1ff.). God has raised Jesus, his Son, from the dead and taken him into his heavenly life. On the Day of the Lord Jesus will come again out of heaven and will deliver those who have turned to the living and true God from God's annihilating wrath. Without God's powerful act of resurrection there would be no deliverance from his righteous wrath.

The plausibility of this narrative of the future wrath and the past resurrection of Jesus does not arise from empirical evidence of the possibility or actuality of resurrection. Rather, it is nourished by the theology of Paul the Jew, who, as such, knows the creative, but also the destructive power of God. Moreover, it stands in the framework of the apocalyptic understanding of time, which counts on an imminent end to this world.

This Jewish apocalyptic theology and cosmology, widespread at the time of Paul, gains something new through the narrative of the resurrection of an individual in the recent past. This event cannot be understood as a mere revivification of a dead man, because this Resurrected One does not continue his prior mode of life. Rather, Jesus has entered into his heavenly life, and indeed did so before the end of the age. Saving power is ascribed to this event, for the Resurrected One himself will be the deliverer. The resurrection of Jesus, having occurred in the recent past, is thus remembered as an eschatological event with a cosmic dimension.

This good news, this gospel, is more than a merely human word. It is the efficacious Word of God because it delivers those who have faith in this Word (cf. 1 Thess 2:13). In support of the divine nature of this Word Paul appeals to the experiences of the Thessalonians to whom he is writing. They have made his proclamation foundational in the constitution of their community. According to 1 Thessalonians, the proclamation of the gospel in Thessalonica did not occur only with the human words of Paul. It also came "in power and in the Holy Spirit and with full conviction" (1:5), so that the Thessalonians received it as that which it truly and effectually is: the reality-creating Word of God (cf. 2:13b). Paul reminds the Thessalonians that they have experienced the wonder working power of the Word of God itself. This is the very power that enabled them to accept the good news of salvation through Jesus, the one raised by God into heavenly life.[13]

The Question of the Resurrection of the Dead

Thus, the narrative of the crucifixion and resurrection of Jesus Christ and of the saving function of the resurrected Crucified One on the Day of God's judgment forms the core of the proclamation that grounds the community. Apparently the question of the resurrection of the dead does not belong to it. The sorrow of the Thessalonians over those from their community who have died threatens their eschatological joy and thus their sanctification. According to Paul they are uncertain whether their dead will have a share in the communion of eternal life with Jesus Christ, whose return is imminent. For this reason, in 1 Thessalonians 4:13-17 Paul imparts his knowledge of the apocalyptic scenario and therein combines traditional motifs of the Jewish hope in the resurrection of the dead with the conviction of the resurrection of Jesus Christ.

The "word of the Lord" in 1 Thessalonians 4:15 solves the fundamental problem of the Thessalonians on the basis of the fundamental conviction that Jesus Christ has been raised from the dead (4:14a) and now communicates with the apostle as Lord of the community. The solution to the problem consists in assuring the anxious Thessalonians with the highest authority, namely that of their Kyrios, "that we who are alive, who are left until the coming of the Lord, will by no means precede those who have died" (4:15).

Verses 16-17 now make clear what will happen at the eschaton: The Kyrios will come down, the "dead in Christ" will rise, those still living at that time will be caught up in the air. The resurrected and those who are caught up will meet their Lord in the air and will be together forever. Verse 14b is grounded in this scenario. As an effective word of comfort, this eschatological knowledge should mitigate the Thessalonians' sorrow.

With a view to the question of the resurrection, let us note the following: In the center of Paul's gospel proclamation in Thessalonica stands the "Jesus-Christ-Story" (Eckart Reinmuth) of death and resurrection. The resurrected Jesus Christ is the Lord of those who believe. At the time of the composition of the letter he is located in the heavenly realm and communicates with Paul, his apostle. He will come at the end of time to save from God's wrath those who trust in the gospel of the resurrected Crucified One and therefore turn to God.

The day of the return of Jesus Christ cannot be dated, but it is so imminent that it is probable that the question of the resurrection of the dead was not a central theme of the proclamation in Thessalonica by which Paul founded the community. The sorrow of the Thessalonians to whom he writes over the uncertainty of the future of those who have died requires Paul to provide information about their fate. According to a word of the Lord, which Paul now communicates to the Thessalonians as apocalyptic-eschatological knowledge, those who have died, who during their lives turned to the gospel and thus at the same time turned to the true and living God and to the Lord Jesus Christ, will rise on the Day of the Lord. Thus, 1 Thessalonians does not speak of an individual resurrection immediately after one's own death.

In view of this eschatological deliverance, the resurrection is not thought of as something necessary, but rather only as a means to the end of the participation of the dead in the eschatological community with its Kyrios. The return of the Kyrios is thought of as so imminent that it is not the resurrection of the dead, but rather the rising of the still living to meet the Kyrios that is regarded as normative.

Galatians

In the Letter to the Galatians the reader encounters the resurrection of Jesus Christ already in the first verse. Paul owes his apostleship to Jesus Christ and to the God "who raised him from the dead." Verse 4 then provides information about the meaning of the death and resurrection of Jesus Christ. Jesus Christ "gave himself for our sins to set us free from the present evil age, according to the will of our God and Father." In this way the Galatians are reminded right at the beginning of the writing of the fundamental conviction of the Pauline Gospel in a pithy and concise manner. Paul does this because he sees that the Galatians to whom he writes stand in danger of deserting this gospel and thus jeopardizing their potential salvation (cf. 1:6–9; 3:1ff.). The letter functions to obligate the Galatians anew to the fundamental convictions of the gospel announced by Paul.[14]

This gospel is bound up with the divine appointment of Paul as an apostle of Jesus Christ, as an exemplar. Therefore, the miraculous story of how God made an apostle out of the persecutor of the church provides argumentative force with which Paul can demand that the Galatians rectify their thinking (cf. 1:6; 3:1). This miraculous story functions also at the same time as a proof of the reality of the resurrected Crucified One, as Paul perceived it. The recounting of the miracle[15] in 1:13-24 is prepared for in 1:11-12 through the presentation of the assertion that is supposed to ground it, namely "that the gospel that was proclaimed by me is not of human origin; for I did not receive it from a human source, nor was I taught it, but I received it through a revelation of Jesus Christ." The narration of the miracle begins in verses 13-14 with the introduction of the problem: the Jewish zealot Paul persecuted the church of God.

Verses 15-16a narrate how the problem was solved. God made Paul an apostle of his church by revealing his Son to him. The confirmation of the miracle proceeds in two steps. First, Paul narrates how he immediately put his new commission into practice without opposition and went into the region of the Gentiles and not to Jerusalem. He had been spontaneously convinced and needed no express proof of the resurrection of Jesus Christ. He did not go to Jerusalem to check perhaps whether the tomb of the Crucified One was in fact empty. Even during his stay in Jerusalem three years later he neither inquired about the tomb of the Crucified One nor questioned reputed witnesses about the veracity of their words of testimony to the resurrection.

Thereafter verses 23-24 offer a doxological conclusion, typical of miracle stories: "I was still unknown by sight to the churches of Judea that are in Christ; they only heard it said, 'The one who formerly was persecuting us is now proclaiming the faith he once tried to destroy.' And they glorified God because of me."

Paul here narrates his existential about-face, his change of mind. This was not something for which he was prepared, however.[16] Rather, it occurred suddenly and indeed not through human action but through an unexpected, powerful act of God. This act consisted in God revealing his Son to Paul the zealous Jew, letting him be seen (cf. 1 Cor 9:1), revealing that the crucified Jesus did not remain in death. In one stroke Paul became aware that God had raised the Crucified One and that he is God's Son and the expected Messiah of Israel. From now on, God is for Paul not only the God of Abraham, Isaac, and Jacob, but also the Father of Jesus Christ, the God who has raised the crucified Jesus Christ from the dead. Paul rethinks everything he knew about God up to this point in light of the death and resurrection of the crucified messiah.

God's enlightenment of Paul changes everything for him. Paul changes from being a persecutor of the church of God to being a proclaimer of the gospel among the Gentiles. One perceives in this miraculous story the revelation of Jesus Christ as a newfound awareness of the resurrection of the crucified Son of God. This fundamental Pauline conviction restructures his thought and shapes all of his wider thinking and action. In 2:20b he writes, "And the life I now live in the flesh I live by faith in the Son of God, who loved me and gave himself for me."

This sentence explains what Paul means just before when he states, "For through the law I died to the law, so that I might live to God. I have been crucified with Christ; and it is no longer I who live, but it is Christ who lives in me" (2:19-20a). Paul is engaging here in language-shaping, metaphorical theology. From an empirical perspective he was not crucified with Christ. With the fundamental metaphor of the cross, of being crucified, he expresses the nature of the paradoxical event of the crucifixion and resurrection of Jesus Christ as the hermeneutical key to his own existence. His words in 6:17b, "I carry the marks of Jesus branded on my body," are similarly to be read as an expression of the metaphorical interpretation of his own bodily weakness (cf. Gal 4:13-14) and infirmity, or illness (cf. 2 Cor 12:7ff.). He can and wants to understand himself, God, and the world only from the perspective of this act of God that alters the entire cosmos. The life he lived before Christ was revealed to him has ended. It belongs to a past that has no future. Never again will he look at himself, the world, or God without the lens of the resurrected Crucified One.

Paul's experience of the apperception of the Crucified One also significantly shapes the structure of his proclamation. In 3:1 he recalls his community-founding proclamation of Christ as crucified. The syntagm "Jesus Christ as crucified" can be regarded as a metonym for the gospel announced by Paul. That Jesus Christ was portrayed as such "before [their] eyes" expresses vividly the structural analogy between their miraculous reception of the gospel and his apostolic proclamation. In fulfillment of his divine commission, the apostle brought the Galatians into the miraculous event of his own transformation by his having written to them of the resurrected Jesus Christ as crucified before their eyes, as he himself had seen him (cf. 1 Cor 9:1).

For this reason, the law can no longer be looked upon as a means to adjudicated righteousness, for it would be a means remaining unaffected by the one event that changes everything, that of the death and resurrection of Jesus Christ: "for if justification comes through the law, then Christ died for nothing" (2:21). According to Paul, everything, the Torah, the promises of God, his covenant with Israel, must be thought through again in light of the cross and resurrection. In this light the faithfulness of the creator God and the reliability of his traditional promises and the cosmological turning of the ages, through God's powerful act of raising the Crucified One, build the hermeneutical system for interpretation the reality of the world.

As is the case with all believers, God sent the Spirit of Christ into Paul's heart, and this Spirit calls God "Father" (cf. 4:6). Paul now lives in this Spirit of Christ and wants to act in accord with it (cf. 5:25). Through the event of the cross all the world's self-determined measures of value are struck through, crucified, and he is no longer accountable to them (cf. 6:14). God has now made him a new creature (καινὴ κτίσις, 6:15) through the revelation of Jesus Christ, through the gift of his Spirit, a new creation with the promise to inherit the kingdom of God. God offers this promise to everyone who believes the gospel.

In the Letter to the Galatians one sees that the resurrection of Jesus Christ possesses emotional and cognitive evidence for Paul. He had an experience that fundamentally convinced him, in a way that altered his existence, that the crucified Jesus was raised by God and that he is the Christ, the Son of God. According to Galatians, no empirical proof, no empty tomb, no proposition convinced him of these things, only the spontaneous certainty of his own experience. The cosmological reach of God's act of raising the Crucified One required Paul to rethink everything about God, his covenants and promises, and the Torah in its light, for the God of Abraham, Isaac, and Jacob is from now on the God who has raised Jesus from the dead. Paul thus remains a Jewish theologian. The God who raised Jesus Christ from the dead is the God of Abraham, Isaac, and Jacob, the God who remains true to his covenant with Israel.[17] Indeed, the one event of the crucifixion and resurrection of the Messiah becomes for Paul the criterion for all speech about God, humanity, and cosmos. Paul was and remained a Jew.[18] But his theological thought changed through his consideration of the paradox of the event of the cross. He neither can nor wants any longer to think about God apart from the word of the cross. Not only Paul's Christology but also precisely his theology take from now on the shape of a *theologia crucis*.[19]

1 Corinthians

In Paul's two Letters to the Corinthians we have the most extensive extant correspondence of Paul with a single congregation. True, these letters represent only a portion of their written communication. The Corinthian letters themselves refer both to written inquiries on the part of the Corinthians, as well as to additional letters of Paul to the Corinthians that have subsequently been lost. As is the situation in every other case of Paul's written communication, we lack the writings of the congregation.

Both extant Corinthian letters show in different ways that the proclamation of the resurrection of the crucified Jesus Christ stands at the center of the Pauline gospel. The resurrection decisively determines not only Pauline language about God, but also in the same way the interpretation of his own apostolic existence and, likewise, the existence of the congregations founded by him.

In 1 Corinthians Paul reminds the Corinthians that the word of the cross, the gospel of the death and resurrection of Jesus Christ, which calls them into communion with the Kyrios, is the foundation of their existence. Their existence owes itself to the wonderful creative power of the merciful and righteous God, and therefore any and every division in the community must be recognized as a dead end directed against this divinely enabled and desired communion. The fifteenth chapter of 1 Corinthians, central for resurrection discourse, reflects the cosmological and soteriological necessity of the resurrection of the dead and its plausibility as regards creation theology on the basis of the undeniable assurances about the reality of the resurrection of the Crucified One, according to Paul shared by sender and receiver.

Baptism, the Lord's Supper, and the interpretation of the congregation as the body of Christ point to the real contemporary activity of the resurrected Crucified One. At the same time, the apostle understands the present time of the congregation as one of waiting for the imminent return of the resurrected Crucified One. This event will bring the communion that already exists with the absent Lord to its completion by achieving its end—that of eternal communion with the present Lord in the kingdom of God.

The Opening of the Letter

In the first eight verses of the writing Paul uses the prescript and the proemium that follows it to present the basic stipulations of communication between the sender and the addressees. That Jesus Christ is the Kyrios of the apostle just as he is Kyrios of the congregation in Corinth therefore rests upon God's act of calling. As those thus called into communion with Jesus Christ (cf. 1:1-2, 9) they should also have communion with one another.[20]

The call to communion with Christ occurs through the effective "testimony of Christ" (1:6). Having become powerful among the Corinthians, this testimony works knowledge and charismatic wonders during the time of waiting for the "Day of the Lord," so that they can await this day "blameless" (cf. 1:7-8).[21]

Verses 10ff., however, show that a problem that disturbs this divinely desired communion has arisen on the part of the addressees. Factions contending against one another have formed in Corinth.

By means of rhetorical questions about the formation of these factions, verses 13-17 counter that Christ is not torn asunder, that he alone was crucified for them, and that they were baptized in his name. At the same time, the apostle emphasizes that his own commission concerns not baptism but the proclamation of the gospel, which should show itself not to have "emptied" the cross of Christ of its power (1:17).

Already the detailed opening of the letter reveals the central position and line of attack of resurrection theology in 1 Corinthians. God issues a call to communion with his Son Jesus Christ, who is the Kyrios of those called (1:9). He was crucified for them (cf. 1:13). The Corinthian congregation's existence is grounded in their communion with the one who was resurrected and crucified. Because of this any sort of division is forbidden.[22]

Christ himself commissioned Paul to proclaim the gospel in this way, so that the significance of the cross of Christ may be seen in all its fullness (cf. 1:17). The gospel *is* the "word of the cross" (1:18).

The resurrection of Jesus Christ is assumed in every line of the opening of the letter as a common conviction about reality. The importance of the abiding significance of Jesus' death by crucifixion, on the other hand, appears for Paul to have been the aspect in need of emphasis at the time of the composition of 1 Corinthians.

The Word of the Cross

The word of the cross is effective. It constitutes reality. Paul regards the congregations he founded through this word as living and experience-rich proof of the effectiveness of the word of the cross. It effects the formation of congregations out of nothing (cf. 1:28). Just as he was made an apostle by God apart from any of his own doing, this word has constituted the church of God in Corinth. The word of the cross proclaimed by Paul has proven to be the "power of God" (1:18).

Those whom this word has called into communion with Jesus Christ, and thus into communion with the church of God, are being saved through their bond to the Crucified One who was raised. Those in whom this call is not effective, however, can perceive the word of the cross only as "foolishness," as nonsense, or as a "stumbling block," as a scandalous misinterpretation of the power of God (cf. 1:23b). Such people show themselves to be "those who are perishing" (1:18).

The *word* of the cross satisfies the Jewish demands for proof of its validity as little as it satisfies the criteria Greek philosophy would employ to validate truth claims. Thus it fulfills neither the Jewish conditions for a sign of the powerful activity of God, nor those of Greek epistemology. Nothing lying outside of it can vouch for it. Paul neither points to an empty tomb that could be seen in Jerusalem, nor argues for the conceivability of the resurrection of a crucified man by means of Greek logic and natural philosophy. The word of the cross would be emptied if it were to be proven by something existing outside of itself. The word of the cross is the power of God that proves itself as such by its effectiveness.

Those whom this word leads into communion with the one who was crucified and resurrected, however, be they Jews or Greeks, recognize in the word of the cross the wisdom and creative power of the merciful and righteous God (cf. 1:24, 28). With this wisdom God serves neither the expectations of the Jews, nor those of the Greeks. In the word of the cross he shows himself to be a sovereign God, who acts in accord with his loving creativity. He does not confirm the hierarchical orders of this world and is not found among the victors who practice the right of the stronger on their way to fame and power and who set themselves in the place of God. He does not simply reverse the balance of power, however. Whoever expects the messiah to drive the Romans out of Palestine will be disappointed. God has not permitted his heavenly host to speak, but rather has transcoded the instruments of torture belonging to the powerful. The cross, the place of agonizing death, becomes an effective *sign* of the creative, new-making love of God precisely in the *word* of the cross. Without the *word* of the cross, the cross remains what it was: a tool of torture belonging to this world, a place of agony without hope. "The cross as such is silent and makes one silent."[23]

The cross is not a qualifying heat in some side arena that can be neglected on the way to greater glory. The cross remains forever the mark of the one who was resurrected and makes it impossible to mistake him. Therefore in 1 Corinthians 1:23 Paul emphasizes that he proclaims Christ as the Crucified One. Jesus Christ, the Resurrected One and as such also the Kyrios of those who are chosen and saved, by virtue of their call to communion with him, is and remains the Crucified One. God does not cancel what has happened. The sorrow and injustice seen in the cross as *pars pro toto*, the guilt of an autonomy that has forgotten God and that fails to see in the other a fellow creature made by God, is not suppressed, forgotten, or ignored. By identifying bodily with the victims of earthly power and violence, the Son of God has destroyed the possibility of forgetting any injustice.

Judgment is coming. "[T]he Day will disclose it, because it will be revealed with fire, and the fire will test what sort of work each has done" (3:13b). The Day of the Lord, which Paul the Jewish Pharisee awaited every bit as much as Paul the apostle of Christ, will deal with every injustice of this world. Those for whom the cross remains what it was before its new coding through the word of the cross are perishing (cf. 1:18) because they will not orient themselves anew in communion with the one who was crucified and resurrected, because they have not identified themselves with the Crucified One (cf. 5:13). Those in whom the word of the cross has become effective, however, have already died the death of Jesus, because by acknowledging Jesus and not the God-forgetting wielders of power in this world as their Kyrios they have stood in solidarity with victims who have suffered injustice. Their guilt will also be dealt with (cf. 3:14-15; 4:4-5), but their solidarity with the murdered confers salvation upon them through their communion with the Resurrected One (cf. 6:11).

That God offers this salvation to all and at all times, and that the church of those saved through their communion with the one who was crucified and resurrected is no closed society, make the word of the cross the gospel: the good news of the enduring new creation of life. This good news has taken away the sting of the finality of death. God offers eternal life to all.

God, the Creator

The resurrection of the crucified Jesus Christ and his establishment as Lord of the church of God folds the times together. The resurrection of the Crucified One lies in the past as a discrete, unique event, which Paul expresses precisely with the aorist ἤγειρεν: "And God raised the Lord" (6:14a). Paul proclaims the resurrected Christ as the Crucified One (cf. 1:23, 2:2b). He employs a perfect passive participle here to indicate that the crucified nature of Christ belongs forever to the identity of him who was raised, and therefore the discrete, closed past event is bound up with the present and the future of him who was raised. He who was raised acts in the present as the powerful Kyrios of the community of God. The bodies of those called into communion with the Lord are already members of Christ in the present (cf. 6:15a), and those called are already now one spirit with the Kyrios (cf. 6:17). Communion with the Crucified One who was resurrected takes on real form in the community. This reality of the community assumes in turn the reality of the resurrection of Jesus Christ. And it is not first mentioned in the fifteenth chapter of the letter, but rather already in the sixth chapter. There the reality of the resurrection of Christ leads Paul to express a statement about the future: "And God raised the Lord and will also raise us by his power" (6:14). As a result, even death will not end communion with the Kyrios.

The power of God, which becomes real and effective in the resurrection event, makes possible the folding together of the times, for it is the power of the creator, who was, is, and will be, in the situation to make everything out of nothing. The folding of the times together in the great story, which generates the coherence of Pauline theology as a comprehensive narrative framework, is indebted to Jewish creation theology, which, more precisely, is a theology of the creative God. With the same power with which he created and sustains the world, he has raised the crucified Jesus Christ; made Paul, the persecutor of the church of God, its apostle; and made the congregation in Corinth out of nothing (cf. 1:28c). With the same power he will raise the dead, making all things new.

The reality of God as the righteous, merciful creator, performer of wondrous deeds, is what provides Pauline theology and Pauline statements about the resurrection in particular with their plausibility. Speaking of the resurrection without speaking of the creator is meaningless, and speaking of the resurrection of the dead without speaking of the resurrection of the crucified Jesus Christ through the power of the righteous and merciful creator God is meaningless. The fullness of the power of the creator God is given short shrift if one fails to speak of the resurrection of the Crucified One and the future resurrection of the dead, because death would be stronger than the creative power of God. Speaking of the overcoming of death through the wonderfully loving, justice-making, and creative God gives God the honor that is owed to him, for, as Paul says, "for us there is one God, the Father, from whom are all things and for whom we exist" (8:6a).

The centrality of creation theology for Paul is seen not least in its embrace of Christology. The Crucified One who was resurrected is the "one Lord, Jesus Christ, through whom are all things and through whom we exist" (8:6b). "Christ's mediation of creation is unmistakably pronounced (the only time in the authentic Pauline letters; cf. Col 1:16; John 1:1-4; Heb 1:2). Early Christian reflection on the salvific significance of Christ could easily have inferred such participation in the first creation from his participation in the new creation (cf. 2 Cor 5:17), having taken recourse to Old Testament and Jewish wisdom speculation (cf. Wis 7:12; 9:1-9; . . .)."[24] The theology of Paul views the whole of the creation and new creation from the perspective of the resurrection of the Crucified One. Paul's theology of creation in turn permits him to grasp the plausibility of the resurrection. The necessary connection between the resurrection of Jesus Christ and the resurrection of the dead inevitably arises from this cosmological perspective, a connection with which 1 Corinthians 15 deals.

The Resurrection of the Dead

1 Corinthians 15 does not seek to prove the resurrection of Jesus Christ.[25] Rather, it is concerned with ending the controversy over the question of the resurrection of the dead, so that this controversy might no longer endanger the community of the called. In 1 Corinthians 15 Paul demonstrates that not even death can place limits on the creative power of God and therefore that death cannot destroy communion with the Kyrios.

According to Richard B. Hays' commentary on 1 Corinthians, chapter 15 has two main parts: "The resurrection of the dead is constitutive of the gospel (vv. 1-34)" and "Resurrection means transformation of the body (vv. 35-58)."[26] I further organize my reading of this very important chapter in seven sections.

The first section is 15:1-11. In 15:1-3a the formulation of the starting point of Paul's argumentation for the acceptance of the resurrection of the dead is introduced in a metalinguistic fashion. These verses remind the Corinthians that what follows concerns the gospel that Paul proclaimed, that the Corinthians accepted, and by which they are being saved, if they hold fast to this gospel. This gospel does much more than simply bind Paul and the Corinthians together, however. It also expresses the fundamental conviction of all those who are called. Paul makes this clear by indicating in the middle of the quotation that he had also received it. The citation begins in verse 3b. Its end is open. Certainly verse 8 does not belong to it. The gospel thus begins with the death of Christ, tells of his resurrection, and confirms that the one who was raised lives indeed, through the mention of the different individuals and groups who have seen him at different times and places.[27] In verse 8, Paul adjusts the quote by making mention of his own vision of Christ. In closing the first section of 1 Corinthians 15 makes a connection to the metalinguistic introduction in 15:1-3a by emphasizing again the commonality of the fundamental conviction of the gospel.

The second section of 1 Corinthians 15:12-19 identifies the Corinthian slogan that there is no resurrection of the dead as a contradiction of the gospel of the death and resurrection of the Crucified One of which Paul reminded them in the prior section.

The third section of 1 Corinthians 15:20-28 now introduces the actual thesis of the whole chapter. It is this: the resurrection of the Crucified One is no isolated, individual case, like, say, the translation of Elijah. Rather, this event marks the beginning of the eschatological resurrection of the dead. Thus, the event of the resurrection of the Crucified One has the eschatological function of the overcoming of death, which affects the entire cosmos (cf. 15:26).

The fourth section of 15:29-34 supports Paul's thesis about the resurrection of the dead by pointing to the actions of the Corinthians and Paul, actions that make sense only on the basis of the acceptance of the resurrection of the dead.

The fifth section of 15:35-49 aids in making the resurrection of the dead comprehensible.

The sixth section of 15:50-56 makes an argument by means of a "mystery" disclosed to the Corinthians.

The argumentation concludes in 15:57 with a doxology and in 15:58 with an appeal to the Corinthians grounded in their acceptance of the resurrection.

Let us look more closely at the chapter's argumentation in view of the question of the reality of the resurrection:

1 Corinthians 15:1-11. The gospel received by Paul and proclaimed by him and by others does not obtain its identity through a formula with fixed wording. Since the beginning of the twentieth century, τίνι λόγῳ in verse 2b has been readily translated as if it were linked to ὅτι in verse 3. But if it is still connected to verse 2a, then the sense would be that salvation is dependent on the preservation of the precise wording that Paul proclaimed. The *Einheitsübersetzung*, for example, translates it thus: "Through this gospel you are being saved, if you hold fast to the wording which I proclaimed to you."[28] *Logos* in the syntagm τίνι λόγῳ in verse 2b does not, however, refer to a fixed *wording*. Rather, it accentuates the reality and the effectiveness of the logos as a reality-creating word, as a power (δύναμις), as Paul formulates it in 1 Corinthians 1:18. This powerfully effective word has a comprehensible and ever-discernible content whose narrative substructure is recalled in 15:3bff.

The effectiveness of the gospel depends not on the sound of the series of signifiers, as with incantations, but rather on the ever-discernible identity of the logos. Paul emphasizes that he always proclaims the same gospel, but every reader immediately perceives the wide variety of linguistic forms in his proclamation.

The ever-discernible identity of the Pauline proclamation of the gospel, of the word of the cross, is indebted to the narrative substructure of the Jesus-Christ-Story,[29] which is already to be found in 1 Thessalonians 1:9-10 as a sermon schema, and which is recalled also in 1 Corinthians 15:3ff as a real, effective, and concrete story.[30]

In order to clarify a misunderstanding, it must be said that neither 1 Thessalonians 1:9-10 nor 1 Corinthians 15:3ff is a fully formed narrative. Both do, however, recall the substance of a narrative in summary ways. The verbs *die–to be buried–to be raised–appear* are the smallest narrative details that in their sequence reveal the narrative plot of the Jesus-Christ-Story in its Pauline version. In 15:3a and 15:11 Paul makes it clear that he knows himself to be united with the other apostles in this fundamental substructure of the gospel narrative.

- Christ died: The aorist ἀπέθανεν (ἀποθνήσκω) indicates that this is a unique, closed event, the absolutely certain death of a man. This thought is underscored by the second narrative item formulated in the passive: ἐτάφη (θάπτω). Christ died the death of a man and consequently his corpse was interred.
- This individual death story becomes a story of life that effectively and enduringly conquers death with the help of the third narrative item: ἐγήγερται (ἐγείρω). The formulation in the perfect indicates that the resurrection has taken place at a concrete point in time in the past and that this act is effective in the present. The passive formulation is to be read as a *passivum divinum*: no one other than God was able to bring about this mighty deed.
- He appeared to a series of witnesses: The fourth narrative item ὤφθη (the aorist passive of ὁράω) indicates that the Easter experiences are an integral component of the Jesus-Christ-Story. They mark the beginning of Christianity but also assume the prior Jesus-Christ-Story.

Discursive developments that make the pragmatic aspects of the text concrete, and permit the perception of the encyclopedic framework by which the pragmatic aspects enable the development of their plausibility, are worked into the narrative plot of 1 Corinthians 15:3b-5: Christ died "for our sins" (ὑπὲρ τῶν ἁμαρτιῶν ἡμῶν). Both the proclaimers and also the recipients of the proclamation are included in the pronoun and written into the Jesus-Christ-Story: *narrator et lector in fabula!*[31] Narrator and reader are situated in the story. Moreover, the Pauline theology of justification appears with the interpretive comment "for our sins," which, embedded in the Jesus-Christ-Story, is perceived by the reader as its discursive development.

He died for our sins and was raised on the third day according to the Scriptures (κατὰ τὰς γραφάς). The receiver can perceive the Jesus-Christ-Story only on the basis of the background of the encyclopedia of the Scriptures of the old covenant. Richard B. Hays remarks, "The two central events of Christ's death and resurrection are said to have occurred 'in accordance with the scriptures.' It is highly significant that this early creed specifies that the story of Jesus' passion and resurrection must be interpreted in light of scripture: the early church understood the gospel as the continuation and fulfillment of God's dealing with Israel."[32] With the twofold "according to the Scriptures" in connection with the *passivum divinum* "he was raised," the Jesus-Christ-Story becomes theology, speech about God.

The Jesus-Christ-Story can be reduced neither to Christology, nor to soteriology, and most certainly not to psychology. It is above all theology: proper speech about the reality of the creative act of God. Paul delineates this wondrous act of God by connecting the traditional formulation to his own story. He was a miscarriage, because he persecuted the Church of God. God altered Paul's reality by transforming him from a persecutor to a proclaimer of the gospel, by making a preacher of life out of a miscarriage.[33] Paul interprets his own apostolic existence within the horizon of the resurrection of Jesus Christ.

This paradoxical structure of creating life out of death interprets the Jesus-Christ-Story in appropriate and effective ways. In its Pauline variant it received its most apposite designation as *the word of the cross* (λόγος τοῦ σταυροῦ, 1 Cor 1:18), which Paul develops in the first four chapters of the same letter. The word of the cross admits of no reduction to a propositional expression, a dogmatic doctrine, or a formula to be handed down word for word. As *pars pro toto* it intends to invoke the whole plot of the narrative theology of the Jesus-Christ-Story. This story narrates how the merciful and just Creator God known through the Scriptures of the old covenant created new life through the cruciform death of his son. In this way Jesus overcomes the finality of the reality of death, thus redeeming men out of their fallen condition whose end is death, to which they are indebted and which they cannot overcome by their own power. The gospel offers them a new life in accord with creation in communion with Jesus Christ. The narrators and recipients of this story are written into this story in either life or death. By accepting and retelling this story, they become bodily signs of its power. The word of the cross becomes for Paul the criterion of all true speech about God and his creatures.[34]

1 Corinthians 15:12-19. Verse 12a again names the commonly accepted conviction about reality, that Jesus Christ has been raised from the dead. The question in verse 12b already makes clear that the denial of the eschatological assumptions about reality concerning the somatic resurrection of the dead stands in irreconcilable contradiction to the common conviction of the resurrection of Jesus Christ. Such a denial, therefore, makes no sense. Verse 13 makes it clear that Paul does not regard the somatic resurrection of Jesus Christ as a special case. Rather, this event belongs to the expected bodily resurrection of the dead at the end of time. Verses 14-19 emphasize that the gospel stands or falls with assumptions about the reality of the bodily resurrection of Jesus Christ. But the latter assumptions would be conceivable only together with assumptions about the reality of the eschatological resurrection of the dead. In this I agree with Dale Martin: "Most important, there is no indication in I Corinthians 15 that the reason why the Corinthians reject the resurrection of the body is because they believe they have already experienced a spiritual resurrection. It is much simpler to assume, as Paul's arguments against them indicate, that what they found objectionable about Paul's teaching was not the *future* aspect of the resurrection but that it was to be a *bodily resurrection.*"[35]

1 Corinthians 15:20-28. The beginning of this section in verse 20 again formulates the commonly accepted assumptions about the reality of the resurrection of Jesus Christ. The interpretation of this event as the beginning of the eschatological resurrection of the dead continues in verse 20b. Paul then details the fundamental thesis of his distinctive argumentation about the resurrection in 1 Corinthians 15: the resurrection of Jesus Christ is accordingly no isolated historical fact of the past that would be subject to the empirical-historical laws of this world. It is, rather, an apocalyptic-eschatological event that reaches into the coming age, or, better, that brings about the dawn of eschatological time and reality and becomes comprehensible from that time. The Crucified One who was raised is therefore no revivified dead man who comes back to his former life. He is rather the beginning of the eschatological raising of the dead. This event conquers death as such and, therefore, has cosmological consequences and effects.

Verses 21-22 give further insight into the logic with which Paul reflects upon the cosmological dimension of the resurrection of Jesus Christ. Through a man, he says here, came death. Therefore, also through a man must come the overcoming of death, the resurrection of the dead. Paul identifies Adam as the man in whose communion all are affected by death, and Christ as the one in whose communion all are made alive.

Verses 24-28 then provide information about the apocalyptic scenario that Paul considers within the interweaving of the times. According to Paul, everything must occur in a proper order: Christ is the "firstfruits" of the eschatological resurrection. His resurrection has already occurred and therefore is also the progression of events guaranteed. He will return. Then those who are dead "who belong to Christ" will be raised (v. 23c). After Christ has annihilated all the powers that oppose God, death the ultimate among them, he will hand over the "kingdom" to God the Father. Verses 27-28 make it unmistakably clear that Jesus Christ the Son does not by his own strength conquer those cosmological powers opposed to God. Rather, God sets "all his enemies under his feet"; God is the sovereign actor in the whole process, so that "God may be all in all" (28c).

1 Corinthians 15:29-34. Verse 29 reveals a denial of the resurrection of the dead as inconsistent, because the practice of baptism for the dead, which, according to Paul, the Corinthians practiced, would therefore be meaningless. Even his own apostolic existence, which again and again endangers his life, would make no sense without the certainty that he will be raised from the dead. Their denial of the resurrection of the dead reveals that God is not known by some of the Corinthians in his creative power. This ignorance of God leads to the logic of the saying, "Let us eat and drink, for tomorrow we die" (32c). And remain dead, were one to make the implication of the saying explicit. Whoever denies God's resurrection power knows nothing of God (cf. v. 34).

1 Corinthians 15:35-49. Verses 35-49 demonstrate that the foundation of Paul's resurrection discourse lies in creation theology. Paul answers the questions "How are the dead raised? With what kind of body do they come?" by making reference to Genesis 1 and 2. Paul seriously endeavors to demonstrate the reality of the resurrection analogically and metaphorically with the cultural encyclopedia of his time. For that, the Jewish theology of creation furnishes Paul's theology of new creation with the decisive requirement: With his wondrous power, the merciful and just creator God testified to in the Torah creates the cosmos and all life by giving to everything and everyone its own body. Bodily life is a good gift of God. God's creation is somatic. "Paul describes the first creation in analogous dependence on Gen 1 by reading and interpreting his Corinthian problem in light of the creation account."[36] Corporeality is the continuum from creation to new creation.

The comparison with the grain (1 Cor 15:36ff.) first of all establishes as a basis the necessity and radicality of death. Death is the all-encompassing end. There is no inherent continuity between the dead body and the newly created body. Paul does not share the Greek conception of a soul that lives on. Death knows no bounds. It devours the whole person. "Here . . . it is chiefly a question of death as an act of discontinuity, which separates temporally both contrary ways of existing. . . . The relationship of seed and plant is understood precisely not in the sense of development, in the sense of the germinal concept, but rather as a new creation of God in the sense of a wonder."[37]

In 1 Corinthians 15:38-41 Paul demonstrates the plausibility of the assumption that God gives to all and to each a specific body. On this basis and on the assumption of the seed analogy, in verses 43-44 he formulates continuity and difference between the first and second creation: the continuous subject of both creations is God, while the continuous kind and way of divine creating consists in the gift of specific bodies. Precisely therein, then, is the decisive difference also grounded. The bodies of the first creation are "natural": weak, mortal, corruptible, and therefore not suited for the eternally enduring kingdom of God. The new "spiritual" bodies, however, are formed for eternal life in the kingdom of God (cf. v. 50). The difference of "natural" (ψυχικόν) versus "spiritual" (πνευματικόν) does not consist in an alleged incorporeality of the pneumatic. The spiritual body is spiritual body because it will be made alive through the Spirit of the Resurrected One (cf. v. 45). It is this divine power (δύναμις) that is accorded to the spiritual body and that the natural body lacks (cf. v. 43b).

It is not only the citation of Genesis 2:7 in 1 Corinthians 15:45 but even more Paul's attempt to understand the new creation analogously and with the help of the differentiation made between ψυχικόν and πνευματικόν, in distinction from the first creation, that shows how strong the theology of creation dominates his entire argumentation: "Thus it is written, 'The first man, Adam, became a living (ψυχην) being'; the last Adam became a life-giving spirit (πνεῦμα ζῳοποιοῦν)" (v. 45). At the same time this formulation binds Christology and pneumatology together. The resurrected Christ functions as the life-giving Spirit.

1 Corinthians 15:50-56. Paul expects the resurrection of the dead at the horizon of his knowledge of the apocalyptic encyclopedia: "For the trumpet will sound, and the dead will be raised imperishable" (v. 52b). The difference from traditional Jewish apocalyptic consists above all in Paul's conviction that the resurrection of the dead has already begun with the resurrection of the Crucified One.

Because Paul assumes the imminence of the end of time and therefore believes that at that point some of his contemporaries will still be living—who will, however, lack a body fit for the kingdom of God, he argues using the idea of transformation or transfiguration (cf. 1 Cor 15:51). He argues this because "flesh and blood cannot inherit the kingdom of God" (v. 50b).

Accordingly, the spiritual body consists no longer of flesh and blood. Nevertheless it can be perceived optically (cf. 1 Cor 15:5-8). Since according to Paul the "second man" is "from heaven," and since Paul distinguishes the sun, moon, and stars on the basis of their "glory" (δόξα), it stands to reason that Paul regarded the spiritual body analogously as a form of light, as he thus perceived the body of the one who was crucified and raised (cf. also 1 Cor 9:1b).[38]

1 Corinthians 15:57-58. The doxological conclusion of the argumentation emphasizes that the God who acts as sovereign subject of the event is owed thanks for the cosmological victory over the powers hostile to God, among whom finally and not least of all death is numbered. It is around this certainty that the Corinthians should orient their lives.

The Embodied Community with the Resurrected Crucified One: Baptism— Lord's Supper—Body of Christ

According to 1 Corinthians the resurrection of the dead occurs as a collective resurrection at the end of time, when Jesus Christ returns from the heavens. This resurrection is no anthropological constant and no end in itself, but rather something necessary for entry into eternal communion with Jesus Christ for those members of the body of Christ who die before his return.

Communion with the Kyrios is not primarily a future promise, however, but rather a reality-constituting present. Communion with the Kyrios engrafts believers into the body of Christ (cf. 6:15a, 12:12ff.). They are "one spirit with him" (6:17b). According to Paul, then, the visible communities are perceptible proof of the reality of the Resurrected One, who is the spirit who gives life (cf. 1 Cor 15:45).

Incorporation into the body of Christ obligates the members of the body of Christ to participate in loving communion with one another and to live a life in a way that gives God the glory. The numerous ethical directives in the Pauline letters arise out of the change of identity that believers undergo in the act of baptism. They do not belong to themselves. Now they are members of the body of Christ. As such, they have to conduct themselves for the benefit of this communal body: "Or do you not know that your body is a temple of the Holy Spirit within you, which you have from God, and that you are not your own? For you were bought with a price; therefore glorify God in your body" (6:19-20).

If believers are incorporated into the body of Christ through the unique act of baptism, then the resurrected Crucified One encounters the members of his body in the materiality of bread and wine in an efficacious manner: "The cup of blessing that we bless, is it not a sharing in the blood of Christ? The bread that we break, is it not a sharing in the body of Christ?" (10:16).

The celebration of the Lord's Supper perpetuates the memory of the crucifixion. The blood of Christ and his broken body are metonymies of the human body killed on the cross. At the same time they are also signs of the absence of the Resurrected One. Precisely the blood as the bearer of life (cf. Lev 17:11a) and the body as the continuum of creation and new creation point to the living corporeality of the Resurrected One. The Lord's Supper proclaims the word of the cross as well (cf. 1 Cor 11:26). The representation of the blood through the wine and the representation of the body through the broken bread make possible the symbolic-bodily incorporation (*Einverleibung*) of the blood and body of Christ and thus also somatic and pneumatic communion with him. Bread and wine are similarly efficacious signs of the presence and absence[39] of the Resurrected One. They are powerful and effective placeholders that are therefore necessary only because he is absent until the day of his final return (cf. 1 Cor 11:26c).

Bread and wine represent his absence in an effective way. The fact that communion with him through the materiality of bread and wine is not spiritually void but is regarded as somatically effective is shown by Paul's explanations of the effects of holy communion taken unworthily. Such unworthy partaking leads to miraculous punishment (cf. 1 Cor 11:27-34).[40] The Lord's Supper, which generates somatic communion with the Resurrected One, is according to Paul the efficacious event of his presence. The plausibility of this line of thought depends on the theology of creation, which permits Paul to think of the resurrection body somatically. If, however, in accord with creation theology the whole of reality is somatic, then the presence of the Resurrected One in the present must also be regarded as somatic. The life-giving Spirit of the Resurrected One presents itself in various ways: in the form in which Paul and the others saw him (cf. 1 Cor 9:1, 15:4-8), in the form of the visible community as the body of Christ, and in the materiality of bread and wine.

2 Corinthians

That the theology of resurrection largely determines 1 Corinthians is apparent throughout the letter, not only in 1 Corinthians 15. By way of contrast, in 2 Corinthians the theology of resurrection is reflected less cosmologically and eschatologically, and more in the significance of apostolic existence in the present. It is also employed apologetically and eschatologically. As a whole, 2 Corinthians bears witness to the certainty of the apostle that the power of the resurrection of the Crucified One does not only concern the significance of eternal life in the kingdom of God but rather is something that is effective already now. As such, it is active now in this world-changing reality for those who believe.

The Construction of 2 Corinthians

It is clear from 1 Corinthians, but also from 2 Corinthians itself, that 2 Corinthians presents a lively and conflict-rich exchange between the Apostle Paul and his coworkers on one side and the congregation in Corinth and its vicinity on the other. Theological themes, news, travel itineraries, plans, reflections on the relationship between apostle and congregation, and thus the common resolution of conflict are woven together much more in this letter than in 1 Corinthians.

The unity of the argumentation of 2 Corinthians is therefore difficult to penetrate. In despairing of finding a coherent line of argumentation, the feeling quickly arises in one that 2 Corinthians is not a single text but rather a collection of letters put together after the fact. Against hypotheses dividing 2 Corinthians, however, I quote Udo Schnelle: "It is not the possibility but rather the absolute necessity of hypotheses of division which must be regarded as a methodological principle. . . . Up to now, however, for none of Paul's letters has the absolute proof been adduced that he can only be sensibly understood on the foundational basis of hypotheses of division."[41]

As Schnelle observes, one cannot speak of such an absolute necessity with reference to 2 Corinthians. Indeed, one can in fact detect a rough argumentative structure:

1:1-2	Prescript
1:3-7	Thanksgiving
1:8-11	Narratio
1:12-14	Propositio
1:15–7:16	Thematic section 1: the glory of the new covenant
8–9	Thematic section 2: the Corinthians put to the test: the collection for Jerusalem
10:1–13:10	Thematic section 3: the Corinthians admonished regarding power in weakness
13:11ff.	Postscript

The prescript not only introduces the sender and addressees, it also names the God-grounded relationship between them as the basis of their communication. Paul is an apostle of Christ Jesus because God wills it so, and the Corinthians are the church of God. Both the existence of the apostle and the existence of the church are not due to their own efforts. They are both the result of the action of God alone. Only on this basis can any communication between apostle and church succeed.

The thanksgiving explains who the God is to whom the apostle and the church are indebted. He is "the God and Father of our Lord Jesus Christ, the Father of mercies and the God of all consolation" (2 Cor 1:3).

The attached *narratio* in 1:8-11 shows that the God of all consolation does not refuse to console but rather intervenes in a saving fashion. The narration of divine salvation from the danger of death confirms the appropriateness of Paul's self-understanding of himself as an apostle through the will of God.

The *propositio* formulates the fundamental pragmatic concern of the letter: The apostolic office of Paul, willed and preserved by God, is exercised by him through the grace of God in a manner sincere, honorable, clear, and comprehensible. If the addressees rely on it, then the apostle of God and the church of God can boast about it "on the day of the Lord Jesus" (1:14), for this boasting would not be praise of one's self but rather the praise of God, to whom both owe their existence. Put another way, the attempt at successful communication between apostle and church is a soteriological necessity in view of the coming judgment.

The three thematic blocks of 2 Corinthians depend upon this pragmatic intent. In the first section (1:15–7:16) Paul explains his service within the new covenant. Next he recounts why this service did not permit him to visit the Corinthians again. Thereafter he explains the glory of the new covenant, his hermeneutical presuppositions, and his relationship to the old covenant, which still is in force. The argument that follows conceptualizes the new covenant as God's act of reconciliation, which effects the "new creation" (5:17). In the example of the Apostle Paul himself the Corinthians should see that belonging to and service to this covenant involve suffering and danger. At the end of the first thematic block Paul again discusses the delay of his visit.

The second thematic section (chapters 8 and 9) prepares the collection of the Corinthians for Jerusalem. The apostle regards this collection as proof of the reliability of the Corinthians (cf. 7:16).

The third thematic section (10:1–13:10) warns the Corinthians against risking a breach by interpreting the sincerity and simplicity discussed in the *propositio* as powerless weakness. In the same way that the resurrection of Jesus Christ has conquered the martial violence of the cross, the power working effectively in the weakness of the apostle will also show itself as mightier than that of the "super-apostles" who are leading the Corinthians astray (cf. 13:4).

If the first thematic section reveals that Paul reliably fulfills his part required for the success of their communication, then the second thematic section challenges the Corinthians to do likewise on their part with regard to the occasion of the collection. The third section emphatically warns against disturbing their communication by disregarding the communicant Paul. All in all, 2 Corinthians attempts to understand the existence of the apostle and that of the church in Corinth as creative works of God analogous to the resurrection of the Crucified One and therefore to esteem each other and on this basis to communicate with each other.

Strength in Weakness: The Death and Resurrection of Jesus Christ
as the Hermeneutical Key of Apostolic Existence

The experiences of the apostle are presented as immediately relevant to the well-being of the Corinthians he addresses: "If we are being afflicted, it is for your consolation and salvation; if we are being consoled, it is for your consolation, which you experience when you patiently endure the same sufferings that we are also suffering. Our hope for you is unshaken; for we know that as you share in our sufferings, so also you share in our consolation" (2 Cor 1:6-7).[42]

Otfried Hofius has pointed out in his instructive essay "Der Gott allen Trostes"[43] that consolation here aims not at the psychic processing of experiences of suffering, but rather, in a way analogous to Old Testament texts, at the "saving care" of God. God, who in 2 Corinthians is introduced as "the Father of mercies and the God of all consolation" (1:3), is here designated not as a pastor or therapist who cares for the interior of the one in need of consolation, but rather as the mighty doer of wondrous deeds, in accord with the Old Testament picture, who intervenes in the course of events and changes exterior adverse circumstances by his divine power: "With the call, 'Comfort, comfort my people!' (Isa 40:1) heavenly messengers are commissioned to announce the 'consolation of Yahweh'— that is, his saving intervention which turns the tide—to the oppressed people of God."[44]

The narration and its accompanying interpretation in 2 Corinthians 1:8-11 functions as an example-rich proof of the divine intervention effective for Paul's benefit,[45] which he asserted in the thanksgiving.[46] With this autobiographical proof of the consoling act of God which had rescued the apostle, Paul asserts that the appositional marking of his name formulated in verse 1 is no empty claim. His claim rests upon a communicable experience. Paul, the apostle of Jesus Christ by the will of God, therefore stands under the protection of the mighty, wonder-working God. The deliverance from the danger of death recounted in 1:8-11 serves the argumentative strategy of 2 Corinthians as proof of the apostle's legitimacy, right at the beginning of the letter.

This narrative proof is recounted as the story of a miracle. Verses 8-9a depict a scene of extreme deprivation. In the Roman province of Asia a threatening situation arose in which the apostle was in real danger of losing his life. The pleonastic formulation in verse 8 reveals with particular clarity that this situation exceeded the power of the apostle and could not be solved by human means.[47] According to a human estimation of the situation, death was inescapable (cf. v. 9a).

According to Paul, only God could provide deliverance from this situation, for he is the "God who raises the dead."[48] To God, then, is actually ascribed the wondrous deliverance from the danger of death, which verse 10a recounts. Paul draws upon the autobiographical miracle of deliverance to show that the same power of God that effected the resurrection of the crucified Jesus Christ from the dead also works to the benefit of the Apostle Paul.

Paul interprets his deliverance from the danger of death within the horizon of the assumption about reality that is the resurrection of Jesus Christ. According to Paul, the power of the resurrection is first effective not at the eschatological resurrection of the dead, but rather already in the midst of the dangers of this world, for it is one and the same power: the wondrous creative power of the just and merciful God.

The miraculous story in 2 Corinthians 1:8-11 is shot through with theological significance. It is employed as a theological foundation that pervades the argumentation of the entire letter. Verse 9b therefore enmeshes the depiction of the situation with a theological significance, which prepares the narration of the interpretation of the miracle. It is clearly set forth that the self-assessment of being given over to death did not arise from some fear of death precipitated by forgetting about God, but rather concerns a richly intentional event.[49] The confession that he could not master the situation with his own powers, and thus the acceptance of his own powerless weakness, enables his confident turning of himself over to God, the mighty and merciful one who raises the dead.

The wondrous deliverance that took place solves the desperate situation[50] on a narrative level and sanctions the theology of the apostle on a discursive level, a theology that rests not least upon the difference between human and divine possibilities. "In delivering the Apostle of Jesus Christ from affliction and from the power of death which seized him in every affliction, God displays his resurrection power made public in the resurrection of Jesus Christ and reveals himself as the God who is 'the God and Father of our Lord Jesus Christ' and the 'Father of mercy and the God of all consolation.'"[51] This correlates with the confession of the powerless weakness of the apostle, a confession that already here shows itself to be a condition of the saving intervention of divine power, and by means of the discourse on the wonders God has wrought serves as a prelude to the paradoxical thesis of the so-called fool speech, "When I am weak, then am I strong" (12:10b; cf. 13:4).

The wondrous deliverance the apostle experienced in turn forms the ground for the hope for further divine deliverance (cf. 2 Cor 1:10b). "Therefore, after his deliverance from deadly danger in Asia, in 2 Cor 1:8-11 he gives thanks not for the strength to endure but rather for the actual removal of the external affliction."[52] The apostle thus respects the sovereignty of God by not counting on an automatic guarantee of further deliverance, but rather asks God specifically for it. In contrast to Stoic wisdom "the δύναμις of the Lord is and remains for Paul a *via aliena* that always comes from the outside and does not become the possession of men."[53]

The Corinthians the apostle addresses are included in this discourse of wonders by means of a direct appeal in 2 Corinthians 1:11. They can contribute to the apostle's grounds for hope for further divine protection by asking God for this protection in the future and by giving thanks for the protection God has already shown. This appeal takes over the function of the acclamation (*Chorschluß*) in other miracle stories. The thanksgiving of the congregation for the evident gift (χάρισμα)[54] of the recounted act of deliverance, and the request for further divine protection, appropriately portray the reaction of the congregation to the wondrous saving action of God and contribute to the further divine protection of the apostle.

If the congregation were to comply with the apostle's appeal, it would at the same time sanction Paul's apostleship and his concomitant authority along with his theology, whose argumentation to a great degree depends on the difference between human helplessness and divine creative power (cf. 1 Cor 6:18c).[55] According to Paul, this is demonstrated in unsurpassable ways in the resurrection of Jesus Christ.[56] The congregation would thus at the same time confirm the reading contract of reciprocal recognition (*Lektuerevertrag*) written in the prescript.

The question concerning the concrete details of Paul's miraculous deliverance—that is, when, where precisely, and above all from which situation Paul experienced rescue—has exercised readers of this section again and again.[57] But it is precisely the indeterminacy of this story of miraculous deliverance that lends it its paradigmatic power within the framework of 2 Corinthians: It serves as a model par excellence for the interpretation of the dangers the apostle faced. With the help of the directions for reading provided by the paradigmatic miracle narrative, all the desperate situations in which the apostle found himself and especially those that according to human measure must be evaluated as mortal danger confirm both the divine protection of and thus the legitimacy of Paul's apostleship and also his thesis that divine power is demonstrated precisely in human helplessness.[58]

Seen from this perspective, the numerous lists of suffering in 2 Corinthians are to be read as metonymies of the wondrous acts of divine deliverance: they are, in other words, concentrated miracle stories that, by means of their theological message distinguishing between divine miraculous power and human helplessness, fulfill the function of confirming the divine calling of the weak Paul as an apostle of Jesus Christ. Again and again God employs the power of the resurrection for the apostle.

Second Corinthians 10–13 is ultimately based on this argumentative strategy. In chapters 10–13 Paul reacts to an accusation that he repeats explicitly in 10:10: "For they say, 'His letters are weighty and strong, but his bodily presence is weak, and his speech contemptible.'" In this accusation, Paul's body is read as a sign that contradicts the office of an apostle. The apologetic argumentation strategy of 2 Corinthians consists not in disputing the accusation of bodily weakness (ἀσθένεια), but rather in the new encoding of the sign ἀσθένεια. With help from the characterization of God as the God of consolation and mercy with his Old Testament connotations in 1:3-7, with help from the paradigmatic story of miraculous deliverance in 1:8-11, and with the theological argumentation of the list of hardships, in the framework of apostolic service the sign of weakness is reevaluated as a sign of the sincerity of the apostle and as a sign of his divine protection, which in turn demonstrates the legitimacy of the claim to be an apostle of Jesus Christ. "Only if he is able to establish weakness as a legitimate side of his apostleship can he make that claim in comparison to his opponents and buttress his opening appeal. The intention of depicting his belonging to Christ and his full authority as an apostle in his weakness therefore forms the thread of the whole of his argumentation in 2 Corinthians 10–13 and also the material assumptions for the authority of his appeals."[59]

With this semantic overcoding, the apostolic description offered by Paul's critics in 2 Corinthians 10:10 is not fundamentally challenged but rather surpassed. The confrontation with his adversaries is not conducted by rebuffing their claims about the signs of an apostle. Paul advances no ideology of weakness and certainly no glorification of suffering and danger. Much more does Paul make clear in his autobiography that his service suffices also for these claims about the signs of apostleship. In this connection 12:11b-13 is of special significance: "Indeed you should have been the ones commending me, for I am not at all inferior to these super-apostles, even though I am nothing. The signs of a true apostle were performed among you with utmost patience, signs and wonders and mighty works. How have you been worse off than the other churches, except that I myself did not burden you? Forgive me this wrong!"

This section illustrates the surpassing integration of the usual signs of an apostle and of the overcoded sign of weakness. The addressees are called upon to serve as signs among whom signs and wonders and mighty deeds were performed in connection with Paul's apostolic activity. By designating these signs, wonders, and mighty deeds with the syntagm "the signs of an apostle," they are sanctioned as legitimately claimed events.[60] The *passivum divinum* makes it clear, however, that the subject of these apostolic signs is not any human commissioned agent but rather God himself. God is the worker of wonders who performs the signs of an apostle.

The paradoxical structure of human helplessness and divine power, which shows itself precisely in the recounted miracles, altogether characterizes the appearance of the Apostle Paul as he depicts it in 2 Corinthians. Thus the body of the Apostle Paul itself functions as an authentic sign of his theological message.

This sign function of the body is emphasized in 2 Corinthians 12:7-10: "Therefore, to keep me from being too elated, a thorn was given me in the flesh, a messenger of Satan to torment me, to keep me from being too elated" (12:7). The "thorn in the flesh" is thus according to 2 Corinthians not a question of an illness arising in some natural way, but rather a question of a sign of memory and admonition carved into Paul's body by God[61] with pedagogical intention. Paul's wounded body is an event willed by divine action. It is the visible locus of a miracle.

This sign of remembrance apparently caused the apostle considerable bodily pains. Therefore the apostle "three times . . . appealed to the Lord" to remove the sign of remembrance from his body (2 Cor 12:8). The autobiographical narrator did not therefore abandon himself to his suffering, but rather appealed to God for help fully in the sense of the Old Testament Psalms of lamentation. The logic of this request is that God, the powerful cause of this bodily infirmity, can eliminate this deficiency once again with his wonder-working power. The apostle thus appeals to God for a new wonder in the knowledge that God has the power to do this wonder—but God refused. Instead, God speaks a promise to him: "My grace is sufficient for you, for power is made perfect in weakness" (12:9a).

It is to Ulrich Heckel's credit that he has drawn attention to the fact that the divine promise here is no appeal by Paul to resign himself to his suffering. According to Heckel, "exegetical works to this point have overlooked that the verb ἀρκεῖν does not in the 2d pers. sg. pass. call Paul to passivity, to self-sufficiency, and to contentment with grace (ἀρκεῖ), but rather standing in the 3d pers. sg. act, which has χάρις for a subject and promises the apostle (σοι is a dative object) the wide-reaching sufficiency of divine grace (ἀρκεῖ σοι ἡ χάρις μου). . . . As the word of the Lord here has not fulfilled the original prayer request of the apostle, the reply does indeed function at first as a denial, but it also in the same breath already surpasses this impression of repudiation through the all-encompassing promise that divine grace suffices and that power is made perfect in weakness."[62] The autobiographical narrator identifies this power made perfect in weakness with the "power of Christ" and thus so interprets the just-cited promise of God.

The syntagm "power of Christ" is not a *genitivus subiectivus*, however, but rather a *genitivus obiectivus*, and thus the phrase does not concern a power whose cause is Christ, but rather the power which also was and is effective in the Christ event. One can see this clearly in 2 Corinthians 13:4: "For he was crucified in weakness, but lives by the power of God. For we are weak in him, but in dealing with you we will live with him by the power of God." The wounded body of the apostle is a sign of the crucifixion. The preservation and deliverance of his wounded body from the astonishing multitude of perils presented in the list of hardships is the wondrous sign of the effect of this power in the present experience of the apostle. Even beyond that, it is a sign of the future life (cf. 12:10, διό). Not only are Jesus Christ's death by crucifixion and the weakness of the apostle set in parallel, but the present life of the resurrected Crucified One is also set in parallel with the power that will work in the apostle when he again finds himself among the Corinthians.[63] Through this strategic parallelism, the proclamation of the working of this divine power becomes a threat to those who would deny Paul's apostleship.

The "life of Jesus" (ἡ ζωὴ τοῦ Ἰησοῦ, 2 Cor 4:11) of which Paul speaks does not refer to any memory of the life of Jesus of Nazareth in flesh and blood before his crucifixion. The life of Jesus before his resurrection is the past, and Paul formulates it in the sharpest relief: "even though we once knew Christ from a human point of view, we know him no longer in that way" (5:16b). The Kyrios, whose apostle Paul claims to be, is the resurrected Crucified One, the living Lord working in Paul's present experience.

New Creation

According to Paul, the creative power of the merciful God works in the present for a great deal more than just his own good. Belonging to the resurrected Crucified One transforms all believers now in the present: "So if anyone is in Christ, there is a new creation (καινὴ κτίσις): everything old has passed away; see, everything has become new!" (2 Cor 5:17). Participation in the community with the resurrected Crucified One, who laid aside flesh and blood and who sits at the right hand of God in a form newly created by God, effects the transformation of believers even now: "And all of us, with unveiled faces, seeing the glory of the Lord as though reflected in a mirror, are being transformed into the same image from one degree of glory to another; for this comes from the Lord, the Spirit" (3:18).

Turning to the resurrected Crucified One affects not only knowledge, which enables one to understand what was already in the Torah in an "unveiled" way (cf. 2 Cor 3:15-16). It also transforms even now the entire human being, something that is again impressively displayed in the apostle himself. The persecutor of the church of God has become the apostle of the church of God. Since he turned to Christ—more precisely, since Christ turned to him and he accepted this turning—he himself is a "new creation" (cf. also Phil 3:7-8).

The new life of the apostle reflects the glory of the Lord, because it portrays a living sign of his resurrection, of the resurrection of the Crucified One brought about by God. The life-giving pneuma of the resurrected Crucified One becomes perceptible for all believers in the transformation of his existence. Paul is "the aroma of Christ to God among those who are being saved and among those who are perishing; to the one a fragrance from death to death, to the other a fragrance from life to life" (2 Cor 1:15b-16a). Whoever does not perceive the resurrection power of God in the transformation of Paul's existence fails to participate in the saving communion with the resurrected Crucified One and thus continues to wallow in death. On the other hand, whoever perceives in Paul that he is the apostle of Christ already savors life as a foretaste of the life eternal that is to come in communion with the Kyrios.

Interpreting the resurrection along the lines of the creation theology, as indicated by the syntagm "new creation," also illuminates 2 Corinthians 4:6. This verse weaves together expressions of creation theology, pneumatology, Christology, and autobiography in a poetic fashion. With the intertextual reference to Genesis 1:3 Paul determines the subject of the action in 2 Corinthians 4:6. It is the God who made light shine in the darkness. The darkness has nothing to do with the light; it has no part in it. God alone is the sovereign creator of the light. With this intertextual reference to creation theology in Genesis 1, Paul sketches the theological horizon of his emotional faith—his existential experience of faith—and theological thought. At the same time this reference provides him with the linguistic material of his metaphorical theology as the verse progresses. Thus he expresses the identity of the God to whom the Scriptures of Israel bear witness with the God whom Paul experienced in his vision of Jesus and whom he proclaims. The God whom Paul the apostle of Christ proclaims is the same God whom Paul the Pharisee had worshiped. Yet, in his vision of Jesus Christ the Jew, Paul recognized the glory of God, his δόξα, the *kabod* of *YHWH* in a new way. In chapter 3 he describes this difference with the metaphor of Moses' veil and with the oppositional pair veiled/unveiled. The God of Israel is and remains the God whom Paul proclaims, but he now knows him in a different way.

The same verb with which Paul brought Genesis 1:3 into play, *to shine* (λάμπειν), carries the verse forward. The God who caused the light to shine in the darkness is precisely the God who has thus acted once more to create out of nothing by shining "in our hearts."

The word "heart" plays a fundamental role in 2 Corinthians. It is the place into which God pours out the Holy Spirit to those who have received the promises of the story of the cross and resurrection as a guarantee of eternal life in communion with the resurrected Crucified One, in communion with God (cf. 2 Cor 1:22; 3:3; 5:5). It is the organ that is responsible for successful communication between Paul and the congregation in Corinth (cf. 2 Cor 6:12 and 7:2ff.). The heart is the instance of human communicative capability with one another, but also of humans with God.

The creative God who caused light to shine out of the darkness has creatively shined into our hearts for the illumination of knowledge. Paul designates the new thing that has illuminated him as a light created and given by the creative God with a certain aim. The preposition πρός points in the direction at which divine illumination aims. God has shined for the illumination of a wholly determined knowledge, for the knowledge of the glory of God—as it was granted to Paul the Jew, the zealot for God, who persecuted the church of Christ—in looking at the visage of Christ, the resurrected Crucified One. In 1 Corinthians 9:1 he describes it as follows: "Am I not an apostle? Have I not seen Jesus our Lord?" And in Galatians 1:15-16, he writes of how it pleased God to reveal his son to Paul. By recognizing in the vision of the resurrected Crucified One the glory of the God of Israel, the glory of his God, the Jewish zealot Paul became a new creation. "So if anyone is in Christ, there is a new creation: everything old has passed away; see, everything has become new!" (2 Cor 5:17).

Paul recognizes the glory of God in the light of his vision of the resurrected Crucified One, and he describes the narrow relationship between God and the resurrected crucified Jesus as the loving relationship of father and son. He recognizes in this God the faithful God of Israel who stands behind all his promises. He recognizes in the unitary event of the death and resurrection the great Yes of God to all his promises: "For the Son of God, Jesus Christ, whom we proclaimed among you . . . was not 'Yes and No'; but in him it is always 'Yes'" (2 Cor 1:19). Paul knows this God from now on as the Father of Jesus Christ, as "the Father of mercies and the God of all consolation" (1:3) and Jesus Christ, the Son of God, as our Kyrios, our Lord.

God's consolation does not fail. God comforts by creating salvation. He is the God who with his creative power "raises the dead" and who also has delivered the apostle several times over from mortal danger and many desperate situations (cf. 2 Cor 1:8-11). Precisely in this consists the glory of God that enlightened Paul in the vision of the resurrected Crucified One: He creates out of nothing, overcomes the cross, raises the Crucified One, chooses the lowly, shows himself merciful and kind, and gives new, eternal life creatively to his hopeless creation, to his damaged and damage-causing creatures again and ever again, giving them ultimate salvation in Jesus Christ. In the act of the resurrection of Jesus, unjustly executed on the cross, the creative God shows forth his mercy and justice at the same time.

Paul does not, however, understand this knowledge that creates new life as the logical conclusion from his own theological or religious-philosophical power of thinking. Rather, he sees it as illumination, as a divine creative act of creation. The metaphor of light in our hearts points to the working of the Holy Spirit. The "guarantee of the Spirit" (2 Cor 5:5) now effects transformation to life. Whomever God spiritually illuminates is already a new creature, and not only metaphorically! According to Paul, believers radiate joy over the life-creating gift of the illuminating Spirit, whenever it is depicted before their very eyes that Jesus of Nazareth, so cruelly executed on the cross, was in fact never abandoned by God, not even in those moments in which he himself perhaps felt desolation. God has drawn him out of death and pulled him into the eternal life of God. According to Paul God offers everyone this eternal life, everyone who through the Jesus-Christ-Story lets himself be shown who God is.

The transformation of believers that has already occurred in the present through the Spirit of Christ does not replace the resurrection of the dead, or the transformation of those who yet live at the return of the Kyrios. The resurrection of the dead remains an event lying in the future. Paul does not employ the terminology of the resurrection for the presently occurring transformation of believers into new creatures in a metaphorical way. "New creation" is instead the syntagm that interprets both the present transformation and also the future resurrection of the dead as well as the eschatological transformation of the bodies of those still living along the lines of creation theology.

Individual Resurrection after Death or Collective Resurrection on the Day of the Lord?

"We know that the one who raised the Lord Jesus will raise us also with Jesus, and will bring us with you into his presence" (2 Cor 4:14). While the resurrection of Jesus Christ has already occurred, the resurrection of the dead remains a future event. By way of contrast to 1 Thessalonians and 1 Corinthians 15, Paul here appears to count on the fact that the return of the Kyrios will occur after his death.[64] In any event it is clear that Paul does not claim to know when the Day of the Lord will come, even though he mentions the eschatological event of the return of the Kyrios in the immediate context.

As in 1 Thessalonians 4 and in 1 Corinthians 15, 2 Corinthians 4:14 also produces the impression that no further individual resurrections follow the individual case of the resurrection of the Crucified One as forerunner, but rather that on the day of the return of the Kyrios all the dead will be raised at the same time.

Second Corinthians 5:1-10 produces another impression, however. Here mortal bodies stand in the way of spatial communion with the resurrected Crucified One: "while we are at home in the body we are away from the Lord." The newly created body of the resurrected Crucified One makes it possible for him to enter into the eternal life of God, to sit at the right hand of God, as Paul expresses it in the words of Psalm 110. Communion between the somatically absent Lord and those members belonging to him is produced through the spirit, who was given as a "guarantee" (cf. 2 Cor 5:5). The bodily distance from the Resurrected One is overcome only when the earthly, mortal body is done away with and the new body created again by God is put on, for as is the case with the body of the resurrected Christ, the other resurrected ones will receive a body that "is from heaven" (cf. 5:2b). In 5:8, however, Paul says, "Yes, we do have confidence, and we would rather be away from the body and at home with the Lord." Here at least Paul counts on the fact that one is raised immediately after death and enters into heavenly life.

In 2 Corinthians 12:1 Paul comes to speak about his "visions and revelations of the Lord" and recounts his heavenly journey in the third person. Within the framework of the universe of discourse of 2 Corinthians, it is neither a matter of providing a psychological explanation for an imagined trip nor a "parody of a tale of a heavenly ascension."[65] Rather, it concerns an event that Paul experienced as rapture. The way the story is recounted in the third person fits stylistically with two observations: (1) Paul here is not the autonomous subject of his own travel itinerary, but rather a passive object of a divine, miraculous rapture, so that he cannot say with any certainty whether the journey was "in the body or out of the body" (12:3). (2) In accord with that fact, neither does Paul want the journey to be considered as something he himself merited (cf. 12:5). In any case, however, it is a question of an individual experience of rapture and heaven is envisaged as a tiered space that can be perceived with or without the body if God brings an individual to it. Paul gives no more precise information regarding how one could conceive a rapture outside of the body. Indeed, he does not work with the Greek distinction between soul and body, but it is clear that with this experience of rapture Paul can now draw on an imaginative way of thinking that permits a conception of entry into heavenly life as an individual act.

In 2 Corinthians 5:1-10 there abruptly appear juxtaposed the collective and individual conceptions of the resurrection of the dead. Verse 10, which concludes the section, belongs in turn to the eschatological-apocalyptic conception of the day of judgment at the end of time.

This irresolvable tension in Paul's resurrection discourse necessitates the insight that Paul's words about the resurrection of the dead should not be conceived as factual knowledge, as quasi-empirical foreknowledge, but rather as metaphorical pictures that express his certainty that death can no longer cancel communion with the resurrected Crucified One. Much more does this communion reach its end through the eschatological resurrection of the dead, that is, through a metamorphosis including the bodies of those remaining alive: "At the consummation, the power of the Lord comes ultimately in God's conquering of human mortal frailty and in eternal life with Christ (13:4). The central problem is not how the all-powerful and merciful God can permit suffering. Rather, in the resurrection of the dead Paul sees proof of the power of the creator and the key to understanding the power of God, who has indeed proven his might in the exaltation of Christ and will bring it to completion in the resurrection of Christians."[66]

The Coherence of Resurrection Discourse in the Corinthian Correspondence

In both Corinthian letters the theology of the resurrection has a fundamental function. In 1 Corinthians Paul develops the gospel as the word of the cross. The message of the cross *is* the gospel proclaimed by Paul, for the complex of the events of the crucifixion of Jesus Christ and his resurrection through the merciful and just creator God, as the Holy Scriptures of Israel have convinced Paul, involves a soteriological and cosmological significance that changes everything. Through that significance God enables communion with the resurrected Crucified One and participation in his somatic solidarity with all who have suffered injustice. This communion preserves one from the righteous wrath of God on the day of eschatological judgment and leads to the eternal communion of heavenly life. This communion with the Kyrios already exists by means of his life-creating Spirit, which one experiences semiotically and somatically in the Lord's Supper. The exchange of believers' identities completed in the act of baptism obligates them to a God-pleasing life that corresponds to the mercy of God. The resurrection of the dead is explained as a necessary consequence that arises out of the resurrection of the Crucified One understood as an event. The defeat of the power of death through the eschatological resurrection ultimately displays the unbounded nature of the merciful creative power of God. The panegyric confession of the resurrection power of God, displayed in the resurrection of the Crucified One, gives the honor to the merciful and just creator God which is his due, and thereby produces a fitting relationship of the creature to his creator.

Second Corinthians relates that this wondrous creative power of God, which effected the resurrection of Him who was unjustly crucified, is effective also in the present experience of believers. By means of this power God saves his apostle from mortal danger again and again. Paul's wounded, powerless body and the success of his proclamation are themselves signs of the reality of the Crucified One who was raised.

The illumination of the Spirit permits all those incorporated into communion with the resurrected Crucified One to become new creatures already in the here and now, just as the persecutor of the church of God became its apostle and just as the congregation in Corinth was produced through the reality-creating power made effective in the word of the cross. This Spirit is the guarantee of eternal life in communion with the Kyrios Jesus, the Son of God, the resurrected Crucified One.

Romans

In his letter to the Roman community, Paul seeks to make preparations for his intended missionary journey to Spain (cf. Rom 15:22-29).[67] He would like to win over the Roman Christians so that they will support his plans. Since there was no contact between Paul and the Roman community before the composition of the Letter to the Romans, he sets forth the fundamental points of the gospel he preaches in fundamental ways. Thus verses 1:16-17 fulfill the task of a *propositio*, and put forth the thesis-like depiction of the fundamental conception, which is then fleshed out from different vantage points and in differing thematic connections in the following chapters. The *propositio* asserts that the gospel is "the power of God for salvation to everyone who has faith, to the Jew first and also to the Greek. For in it the righteousness of God is revealed through faith for faith; as it is written, 'The one who is righteous will live by faith.'"

The section of 1:18–3:20 describes the sinfulness of all men and thus provides the reason why it requires an actual rescue. Paul names the danger from which one must be rescued as the annihilating "wrath of God" (Rom 1:18).

The section of Romans 3:21-31 functions first and foremost as an indication of time. The time of God's patience, which has postponed the annihilating exercise of his just wrath, is now over. "Now" (3:21) has the time of decision broken in, for the righteousness that matters before God was revealed, the "righteousness of God through faith in Jesus Christ for all who believe" (3:22). Chapter 4 relates how this faith is created. The section of 5:1-11 explains that the event of the death and resurrection of Jesus Christ achieves reconciliation with God and hope in eternal life. The Adam–Christ typology in 5:13-21 thematizes how general sinfulness came into being and how it is conquered. Through reflection on the act of baptism, chapter 6 presents how one comes to participate in communion with the resurrected Crucified One and what it effects. Chapter 7 is dedicated to the theme of the law and discusses the position of those who believe in Jesus Christ relative to the law. Chapter 8 is concerned with the new life already made possible through faith and its cosmological dimensions. Chapters 9–11 inquire about the effects of the *propositio* for the chosen people of Israel. The section of 12:1–15:13 makes the *propositio* concrete for the congregation's life in relation to the life it shares with wider Roman society. In 15:14-33 the work of the apostle is then reflected and his further plans are related. A detailed list of persons to greet, warnings against heresies, greetings to the Roman congregation, and a closing doxology bring the letter to an end with chapter 16.

In the Letter to the Romans we find mention of the resurrection in almost every chapter.[68] More than that, though, we also find that the resurrection of the Crucified One forms the cosmological turning point and the fixed hermeneutical point for the apostle's theology, with which the entire writing is shot through. The gospel that Paul sets before the Romans as the saving power of God is the Jesus-Christ-Story of the death and resurrection of the Crucified One. The gospel is the word of the cross also in the Letter to the Romans.

The Gospel of the Resurrection of the Crucified One as the Saving Power of God

"For I am not ashamed of the gospel; it is the power of God for salvation to everyone who has faith, to the Jew first and also to the Greek. For in it the righteousness of God is revealed through faith for faith; as it is written, 'The one who is righteous will live by faith'" (Rom 1:16-17). With these words, Paul provides the Romans with a precise and pithy summary of the gospel he proclaims and means to bear to Spain. These phrases do not simply repeat the content of the gospel, but rather clarify its character and function. They identify it namely as the power of God. It is no human word, no wise speech, no philosophical proverb. It is something other and indeed much more than that: It is good news that unfolds as the effectual power of God. This power of God effects the salvation of all believers. Again, what is communicated is not what, or in what, one should believe, or even from what salvation is necessary. But verse 17 does, at the very least, tell why the gospel permits this saving effectual power to unfold. In this gospel, in this good message, the righteousness of God is being revealed publicly, visibly, perceptibly, and experientially, though not apparently for everyone, but rather "through faith for faith."

The righteousness of God can be perceived in this good news as nothing other than a turning to the gospel in assurance and confidence. It leads neither to a knowledge of nor a proof for the validity of this good news that could be grasped apart from faith. One need not believe in any empty tomb, any neutral witnesses, any chain of evidence, that could force one to come to the inductive conclusion of the experiential wisdom of this world, because that would be something empirically or historically demonstrable. No coercive list of facts is employed. The gospel reveals itself as the saving power of God only through faith, and it also leads to nothing other than faith.

The characterization of his gospel in Romans 1:16-17 raises questions that the letter as a whole answers: What is the gospel about? In what or in whom does one believe? For what is the saving power of the gospel necessary? Put differently, from what must one be saved? In which ways does the gospel reveal the righteousness of God? How does one come to the faith that enables one to see and hear the gospel as the revelation of the righteousness of God, or how can one enter into this saving faith? And finally, why does Paul, the writer of the letter, never simply communicate the content of the gospel?

The answer to this last question is easy to give, and from that answer the answers to the other questions formulated above open up to readers of the Letter to the Romans. Paul has already delineated the content of the gospel in Romans 1:2-15. He has already in 1:1-4 set himself forth as the one who proclaims the gospel by divine commission, as the prophets of Israel received it: "Paul, a servant of Jesus Christ, called to be an apostle, set apart for the gospel of God, which he promised beforehand through his prophets in the holy scriptures, the gospel concerning his Son, who was descended from David according to the flesh and was declared to be Son of God with power according to the spirit of holiness by resurrection from the dead, Jesus Christ our Lord." The gospel Paul proclaims is the gospel of God. This gospel is announced in the Scriptures of Israel. Paul thus makes the continuity of the gospel with the Old Testament witness clear. Its content, however, consists in the Jesus-Christ-Story, the narrative of the Son of God who was according to the flesh a descendant of David, but who, as the Son of God, has a second origin as well: his resurrection from the dead. This event does not obey the laws of human possibilities and human categories of experience.[69] The resurrection happened not κατὰ σάρκα (according to the flesh) but rather is an event κατὰ πνεῦμα ἁγιωσύνης (according to the Spirit of sanctification). Jesus Christ was not made Son of God according to his genealogical origins, which belong to the realm of reality according to human expectations. Rather, he was made Son of God effectively (ἐν δυνάμει) according to the reality that arises from the Spirit of sanctification, the spirit of the creative God.[70] The mention of his human heritage points to the fact that this Jesus, witnessed by humans, this bodily man has been raised from the dead by God. This resurrected Jesus was determined by God to be the Son of God. Thus the gospel of God Paul proclaims tells the Jesus-Christ-Story, and its center and pivot is the resurrection of the crucified Jesus Christ.[71]

This gospel has saving power: "because if you confess with your lips that Jesus is Lord and believe in your heart that God raised him from the dead, you will be saved" (Rom 10:9). But from what must one be saved? The section of 1:18–3:20 elucidates and answers this question. One needs to be saved from the coming wrath of God (cf. 1:18), which represents the just answer to the sins of his human creatures.

The wrath of God is no emotional mood of an unmerciful potentate. It is instead a reaction of the righteous creator God. God cannot tolerate the injustice of this world because he is the just and merciful creator.[72] His mercy makes him a God who is involved whenever injustice happens. He suffers with the weak, the scandalized, the oppressed, the exploited, the hungry, the tortured, the crucified. Injustice has many names, but in his creation-theological argumentation Paul returns to a cause that is also recounted in Genesis 3. Man does not regard his existence as creature. He does not give his creator honor, but rather wants to be like God (cf. Gen 3:5-6). Thus he loses the way of life, of the creaturely life of the solidarity of male and female and refuses God the honor that is owed to him as the creator of life.

The German language designates this lapse (ἁμαρτία) of creaturely life, this misstep (παράπτωμα), in which all injustice has its ultimate ground, with the word *Sünde* (sin). In his argumentation in Romans 1:18–3:20 Paul makes clear that all, be they Jews or Greeks, have made themselves guilty of this fundamental lapse; "For what can be known about God is plain to them, because God has shown it to them. Ever since the creation of the world his eternal power and divine nature, invisible though they are, have been understood and seen through the things he has made. So they (all) are without excuse" (1:19-20). This human sinfulness calls forth God's wrath, and it is precisely from this immeasurable, powerful, and annihilating wrath that man needs to be saved.

In Pauline thinking, as it is handed down to us in his letters, God is the powerful creator who remains turned toward his creation through his justice and mercy. Justice and mercy are the fundamental expressions of the relationship of God to his creation. The righteousness of God consists in the fact that he alone administers the position of God with his power and releases humanity into a caring life of creaturely solidarity. It would be unjust if humanity were required to take on the tasks of God. Humanity may rather know itself to be kept by the creative reality of the God who shepherds them. According to Paul we may know ourselves to be accepted and loved by the life-creating mercy of God, a love so almighty that nothing and no one can destroy it (cf. 8:31-39). We may know ourselves to be wanted by the God who has made everything by his caring will. God's righteousness demands this relationship between creator and creature because it is only in this way that a human and creaturely life of solidarity is possible. God's righteousness consists in his forbidding of any injustice that befalls his creatures to be forgotten. Whoever gives God honor as creator recognizes at the same time his own position as a creature wanted and loved. Only such a one can see his fellows and his "world" as the creation of God wanted and loved. He will then strive for a way of life and conduct that gives thanks for his creaturely existence.

According to Paul, God, however, is not a God who says, "Hey! No hard feelings." For God cannot and will not tolerate injustice.[73] Were he to tolerate or forget an act of injustice, he would be leaving victims of power and violence in the lurch and would even then be setting himself on the side of the perpetrators. Injustice permits no neutrality. God stands by and with the victims. God will hold court (cf. 14:10c). His annihilating wrath gives the answer to all injustice on the day of judgment. Paul is convinced that this day is immediately imminent (cf. 13:11) and that there is only one thing that saves one from this wrath: the gospel of God.

In light of this background, we can now understand in which ways the gospel reveals the righteousness of God (cf. Rom 1:17). The gospel narrates the Jesus-Christ-Story with the hermeneutical fixed point of the resurrection of the Crucified One at the center. The cross functions as a metonymy for the injustice of this world. On the cross Jesus was unjustly beaten, tortured, killed. God attacked this injustice, for it abused the creaturely solidarity of the one killed and thus at the same time his creator. The resurrection of the Crucified One exposes the injustice of the act and makes God's righteousness known. It consists in the concerned intervention of God, which restores to the one killed his right to life, and even more takes him up as the Son of God into the eternal divine life. The power of God made visible in the resurrection of the Crucified One is the immeasurable power of the creator, against which even death itself is powerless. God restores justice with his immeasurable might.

Whoever gives God honor as the creator will live and enter into the eternal life of God. Whoever continues to refuse to give God honor in light of the saving story the gospel narrates must reckon with the annihilating power of his wrath. Believing the narrative of the resurrection of the Crucified One in accord with the Spirit of sanctification means giving God honor and understanding oneself as created. The righteousness of God thus emerges, however, as a fitting relationship between creator and creature.[74]

Faith as Confidence in the Limitless Creative Power of God

Because the event of the resurrection of the Crucified One does not follow the regular laws of the created order (κατὰ σάρκα) but rather results from the reality-making power of the creator (κατὰ πνεῦμα ἁγιωσύνης), it can neither be grasped nor proven by the empirical or logical wisdom of this world. This truth is grasped only "through faith for faith" (cf. Rom 1:17). Chapter 4 elaborates this aspect of the *propositio* using the example of Abraham. This example grounds the thesis "that a person is justified by faith apart from works prescribed by the law" (3:28b). In 4:3 Paul cites Genesis 15:6: "For what does the scripture say? 'Abraham believed God, and it was reckoned to him as righteousness.'"

Abraham's faith made him the father of all who believe (cf. 4:11-12). His faith serves for Paul as a model for the sort of faith that the gospel he proclaims seeks to ignite.[75] It is a faith that requires no sign, no empirical or philosophical proof. This faith follows neither the force of fact nor the inevitability of deductive or inductive conclusions. Rather, it is a faith that binds itself to the power of the merciful and just creator God without any validation. It is the God whom Abraham believed "who gives life to the dead and calls into existence the things that do not exist" (4:17b). Käsemann's comments are fitting: "As in 2 Cor 1:9, Paul takes up the Jewish predication of God from the second of the Eighteen Benedictions: 'Yahweh, who gives life to the dead.' This explains his unusual use of the verb 'to give life' instead of 'to raise.' Another common Jewish formulation is also involved. . . . It reveals that God's sovereign act of creation occurs, the call of the creator endures, and the resurrection of the dead must be advanced in such a connection. The resurrection does not concern surviving the grave, but rather the eschatological *creatio ex nihilo*, as it is the work of the creator who acts in his Word since the beginning of the world."[76]

According to Paul, the faith of Abraham is shown in an exemplary way in the story of the miraculous arrival of Isaac: "Hoping against hope, he believed that he would become 'the father of many nations,' according to what was said, 'So numerous shall your descendants be.' He did not weaken in faith when he considered his own body, which was already as good as dead (for he was about a hundred years old), or when he considered the barrenness of Sarah's womb. No distrust made him waver concerning the promise of God, but he grew strong in his faith as he gave glory to God, being fully convinced that God was able to do what he had promised. Therefore his faith 'was reckoned to him as righteousness'" (Rom 4:18-22).

As Paul presents it,[77] the faith of Abraham reckons with the immeasurable creative power of God. This faith is therefore reckoned as righteousness, because Abraham sets himself as a creature in the appropriate relationship with the creator. With his confidence in the creator's ability, he gives the creator honor. The God of Abraham calls that which is not into being, just as Genesis 1 recounts. This wondrous power of God is not bounded by death. Paul purposely chooses the metaphor of the state of death for Abraham's inability to sire offspring at a hundred years old and his wife Sarah's inability to conceive. The creator God creates new life out of their dead bodies, Isaac, the child of the promise of the God who makes the dead live.

Paul explicitly writes himself and his readers into this miracle story: "Now the words, 'it was reckoned to him,' were written not for his sake alone, but for ours also. It will be reckoned to us who believe in him who raised Jesus our Lord from the dead, who was handed over to death for our trespasses and was raised for our justification" (Rom 4:23-25).

The Holy Scriptures of Israel contain a message that expands its realm of validity over what is narrated into the present situation of Paul and his addressees. In view of the miraculous promise of an heir, the story of Abraham's faith not only narrates Abraham's holding fast in faith but also illustrates how God's righteousness is continued through faith. That is, to the believer who counts on God's creative power over that which is possible and that which a person can expect, it is precisely his faith that is reckoned as righteousness.[78]

This reciprocal logic also holds true for the gospel of the resurrected Crucified One. Whoever counts on God's creative power, and therefore ascribes truth to the narrative of the death and resurrection of the Crucified One, will be ascribed righteousness by God, because such a one gives God honor. If the sinfulness of creatures, their individualistic injustice, brought Jesus to the cross, then the resurrection of the Crucified One brings those who believe the gospel into justification. God reckons righteousness to them because they believe God raised Jesus, for thus the creatures give their creator the honor due to him alone (cf. also 10:4).

The Work of the Spirit, the Efficacy of Baptism, and the Future of the Resurrection of the Dead

God thus now grants his righteousness to those who believe the gospel narrated in this way (cf. Rom 5:1). God is reconciled with believers already in the here and now (cf. 5:10). Believers can even now live in "peace with God" (5:1), for the just and merciful God grants them grace through their Kyrios Jesus Christ. This grace of God reveals itself in believers as efficacious, because God pours out his love into their hearts "through the Holy Spirit that has been given to us" (5:5). This love of God, poured into the hearts of believers through the Spirit of God, effects hope, just as the resurrected Crucified One entered into the glory of God (cf. 5:2b).

That the resurrection of the dead that is still to come is thus meant is clearly seen in Paul's explication of the reality-changing event of baptism. Baptism effects the identification of the one who is baptized with the crucified Jesus Christ. This solidarity with the one who was unjustly killed effects the cessation of the entanglements and bondages of the prior existence of the one baptized. He does not remain in this condition without connections, but rather receives even now, as a gift, the new existence of a life in communion with the resurrected Crucified One and in communion with other believers. This exchange of existence is made complete through the act of baptism and interpreted in a way analogous to the death and resurrection of the Crucified One (cf. 6:2-11).

But even the new life after baptism still stands under the eschatological condition of the resurrection of the dead yet to come. The only one raised already, over whom death can claim nothing more, is the resurrected Crucified One, Jesus Christ (cf. Rom 6:9).

The resurrection of the dead does not only amount to a new understanding of existence on the part of believers. Rather, it is an event still to come in which is contained the hope of transformation. The Spirit of God's love poured into the hearts of believers permits them to perceive, but not see, the divine promise of entry into God's glory, into God's eternal life even now. It is not yet an existence they have fully entered. Eternal life still remains a future hope. But they live with this hope, grounded in the gift of the Holy Spirit, that they too will be raised, that is, transformed bodily, and will enter into the glory of God: "If the Spirit of him who raised Jesus from the dead dwells in you, he who raised Christ from the dead will give life to your mortal bodies also through his Spirit that dwells in you." It is this Spirit of God who permits the creature to feel his or her status as a child of God and thus to know to address the creator as a loving Father, in confidence: "For you did not receive a spirit of slavery to fall back into fear, but you have received a spirit of adoption. When we cry, 'Abba! Father!' it is that very Spirit bearing witness with our spirit that we are children of God, and if children, then heirs, heirs of God and joint heirs with Christ—if, in fact, we suffer with him so that we may also be glorified with him" (8:15-17).

The Resurrection of the Crucified One as the Cosmological Turning of the Ages

Believers live in the in-between times. The time of God's patience is past. The day of judgment stands immediately at hand (cf. Rom 13:11). The resurrection of the Crucified One marks the turning of the ages: "For to this end Christ died and lived again, so that he might be Lord of both the dead and the living" (14:9). The resurrected Crucified One has been raised into the divine life. He sits "at the right hand of God" and represents those who believe his gospel (cf. 8:34).

"But now," as Romans 3:21 formulates it, "apart from law, the righteousness of God has been disclosed, and is attested by the law and the prophets, the righteousness of God through faith in Jesus Christ for all who believe. For there is no distinction, since all have sinned and fall short of the glory of God; they are now justified by his grace as a gift, through the redemption that is in Christ Jesus, whom God put forward as a sacrifice of atonement by his blood, effective through faith. He did this to show his righteousness, because in his divine forbearance he had passed over the sins previously committed; it was to prove at the present time that he himself is righteous and that he justifies the one who has faith in Jesus" (3:21-26).

God would be well within his rights to react to the injustices of this world with his annihilating wrath, but his mercy results in his patience. Thanks to his caring mercy, he opens to all a way out of the Devil's circle of guilt and increasing distance from God. He determines that the crucified Jesus should achieve atonement through his violent death. God regards[79] the blood he poured out on the cross, the blood of one unjustly killed, as a means of atonement for all the injustice that has ever been committed.

This means of atonement does not work in a magical manner, however. It is no magic remedy that would unleash its power against the free decision of an individual. The blood of the innocent, murdered Jesus as the means of atonement becomes effective first in the interpretation of faith, which identifies the believer with Jesus on the cross, the victim of man's injustice and brutality. Faith, which decides for communion with this murder victim, for solidarity with this one who was executed unjustly and thus declares the old, godless bonds null, is that which first receives a share in the atoning power of this blood. With this new bond, which even death cannot sunder, believers receive the promise that God declares them to be just and that they receive new life as a gift.

God did not kill his Son, but rather the injustice and ready violence of human power fixed Jesus of Nazareth to the cross. God shows forth his justice in the present not by repressing, downplaying, or masking the injustice committed, but rather in his measureless mercy by regarding the blood of the one unjustly killed as a means of atonement for all who show solidarity with this innocent victim. He thus shows forth his righteousness as truly divine, merciful justice, which is not a matter of revenge but rather a matter of the enabling of new life within the communion of creatures.

That man alone is not the only thing in view of this new life but rather the entire cosmos is seen in Romans 8:18-39.[80] "[T]he creation itself will be set free from its bondage to decay and will obtain the freedom of the glory of the children of God. We know that the whole creation has been groaning in labor pains until now; and not only the creation, but we ourselves, who have the first fruits of the Spirit, groan inwardly while we wait for adoption, the redemption of our bodies. For in hope we were saved" (8:21-24a).

The whole cosmos is included in the grounded hope of the gospel of the death and resurrection of Jesus Christ. It concerns much more than merely the existential understanding of the individual. In dramatic ways it concerns the fate of the entirety of God's creation. God's almighty love, whose cosmological power Romans 8:31-39 expresses in unsurpassable ways, counts for his entire creation. God remains true to it, as he also remains true to Israel, his chosen people.

Chapters 9–11 revolve around one single question along ever new lines of argumentation: Why on the whole do the chosen people of God, of all peoples, not believe the gospel of their God? This question too Paul considers in the light of the gospel of the death and resurrection of the Crucified One. Paul can explain his Jewish coreligionists' rejection of his gospel only by claiming that God has hardened them so that the gospel might be preached to the entire world. But finally even Israel's hardening will end. God, the wonderful creator, will enable them to be once more "grafted in" (Rom 11:23c). As Paul, employing the Jewish way of drawing conclusions from the lesser to the greater, writes in 11:15-16, "For if their rejection is the reconciliation of the world, what will their acceptance be but life from the dead! If the part of the dough offered as first fruits is holy, then the whole batch is holy; and if the root is holy, then the branches also are holy."

Philippians

The Letter to the Philippians is concerned with supporting the Philippians in their decision for the Pauline gospel, in view of the eschatological knowledge of the nearness of the coming of the Lord (cf. Phil 1:6, 4:5b). Paul also wants to advise them regarding their behavior in connection with that knowledge that they "may be pure and blameless for the day of Christ" (1:10). The chief thesis of the letter flows from this, namely that the purity and blamelessness for which they are to strive is achieved through a change that is in accord with the gospel of Christ (cf. 1:27a). This challenge regarding their conduct (πολιτεύεσθε) corresponds to the heavenly "citizenship"[81] (3:20a) of both the sender and the addressees. The "story of Christ"[82] as delineated in 2:6-11 serves as their model. Therein the cosmological dimension of the Jesus-Christ-Story is employed to very good effect.

The resurrection of the Crucified One is also shown to be the fundamental conviction of the gospel in the Letter to the Philippians. In relation to this, Paul regards the role of the Philippians just as he regards his own situation.

The Cosmological Dimension of the Resurrection of the Crucified One

The cosmological dimension of the resurrection of the Crucified One becomes apparent in the so-called Philippian hymn of 2:5-11. In his seminal work *Kyrios Jesus. Eine Untersuchung zu Phil 2,5-11*, in which he set forth the thesis that Philippians 2:6-11 was a pre-Pauline,[83] poetic[84] "Psalm,"[85] Ernst Lohmeyer was driven by his interest in illuminating "the meaning of the early Christian conception of the *kyrios*."[86] Lohmeyer's work proved and still proves so stimulating for research[87] that it is indeed to be mourned that he made little use of the insight that the hymn in praise of Christ in 2:6-11 narrates a story. In contrast, and in fundamental criticism of the older Protestant moralizing interpretations, Ernst Käsemann rightly emphasized that "[t]he concern here is not with the identity of a person in different phases, but rather the continuity of a miraculous event."[88] The hymn of praise narrates "what Christ did, not what he was."

"The heavenly being is set aside, the earthly put on. This indicates that here one should observe the miracle. An explanation of the miracle is omitted, as throughout the NT."[89]

The relative conjunction in verse 6 binds the Christ hymn,[90] which derives its paranetic function from verse 5. Moreover, verse 6 introduces the point of departure for the event. Christ Jesus was "in the form of God."[91] Thus the divine status of Jesus Christ is announced in contradictory opposition to his later human status. The miracle of the transformation of the divine form into a human form (μορφὴν δούλου λαβών) is recounted in verse 7. This disadvantageous and altruistic transformation occurred not only on his own initiative but also from his own power. The miraculous power of this transformation is grounded in Christ Jesus being "equal with God" (2:6c). As such, he was provided also with the miraculous power for this transformation. But he laid aside the divine form and entered totally into human existence. "One should observe that in the first section (vv. 6-8) God is not named as the one who acts, sends, or commissions; the Son acts out of his own will. Naturally his will agrees with that of his Father (as v. 9 then shows), but without the text saying so expressly. It is thus already clear that the song's chief Christological motif is not that of obedience to the Father; ὑπήκοος in v. 8 means the free, conscious, and consequent submission to the lot of human existence."[92]

All the actions of Christ Jesus narrated up to verse 8 present him as the subject of his actions. It is precisely this way of self-humiliation, undertaken under his own power and drive and prescinding from his own advantage, that leads to the absolute instance of the incapacity to act, death on a cross (v. 8b).

This death is no glorious hero's death. The self-humiliation of God's former equal leads him to the most extreme limits of his original divine quality, to the crucifixion (2:8c). The crucifixion demonstrates the unsurpassable degree of humiliation of the one who took the form of a slave.[93]

Seen from the perspective of human possibilities, the crucifixion is an absolute nadir and marks the absolute incapacity of the protagonist of verses 6-8 to act, but this does not signify the end of the story. Its course discloses itself therefore as a miracle story. The point of the *story* can be understood only in the interplay of what has been narrated up to this point with what follows. In the shift from verse 8 to verse 9, we find the peripeteia in the sense of Aristotelian poetics. "Vv. 6-8 depict the premise on the ground of which God acts toward his Son (v.9)."[94] The miraculous intervention of God proceeds out of the humanly determined incapacity to act out of death. God alone enables and effects the turning point of the plot. Verse 9 recounts the miracle of the exaltation of the unsurpassably humble one through God's power. God repays the selfless conduct of him who humbled himself, by giving him his own mighty divine name: Kyrios (cf. v. 9b and v. 11b). In accord with this name, he provides him with Lordship over all (cf. vv. 10-11). "It is to be observed that the way of the Son is not described in cosmic-spatial categories (according to the schema of katabasis/anabasis). It is rather a way that is measured according to the parameters of power and powerlessness. Out of a privileged status . . . the Son enters into the powerlessness of the enslavement of humanity. There-upon he is wonderfully exalted by God and given the highest rank, the highest authority next to God. The hymn thus does not intend the return of the Son to a status of departure, but rather expressly emphasizes the conferral of new power. He is now the '*kyrios*' for humans and cosmic powers, and thus YHWH (LXX: κύριος), equal in power."[95]

The paranetic function of this narrative becomes clear when one notes the connection to the paranesis of Philippians 2:3-4. Being one's own subject, having the active agency of a citizen of heaven, should not mean looking out for one's own advantage but rather looking to the advantage of others. Acting in this way leads to the inability to act, which is one's task as an existing subject; it leads to death as an ultimate consequence. Through the *story* of the Christ hymn, action directed outward while taking the fate of Christ Jesus into account receives the promise of God's wonderful intervention, the promise that we will not remain in death.

The Resurrection of the Dead and the Individual Hope of Paul

With this model, the author signals his own apostolic existence as well. Seen from this perspective, the self-designation of "slave" (δοῦλοι, Phil 1:1), which Paul provides in the prescript, becomes a title of honor that conceptualizes both the fate of the senders (Paul, Timothy, and also Epaphroditus) in a way analogous also to the fate of the one who sent them. Or, as Paul formulates it in 3:10-13, "I want to know Christ and the power of his resurrection and the sharing of his sufferings by becoming like him in his death, if somehow I may attain the resurrection from the dead. Not that I have already obtained this or have already reached the goal; but I press on to make it my own, because Christ Jesus has made me his own."

Paul writes to the congregation in Philippi from prison. The outcome of any trial is uncertain. He ponders both the possibility of his release as well as that of his death (cf. Phil 1:20b-21). The tone of the Letter to the Philippians is in no way marked by the uncertainty of despair, however.

The letter conveys instead the eschatological joy and confidence that Paul also recommends to its addressees in 4:4ff.

The eschatological joy of the letter is nourished by the certainty of the cosmological and soteriological power of the resurrection of the Crucified One and by the confidence it evinces in the imminent coming of the Kyrios Jesus Christ, whom Paul expects to come from the heavens (3:20). The expectation of the resurrection of the dead and the transformation of fleshly bodies into a new and glorious corporality, just as the resurrected Kyrios has already received, is bound up with this coming. "But our citizenship is in heaven, and it is from there that we are expecting a Savior, the Lord Jesus Christ. He will transform the body of our humiliation that it may be conformed to the body of his glory, by the power that also enables him to make all things subject to himself" (3:20-21). The body thus transformed will no longer be fleshly (cf. 1:23-24).

As with his other letters, Paul interprets his concrete situation within the horizon of his gospel of the resurrection of the Crucified One in his Letter to the Philippians. He also here expects the collective resurrection of the dead and the transformation of fleshly bodies into a new corporality that opens the way to eternal life in communion with the Kyrios at the end of time. But the formulation in Philippians 1:23 counts on the fact that he himself will arrive directly in Christ's presence upon his potentially imminent death before the coming of the Kyrios.

Paul can apparently hold both possibilities together without contradiction. How can this state of affairs be explained? One possibility lies in the recognition that Paul never authored a textbook of systematic theology. This consideration suggests either that Paul did not notice this contradiction, or that for him it was simply of no significance for his gospel.

A second possibility consists in the fact that the expectation of one's own immediate resurrection and transformation is based on a kind of martyr theology such as one finds in the book of Daniel or in the Maccabean literature. Accordingly, for those who die in service to the gospel or who suffer a violent death, Paul anticipates an immediate resurrection and transformation. The majority of believers who have died, however, would not be raised and transformed until the coming of the Kyrios, expected in the near future.

It is not possible to come to a decisive judgment between these two positions. The second possibility, though, has the clear advantage of permitting Paul to think within his Jewish context. Moreover, this option has the advantage of not needlessly imputing to him obvious carelessness of thought. In neither case, however, can Paul's individual hope as formulated in Philippians 1:23 be accounted of such significance that it overshadows the predominant expectation about the collective resurrection of the dead at the eschatological coming of the Kyrios.

The Letter to Philemon

The letter to Philemon is the shortest writing in the Corpus Paulinum. It offers hardly any new insights whatsoever for the theme of the present investigation, but in light of the proto-Pauline letters already discussed, its concluding greeting becomes a clue that the syntagm "Kyrios Jesus Christ" would make no sense apart from the conviction of the resurrection of the Crucified One. In the logic of the proto-Pauline letters, only the resurrected and exalted Jesus Christ can be Kyrios. The concluding verse prays, "The grace of the Lord Jesus Christ be with your spirit." The resurrected Crucified One is revealed as the Kyrios, because he can be called upon in the present as the effective Lord of those who believe. His grace enables the strengthening of the spirits of believers. As verse 3 shows, the Kyrios Jesus Christ is experienced just as effectually as is God, his Father.

The Deutero-Pauline Letters

The deutero-Paulines bear witness to a struggle for the correct interpretation and actualization of Pauline theology. They cannot be determined to have come from a common "Pauline school," for with respect to the theme of the resurrection being treated here they represent very different positions. The Pastoral Letters, along the lines of the proto-Paulines, forcefully repudiate every formulation claiming the resurrection has already happened. Thus they preserve resurrection language from evaporating into spiritualizing language. In discontinuity with Romans 6, however, Colossians and Ephesians see the resurrection of the dead already completed in baptism. Colossians preserves a future element in a manner stronger than Ephesians. Second Thessalonians in contrast struggles precisely for the future concern of apocalyptic eschatology.

The Letter to the Colossians

Although the Letter to the Colossians displays the formal characteristics of a real letter, the majority of scholars, I think rightly, assume that both the sender and addressees are to be regarded as fictions.[96] The style of the Letter to the Colossians as well as several expressions distinctive in content demonstrate that the letter was neither written nor dictated by Paul.

The issue of the resurrection of the dead is directly affected by the differences between the proto-Paulines and the Letter to the Colossians.

Individual aspects like this one, however, are not the only problem with supposing Paul wrote this letter. An issue that more seriously complicates attempts to ascribe this letter to Paul is the fact that the entire perspective of the letter looks back on Paul's life's work in order to bring to memory the significance of his apostolic work in the present.[97] Above all, without the rich intertextual fabric found in the proto-Paulines, the letter lacks the paradoxical yet fundamental tension of the Pauline theology of the cross. This tension not only paints the Resurrected One always and everywhere as the Crucified One, it also enables him to interpret his own apostolic existence and that of his congregations from the perspective of the theology of the cross in rich and tensive ways. In so doing he can keep the experiences of their own vulnerability and failure in view while also highlighting the certainty of the reality of the saving eschatological action of God.

Colossians, on the other hand, with its emphasis on Christology, on the soteriological significance of the cross, and also its numerous intertextual allusions to and appropriations of the letters to Philemon and to the Romans (and probably also of 1 Corinthians), displays such a strong continuity with the theology of the Pauline letters that many exegetes hold that its author might have been a companion or secretary of Paul.[98]

Since it is assumed that the letter was written after the death of Paul at the beginning of the 60s, the addressees of the letter are shown to be fictional, for Colossae was destroyed by an earthquake in A.D. 61 and rebuilt only in the third century. We need not here decide whether the intended address of the letter was Laodicea, a conclusion for which Andreas Lindemann makes good arguments,[99] or whether the letter was sent first to Ephesus, as Michael Theobald contends with arguments every bit as good as Lindemann's.[100] What is clear is that the writing belongs in the orbit of Asia Minor and must be treated as a separate writing of an unknown author. There are intertextual references to the letters of Paul, however, which can be cautiously considered within his thought horizon in the interpretation of the Letter to the Colossians.

The Intratextual Communication Situation

Paul and Timothy are explicitly named as the senders of the letter in Colossians 1:1, while the addressees are introduced as "the saints . . . in Colossae." The repeated use of "I" by the explicit author and the concluding greeting "with my own hand" in 4:18 leave no doubt that Paul is supposed to be regarded as the author of the letter.

The communication situation is determined in Colossians 1:4, which reveals that Paul and the saints to whom he writes do not know each other personally. In verse 7 Epaphras is introduced as the intermediary for their communication. The information about Paul is thus sanctioned as true by this coworker. The picture that the letter paints about the saints in Colossae appears extremely positive. In verse 4 they are being praised for their "faith in Jesus Christ" and "the love that [they] have for all the saints." The letter confirms their "hope" as well (v. 5), with which the Pauline triad of faith, hope, and love is made complete. The individual members are set in a relationship different than that which one finds in the proto-Paulines, however. If 1 Corinthians 13 presents "love" as having singular significance because it alone will transcend the eschatological turning of the ages and will also exist in the kingdom of God, in the Letter to the Colossians hope functions as the foundation for faith and love. It is thus spatial, considered something already laid up in heaven (cf. 1.5), so that one finds in the Letter to the Colossians a spatial eschatology derived from the futurist eschatology of the Pauline letters without wholly surrendering futurist notions.

In what does this hope that has already been laid up consist? What still remains to hope for when Colossians 2:14 tells us that "[he] eras[ed] the record that stood against us," or again, shortly before, when 2:12b tells us, "you were also raised with him"? Moreover, the author writes about the cosmic Christ that he "disarmed the rulers and authorities and made a public example of them, triumphing over them in it" (2:15). For what, then, should one still hope? The answer to this question depends on two decisions: (1) How does one understand the assertions that the resurrection has already happened? (2) How broadly does one see intertexual references in Colossians to the proto-Paulines?

The picture that Colossians sketches of the "saints in Colossae" presents in any case neither political oppression nor conflicts within the community. Instead, the text warns of the danger of not living in the sovereignty belonging to those who have been raised, of the Colossians orienting themselves toward regulations of food and drink and concerns for festal calendars (cf. 2:16), toward "philosophy" as "human tradition" (cf. 2:8). These things stand counter to the fundamental conviction of the Letter to the Colossians: Those who have "died to the elemental spirits of the universe" with Christ (2:20a) and who "have been raised with Christ" (3:1a) have oriented themselves to Christ Jesus alone, to "the firstborn from the dead" (1:18c), who sits "at the right hand of God" at the very time of the reading of this writing. Here also the spatial notion of the Letter to the Colossians becomes clear. The letter's perspective does not so much wait for the second coming of Jesus Christ as direct its gaze "above."

The Letter to the Colossians gives special warning against the danger of being bound to something or someone other than Jesus Christ alone, who is the head of the church (cf. 1:18). As those who have died with Christ and who have been raised with Christ, its readers should thus be empowered to live in a way orientated to that which is above. But what does "resurrection" mean in this connection?

The Christological Argumentation

The theological basis upon which the Letter to the Colossians constructs its argumentation is this: in Christ "the whole fullness of deity (τὸ πλήρωμα τῆς θεότητος) dwells bodily (σωματικῶς)" (Col 2:9).

The special status of Jesus Christ is portrayed in the so-called Colossian hymn in Colossians 1:15-20, which begins with the relative pronoun "who," as does the hymn in Philippians (cf. Phil 2:6). Like the Philippian hymn, the Colossian hymn brings out the cosmological dimension of Christology. This is accorded to Jesus Christ in Colossians because Christ is the "image" (εἰκῶν) of the "invisible God" (cf. 1:15). "Image" here should not be regarded as pejorative. With the intertextual link to Genesis 1:26, the word here means the realization of the embodiment of God, the present somaticizing of God, who himself cannot be depicted within the limitations of time and space. In Jesus Christ the divinity of God (cf. Col 2:9) has so fully taken form that nothing can disturb his existence as the image of God. Therefore, having become the form of the divinity of God, the creative qualities of God belong also to Jesus Christ, which indeed decisively constitute his own divinity. The first part of the Colossian hymn deals with this. Christ is the "firstborn of all creation" (1:15b). God created him first, and God made everything else by this first work of creation. Nothing was made without connection to the firstborn of creation. He is, therefore, the center of creation, its cosmological center, the head of every embodied created thing and also "the body" of "the church" (1:18a).

The second part of the hymn again begins with a relative pronoun and a fundamental designation: He is the "beginning" (ἀρχή) (1:18b). He is in the same sense the beginning as he is the image of the invisible God. God has no other beginning other than his Christ. God himself cannot be thought of as a form with a beginning. That is precisely the designation of one who is created, and that also displays the concept of the body in the Letter to the Colossians.

Since Jesus Christ is now the center of the whole creation, he must also be so for the new creation as well, which arises from his birth out of the realm of the dead. He is therefore the beginning par excellence, the "firstborn from the dead" (Col 1:18d). But this second creation also remains somatic; it remains creation and does not itself become creator. In spite of the cosmological Christology of the Letter to the Colossians, the limitless God and his corporeal Son remain just as differentiated from one another as the cosmic Christ, head of the church, is from the church itself.

But in Jesus Christ "dwells" the whole fullness of the divinity. In him divinity takes visible form. From this notion of the absolute perfection of the image of God in Jesus Christ a good intertextual bridge from Genesis 1 to the Johannine Prologue can be built. By the same token, the Letter to the Colossians can also be regarded as a bridge between the Corpus Paulinum and the Corpus Johanneum.

As the cosmic Christ is the unsurpassable reference point not only as the head of the church but also as the linchpin of the entire creation, so also everything can be reconciled with God only in connection with him as the firstborn from the dead. Without a connection to this Resurrected One, God exists in irreconcilable strife with his creation. It is only through reconciliation in an enmeshed relationship with Jesus Christ that God grants peace (cf. Col 1:20).

Mention of the "blood of [Jesus'] cross" (Col 1:20c) first appears at the conclusion of the Colossian hymn. The entire understanding of the hymn depends to a considerable degree on whether one conceives of the cross as an appendage added after the fact to the hymn's cosmological Christology of exaltation, or whether the "blood of his cross" is read within the horizon of Pauline theology. The intertextual interweaving with the Pauline letters, especially with Philemon, Romans, and probably also with 1 Corinthians, permits one to bring the Pauline word of the cross into the discussion. Thus, one should make the assessment that the cosmological Christology of the Letter to the Colossians likewise has its foundation in the event of the cross. As with the other letters, the firstborn from the dead, the resurrected Crucified One, remains the beginning of the eschatological resurrection of the dead (cf. 1 Cor 15:20) in the Letter to the Colossians.

The Soteriological and Appellative Function of the Language of the Resurrection of the Dead

The creation-theological and soteriological basis of the Letter to the Colossians is thus as follows: in Christ "the whole fullness of deity dwells bodily" (Col 2:9). Immediately after follows the fundamental soteriological expression of this conviction: those who believe in Jesus Christ already participate in his bodily fullness (cf. 2:10).

As the Colossian hymn specifically states in 1:20, in the event of the cross, God has reconciled himself with his entire creation when creation understands itself in its cosmological connection to Jesus Christ, the firstborn of creation, and in its eschatological connection to Jesus Christ, the firstborn from the dead. Colossians 1:13-14 is true for those who can already understand the world and themselves in this way: "He has rescued us from the power of darkness and transferred us into the kingdom of his beloved Son, in whom we have redemption, the forgiveness of sins."

The Letter to the Colossians regards being determined by the power of darkness and thus sin, as well as letting these powers serve as points of reference for one's own life, as existential death: "you were dead in trespasses" (Col 2:13b). In the act of baptism everyone dies to their old self, with Christ. In this way all connections to sin-generating powers are ended. Up to this point the author of the Letter to the Colossians can call upon the theology of the proto-Paulines. In Romans 6:6 Paul himself says that we have died with Christ. Also according to Paul faith brings about the transformation into a "new creation" (cf. 2 Cor 5:17) already in the here and now. This makes new life possible. The eschatological difference between this new life in the body of flesh and blood and life in the kingdom of God in new bodies (cf. 1 Cor 15:50-51), however, can hardly be perceived in Colossians. Whereas in Paul one's resurrection from the dead remains a future hope, Colossians says, "when you were buried with him in baptism, you were also raised with him through faith in the power of God, who raised him from the dead. And when you were dead in trespasses" (Col 2:12-13a). Faith in the resurrected Crucified One is qualified through the same power of God that raised the Crucified One, to such a degree that this faith not only hopes for one's own resurrection, but in Colossians is regarded already itself as the completion of one's own resurrection. As with Paul, faith is not one's self-achievement. But going far beyond Paul it is also the eschatological resurrection. As Paul does in Romans 6:13, the Letter to the Colossians teaches that the baptized not only die to the old, sin-generating relations, but—at the same time in faith, and as those who have faith—enter into the life-giving relationship to the firstborn from the dead. But, unlike Paul, in Colossians this is now understood as a resurrection already completed and the eschatological scenario becomes an ecclesiological reality. The somatic realization of this new birth occurs as incorporation into the body of the church, whose head is the cosmic Christ from time immemorial.

This connection is in the present age, however, still hidden. Only faith permits one to see the truth. The Letter to the Colossians decisively brings in the futurist element of its eschatology as the ongoing revelation of that which has already happened (cf. Col 3:3-4). Because the Letter to the Colossians can address its recipients on the basis of this argumentation as those who "have stripped off the old self with its practices and have clothed yourselves with the new self" (3:9b-10a), it can now totally maintain that as those who are eschatologically clothed, they should live according to their eschatological new creation and should "put to death" all sinful powers (cf. 3:5).

The letter's language about one's own, already-completed resurrection thus stands in the service of paranesis. Nevertheless, it can be conceptualized only metaphorically. The Letter to the Colossians is not interested in the problem of one's own coming bodily death or of the deaths of beloved brothers and sisters, as in 1 Thessalonians 4:13-18. Colossians also lacks consideration of the problem with which the Apocalypse of John deals, namely that the powers and forces hostile to God always bring suffering and death to the "saints." The Letter to the Colossians is wholly animated by the conviction that the eschatological turning of salvation history was completed once and for all in the event of the cross. Everyone who lays hold of that event by faith has already even now been made alive in an eschatologically effective way on the basis of his relationship to the first-born from the dead. Now it remains only to live in a manner corresponding to this dignity, to this gift.

And what of the hope that is "laid up for you in heaven" (Col 1:5)? Perhaps we still have here a futurist element of eschatology. If with Andreas Lindemann one accepts that the "saints in the light" are the angels,[101] then we may have a clue that the Letter to the Colossians also assumes that the saints who have already been made alive through faith receive a body of light like the angels after their death. But in Colossians, this depiction is not central when the letter speaks of the resurrection of the dead. If the author of the Letter to the Colossians was familiar with 1 Corinthians, then it appears that the question about the nature of the resurrection body in 1 Corinthian 15 did not make a great impression on him.

Ephesians

The close literary relationship[102] between the Letter to the Ephesians and the Letter to the Colossians can be plausibly explained by the hypothesis that the author of the Letter to the Ephesians reworked the Letter to the Colossians. In agreement with the Letter to the Colossians and in contrast to the proto-Paulines the Letter to the Ephesians emphasizes the cosmological significance of Christ and the church bound up with the cosmic

Christ. It takes its language about the already-occurred resurrection of believers from the Letter to the Colossians, but it emphasizes the significance of the Holy Spirit more clearly than the Letter to the Colossians. It also produces closer formal connections to the proto-Paulines through its explicit references to the Holy Scriptures of Israel. One can therefore look upon the Letter to the Ephesians as a systematically expanded copy of the Letter to the Colossians, reworked using some of the proto-Paulines.

Like the Letter to the Colossians, the Letter to the Ephesians belongs in Asia Minor and came into being before the reign of Domitian but with some gap after Colossians. Thus it was probably written sometime between A.D. 80 and A.D. 95. With Michael Theobald, one can see its intention as "legitimizing its ecclesiological schema of a Christian way of life in the biblical Spirit as the abiding 'bequest' [*Vermächtnis*] (M. Gese) of the apostle to the post-apostolic church, and thus letting Paul himself speak indirectly."[103]

The theology of the Letter to the Ephesians can nevertheless hardly be designated as a mere repetition or actualization of Pauline theology. In addition to the above-named commonalities with the Letter to the Colossians, the text's understanding of marriage must be regarded as a discontinuity with Paul. Further, the entire salvation-historical argumentation is based on a temporally and spatially differentiated universalistic cosmology[104] and no longer on a Pauline theology of the cross. The author of the Letter to the Ephesians regards the cosmos as the creation of God, but at the same time he sees it as the place of the battle between God and those who belong to him on the one side, and Satan and his demonic powers of darkness on the other. This fractured cosmos is overcome through the self-sacrifice of Jesus out of love for the *ekklesia* (church) (cf. Eph 5:25). In place of this fractured state of alienation from God enters unity supported by the Spirit of Love: "[L]ead a life worthy of the calling to which you have been called, with all humility and gentleness, with patience, bearing with one another in love, making every effort to maintain the unity of the Spirit in the bond of peace. There is one body and one Spirit, just as you were called to the one hope of your calling, one Lord, one faith, one baptism, one God and Father of all, who is above all and through all and in all" (4:1b-6). Gerhard Sellin's words are fitting: "The main theme of Ephesians is the motif of 'one-ity [*Ein(s)heit*],' which as a term governs above all the sections of 2:14-18; and 4:1-6, 13-16. Behind it stands a Platonic-Pythagorean metaphysic, which Philo also assumed, according to which the number *one* stands for the existing, spiritual, eternal, divine (and thus for universality, peace, concord, identity), but the number *two* stands for the divisible, material, becoming, and transitory (and thus for war, strife, dissonance, and difference)."[105]

The Letter to the Ephesians therefore interprets the event of the cross as an overcoming of the fracturing of the cosmos through the love that supports unity, a plan that had already been determined in the divine economy of salvation. The significance then accorded to the detailed paranesis of chapters 4–6 concerns accepting the universal form of this cosmic peace. This peace was already determined in the divine plan of salvation and disclosed in the death and resurrection of Jesus Christ (cf. Eph 2:16). The universal *ekklesia* is the corporeal realization of cosmic peace. Its growth realizes the entire fullness of the resurrected cosmic Christ in the constant progress occurring in accord with the divine plan of salvation: "But speaking the truth in love, we must grow up in every way into him who is the head, into Christ, from whom the whole body, joined and knit together by every ligament with which it is equipped, as each part is working properly, promotes the body's growth in building itself up in love" (4:15-16).

Baptism effects incorporation into this cosmic body of Christ and thus not only the dying off of the fracture of the cosmos, which is alienated from God, but also just as much the resurrection of those into the body of Christ who, through their sins, have fallen in death (cf. 2:1, 5-6). The baptismal liturgy can therefore even be formulated as an imperative: "Sleeper, awake! / Rise from the dead / and Christ will shine on you" (5:14b).

The futurist element of this cosmic eschatology consists less in the expectation of eschatological judgment, at which the dead are raised by God so that in the end God speaks his justice, and more in the expectation that the *ekklesia* as the body of the Resurrected One—already established before all time in the plan of God as the locus of unity and peace—stretches over the entire cosmos and thus gives the powers of darkness no quarter any more (cf. Eph 2:20ff.; 4:27; 6:12).

With this spatial eschatology of the cosmic *ekklesia* (cf. Eph 3:10; 4:12-13) the author of the Letter to the Ephesians removes himself further from Paul than appears at first glance. With its ecclesiology of universal expanse, its eschatology stands closer to the presentist eschatology of the Roman Imperium than to that of the proto-Paulines.[106] The resurrection hope of Ephesians, transformed into an imperative, may contribute to the growth of the church and to the moralistic engagement of its members, but at the same time it robs resurrection theology of the humility to rely wholly on God's righteousness. It also robs the victims of the cosmos, given its alienation from God, of their certainty that they will not be forgotten. An eschatological resurrection theology as the word of the cross does not ground this ecclesiology of unity. Rather, the metaphysics of unity determine the function of resurrection discourse in a new way.

2 Thessalonians

Although the Second Letter to the Thessalonians does not contain any of its own statements about the resurrection of the dead nor any statements about the resurrection of Jesus, it must at least be pointed out here that neither dies its intertextual relationship to 1 Thessalonians contain any corrections or interpretive necessities pertaining to the question of the resurrection of the dead. The occasion for conflict is not the resurrection, but the significance of the present. Second Thessalonians assumes the expectation of the return of the resurrected Crucified One from heaven (cf. 2 Thess 1:7) and also emphasizes the eschatological judgment that will take place on the Day of the Lord. It rejects the simple identification of the present with the Day of the Lord, however (cf. 2:1-2), and in support calls upon oral and written traditions about Paul (cf. 2:15). It employs this authority to further its own concerns.

If the use of this Pauline authority already signifies that 2 Thessalonians was probably written shortly after the death of the apostle, this impression is strengthened even more through the tone of the writing. While in the proto-Paulines the eschatological day of judgment is introduced principally as an ultimate and cosmological realization of the kingdom of God, 2 Thessalonians emphasizes the vengeance of God upon those whom 2 Thessalonians criticizes (cf. 1:6). Even the cosmological battles in which Christ will "destroy" the "lawless one" with "the breath of his mouth" (2:8) are reminiscent more of the atmosphere of the Johannine apocalypse than the tone of the proto-Paulines and, above all, their respective occasions. The letters produced for these occasions, for all their sharp criticism, especially in Galatians, encourage fresh thinking in argumentative ways and even contribute to that more than they bully opponents with violent vengeful fantasies.

Determining a precise date of composition for the writing by identifying the "lawless one" with a particular Roman emperor fails to convince due to the lack of any impressive indications in the letter. Such attempts are accompanied by so many hypotheses that their historical chain of assumptions must be evaluated at best as "could be, but probably not."[107] The hypothesis that 2 Thessalonians was supposed to replace 1 Thessalonians also fails to convince.[108]

Indeed, the difficulties involved in locating 2 Thessalonians more precisely do not contribute greater understanding. Rather they throw the question wholly back on the writing and its intertextual relationships. Eckart Reinmuth's commentary proceeds from this interpretive position to a comprehensive view of the text: "With his letter, Pseudo-Paul reworks a disconcerting position in the church of his time that combines contemporary experiences of persecution, eschatological impatience, and a denunciation of prior social behavior. He continues Paul's communication with the congregation in Thessalonica because he found the connection of these problems represented in the first letter and its eschatological sections could be understood as prooftexts of imminent expectations in need of correction."[109] However, the basis of the apocalyptic eschatology of 1 Thessalonians, namely the conviction regarding the eschatological resurrection of the Crucified One through the creative and just God of Israel and the hope of the resurrection of the dead based upon it, can be seen as valid also for 2 Thessalonians in the affirmative manner in which 2 Thessalonians makes intertextual reference to 1 Thessalonians.

The Pastoral Letters (1 Timothy/2 Timothy/Titus)

There is some indication not only that both of the Letters to Timothy and the Letter to Titus come from one and the same author, but also that these letters were composed as a coherent literary unit that can be located in the literary-historical realm of the epistolary novels of antiquity.[110] Both the author and also the addressees must be regarded as fictions to whom is accorded exemplary character.

In the words of Michael Wolter, 1 Timothy and Titus can "be understood as epistolary instructions to office holders and chosen leaders in need of instruction from their superior,"[111] while in the words of Alfons Weiser, 2 Timothy can be conceived of as "a testamentary admonitory writing in the form of a friendship letter."[112] The author of the Pastoral Letters thus employs the authority of Paul in order to deploy his own conceptions of the organization, dignity, and tasks of the church in the struggle for the true understanding of Christian tradition in the first half of the second century. He grounds organizational and moral directives in the theology and works of Paul as he depicts him above all in 2 Timothy. Thus, in the Pauline theology of the Pastoral Letters, the Jesus-Christ-Event as understood from the perspective of the cross stands at the center of their argumentation.

The Pastoral Letters are shot through with their patriarchal ecclesiastical structures. In line with their hierarchical conception, the rather general presentation of the political situation supports the power of those who rule. It is not only these positions, unacceptable for those of a democratic disposition, however, that have led to criticism of the Pastoral Letters. The opinion that they are not theologically fruitful also comes into play. It is relevant that the Pastoral Letters are removed from the radical nature of the Pauline theology of the cross and from the apocalyptic eschatology that is certain of the imminent eschatological Judgment Day that accompanies it. It would be a mistake, however, to undervalue the unique merit of the theology of the Pastoral Letters. These are letters that, at the beginning of the second century, faced the task of preserving a Pauline theology, which in their understanding and in their application was far from undisputed, in a manner suitable for day-to-day Christian life in their time. Whether the Pastoral Letters were written especially for a collection of Pauline letters, as Annette Merz argues, may remain here an open question.[113] It can be said on good grounds, however, not only that the author wanted to secure the legacy of the Pauline letters through their wider reading and circulation, but also that he saw the necessity of formulating something new, so that the voice of Paul, as the author of the Pastoral Letters understood it, could also advance his understanding of the gospel of Jesus Christ in the second century after Christ's birth. Therefore, the theology of the resurrection of the Crucified One remains central in the theology of the Pastoral Letters, even if the accent shifts from the Pauline "word of the cross" (1 Cor 1:18) to "the goodness and loving kindness of God" (Titus 3:4), which, however, appears in every significant way in the Jesus-Christ-Story.

The Resurrection of Jesus Christ as Proof of the Loving Kindness of God

At the beginning of 1 Timothy Paul instructs Timothy to act against those who teach something other than what Paul teaches. The content of the difference is not precisely delineated, but it has at its root "myths and endless genealogies" (1 Tim 1:4) and confusing interpretations of Scripture (cf. 1:7). In opposition to this, 1 Timothy emphasizes the clarity and simplicity of Pauline instruction, whose sense and purpose is nothing other than "love that comes from a pure heart, a good conscience, and sincere faith" (1:5b).

This love has appeared in Jesus Christ, who "came into the world to save sinners—of whom I am the foremost" (1 Tim 1:15b). Paul is introduced as an example of a sinful man with whom God and Jesus as savior have dealt mercifully. Thus Paul has been brought into the way of love observed in Jesus Christ (cf. 1:16). As one given the gift of true faith, it is Paul's apostolic task to announce this love in Jesus Christ to all, especially the nations, so that they themselves may be saved by this faith. Faith unstained consists in nothing other than faith in Jesus Christ, and only this unvarnished faith in him leads to "eternal life" (1:16).

The congregation as a whole should adopt the exemplary function of the apostle and thus contribute to the promotion of the gospel of Jesus Christ. Soteriological significance is thus accorded to church order. This stands in discontinuity with the proto-Paulines, since it is supposed to contribute to generating outsiders' interest in the church and its teaching and to win them for the true faith by means of an order that avoids conflict and neighborly amiability: "First of all, then, I urge that supplications, prayers, intercessions, and thanksgivings be made for everyone, for kings and all who are in high positions, so that we may lead a quiet and peaceable life in all godliness and dignity. This is right and is acceptable in the sight of God our Savior, who desires everyone to be saved and to come to the knowledge of the truth" (1 Tim 2:1-4). The soteriology of the Pastoral Letters is interested in the universal salvation of humanity. The congregations should be islands of peace and piety, whose quiet lives radiate outward, and who concern themselves with the approval of the wider society. In this way all men may perceive the "truth" of the gospel of Jesus Christ, engage it, and be saved by it.

The church also has a soteriological function for its own members, however. In particular, it contributes to the living of their faith in orderly ways in everyday life. It is not a matter of order for order's sake, but rather a matter of the organization of the common life of believers together so that they may obtain eternal life on the expected eschatological day of judgment.

The universalistic soteriology of the Pastoral Letters is grounded in the "Pro-Existence"[114] of Jesus Christ, who does not balk before the cross. The event of the cross itself forms the fundamental story upon which the church as the "house of God" (1 Tim 3:15) is built in the Pastoral Epistles. "For there is one God; there is also one mediator between God and humankind, Christ Jesus, himself human, who gave himself a ransom for all—this was attested at the right time. For this I was appointed a herald and an apostle (I am telling the truth, I am not lying), a teacher of the Gentiles in faith and truth" (2:5-7). This soteriology is grounded in the love of God, to which witness is borne in the pro-existence of Jesus Christ by his way to the cross, and by the apostle who himself functions as an example of the effective mediation of the Son, which is now being proclaimed and taught faithfully and in accord with the truth.

The apostle summarizes the "mystery of the faith" he hands on in a short and succinct manner, for Timothy should know "how one ought to behave in the household of God, which is the church of the living God, the pillar and bulwark of the truth. Without any doubt, the mystery of our religion is great: He was revealed in flesh, vindicated in spirit, seen by angels, proclaimed among Gentiles, believed in throughout the world, taken up in glory" (1 Tim 3:15b-16). The church as the bulwark of the truth is no longer designated as the body of Christ as it is in the proto-Paulines, but rather as the "house of God," which operates according to its own economy. Only if it preserves the mystery of the faith and passes it on faithfully does it do justice to its special task. In all its decisions, in its organization, and above all in every aspect of its life it must make clear that it owes its existence to the love of God, the creative maker, and to the pro-existence of Jesus Christ, who walked his path though it lead to the cross. The church must not think of itself, however, as an end in itself. The church is not the goal itself, but rather the means of proclamation. It does not stand at the end of time, but rather waits for the epiphany of the res-urrected and exalted Crucified One: "In the presence of God, who gives life to all things, and of Christ Jesus, who in his testimony before Pontius Pilate made the good confession, I charge you to keep the commandment without spot or blame until the manifestation of our Lord Jesus Christ, which he will bring about at the right time—he who is the blessed and only Sovereign, the King of kings and Lord of lords. It is he alone who has immortality and dwells in unapproachable light, whom no one has ever seen or can see; to him be honor and eternal dominion. Amen" (6:13-16).

First Timothy makes one think of the connection between the creative power and love of God on the one hand and the event of the cross on the other. Moreover, it emphasizes the soteriological dimension of this event and thus grounds the hope for eternal life. But only 2 Timothy 2:8 speaks explicitly of the resurrection of Jesus Christ: "Remember Jesus Christ, raised from the dead, a descendant of David—that is my gospel."

The Resurrection of the Dead Has Not Yet Taken Place

2 Timothy 1:9-11, similar in content to 1 Corinthians 15 though retaining its own accent, expresses the fact that the event of the cross signifies not only the singular resurrection of Jesus, but also the fact that death itself has been deprived of power: "[He] saved us and called us with a holy calling, not according to our works but according to his own purpose and grace. This grace was given to us in Christ Jesus before the ages began, but it has now been revealed through the appearing of our Savior Christ Jesus, who abolished death and brought life and immortality to light through the gospel. For this gospel I was appointed a herald and an apostle and a teacher."

Second Timothy is clearly directed against the understanding that "the resurrection has already taken place" (2 Tim 2:18b). Second Timothy does not betray what is meant by this slogan. It is entirely possible, though this cannot be proven, that the Pastoral Letters have Colossians 2:12, Ephesians 2:6, and Ephesians 5:14 in view here. Certainly the talk of being raised with Christ in baptism in those texts is in need of considerable interpretation and can cause confusion.

If the Pastoral Letters are directed against a gnostic understanding of the resurrection, as one sees in the Gospel of Philip, that would signify that it is more likely that they came into being in the middle of the second century than at the beginning of the new century. That would also fit well with the Pastoral Letters' repeated refusal of myths, such as the enigma in the Gospel of Philip 90a: "Those who say they will die first and then rise are in error. If they do not first receive the resurrection while they live, when they die they will receive nothing."[115]

Be that as it may, it is precisely the intertextual connection to Romans 6 that summons the church to preserve this differentiation in Pauline resurrection theology, and, indeed, the resurrection of the dead is bound up with the expectation of eschatological judgment, as 2 Timothy 4:1b states when it speaks of "Christ Jesus, who is to judge the living and the dead."

In a manner analogous to Romans 6, the Pastoral Letters preserve the difference between the Crucified One who has already been raised and exalted on the one hand and those who believe in him and his gospel on the other. They can die even now in their identification with the cruciform death of Jesus Christ under the conditions of this world, but sharing eschatological life remains a new and eternal existence to be hoped for in the future (cf. 2 Tim 2:11b). On the basis of God's mercy, and not on the ground of their own achievements but rather through "Jesus Christ, our Savior," in baptism, in the "water of rebirth," they experience "renewal by the Holy Spirit" (cf. Titus 3:5-6). Just as Jesus Christ became the Savior, by "[giving] himself for us that he might redeem us from all iniquity" (2:14a), so those who believe his story of the cross receive the hope of receiving eternal life like their savior himself. Their present life is still not eternal life. They are "heirs according to the hope of eternal life" (3:7b).

This hope has its ultimate ground in the "goodness and loving kindness of God" (Titus 3:4), in which all life, and even more the hope for an eternal life free from all injustice, is rooted.

Chapter 2

Hebrews

Although the Letter to the Hebrews was handed down as a component of the Corpus Paulinum, Paul is not its author and Hebrews is not a letter. The "Letter" to the Hebrews designates itself fittingly as "a word of comfort and exhortation" (λόγος τῆς παρακλήσεως).[1] This word comprises the chief part of the writing (1:1–13:19). In Vanhoye's opinion, only the "final verses (13:22-25) are proper to a letter, while the first sentence (1:1-4) is not in any way." In Vanhoye's judgment, which he prefers on the basis of his in-depth and plausible structural analysis, the Letter to the Hebrews is a "sermon . . . onto which a short accompanying note is affixed."[2] According to Vanhoye, Hebrew's word of exhortation can be properly understood only if its interwoven theological argumentation and the resulting exhortations are perceived as the fundamental syntagmatic structure of the writing.[3]

The pragmatic concern of the Letter to the Hebrews' "word of comfort and exhortation" is to strengthen believers to hold fast to their "confession" (cf. 4:14c), and to continue along the way of faith marked out for them, even if it brings suffering and affliction (cf. 10:32ff.; 13:3). Those who abandon this way after confessing faith in Jesus Christ are accused of "crucifying again the Son of God and . . . holding him up to contempt" (6:6b).

The confession that the readers have to hold on to is a confession about the one who was crucified, brought back "from the dead," and exalted by "the God of peace," the one who is "the pioneer and perfecter of our faith, who for the sake of the joy that was set before him endured the cross, disregarding its shame" (12:2).

The Letter to the Hebrews expresses the honor and significance of Jesus Christ, who is above comparison with any creature of God, through its metaphor of the heavenly high priest (cf. 8:1-2) who is "the mediator of a better covenant" (8:6; cf. 12:24). This depiction of Jesus works by way of metaphorical transformation of the sacrificial language of the Jerusalem temple cult. The development of the letter's Christology by means of the semantics of the high priesthood, which juxtaposes the heavenly high priest after the order of Melchizedek with the high priest of the Jerusalem temple cult after the order of Aaron (cf. 7:11), forms an independent and distinctive contribution to the theological representation of and soteriological reflection upon the Jesus-Christ-Story. This distinctive Christology, in spite of its obvious points of contact with Paul's letters,[4] suggests that its author, who was clearly learned in the Scriptures,[5] is more an independent creative theologian of early Christianity than a disciple of Paul. "The move to locate ultimate salvation 'in the heavens' (8:1) through Christ the high priest is in a sense directly connected to the fundamental concern of the author. In this connection the unshakeable foundation of their faith, unaffected by earthly change and earthly transience, is brought before the eyes of the addressees, and thus at the same time they are again motivated by the certainty of salvation and faith—which is the author's concern in his 'word of comfort and exhortation.'"[6]

However much the metaphor of the heavenly high priest according to the order of Melchizedek may also determine the semantics of the Letter to the Hebrews, one must not overlook the fact that the letter's argumentative foundation is formed by the soteriologically significant connection between the cross and resurrection of Jesus Christ.[7] The criticism of "dead works" (cf. Heb 6:1b) and the import of the citation from Habakkuk, "My righteous one will live by faith" (10:38; cf. Hab 2:4b; Rom 1:17b), are not the only elements in the homily that provide occasion for the justified impression of a material point of contact with Pauline theology. The shape of the Jesus-Christ-Story itself, which forms the theological structure of the letter, understands the cruciform death of Jesus as the eschatological event that effects salvation on the basis of Jesus' being brought back from the dead (cf. Heb 13:20). The exaltation of the crucified one through the creative power of the merciful and righteous "God of peace" (13:20), an event that has already happened "once for all" (9:26b), has changed everything and made salvation possible. If metaphorical language about the soteriological function of the high priest, Jesus Christ, shapes the presentation of the Christology of Hebrews, then the ground of its material possibility is expressed in the confession that the crucified one was brought back "from the dead" and exalted (cf. 13:20). I agree with David M. Moffitt: "[N]ot only does the author make allusions and references to Jesus' resurrection in the sermon, but the confession of this event stands at the heart of his explanation for how Jesus, the Judahite, *became* the great high priest he now is (Heb 5–7). After he died, Jesus arose to the power of an indestructible life. Because he now possesses a life that remains, he is qualified to serve as *the* high priest of the heavenly order of priests."[8] The sermon's fascinating rhetoric of the heavenly high priest is grounded in the word of the cross.

The Jesus-Christ-Story and Its Significance in Its Presentation in Hebrews

In 1:1 the Letter to the Hebrews designates its theology and Christology as speech of the word of God. The same God who spoke to the fathers through the prophets has "in these last days . . . spoken to us by a son" (Heb 1:2a). As God directed himself to the fathers through the word of the prophets, so has he turned "to us" again, once and for all, in the Word of his Son at the end of time. Since the precise addressees of the writing are not mentioned, the phrase "to us" includes all who read the Letter to the Hebrews with consent and who thus permit themselves to be included in the "us" through their cooperative reading of the letter. Those who read in this way are situated with the author of the writing at the end of time, the situation determined by the letter. Given this time, it is now paramount to understand Jesus as the ultimate word of God, to become conscious of the eschatological certainty of this communicative act of God, and to align oneself with it.

Therefore verses 1:2b-3 first sketch the dignity and function of the Son. He was "appointed heir of all things" by God. This cosmic dimension of divine sonship is developed through the inclusion of the Son in the theology of creation (cf. Heb 1:2b). His participation in the glory of God is seen in 1:3a. And 1:3b speaks of the soteriological function of the Son: "he sustains all things by his powerful word. When he had made purification for sins, he sat down at the right hand of the Majesty on high." On the basis of this soteriological plot he became greater than the angels and his name therefore even outshines the names of angels (1:4). In the center of Hebrews' Christology thus stands the act of the Son of God. This act receives its soteriological power through the connection of the events of the cross and resurrection and raises the Son's dignity even higher through the components of his humiliation and exaltation.

In the course of its argumentation, the Letter to the Hebrews reveals how this act is to be seen and how it effects salvation. The narrative of the Jesus-Christ-Story in its fundamental lines is interwoven into Hebrews' argumentation in the context of the rhetoric of "comfort and exhortation."

The salvation (σωτηρία) effected by the Son "was declared at first through the Lord, and it was attested to us by those who heard him, while God added his testimony by signs and wonders and various miracles, and by gifts of the Holy Spirit, distributed according to his will" (Heb 2:3b-4). The powerful word of the Son, which sustains all things (cf. 1:3b), began on earth with the proclamation of Jesus even before his crucifixion. This word was confirmed by God as the divine word by the miracles accompanying it and by the gift of the Holy Spirit. The preaching of this word was effective and, because of the positive reception of those who had already heard it, it spread so widely that even the author of the Letter to the Hebrews and his readers heard it and received it.

The Son of God assumed a human existence, one "of flesh and blood," in order to take up the likeness of the "children of Abraham" and to liberate them from the sin-causing power of death, wielded by the devil (cf. 2:14ff.). "Therefore he had to become like his brothers and sisters in every respect, so that he might be a merciful and faithful high priest in the service of God, to make a sacrifice of atonement for the sins of the people. Because he himself was tested by what he suffered, he is able to help those who are being tested" (Heb 2:17-18). Through this experience, he has achieved the ability to suffer "with our weakness," for he has been "in every respect tempted as we are, yet without sin" (4:15b). Jesus lived the limited and oppressed life of a mortal human with all its temptations, wishes, and fears. Nevertheless, during his experience of mortality he remained fully obedient to God in all things. In this obedience nothing was spared him—not suffering, not shame, not even the fear of death on the cross. "In the days of his flesh, Jesus offered up prayers and supplications, with loud cries and tears, to the one who was able to save him from death, and he was heard because of his reverent submission. Although he was a Son, he learned obedience through what he suffered" (5:7-8).

He was mocked (cf. Heb 6:6b) and suffered a bloody death on the cross (cf. 2:9; 6:6b; 12:2), but his prayers and supplications in the face of his death on the cross were answered by God when he brought him back from the dead: "The God of peace" has "brought back from the dead our Lord Jesus, the great shepherd of the sheep" (13:20).[9] He was exalted to the position of high priest in the heavens "through the power of an indestructible life" (7:16c). "Consequently he is able for all time to save those who approach God through him, since he always lives to make intercession for them" (7:25). "For this reason he is the mediator of a new covenant, so that those who are called may receive the promised eternal inheritance, because a death has occurred that redeems them from the transgressions under the first covenant" (9:15; cf. 8:6).

He is the "pioneer and perfecter of our faith" (Heb 12:2), because nothing pulled him from the path of obedience, and thus salvation is made possible for those who now trust in his mighty word and cleave to him and who align themselves with God through his story (cf. 5:9-10).

With his unconditional and constant listening to God, that is, his obedience, he displays the right way to serve God. "If Jesus thus . . . shares in human weakness (Heb 5:2), then, unlike other men, he does not fail, but rather maintains his fellowship with God. Unlike other men, he remains sinless and maintains obedience in suffering (5:8)."[10] He followed this path even when he became a bloody victim of the power of death. In spite of his fear of death he entrusted himself to the God through whose word all things have been created (cf. 11:3), the same God of whom Abraham already thought, "God is able even to raise someone from the dead" (11:19). The acceptance of his own suffering and the distress, anguish, and fear of death are not blocked out in a stoic manner. Rather he turns crying, praying, screaming to God the creator, the one who raises the dead. This shows him to be the powerful word of God. This is the sign of the right service of God. This is what it looks like to give God honor as the creator of all life in every situation in life. God does not require his Son's death in order to placate himself. His violent death on the cross makes it apparent that God's adversary would not wince before the blood of the one who was without sin. Jesus has fear, but he does not run away. He sets himself on the way of obedience and makes himself a representative of all the victims of the power of death. The blood of this self-sacrifice, poured out on the cross (cf. 8:27b), becomes an effective sign for those who obey Jesus Christ and let themselves be reoriented by his story. From now on, no other way of dealing with sin is necessary. The crucified one, resurrected and exalted to heaven as high priest, "has no need to offer sacrifices day after day, first for his own sins, and then for those of the people; this he did once for all when he offered himself" (7:27; cf. 9:11-12). "Now the main point in what we are saying is this: we have such a high priest, one who is seated at the right hand of the throne of the Majesty in the heavens, a minister in the sanctuary and the true tent that the Lord, and not any mortal, has set up" (8:1-2).

Through the narrative of the self-offering of the sinless Son of God, the one who also suffers with us, the Jesus-Christ-Story has become the saving story for all those who are victims. But this story has not yet achieved its goal. Through his consistent and courageous service to God, Jesus has broken the power of death. Nevertheless, "we do not yet see everything in subjection to him" (Heb 2:8c). Only faith, of which Hebrews 11 expressly speaks, can already see the Savior in the Crucified One. In patient confidence faith expects him, and thus also expects the end of violence. This confidence determines the conduct of the lives of the faithful: "But as it is, he has appeared once for all at the end of the age to remove sin by the sacrifice of himself. And just as it is appointed for mortals to die once, and after that the judgment, so Christ, having been offered once to bear the sins of many, will appear a second time, not to deal with sin, but to save those who are eagerly waiting for him" (9:26b-28).

"God Is Able Even to Raise Someone from the Dead"

God speaks through the prophets and ultimately through the story of his Son, Jesus Christ, the Crucified One who has been raised and exalted (cf. Heb 1:1-2). The story receives its plausibility on the basis of language about God found in the Scriptures of Israel. The author of the Letter to the Hebrews assumes these Scriptures as God's own word given to the fathers as a witness on the basis of their faith. The Scriptures of Israel are thus the charter of faith, which the Letter to the Hebrews defines as "the assurance of things hoped for, the conviction of things not seen" (11:1). Consequently, the Scriptures of Israel provide the believer with the testimony about God and his acts. To talk about God and his Son apart from faith would make no sense for Hebrews.

"By faith we understand that the worlds were prepared by the word of God, so that what is seen was made from things that are not visible" (Heb 11:3). From this foundation arises the plausibility of all "signs and wonders and various miracles" (cf. 2:4a) that God works and about which the "cloud of witnesses" (12:1a) speaks; they are called up intertextually in chapter 11.

To these wondrous, mighty deeds of the creator God belong also resurrections from the dead. Abraham is convinced already: "God is able even to raise someone from the dead" (Heb 11:19a). Hebrews 11:35a alludes to the stories of Elijah (1 Kgs 17:17-24) and Elisha (2 Kgs 4:18-37): "Women received their dead by resurrection." One should probably think of martyrologies such as 2 Maccabees 7 and perhaps also Daniel 12 when in the same verse Hebrews continues, "Others were tortured, refusing to accept release, in order to obtain a better resurrection." The Letter to the Hebrews thus distinguishes the revivification of the dead who return to earthly life—in the way that Elijah restored the dead son to the widow of Zarephath—from the resurrection of the dead "through the power of an indestructible life" (Heb 7:16b). In contrast with Paul, however, the Letter to the Hebrews places no value on the fact that Jesus Christ, the resurrected, Crucified One, is the first and the beginning of this eschatological resurrection (cf. 1 Cor 15). The resurrection of the Crucified One as his being led out of the dead (cf. Heb 13:20) is neither more nor less than the indispensable assumption for his exaltation as the heavenly high priest, where he now exercises his saving office as mediator. Like Paul, the Letter to the Hebrews emphasizes the saving significance of the crucifixion, but into the place of the eschatological power of the resurrection steps the eschatological significance of the exaltation of the Crucified One brought back from the dead. For the Letter to the Hebrews, the doctrine of the resurrection of the dead belongs to the essential assumptions of Christian doctrine (cf. 6:1-2), but it possesses no independent eschatological significance. It is precisely in the theology of the resurrection that one sees marked agreements, but also considerable differences between the Pauline letters and the Letter to the Hebrews.

One certain point of agreement concerns the fact that the Letter to the Hebrews and Paul accept the fact that a transformation is needed because the first creation is not suitable for eternal life. The Letter to the Hebrews assumes "that what cannot be shaken may remain. Therefore, since we are receiving a kingdom that cannot be shaken, let us give thanks, by which we offer to God an acceptable worship with reverence and awe; for indeed our God is a consuming fire" (12:27b-29).

Because the Crucified One has experienced this transformation in his resurrection, the Letter to the Hebrews can proclaim, "Jesus Christ is the same yesterday, today, and forever" (Heb 13:8). The transformation from a limited life in flesh and blood to a limitless life "through the power of an indestructible life" (7:16b) releases indestructible, eternal life from the limits of the temporality of life in flesh and blood. Therefore, Jesus, whom God "appointed heir of all things" as a Son, can also now be praised as the one "through whom he also created the worlds" (1:1, 2b). The so-called expressions of preexistence are absolutely not expressions of existence in the sense of an empirical explanation of the world according to the laws of space and time that limit the first creation. It is much more a question of expressions within the logic of the second creation, for which the temporal order merges into the contemporaneity of eternity.

The "better hope" (Heb 7:19b), by which the Letter to the Hebrews is moved, is the promise that all suffering, all fear-inducing limits of life in mortal flesh and blood have come to an end through the complex of events of the crucifixion, resurrection from the dead, and exaltation of Jesus. The way into the heavenly sanctuary has been opened by Jesus, the heavenly high priest according to the order of Melchizedek, for all who continue to confess his story and let themselves have their lives directed by it. "For Christ did not enter a sanctuary made by human hands, a mere copy of the true one, but he entered into heaven itself, now to appear in the presence of God on our behalf" (9:24). The great hope of which the Letter to the Hebrews speaks consists in the trusting confidence that death will not have the last word. It also consists in the confidence that the judgment of God, who himself is "a consuming fire" (12:29), does not determine the future of believers. Rather, believers already have "hope" offered through the Jesus-Christ-Story as "a sure and steadfast anchor . . . , a hope that enters the inner shrine behind the curtain" (6:19). Those who wait for him, however, by pursuing "peace with everyone, and holiness" (12:14) will enter "the city of the living God, the heavenly Jerusalem" (12:22) and live eternally in peace in communion with God, his Son, and the angels.

Chapter 3

The Synoptic Gospels and Acts

The Synoptic Gospels, which probably came into being between A.D. 70 and 90, can as Martin Kähler put it be regarded as "passion narratives with extended introductions."[1] They bear the impression of the fundamental eschatological significance of the resurrection of the crucified one every bit as much as the Pauline letters. They also, however, wish to tell who this Jesus of Nazareth was, and how it happened that he was murdered by crucifixion.

This does not mean, however, that the Gospels are completely absorbed with questions of historical interest. That Jesus' proclamation of the in-breaking of the kingdom of God, and above all his parables pertaining to the kingdom of God, should be understood in continuity with the God who raised him from the dead is clear from the scriptural foundation of the Gospels' Christian memory. God's merciful and just action in the resurrection becomes comprehensible as the identification of God with Jesus' own portrayal of God. In his eschatological act of raising Jesus from the dead, God is shown as the one about whom Jesus of Nazareth spoke. Moreover, through the resurrection God gives Jesus justice.

The Gospels fulfill yet another task. They accomplish what Paul also said about his own proclamation: they portray Jesus as the Resurrected One who was crucified, the Son of God exalted to the Lord and active for believers in the present. In significant ways the Gospels also represent the absent body of the Resurrected One who was crucified. In this way the Gospels are themselves signs of his resurrection.

That the proclamation of the resurrection of the Crucified One and not just the memory of the words and deeds of Jesus stands at the theological center of Luke's Acts of the Apostles, however, points clearly to the theological intention of Christianity's first church historian.

In any event, the differences among the Synoptics cannot be overlooked, for they narrate the Jesus-Christ-Story with rather differing conceptions, something which in turn is seen in their respective presentations of resurrection theology.

The Gospel of Mark

For the interpretation of the gospel of Mark and especially for the present question of its resurrection discourse, the question of where the gospel ends plays an important role. The text-critical witness points to the problem of Mark's ending: If we follow the most ancient witnesses, then Mark 16:9-20 does not belong to the earliest text of the gospel. Verses 9-20 complete the gospel of Mark by adding references to stories about encounters with the resurrected "Jesus" (cf. 16:9). We find similar accounts in other gospels but not in the original Mark. The gospel of Mark thus originally ended with the tantalizingly abrupt comment of verse 8: "And they"—the women—"went out" from the tomb of Jesus "and fled from the tomb, for terror and amazement had seized them; and they said nothing to anyone, for they were afraid."

Can a gospel end with the message that the women were seized with paralyzing fear at the tomb of the Crucified One, fear that prevented them from understanding the empty tomb as a sign of good news rather than their proclaiming this fact with joy? Can a gospel conclude without stories of encounters with the one raised from the dead? These questions probably confronted readers already in the second century,[2] and they answered them by annexing stories culled from reading other gospels. From then on the gospel of Mark was more often than not handed down with this longer ending (16:9-20). Thus it stands recorded even today in many contemporary editions of the Bible.

There is also a shorter addition to the original conclusion to Mark. It reads, "And all that had been commanded them they told briefly to those around Peter. And afterward Jesus himself sent out through them, from east to west, the sacred and imperishable proclamation of eternal salvation. Amen." This variant ending of the gospel of Mark, attested by an old Latin manuscript, also shows how intolerable the original ending of Mark has appeared to many readers. Several manuscripts even combine both additions.

Readers of the first centuries are not the only ones who have had problems with the original ending of Mark. Academic exegesis of the twentieth century has also attempted to evade the challenges of this conclusion. Since the text-critical witness permitted neither verses 9-20 nor certainly the shorter, old Latin ending to be seen as original, the conjecture was contrived that the original gospel of Mark did not end with 16:8 but rather with a lost ending that could be produced once again by means of literary-critical hypotheses.[3] The hypothesis of a lost ending to Mark stands on clay feet, however, for it is supported neither by a textual witness nor by any recipients of the gospel of Mark in the early church. It is thus a question of exegetical conjecture that, like both of the early endings of Mark that have been preserved, wants to mitigate both literarily and theologically the abrasive original ending of Mark. But, ever since Henning Paulsen's investigation of Mark's ending, one must confront the difficulty of a gospel of Mark that ends at 16:8.[4]

How then should one understand Mark's conclusion? Why does the gospel end without euphoria, but rather with the dissonance of a terror that produced persistent silence on the part of the first recipients of the message of the resurrection? Only an interpretation of the gospel of Mark as a whole can answer these questions. In order to focus on this larger interpretation of Mark's gospel, we will first analyze the conclusion itself, and then approach the beginning of the gospel. From there we will move out to investigate the narrative and the rhetorical strategies of the gospel. All of this will be done with a view to the pragmatic question of how Mark shaped his gospel to prepare his readers for the conclusion that one can understand the message of the resurrection in a way that differs from the initial assessment of the women at the tomb.

The Incomprehension of the Women at the Tomb

Chapter 15 relates the crucifixion of Jesus, which leads to his death. Jesus' death is expressly recorded in Mark 15:37: Jesus completely breathed out his life (ἐξέπνευσεν). As the inspiration of the breath of life described in Genesis 2:7[5] makes the man into a living creature, so the expiration of this breath of life makes him a lifeless corpse. Jesus is dead without any reservation whatsoever. There is no talk of a soul that lives on. Joseph of Arimathea, "a respected member of the council, who was also himself waiting expectantly for the kingdom of God," as Mark 15:43 has it, requests the corpse from Pontius Pilate. He then wraps it in a shawl, lays it in a stone tomb, and shuts the entrance of the tomb by rolling a stone in front of it (cf. 15:45-46). Mary Magdalene and Mary the mother of Joses observe this (cf. 15:47). All of this happens on the day before the Sabbath (cf. 15:42).

The concluding section of the gospel of Mark now begins in Mark 16:1 with the temporal declaration "When the sabbath was over." Both Marys go together with Salome to the tomb knowing where the corpse of the crucified one is to be found. They do this with the intention of anointing the corpse. When they ask themselves who can roll the stone away from the tomb for them, they see "that the stone . . . had already been rolled back" (16:4). They enter the tomb, see a young man wearing a white garment sitting there, and are seized with fear. This reaction is in the Greek text expressed passively in the aorist, a time form peculiar to the Greek used to designate punctiliar action: they were *abruptly* seized with fear.[6] This spontaneous reaction shows that the three women are in no way prepared for the message of the resurrection. Their intention to anoint the corpse of the Crucified One (16:1) unreservedly assumes the facticity of death. The women observed how the corpse was laid in the tomb before the Sabbath. The power and reality of death is so indisputable to them that they can comfortably wait out the Sabbath, for in the logic of death the corpse has no power to get up and walk away. What they see at and in the tomb, however, shatters their expectation and intention, shaped as they were by the plausibility structure of death.

The young man, the description of whose clothing identifies him in the gospel of Mark as a heavenly figure (cf. Mark 9:3), and whose words cause him to be perceived wholly as a heavenly messenger, perceives the women's terrified paralysis and rejects it as an inappropriate reaction to what they have seen. He commands them with the same verb: μὴ ἐκθαμβεῖσθε.[7] With the change from aorist to present he repudiates the punctiliar paralyzed terror of the women with the command to no longer be seized by fear generally. Then he gives the ground for this command: "You are looking for Jesus of Nazareth, who was crucified. He has been raised; he is not here. Look, there is the place they laid him" (16:6b). The heavenly messenger thereby tells the women that he knows whom they seek: Jesus of Nazareth, the Crucified One (τὸν ἐσταυρωμένον). Ἐσταυρωμένον is a passive participle that stands in the perfect. The perfect designates an action that lies in the past whose effects extend into the present. Jesus of Nazareth has been crucified, and the crucifixion belongs from then on to his enduring bodily identity. It is this Crucified One who has been raised from the dead in a unique event. The verb ἠγέρθη, which expresses his resurrection, stands in the aorist indicative passive and thus likewise designates a punctiliar event that lies in the past. The passive is to be understood as a *passivum divinum*, a reverent way to express an act of

God. The heavenly messenger announces to the women the resurrection of the crucified Jesus of Nazareth by God.

Connected to this message is the commission to become messengers themselves: "But go, tell his disciples and Peter that he is going ahead of you to Galilee; there you will see him, just as he told you" (Mark 16:7). The appropriate reaction to the message of the resurrection is not to be paralyzed by fear but rather to become a messenger of this good news, a messenger of the gospel.

The women are not, however, in a state to hear the message of the resurrection as good news. The concluding verse of the gospel of Mark cited above expressly states this: "So they went out and fled from the tomb, for terror and amazement had seized them; and they said nothing to anyone, for they were afraid" (Mark 16:8).

Neither the visual perception of the empty tomb nor the auditory perception of the message of the resurrection is sufficient for understanding the event as gospel. The women at and in the tomb see with eyes that see, and yet they do not perceive; they hear with ears that hear, but they do not understand (cf. Mark 4:12).

But why do they not perceive and understand, and what is the reader of the gospel of Mark to make of its frustrating ending? It is necessary to read the whole gospel of Mark in order to be able to understand its ending appropriately. Mark prepares its readers step-by-step to be able to understand the event of the cross and resurrection of Jesus as gospel. In terms of pragmatic function of the text, the women at the tomb form negative examples that in the rhetoric of hardening serve to warn readers of their own incomprehension. They are therefore set in the pragmatic motif of the incomprehension of the disciples, which again and again shows the disciples seized with fear.[8] With this recognition an interesting rereading of the gospel of Mark becomes plausible. Specifically, one can now ask how readers are shaped by reading the gospel so that they can perceive the message of the resurrection without being seized by fear.

The Beginning of the Gospel

The word sequence from ἀρχή to τῷ προφήτῃ at the beginning of the gospel of Mark forms one coherent sentence, which is to be translated as follows: "The beginning of the gospel of Jesus Christ as it is written in Isaiah, the prophet."[9] Thus Mark instructs its readers to read the Jesus-Christ-Story, which the gospel tells as the continuation of the Scriptures of Israel. The subordinate clause beginning with καθώς refers to ἀρχή (beginning) and thus defines where the beginning of the gospel narrated by Mark is to be found. The word ἀρχή thus does not designate the beginning of the text of Mark, but rather the beginning of the gospel narrated by it, the beginning that Mark sees given in the book of Isaiah the prophet, not in his own writing.[10] The gospel of Mark presents itself as the written continuation of the written prophecy of Isaiah (γέγραπται). The first sentence of the gospel provides the encyclopedia,[11] the conventionalized knowledge, in whose plausibility assumptions the story narrated by Mark makes sense.

The word "gospel" raises expectations for a story with a good outcome. Jesus Christ is introduced as the protagonist of this story. His proper name, Jesus, locates him within the plausibility structures of human relationships. The title of Christ grounds his elevated position as the protagonist of the narrative, for he therefore fulfills the messianic expectation produced by the Scriptures of Israel and especially by the prophetic Scriptures. The designation υἱοῦ θεοῦ (Son of God), on the other hand, is a later addition that was motivated by the decisive significance of this title for the gospel of Mark.[12]

Verse 2 introduces the messiah's messenger, who in verse 4 is identified as John the Baptist and who through the description of his clothing in Mark 1:6 reminds the reader of Elijah (cf. 2 Kgs 1:8). The messenger is supposed to prepare the way for the promised messiah, and he completes his commission by summoning the addressees of the messiah to prepare the way for the Lord.

In pragmatic perspective, the address in verse 3 is directed to the readers of the gospel of Mark. They are held fast by the prophetic voice that proclaims the summons of God to hear the message of the gospel of Mark in such a way that the Lord will be received by them rightly. Thus the title κύριος, which is a divine designation in the LXX, the Greek version of the Scriptures of Israel, refers both to the speaking I and also to the addressed You. It thus refers both to God and to his messiah. On the basis of this intertextual interweaving it is better to refer the title first to God, but in the coming of his messiah God himself is seen to arrive at the same time.

Verses 1-3 not only open up the universe of discourse[13] of the gospel of Mark, but also provide at the beginning of the gospel the decisive direction for proper reception: the gospel of Mark itself should be heard as a prophetic voice of the Lord's messenger. One ought therefore to let oneself be shaped by it. At the level of their pragmatic function, verses 1-3, the very beginning of the gospel of Mark, thus provide an intertextual[14] introduction to the story that follows.

The Introduction of the Protagonist

In Mark 1:9 the protagonist of the narrative enters. He is identified as Jesus of Nazareth from Galilee (1:9a). After being baptized by John with water (1:9b), he receives the πνεῦμα, the Spirit (1:10), and the heavenly voice addresses him as the beloved Son of God (1:11). The Spirit plays an active role and makes Jesus an object by casting him out into the wilderness (1:12). There Jesus withstands the trial of testing through Satan, God's accuser (1:13). The protagonist, Jesus of Nazareth in Galilee, is now equipped with the power that makes his works, which transcend all human possibility, appear plausible, and through his endurance in testing, his words and works are designated beforehand as conforming to the will of God. From the first thirteen verses of the gospel of Mark readers know who Jesus of Nazareth is: the beloved Son of God, equipped with the Spirit, and as such the expected messiah. They do not yet know, however, for what purpose the Spirit has empowered him and with what resistance he will meet.

The Beginning of Narrative Tension

Verse 14 introduces the first dysphoric element and thus opens up the narrative thread of antagonism: Jesus comes to Galilee, after John has been arrested. At this point readers learn nothing about the circumstances of the messenger's arrest. But the arc of tension is built upon the two narrative threads running counter to each other: the euphoric story of the arrival and works of the protagonist on the one hand and the dysphoric story of the threats to these deeds on the other.[15]

As Willi Marxsen has already shown,[16] the announcement of the cosmological-eschatological turning of the ages stands at the beginning and in the center of the public activity of Jesus: "The time is fulfilled, and the kingdom of God has come near" (Mark 1:15). From this announcement follows the appeal to repentance and faith in the gospel. The protagonist names the proclamation of the kingdom of God as the reason for his coming (cf. 1:38c).

Up to and including chapter 3, the euphoric narrative thread of the success of the works of Jesus through the calling of the disciples (cf. Mark 1:16-20) is driven by the presentation of his power in word and deed and by the determined increase of his disciples (cf. 2:2, 15; 3:7-8). At the same time the dysphoric narrative thread is depicted in the conflict narratives such as the conflict about fasting (cf. 2:18-22) and about plucking grain on the Sabbath (2:23-28). Above all the conflict is made concrete through the scribe's accusation of blasphemy in 2:7 and the murderous intention of the Pharisees and Herodians in 3:6.

This conflict is fueled not only through the depiction of Jesus' opponents, but also through the depiction of the protagonist himself. The Jesus of the gospel of Mark is an angry messiah (cf. Mark 1:43; 3:5) ready for a fight. His claims to authority prove provocative. He openly claims divine competence when he forgives sins (cf. 2:5) and employs the divine designation κύριος for himself: "So the Son of Man is *kyrios* even of the Sabbath." The syntagm "Son of Man" as the self-designation he himself emphasizes[17] also underscores the protagonist's claim to authority. The protagonist's solidarity with sinners and tax collectors fuels the fires of conflict as well.

The two narrative threads do not play out next to each other; rather, precisely because of their restrained narrative intertwining they produce a high degree of tension. This is seen already in the story of the first appearance of Jesus in Capernaum (Mark 1:21-28). Jesus teaches in the synagogue there, and the listeners are overpowered by the effect of his teaching. The verb ἐκπλήσσω, which expresses this reaction to Jesus' teaching repeatedly in the gospel of Mark,[18] is also employed as a reaction to Jesus' wondrous deeds (cf. 7:37). The narrator comments on this reaction as follows: "For he taught them as one with divine authority, and not as the scribes." Mark 1:23 then tells of a man in the synagogue who had an unclean spirit. He screams, "What have you to do with us, Jesus of Nazareth? Have you come to destroy us? I know who you are, the Holy One of God." Jesus commands the spirit to come out of him, which the unclean spirit then does in a dramatic fashion.

The reaction of those present to this proof of authority is now described with the same verb that designates the instance of fear seizing the women at the empty tomb (θαμβέω in Mark 1:27, ἐκθαμβέω in 16:5). As at the tomb, the paralyzing fear in the synagogue in Capernaum displays the lack of understanding that, as a consequence of fear, fails to perceive in each instance what has actually happened.

Admittedly one must observe also a distinction between Jesus' first public working of wonders in Capernaum and his wondrous resurrection effected by God at the end of the gospel. If in Capernaum Jesus is not recognized as the expected messiah whose coming marks the breaking in of the kingdom of God, then at the very least the full authority of his works is named and a congruence between the narrator's comment (Mark 1:22b) and Jesus' audience in the synagogue (1:27c) is created. At the beginning of Jesus' ministry, when his works produce fear, those present at least ask what has happened (cf. 1:27). The women at the tomb, however, remain in terrified silence (cf. 16:8).

The healing of Peter's mother-in-law is told in connection with the scene in the synagogue (Mark 1:29ff.). This miracle story contributes something to the resurrection discourse of the gospel of Mark as well. Werner Kahl has impressively pointed out the fact that in antiquity as also today in regions lacking adequate medical care, fever is frequently a harbinger of death.[19] The illness of Peter's mother-in-law is thus designated as life-threatening. It is therefore conspicuous that in the description of the process of her healing by Jesus, the first instance of resurrection terminology, the same language employed in 16:6, occurs. After Jesus takes her by the hand, he raises (ἤγειρεν) her. His own resurrection is later announced by the heavenly messenger at the tomb with the passive form of the same verb: ἠγέρθη.

This is not the only place where the verb ἐγείρω is found in connection with a miracle story, that is, in resurrection discourse. It is also employed in Mark 2:9, 3:3, 3:38, 5:41, 6:14, 6:16, 9:27, 10:49, and 14:28. This observation should not be overinterpreted, for the verb in question first of all means "to wake up, to get up." From this meaning it comes to be used metaphorically for the event of the resurrection. But because of the frequent appearance of ἐγείρω in conjunction with miracle stories and resurrection discourses in the gospel of Mark, readers are semantically prepared for the all-decisive ἠγέρθη in 16:6.

The Warning Against Hardened Reading

The fourth chapter drives both the euphoric and the dysphoric narrative strands forward by weaving them ever more tightly into one another. If in the first three chapters the disciples line up on the side of the protagonist, their estrangement from the hero begins in chapter 4 with their lack of understanding regarding the parable of the Sower. They see and hear, but they do not understand. Winds and waves listen to Jesus, but the disciples are afraid (cf. 4:41).

After Jesus tells the so-called parable of the Sower in Mark 4:3-9, the text continues in verses 10-12 with the following: "When he was alone, those who were around him along with the twelve asked him about the parables. And he said to them, 'To you has been given the secret of the kingdom of God, but for those outside, everything comes in parables; in order that "they may indeed look, but not perceive, and may indeed listen, but not understand; so that they may not turn again and be forgiven."'"[20]

Inside and outside are not static categories in the gospel of Mark.[21] If the disciples appear in Mark 4:10 as insiders, it is a consequence of their following of Jesus as told in the preceding chapters. Where they do not follow the words and deeds of Jesus they are outsiders. As an example, consider 6:52: "for they"—the disciples—"did not understand about the loaves, but their hearts were hardened." On the other hand those who are outside are no static mass. The message of the resurrection is first for those who left Jesus of Nazareth in the lurch and betrayed him, namely his hardened disciples (cf. 16:7). It depends on the question of how one hears and sees. Lack of understanding and hardening are considered co-original. Hearing with understanding as the gospel of Mark portrays it proves that readers who grasp the point are not hardened and are thus insiders. The gospel of Mark requires a reading in which readers show themselves to be those who understand. As such they are not hardened and therefore are insiders. Whether readers are numbered with those who are insiders or are among those who are outsiders is shown by their way of reading.

Reading the gospel of Mark is itself a visual and auditory process. *Scriptio continua* was a common way of writing in antiquity. The letters were arranged right next to one another without spaces between them. There were a great many abbreviations in the text, and usually there was no punctuation. This mode of writing made reading a visual and acoustic process. Reading was done out loud.[22] In her University of Frankfurt dissertation investigating the significance of hearing in Mark 4, Kristina Dronsch has shown convincingly that hearing in Mark 4 thematizes hearing with understanding in the act of reading.[23] Moreover, she finds the typology of hearers in the interpretation of the parable of the Sower in Mark 4:13-20 again and again in Mark. The first group of hearers comprise accordingly the opponents of Jesus, those who hear him but who immediately stand against him. As an example, one can point to the scribes in 2:6-7, who hear Jesus and classify that which they hear as blasphemy. This is also the accusation in 14:64 that takes Jesus to the cross. The second group of hearers are those who immediately receive his word but who when encountering "trouble or persecution . . . on account of the word" immediately fall away. The word used here for "immediately," εὐθύς, actually appears in the story of the call of the first disciples in Mark 1:16-20: After Jesus' call to discipleship, the narrator says, "And immediately (εὐθύς) they left their nets and followed him." In the desperate situation in Jerusalem after the arrest of Jesus, however, they all fall away. Peter's threefold denial is portrayed in an especially powerful way

(14:66-72). The third group of hearers, among whom riches and desires hinder the fruitfulness of the word, is portrayed in the example of the rich young man whom Jesus came to love during their exchange. Jesus therefore says to him in 10:20-21, "'You lack one thing; go, sell what you own, and give the money to the poor, and you will have treasure in heaven; then come, follow me.' When he heard this, he was shocked and went away grieving, for he had many possessions."

The fourth group, which hears the word, accepts it, and bears fruit thirty-, sixty-, and even a hundredfold, cannot be found in the narrative of the gospel of Mark, according to Dronsch. It is a gap that the readers of Mark have to fill. They show themselves to be those who are insiders if they read the gospel with understanding and agree with it and bear fruit. Continuing Dronsch's interpretation, fruitfulness may be interpreted as fulfilling the command of the heavenly messenger at the grave of Jesus. Readers of Mark reveal themselves to be insiders when they hear or read the gospel with understanding, accept it as the gospel of Jesus Christ the Son of God, and bear forth his message of the resurrection of the Crucified One as the gospel.

Narrative and Discursive Preparation
for the Resurrection Message

The gospel of Mark itself enables its readers to perform such fruitful hearing, for already after chapter 4 they know not only who Jesus is but also the secret of his wonder-working power. They do not yet know, however, that this authority is also in the position to conquer death. It is precisely that knowledge which is now thematized step-by-step in the gospel.

Jesus frees the tomb-dwelling Gerasene demoniac from an entire legion of unclean spirits and thus brings him out of the tombs back into the life of the community (cf. Mark 5:1-20). Directly in connection with this story, the power that flows out from Jesus heals the hemorrhaging woman. More than that, however, his authority over death becomes apparent in the story of the raising of Jairus' daughter (cf. 5:21-43). And here also is found the terminology of resurrection: Jesus takes the girl's hand and says to her, ἔγειρε (arise) (5:41c). The similarity of this procedure of raising the girl and the agreement of the semantics brings to mind again the healing of Peter's mother-in-law. If Jesus saved her from her death-signifying fever, then he calls the dead girl back to life in a comparable way. The resurrection from the dead effected by Jesus is clearly a wondrous deed that transgresses the boundary of death. As with his other miracles, however, this act does not bring with it any enduring cosmological change. It aims instead to temporarily remedy the deficiencies of the present situation.

The following sixth chapter joins both narrative threads together. It continues the euphoric theme of the defeat of death found in chapter 5 in a dysphoric way. In the story of the rejection of Jesus at Nazareth (ἐσκανδαλίζοντο ἐν αὐτῷ, Mark 6:3), the fate of the prophets plays out in the narration (cf. 6:4). Not only does the story make clear the dangerous nature of the related sending of the disciples (6:7-13), but the story of the execution of the messenger who herald the protagonist is also bound to the same horizon of meaning. John dies the death of a prophet of God. The violent death of John (6:17-29) in turn prepares readers in narrative ways for the violent end of Jesus and his burial in the tomb even before Jesus' discursive passion predictions.

The successful mission of the disciples grounds Herod's knowledge of Jesus and his extraordinary deeds. Of the three current interpretations of Jesus as being either John raised from the dead, or Elijah, or one of the prophets, Herod chooses the first because this seems to him to explain Jesus' ability to work his wonders (cf. Mark 6:14ff.). With the question of Markan resurrection discourse in view, it is important to note that the temporal raising of a dead person stands within the horizon of expectations of the broader public as well as in the expectation of Herod, the political authority. Readers know, however, that Herod's conclusion is an instance of the kind of mistaken judgments that do not perceive the true identity of the messiah as the Son of God.

But it is not only the incomprehension of the crowds and of Herod that drives the dysphoric plotline. The incomprehension of the hardened disciples (cf. 8:14-21) also contributes to the plotline. The disciples do not perceive the symbolic message of the miracles of Jesus and especially the dual feedings of the four and five thousand (cf. 6:30-44; 8:1-10). Moreover they are seized by fear at Jesus' walking on the water (cf. 6:50). Indeed, Jesus' own companions are as caught up in this plotline, as are the Pharisees who engage in a polemical confrontation with Jesus over the question of what is clean and unclean (cf. 7:1-23).

Thus, when taken together, chapters 5–8 strengthen and accelerate the interweaving of the euphoric and dysphoric plotlines. Importantly, though, Jesus' first announcement of his death and resurrection (8:31-32a) following Peter's messianic confession (cf. 8:29) form a peripeteia, a reversal, in the narrative. The announcements of death and resurrection interweave the euphoric and dysphoric plotlines through the necessity (expressed by δεῖ) of the suffering of the Son of Man by explaining the dysphoric element as a necessary function of the euphoric element.

The peripeteiac function of the first passion prediction is seen especially in the narrator's commentary: Jesus speaks this word in uncoded language, clearly and openly (παρρησία). Peter, who identifies Jesus rightly as the messiah in Mark 8:29, steps in decisively against this interweaving by seeking to remove the dysphoric element, the suffering and death of Jesus, from the euphoric plotline of the works of the messiah. Jesus' harsh reaction to Peter disqualifies this separation as not in conformity with that which God wills (cf. 8:33). Jesus' way, and thus also the way of those called to follow him, is the way of the cross, as 8:34ff. makes plain.[24] This way of the cross leads to life.

Because the disciples do not understand this connection, they do not understand Jesus' words about his resurrection, which their reaction to the transfiguration scene reveals just as much as the second and third passion predictions. Thus, through the appearance (ὤφθη, Mark 9:4) of Elijah and Moses at the transfiguration of Jesus (9:3), it becomes clear to the disciples present that there is a heavenly life. Additionally, the heavenly voice, which now addresses them directly, reveals to them that Jesus is the Son of God (cf. 9:7), and on the way down Jesus plainly tells them that he will rise from the dead (cf. 9:9). They see, but they do not perceive. They hear, but they do not understand. The disciples do not understand what this talk of the resurrection from the dead might mean (cf. 9:10). They also fail to understand that John was the messenger of Jesus the messiah (cf. 9:11-18). For readers, on the other hand, the identification of John with the prophet Elijah and John's violent death as the fate of a prophet are confirmed again from the mouth of Jesus (cf. 9:13).

The story of a possessed boy that follows (9:14-29) can be designated a masterpiece of narrative theology. The disciples are unable to heal the boy. The father of the boy turns to Jesus, who is approaching the scene. Jesus' reaction shows the increasing isolation of the protagonist clearly. His raging outburst at his disciples at the same time sets the theological theme of faith in the discursive center of the story: "You faithless generation, how much longer must I be among you?" (9:19b). The accusation of faithlessness refers not to those who do not follow Jesus but rather to his closest companions.

The father turns to Jesus not because he desires to follow Jesus' message, but because he has hope in the miraculous powers of an extraordinary man. This becomes clear through his words, which express a limited hope: "If you are able to do anything, have pity on us and help us" (9:22b).

Jesus' answer sets faith in the center of the event: "All things can be done for the one who believes" (9:23b). The emotional reaction of the father to this comment is a cry that expresses the incapacity for a self-constitution of faith. He gives himself over to the hands of Jesus, both trusting and fearful at the same time: "I believe; help my unbelief!" (9:24b). With his confession of unbelief, the father becomes like the unbelieving disciples. Yet his insight shows at the same time the way out of hardening.

If the gospel of Mark aims for a reading that leads to faith, which in addition enables one to take up one's own cross as a follower of Jesus in the hope of achieving life, then the despairing father, who perceives and expresses with deep emotion the impossibility of securing one's own faith, is the model of faith in the gospel of Mark. Readers who understand will connect the empty tomb with this father's cry of concern for his child: "I believe; help my unbelief!" This attitude will prevent them from setting themselves above other followers of Jesus who are seized with fear. This attitude also helps one encounter the message of the angel at the tomb without the expectation that this message will produce a permanently doubt-free faith. Nevertheless this faith will also not let itself be seized by fear that strikes one dumb. Faith like this will answer the message of the angel: "I believe; help my unbelief!"

After the spirit that made the boy deaf and dumb has been effectively cast out of him, the child lies on the ground as dead, "so that most of them said, 'He is dead'" (9:26). The next verse (v. 27) confirms, however, that the exorcism has been successful. Interestingly, Mark uses phrasing here found already in the accounts of the healing of Peter's mother-in-law and of the raising of Jairus' daughter. Jesus takes the boy's hand and raises (ἐγείρω) him so that he stands up (ἀνίσταμαι). For the first time in this gospel, both resurrection terms appear in the same story, and their sequence is significant. The activity of the wonder worker is expressed through the verb "to raise" [*erwecken*], while the action of the object being raised up is said "to stand up" [*aufstehen*].

One must certainly guard against overinterpretation here. The resurrection terminology employed in the passion predictions (ἀνίσταμαι) reveals itself to be just as metaphorical as the terminology of rising (ἐγείρειν). Both are common words in everyday speech. If ἐγείρειν designates rising and getting up [*sich erheben*], then ἀνίστημι signifies standing up [*aufstehen*] or setting oneself up [*aufstellen*], and they are often synonyms.[25] In terms of theological content, however, the sequence in 9:27 expresses the fact that resurrection is an act of God that makes a rising to new life possible.

It is probably not an accident that the narrative staging of the story of this exemplar of faith is joined to the second passion prediction of Jesus' death and resurrection. The reaction of the disciples to the event shows their ongoing hardness and incomprehension. In fact their failure to apprehend the situation now devolves into a fearful silence: "But they did not understand what he was saying and were afraid to ask him" (Mark 9:32).

Instead, the disciples argue about who is greatest among them (Mark 9:33ff.). This provides Jesus with an occasion to speak about the order determined in the kingdom of God for service to others. Service to the other is explained as service to Jesus, and service to Jesus is service to God (cf. 9:37). From then on the theme of future reward and punishment is developed (cf. 9:41-50).

The section of 9:41-50 introduces the Jewish conception of eschatological punishment into the gospel's universe of discourse. Two offenses merit the punishment of hell: leading another into apostasy and one's own apostasy. Positively, the kingdom of God is promised to those who remain on the way of discipleship. The section displays the seriousness of the Markan message: The gospel of Mark is not concerned simply with telling a nice story, but rather with saving readers from the way that leads to Gehenna.[26] Readers who understand recognize that the way that leads to life is the way of cruciform discipleship. One can win that life, but one can also lose it.

The tenth chapter depicts Jesus' arrival in Judea and his way to Jerusalem. Thus the theme of discipleship deepens. One should receive the kingdom of God in trust like a child (10:13-16). Riches hinder discipleship considerably (10:17-27). Discipleship will soon be repaid, even now (10:28-31). Eternal life is the reward of discipleship in the coming world (10:30c).

The theme of discipleship is bound up narratively with the theme of the cross and resurrection by means of the third passion prediction: "They were on the road, going up to Jerusalem, and Jesus was walking ahead of them" (Mark 10:32). In Jerusalem Jesus will say to them that his going ahead of them will not end with his death, but rather he will go ahead of them to Galilee after his resurrection (cf. 14:28). And it is precisely this promise about which the messenger at the tomb reminds the women (cf. 16:7).

Jesus' way to Jerusalem is perceived by his followers as threatening: "They were amazed, and those who followed were afraid." Thereupon Jesus turns to the twelve and announces to them again his way of suffering and resurrection (cf. Mark 10:32ff.). Again the theme of ruling and serving is connected to Jesus' announcement as a reaction and in this connection comes the only explicit explanation of the death of Jesus in the gospel of Mark: "For the Son of Man came not to be served but to serve, and to give his life a ransom for many" (10:45). The life and death of Jesus is also conceptualized in the gospel of Mark as pro-existence.

The story of the healing of blind Bartimaeus in Jericho connected to the former story continues the themes of discipleship. Its concluding sentence confirms the success of the miracle on the narrative level. The pragmatic message uses the symbolism of blindness and seeing: faith creates sight and leads to the way of discipleship (cf. 10:52).

The entry of Jesus into Jerusalem told in Mark 11:1-10 seems to belie the disciples' fear. Jesus is received euphorically as the son of David. Indeed, even the odd note that Jesus scouted out the temple and then left Jerusalem in order to stay overnight with the twelve in Bethany (cf. 11:11b) stokes the euphoric attitude of expectation of the preceding story.

The story continues on the next day in Mark 11:12, and sharpens the conflict even further. In the story of the fig tree, Jesus' divine wrath and his power to bring absolute annihilation are introduced (cf. 11:12ff., 20-25). This story shows that through his solidarity with God, Jesus possessed the means to slay his tormentors. According to the gospel of Mark, Jesus' way to the cross is not the way of a powerless victim. From his first public act in Jerusalem at the beginning of the second day on, the story permits no doubts about the extent of his power. Jesus' opponents are playing with their own destruction.

The so-called "cleansing of the temple,"[27] which leads to the ultimate sentence of death for Jesus at the hands of the high priests and scribes, signifies precisely this. They thus react to the provocative act of an aggressive Jesus. That they do not arrest him immediately is due to their paralyzing fear, which is expressed with the same verb used of the disciples and the women at the tomb: ἐφοβοῦντο γὰρ αὐτόν.

The dispute that follows is initiated by Jesus' opponents. Jesus, however, shows himself superior to them in his defense. One of these disputes deals explicitly with the resurrection of the dead.

The dispute with the Sadducees about the resurrection of the dead (Mark 12:18-27) lets readers of the gospel of Mark learn to think about resurrection. The "Sadducees, who say there is no resurrection" (12:18) want to lead Jesus with a question *ad absurdum*: "In the resurrection whose wife will she be?" (12:23a). Jesus, however, advocates for the reality of the resurrection: "Is not this the reason you are wrong, that you know neither the scriptures nor the power of God? For when they rise from the dead, they neither marry nor are given in marriage, but are like angels in heaven. And as for the dead being raised, have you not read in the book of Moses, in the story about the bush, how God said to him, 'I am the God of Abraham, the God of Isaac, and the God of Jacob'? He is God not of the dead, but of the living; you are quite wrong" (12:24b-27).

This pericope is illuminating in many ways. It shows that faith in the God of Israel was not necessarily bound up with the expectation of the resurrection of the dead.[28] Jesus does not accuse the Sadducees of unbelief but rather of a lack of knowledge of Scripture and God. Moreover, it becomes clear that what is meant by the resurrection of the dead was disputed. The Sadducees regard resurrection as the reproduction of relationships as they existed before death. Since this assumption leads to absurd consequences, however, they reject it. Jesus, on the other hand, understands the resurrection of the dead not as a reproduction of prior conditions but rather as a transformation into an angelic state, whose reality for him and his Jewish opponents is indubitable. That the question of the reality of the resurrection turns for Jesus on one's understanding of Scripture and God receives special emphasis. Because the Sadducees know neither "the scriptures" nor "the power of God," they fall into error. And finally, in this pericope the reality of the resurrection is no question of emotional opinion, but rather a question of theological thinking. Jesus argues against the Sadducees not with verbs of faith or opinion but rather with verbs of knowledge. Whoever is familiar with the Scriptures and knows the power of God knows also the reality of the resurrection.

From the point of view of theological history, the Sadducees represent the older position. "The conception of the resurrection from death as the beginning of a new, everlasting life is foreign to the greatest part of Old Testament traditions."[29] It is exclusively Daniel 12 that stands as uncontroversial proof of a hope in the resurrection. Not much changes regarding this evidence when one also adds the (late) texts of Isaiah 25:8, Isaiah 26:19, Psalm 22:28-32, and perhaps still a few others such as Psalm 49. All other texts adduced from the Old Testament are at least polyvalent. And this is due not least to the fact that in the sacred Scriptures of Israel the concept of death means much more than a medical judgment. The danger of death that breaks in through illness or overpowering enemies or even a life perceived as wholly full of suffering can be designated as death, and the change of this awful condition can be understood as deliverance from this death (cf. Ps 88).[30] Further afield important passages such as Isaiah 24–27 and Ezekiel 37 deal with a collective resurrection in the sense that the oppressed, defeated, deported people of Israel will experience new life in the progress of history.

The Sadducees—who would be the biblicists of our present day—would have been able to counter Jesus very well with an isolated citation: "The dead do not live; shades do not rise" (Isa 26:14). Jesus then would have been able to cite Isaiah as well: "Your dead shall live, their corpses shall rise. O dwellers in the dust, awake and sing for joy! For your dew is a radiant dew, and the earth will give birth to those long dead" (Isa 26:19). But in the actual argumentation strategy in Mark 12 any battle of isolated citations lies far in the distance.[31] The argumentation in the pericope much more involves conclusions on both sides and makes the conclusion of Jesus appear as the appropriate conclusion, which at the same time lays bare the Sadducees' erroneous thinking.

Jesus cites the Scriptures as the point of departure for the correct conclusion: "I am the God of Abraham, the God of Isaac, and the God of Jacob" (cf. 12:26c; Exod 3:6, 15b). Jesus chooses the self-revelation of God to Moses as the basis for his position, a basis that in the framework of Jewish encyclopedic knowledge could not be stronger. Jesus attaches a second phrase to the prior noncontroversial one: "He is God not of the dead, but of the living." The phrase directed to the Sadducees, "You are quite wrong," requires readers at the same time to draw the conclusion: God enables the dead to rise. Readers are prepared for this conclusion by the declaration that God can raise the dead with his very own power, the power of God (cf. Mark 12:24). Hope in the resurrection is made conceivable through the reference to the resurrection existence as angelic. The ability to raise the dead is ascribed to God alone, and indeed not to just any god but to the God of Israel.

The resurrection of the dead takes place as a raising through the power of God. The dead possess no inherent property with which they could contribute something to their resurrection. They are wholly dead and therefore incapable of any action whatsoever. According to the gospel of Mark, resurrection is no anthropological component, but rather exclusively a theological component. It belongs to language about God and indeed language about the God of Abraham, Isaac, and Jacob, as Jesus proclaims him in the gospel.

It is characteristic that Jesus does not draw upon the revivifications of the dead wrought by Elijah (1 Kgs 17:17-24) and Elisha (2 Kgs 4:31-37; 13:21) in his argumentation, which did indeed show that God's power is not limited by death. Even the citation of 1 Samuel 2:6 would not have been extensive enough were it not for Jesus' argumentation: "The LORD kills and brings to life; he brings down to Sheol and raises up." With his answer, Jesus makes clear that the resurrection of the dead does not involve the continuation of a life with which one is already familiar, but rather a new and ultimate way of being that has left death behind after it has been endured.

The eschatological aspect of resurrection is strengthened through the apocalyptic discourse of Jesus in Mark 13. Jesus speaks to his disciples Peter, James, John, and Andrew about the coming time of his absence, a time of horrors ordered before the ultimate end of the present age. Before the end can take place, "the good news must first be proclaimed to all nations" (13:10). Since the gospel of Mark is itself the medium of this proclamation, reading the gospel of Mark becomes an apocalyptic act that like the passion and resurrection of the Crucified One and the suffering of the end times (cf. 13:7c) is a necessary requirement of his coming. Umberto Eco's *Lector in fabula* succinctly makes the point about the pragmatics of the gospel of Mark. Through the intertwining of the times in the act of reading, readers are situated in the middle of the story being narrated. A distanced reading is impossible for a purposeful reception of the gospel of Mark. Rather, reading Mark is much more a question of readers themselves becoming proclaimers of the gospel. Reading occurs in the midst of the apocalyptic tribulations of the end times.

Verses 24-27 in chapter 13 formulate the shape of the end of the end times and indicate where the absent Son of Man remains during the end times: "Then they will see 'the Son of Man coming in clouds' with great power and glory" (13:26).

To the desire of the disciples to learn the precise time of the beginning of the end Jesus responds with the call to watchfulness and the certainty that the end times stands immediately before the door: "Truly I tell you, this generation will not pass away until all these things have taken place. Heaven and earth will pass away, but my words will not pass away" (Mark 13:30-31). No one—not the angels, nor even the Son of God—knows the timing of the end (cf. 13:32), but all readers of the gospel of Mark are familiar with the words of Jesus, and with this knowledge they confirm the permanency of his words. They are even addressed in the end time discourse as readers with an imperative: "Let the reader understand!" (13:14b).

As with the parables discourse in Mark 4, so also the apocalyptic discourse in Mark 13 has an interpretive function for the entire gospel. Reading the gospel of Mark with understanding is part of the cosmological act to which the death and resurrection of the Crucified One belong. The end of this act will come with the coming of the Son of Man. Then eternal life in the kingdom of God will be given to those who follow him, those who have carried out the message of the gospel of Mark in their own lives by taking up their cross (cf. 8:34).

The tragic escalation of the dysphoric narrative strand in chapters 14 and 15 comprises Judas' betrayal, Peter's denial, the protagonist's torture, mocking, and murder, as well as his cry of dereliction at his death on the cross. This strand is, however, interrupted by two passages that point to the time of the reading of the gospel.

Directly connected to the apocalyptic discourse is the repetition of the intention of Jesus' opponents to kill him. The story of the anointing with costly oil at Bethany anticipates what the women at the tomb mean to do. Jesus defends the actions of the woman who anoints him and concludes the story with these words: "Truly I tell you, wherever the good news is proclaimed in the whole world, what she has done will be told in remembrance of her" (Mark 14:9). The reading of the gospel of Mark itself confirms this prediction.

Immediately thereupon Judas decides to betray Jesus (cf. Mark 14:10-11). Then follows the story of the Last Supper (14:12-25). In this story, the identification of the bread with the body of Jesus and the identification of the wine with his blood supports a sign relation that enables corporeal communion with Jesus well beyond the presence of his earthly body. The materiality of bread and wine represents his body even when he is absent.[32]

The poignant scene in the Garden of Gethsemane (cf. Mark 14:32-42) rejects any martyr ideology that longs for death. Jesus does not want to die. He begs God to find another way, and at the same time agrees to follow the way of the cross if it is God's will (14:35-36).

Thus also the scene of condemnation receives its power. The death sentence given to Jesus for blasphemy merely takes up what his opponents already planned in Mark 3:6. In the course of the narrative, they make no progress in perception. Jesus speaks out openly about his being the messiah, and identifies himself with the coming Son of Man: "I am; and 'you will see the Son of Man seated at the right hand of the Power,' and 'coming with the clouds of heaven'" (14:62). Jesus here takes up a passage from his apocalyptic discourse in Mark 13 (cf. 13:26), and readers can make for themselves a concrete picture of where Jesus abides after his death.

The darkness that accompanies his crucifixion (cf. Mark 15:33) also produces intratextual references to the apocalyptic discourse and underscores the apocalyptic horizon of the event.

At the Tomb Again

With this knowledge of the larger narrative of the gospel of Mark, readers can accompany the women to the tomb again. This time, however, they are well prepared not to be struck dumb when faced with the empty tomb. Now readers can respond to the interpretation and directive of the heavenly messenger: "I believe; help my unbelief!" One way to help further one's understanding of Mark along these lines is to read and reread this gospel. Every reading will discover something new and further the knowledge that we are not to seek a rotting corpse as the logic of death would have us believe. But where is the body of the resurrected Crucified One?

The words of the heavenly messenger give a clear answer for the world that is narrated in Mark: He is no longer in the tomb. The resurrected Crucified One goes ahead to Galilee. The risen Lord goes back to where his work began. The protagonist of the story had announced this very thing to his disciples even before the crucifixion: "But after I am raised up, I will go before you into Galilee" (Mark 14:28).

But how can readers follow the resurrected Jesus? The syntagmatics of the textual signs open up the possibility of returning to the beginning of the gospel of Mark and following the protagonist again on his way from Galilee to Jerusalem with knowledge provided by prior reading(s). The resurrected crucified one is now found in the materiality of the *Sprachkörper*—the written text—that represents him and causes him to be seen and heard by means of the presence of its written signs. The gospel of Mark represents the absent body of the Crucified One who was raised.

In repeated readings, readers will discover that the body of the resurrected Crucified One was absent also for the first readers of the gospel: "The days will come when the bridegroom is taken away from them" (2:20). The time of the composition of and reading of Mark is this time of absence.

Whoever seeks the resurrected Crucified One outside of the written signs of the gospel of Mark receives from those same signs a twofold localization. According to Mark 14:62, he is seated "at the right hand of the Power," and we at the end of the world will see him sitting there "coming with the clouds of heaven" (cf. 13:26).

The absent body of the resurrected Crucified One is, however, not only represented through the materiality of the written signs composing the gospel of Mark. Rather, the narrative of the gospel produces a second sign complex, one that the community opens up outside the reading of the gospel of Mark in the space between the resurrected Crucified One and his disciples. The absent body is represented in the event of the Lord's Supper and indeed in, with, and under the materiality of bread and wine. Read from the perspective of the resurrection message, the words of institution in Mark 14:22ff. make the resurrected Crucified One heard and seen and tasted in bread and wine.

Readers who read with the kind of understanding that the gospel of Mark seeks to produce are now endowed with the extensive theological formation needed to apprehend the resurrection message:

1. Jesus of Nazareth, the Crucified One, *was raised*. He was not pulled out of the grave like the Gerasene demoniac, who then went on to wear orderly clothing and to return to his earthly life with his senses intact. Jesus was also not merely revivified, as was the daughter of Jairus, who shows by eating that she also stands in the domain of earthly life and exists under the conditions of this life. Jesus, on the contrary, was raised to heavenly life.

2. Jesus of Nazareth, the Crucified One, was raised *by God*, and indeed by the God whom he proclaimed, the God of Abraham, Isaac, and Jacob.

3. Jesus of Nazareth, the Crucified One, was raised by God *through the power of God, to which the sacred Scriptures of Israel bear witness*. It is the same power that the Spirit (πνεῦμα) imparted to him and through which he did his wonders, by which he pulled the Gerasene out of the tombs, and which revivified the daughter of Jairus. These things are possible only in the power of God to which the Scriptures bear witness.

4. Jesus of Nazareth, the *Crucified One*, was raised. The identity of Jesus of Nazareth with that of the one who was raised is marked by the cross. The cross is no transitional phase to be left behind, but rather an identity marker of the Resurrected One.

5. God's act of raising Jesus Christ is no isolated event, but rather something bound up with the cosmological turning of the ages that is determined by God.

6. The resurrected Crucified One, Jesus of Nazareth, is seated at the right hand of God until the end of the present age. At the end of time he will come from there to gather his followers to him.

7. The resurrected crucified one is encountered in the present time in reading (hearing) the gospel of Mark with understanding and in the celebration of the Lord's Supper in, with, and under bread and wine.

8. The appropriate reaction to the resurrection message is the cry, "I believe; help my unbelief!"

9. This honorable and uncertain faith that knows that it cannot constitute itself will contribute to multiplying the gospel, be it thirty-, sixty-, or a hundredfold. Those who understand the resurrection message in the sense of the gospel of Mark will become messengers themselves and thus follow Jesus.

10. Discipleship means taking up one's own cross in the certainty of receiving heavenly life through the power of God.

Those who see and perceive, who hear and understand in this way, in the sense of the gospel of Mark, are drawn into the presence of the resurrected Crucified One by the Spirit of the gospel of Mark's resurrection message. Mark's gospel represents the absent Jesus of Nazareth as the resurrected Crucified One, the Christ, the Son of God. It points to his future coming and shows the place where readers can encounter him bodily in their present reality. In any event, according to the gospel of Mark he is not to be found in the tomb.

The Gospel of Matthew

With the genealogy at the beginning of the book, the gospel of Matthew lays out the universe of discourse in whose framework its assumptions about reality, plausibility structures, and inherent values and judgments develop their meaning. The names listed in the genealogy remind the reader by metonymy of the stories and narrative complexes of the history of Israel, most of which may be found in the sacred Scriptures of Israel. If one takes together all the texts that maintain intertextual connections in this way to the gospel of Matthew, then one easily gets the impression that the Matthean genealogy functions as "the Old Testament's Table of Contents."[33] But this designation is erroneous to the extent that it neglects the moment of selection that instructs the reader which stories to have in mind during the act of reading Matthew's gospel. Moreover, it permits only canonical texts to come into view, a canon of the Christian "Old Testament" that did not exist when Matthew wrote his book. Nevertheless, the genealogy at the beginning of the gospel of Matthew serves as a theological and hermeneutical selection from the sacred Scriptures of Israel that call to mind the faithfulness of God, the sinfulness of the chosen people, and the calling of the gentiles into the covenant with God.[34]

But this genealogy also highlights a problem with this history. It is shaped not only by Abraham's confidence, but also by individual injustices such as adultery and murder. The prime example of this is found in the allusive reference to King David (cf. Matt 1:6) and the collective unfaithfulness of Israel, which led to the exile.

Nevertheless, the history of the genealogy is an ordered history, arranged in three groups of fourteen names, and thus the purposeful acts of God are made known.[35] The break in the stereotypical formula by the cumbersome introduction of Jesus at the end of the genealogy inscribes the name "Jesus" into this history. At the same time, however, it demonstrates that something else has begun that does not simply continue the natural, usual course of things. The appended story of his conception makes known the meaning of his coming. The angel says to Joseph, "She will bear a son, and you are to name him Jesus, for he will save his people from their sins" (1:21).

Through the intertextual connection with the prophecy of Isaiah, the following verse makes clear that this Jesus is therefore in a position to save his people, because he is the Emmanuel announced by God through Isaiah. The significance of this name is programmatic for the narrative of Matthew. This is already evident in the translation the gospel gives: "which means, 'God is with us'" (Matt 1:24c). Now the Scriptures are being fulfilled. The gospel of Matthew tells the story of Jesus Christ, the Son of David, the Son of Abraham (cf. 1:1), as the fulfillment of the promise of the royal rule of God, which begins with the miraculous birth of Emmanuel. In his preaching, Jesus proclaims the righteousness and mercy that characterize this kingdom.

Jesus will free Israel from the sins that the genealogy calls to mind. He can do this because he is "God with us." Following him through the narrative reveals how he fulfills his commission. But it is already clear at the beginning of the gospel that it is a question of a way of discipleship that involves the problem of a failed life. It concerns the alternative of walking a way of life that corresponds to the values of the rule of God as depicted in the sacred Scriptures of Israel, and as that rule is interpreted as the will of God in Jesus' speeches in the gospel of Matthew, or on the other hand to stray from this path and to come finally into perdition.

From the very beginning Jesus' way is threatened. The political authority in the form of the Roman client king Herod the Great endeavors to take the life of the child Jesus. The indiscriminate cruelty of this particular political authority is powerfully portrayed in a paradigmatic manner that influences the entire reading of the gospel in the narrative of the slaughter of the innocents in Bethlehem (cf. 2:16ff.). The royal rule of Herod stands in direct opposition to the royal rule of God, whose representative is Jesus, Emmanuel. The gospel of Matthew builds an arc of narrative tension through the irreconcilable, conflict-rich opposition of human and divine rule. Moreover, the gospel calls readers to decide between them: "But Jesus called them to him and said, 'You know that the rulers of the Gentiles lord it over them, and their great ones are tyrants over them. It will not be so among you; but whoever wishes to be great among you must be your servant'" (Matt 20:25-26).

In order to display the royal rule of God in a concrete way, Matthew places the Sermon on the Mount at the very beginning of Jesus' ministry (Matt 5–7). This sermon points in a programmatic way to the values of the kingdom of God. Jesus begins the sermon with the merciful affirmations of the Beatitudes (5:1-12) and thus sketches at the outset a picture of the kingdom of God. In God's kingdom neither power, strength, possessions, nor the assertion of one's rights count for anything. Rather, meekness, peacefulness, childlike trust in God, and forgiveness are what matter. The Antitheses (5:21-28) flesh out the outline of the merciful affirmations of the Beatitudes, and these proceed from the thankful acceptance of the mercy of God: They depict an ethic oriented to justice toward the other, precisely because the other is a creature of God. With this orientation to justice toward the other, the meaning of the law is fulfilled (cf. 5:17-20), namely making the mercy of God the measure of the living of one's own life.

Jesus' resolute Way, a way lived in accord with the royal rule of God, does not, however, lead him into a care-free and sheltered life. Instead, it leads him to the cross. The royal rule of the authorities seems to triumph at first. The representative of the royal rule of God is violently killed as a criminal by means of the tool of execution reserved for those who do not possess Roman citizenship. He dies at the initiative of the high council of Jerusalem on the cross of the *imperium Romanum.*

It is principally the narrative of the resurrection of Jesus that makes the book of Matthew become a gospel. The resurrection of the crucified one confirms that the values Jesus proclaimed are in fact the values of the royal rule of God. At the same time they point to the immeasurable power of the royal rule of God, a power that exceeds all other claims to rule. Through this act of divine power, the resurrected crucified one changes from "God with us" to "I am with you": "And remember, I am with you always, to the end of the age" (Matt 28:20b). With these words of the resurrected Crucified One, the book of Matthew closes its narrative. On the pragmatic level the gospel promises to all readers who agree with its message and who order their lives after it the enduring presence of the resurrected crucified one. Thus the final words of this sentence sharpen the eschatological conviction that the present world will finally arrive at its God-ordained goal. Both convictions shape the narrative and the pragmatic message of the gospel as a whole.

Death or Life?

The gospel of Matthew calls for a decision: "Enter through the narrow gate; for the gate is wide and the road is easy that leads to destruction, and there are many who take it. For the gate is narrow and the road is hard that leads to life, and there are few who find it" (Matt 7:13-14). Perdition or life: that is the choice the gospel sets forth. Its claim is that only the way conforming with the values of the royal rule of God represented by Jesus leads to eternal life. The way of the royal rule of Herod or of the *imperium Romanum*,[36] or the way of the high council, or the way oriented to mammon, to one's own rights, to one's own power and strength, leads to perdition.

The plausibility of this conviction stems from the eschatological expectation of the judgment of God. In the gospel of Matthew's presentation, the royal rule of God encompasses both heaven and hell.[37] Hell is not the kingdom of the devil, but the annihilating side of the power of God. The devil and his angels will be annihilated with its unquenchable fire just as much as those who are condemned at the eschatological judgment on the basis of their selfish way of living (cf. 25:41-46).

No one will escape this judgment, not even the dead. It is precisely the resurrection of the dead that enables the eschatological judgment to be a universal judgment of the entire world, at which those resurrected also serve as accusers and judges. Jesus responds to the scribes' and Pharisees' demands for signs with the following words:

> An evil and adulterous generation asks for a sign, but no sign will be given to it except the sign of the prophet Jonah. For just as Jonah was three days and three nights in the belly of the sea monster, so for three days and three nights the Son of Man will be in the heart of the earth. The people of Nineveh will rise up at the judgment with this generation and condemn it, because they repented at the proclamation of Jonah, and see, something greater than Jonah is here! The queen of the South will rise up at the judgment with this generation and condemn it, because she came from the ends of the earth to listen to the wisdom of Solomon, and see, something greater than Solomon is here! (Matt 12:39b-42)

The use of the sign of Jonah as an allegory for the burial and resurrection of Jesus Christ as well as the resurrection terminology of "to rise up"—that is, "to be raised"—with the pronouncement of judgment reveals the function of the gospel of Matthew's resurrection theology. The eschatological resurrection of the dead is not an end in itself, but rather something necessary for eschatological judgment, which will finally permit justice to be achieved. The eschatological judgment knows no bounds, not even those between the dead and the living. The royal rule of God works in all-encompassing ways and brings about not only eternal life but also eternal damnation.

That the verbs "to rise up" ἀναστήσονται and "to be raised" ἐγερθήσεται in verses 41 and 42, respectively, standing as they do in parallel construction, have no perceptible difference in meaning demonstrates in an exemplary fashion that they are employed as synonyms in the gospel of Matthew. It is clear that only God has the power to raise the dead. But according to Matthew God deploys this immeasurable power also to punish. The "royal rule of heaven" proclaimed by Jesus encompasses God's power in all its fullness.

It is precisely at this judgment that death and life are ultimately decided. Neither the earthly nor the demonic powers are in the position to effect eternal death or eternal life. The words of commissioning that Jesus utters in Matthew 10:28 set this forth clearly: "Do not fear those who kill the body but cannot kill the soul; rather fear him who can destroy both soul and body in hell." But this it not something the devil intends. It is something God intends. Only he has power over the whole person. And the full effect of this power will finally come be shown at the eschatological judgment.

John the Baptist's call to repentance warns of this (Matt 3:2-10) just as much as Jesus of Nazareth's sermons of judgment do. John warns the Pharisees and scribes against calling themselves children of Abraham without real and true repentance. He warns them not only of "the wrath to come" (3:7) and the "burn[ing] with unquenchable fire" (3:12d). But God's immeasurable creative power is emphasized much more than the destructive side of his power. God is the one whose creative power can create life out of death: "God is able from these stones to raise up children to Abraham (ἐγεῖραι)" (3:9c).

In the presentation of the gospel of Matthew, Jesus' proclamation receives its plot-oriented culmination from the perspective of the royal rule of God with its eschatological judgment. One's fate at the eschatological judgment, whether one receives heaven or hell, is not merely a matter of confessing particular words. Rather, it is a matter of doing the will of God just as Jesus did in his words and deeds (cf. Matt 25:31-46). According to the gospel of Matthew, one does not simply believe in the dogmatic topos of "the resurrection of the dead." One must embrace the righteous and merciful God as Jesus proclaimed him. This God will raise the dead so that he can execute universal judgment at the end of the world.

Jesus' answer to the Baptist's question, communicated by John's disciples, regarding whether Jesus was the messiah is as follows: "Go and tell John what you hear and see: the blind receive their sight, the lame walk, the lepers are cleansed, the deaf hear, the dead are raised, and the poor have good news brought to them. And blessed is anyone who takes no offense at me" (Matt 11:4b-6). Jesus' answer brings the prophecy of Isaiah into intertextual play and thus receives its fulfillment through his works. The final sentence of Jesus' answer underscores Jesus' eschatological saving significance. In its presentation of Jesus' deeds and words, the gospel of Matthew as a whole and especially here emphasizes the eschatological dimension of the Jesus-Christ-Story. Now the Scriptures are being fulfilled. Now the royal rule of heaven has broken in with the works of Emmanuel, born of the Virgin, which will end in final judgment. Now the final hour in which one can make a decision for the royal rule of God has broken in, and like the laborers in the vineyard who begin their work at the last opportunity but nevertheless receive a full wage for it (cf. 20:1-16), God will repay with eternal life all who repent in this final hour and follow Emmanuel.

The plausibility of Jesus' answer depends upon the context of the gospel of Matthew and its intertextual connections to Isaiah: "On that day the deaf shall hear the words of a scroll, and out of their gloom and darkness the eyes of the blind shall see. The meek shall obtain fresh joy in the LORD, and the neediest people shall exult in the Holy One of Israel" (Isa 29:18-19). "Then the eyes of the blind shall be opened, and the ears of the deaf unstopped; then the lame shall leap like a deer, and the tongue of the speechless sing for joy" (35:5-6a). And in Isaiah 26:19, we read, "Your dead shall live, their corpses shall rise. O dwellers in the dust, awake and sing for joy! For your dew is a radiant dew, and the earth will give birth to those long dead."

In light of this background, one can read Jesus' miraculous healings altogether as eschatological sign acts, for which Jesus also empowers his disciples. These acts include instances of raisings from the dead. For example, the revivification of Jairus' daughter is narrated in Matthew 9:18-19, 23-26. This story is syntagmatically necessary before the Baptist's question. Then in 10:7-8 Jesus commissions the disciples: "As you go, proclaim the good news, 'The kingdom of heaven has come near.' Cure the sick, raise the dead, cleanse the lepers, cast out demons."

The raising of Jairus' daughter in Matthew 9:18-29, 23-26 narrates the revivification of a recently deceased girl. Through Jesus' answer to the

Baptist's question and through his commission to his disciples, this story becomes an example of an indeterminate multiplicity of such raisings. These dead do not receive a new body. Instead they return to their old life with their reanimated but ultimately mortal body of flesh and blood.

The eschatological raising of the dead must, however, be categorically distinguished from stories such as this. The argument that Jesus has with the Sadducees in Matthew 22:23-33 concerns this eschatological event. Here it is precisely the otherness of life after the eschatological resurrection that is used by Jesus as an argument against the denial of the resurrection as the Sadducees understand it. The Sadducees err because they regard the eschatological resurrection as a mere revivification of the dead who then return to their old life. Jesus, however, points to the categorical difference of life after the eschatological resurrection when he draws an analogy to the nature of the angels: "For in the resurrection they neither marry nor are given in marriage, but are like angels in heaven" (22:30). The dead who are raised up at the end of the world are created anew by God's creative power as heavenly creatures.[38]

The opening of the tombs at Jesus' death on the cross must be conceptualized as an intertextually motivated eschatological sign act: "The tombs also were opened, and many bodies of the saints who had fallen asleep were raised. After his resurrection they came out of the tombs and entered the holy city and appeared to many" (Matt 27:52-53). This episode narrates what Isaiah had announced: "Your dead shall live . . . and the earth will give birth to those long dead."

Intrigues, Lies, and Betrayal; or, The Judicial Murder of the Righteous One

Jesus not only knows the will of God, he also directs all his works to him. He knows that his way will lead him to the cross. Several times he predicts his suffering, but also his resurrection (cf. Matt 16:21; 17:9; 17:22; 20:17-18; 20:28; 26:32). The scene in Gethsemane makes it impressively clear, however, that Jesus does not want to die. The gospel of Matthew depicts him neither as a hero who has tired of life nor as a mythic figure who is insensitive to suffering. He is also, however, not a powerless victim. The destruction of the fig tree (21:19) makes this fact clear, as do his words at his arrest: "Do you think that I cannot appeal to my Father, and he will at once send me more than twelve legions of angels?" (26:53).

The astounding impression that Jesus' action produces consists much more in the fact that he not only prays the "Our Father," he also lives it:

"Your will be done" (Matt 6:10b) applies even to him, even in view of his impending death on the cross (cf. 26:36-42).

But it is not the will of God that threatens Jesus. Rather, the threat comes from the deceitful exploitation of human power. It is not the royal rule of God that nails the innocent one to the cross. It is the knowing tolerance of injustice that does this. No divine plan requires a bloody victim. Human intrigue, however, devises lies in order to rationalize its desire to kill.

Judas, one of his disciples, betrays him with a deceitful kiss (cf. Matt 26:38ff.). Instead of the truth, the high council seeks false eyewitness testimony in order to pin a crime on Jesus that will form the basis for his intended execution (cf. 26:59). When this plan fails, however, the high priest seizes the opportunity and misuses the authority of his honorable office to interpret Jesus' utterance as blasphemy and demands the sentence of death (26:65-66). Jesus is spit upon, beaten, and mocked (cf. 26:67-68). Even Peter makes himself guilty of lying. He slanders Jesus three times (27:3-10).

Pilate, warned through his wife's dream, tries at first to get the Jews to agree to set Jesus free, for through his wife's dream he knows Jesus is innocent. Even more, he knows that Jesus is a righteous man (Matt 27:11-23ff.). But he consciously permits injustice to happen (27:24ff.). Then Jesus is tortured and mocked by the Roman soldiers and nailed to the cross (cf. 27:27-36). An inscription affixed over his head gives the grounds for his execution: "This is Jesus, the King of the Jews" (27:37b).

Jesus, nailed to the cross, is mocked by the masses of his own people. Even the robbers crucified with him join in the mockery.[39] Jesus dies an agonizing death. With his last words, a psalm verse, he directs himself to God: "My God, my God, why have you forsaken me?" (Matt 27:46b/Ps 22:2).

If the story were to end here, it would be a tragic story of a good man, or, read more cynically, a story confirming the power of human rule and the powerlessness of justice. The structures of power in the realm of fact would once again have the last word.

The Resurrection of the Crucified One: Deception or Act of God?

The events that happened during Jesus' crucifixion—the darkness, the tearing of the temple curtain, the earthquake, the opening of tombs, and the resurrection of many saints—demonstrate that the depiction of the crucifixion of Jesus does not follow the empirical laws of the realm of the factual. Rather, Matthew thematizes precisely the breaking of the power of the realm of the factual through the eschatological act of God, an act that affects the entire cosmos. The cosmological-eschatological signs are understood by the Roman soldiers who carry out the crucifixion as signs that the crucified one was the Son of God, but the reaction of others present is not recounted. If it were a question of an eyewitness report oriented to empirical facts, however, the question would arise: Why then did others present not come to the insight of the Roman soldiers on account of the signs of darkness, earthquakes, and open graves? And why does not the whole of Jerusalem repent, like Nineveh of old, in sackcloth and ashes because of the injustice that has been perpetrated? Even the reaction of the women followers of Jesus who were there is not reported (cf. Matt 27:55). The intention of the narrative runs instead in another direction, with the fundamental theme of how the resurrection of the Crucified One is confirmed, and thus, too, the teaching of Jesus about the royal rule of God is confirmed.

After the death of Jesus he is, with Pilate's permission, buried by one of his rich followers, Joseph of Arimathea. Joseph laid him in his own stone tomb and "then rolled a great stone to the door of the tomb and went away" (Matt 27:60b). Both Marys, whose presence was already noted at the crucifixion scene, are also mentioned here.

The following section (Matt 27:62-65)—a master achievement of ironic staging—has the high priests (to speak of them in the plural is inappropriate in historical perspective) and the Pharisees ask Pilate for a guard to watch the tomb. These perverters of justice fear the deceit of the disciples: "Sir (κύριε), we remember what that impostor said while he was still alive, 'After three days I will rise again.' Therefore command the tomb to be made secure until the third day; otherwise his disciples may go and steal him away, and tell the people, 'He has been raised from the dead,' and the last deception would be worse than the first" (27:63-64). They do not name Emmanuel as κύριος, but instead they honor Pontius Pilate, the Roman governor, by addressing him with this title. And they themselves, the ones who sought false statements from false witnesses in order to cause Jesus' execution, now fear deceit on part of their opposition. Their desire is granted and a guard seals the tomb of Jesus (27:65-66).

On the third day, however, both Marys come to the tomb, and again an earthquake occurs:

> And suddenly there was a great earthquake; for an angel of the Lord, descending from heaven, came and rolled back the stone and sat on it. His appearance was like lightning, and his clothing white as snow. For fear of him the guards shook and became like dead men. But the angel said to the women, "Do not be afraid; I know

that you are looking for Jesus who was crucified. He is not here; for he has been raised, as he said. Come, see the place where he lay. Then go quickly and tell his disciples, 'He has been raised from the dead, and indeed he is going ahead of you to Galilee; there you will see him.' This is my message for you." So they left the tomb quickly with fear and great joy, and ran to tell his disciples. (Matt 28:2-8)

When the women come to the tomb, the stone is not yet rolled away. The tomb is sealed and the Romans are guarding it. Both these female followers of Jesus and the Roman guard witness an angelic appearance. It is precisely this angel who rolls away the stone before the very eyes of those present, sits upon it, and then announces to them that the crucified Jesus has been raised from the dead. The body of the crucified and Resurrected One has thus left the tomb before the stone was rolled away. His raised body does not any longer follow the possibilities afforded by empirical laws. The tomb is opened by the angel only in order to make visible to the women that the Resurrected One is no longer there.

The figure of the angel is impressively depicted. He is like lightning. Thus his appearance is like light, and the brilliant white of his clothing coheres with this. In the dispute about the resurrection of the dead (Matt 22:23-33) Jesus had declared against the Sadducees that those raised from the dead will be like angels (cf. 22:30). According to the universe of discourse of the gospel of Matthew, that state holds also for the resurrected crucified one. He is no revivified dead man who returns to his old life only to die again. Rather his resurrection transforms him and gives his resurrected body the capacity for eternal life and enduring presence. This body does not need the gravestone to be rolled away in order to free him from the grave. This body does not live within the boundaries of empirical facticity.

If the angel frightened the Roman guards to death, then so too are the women whom the angel addresses afraid, but joy and thus trust in the truth of the angel's message predominate. On their way to meet Jesus' disciples, they encounter the Resurrected One himself and are persuaded that he is neither ghost nor illusion. The resurrected Crucified One is visible, speaks, and is tangible (cf. Matt 28:9-10). He repeats what the angel has already said. He speaks to them, "'Greetings!' And they came to him, took hold of his feet, and worshiped him" (28:9b).

A change of scene: A few guards have also left the tomb and have gone to the high priests to report the event. The high priests convene the council and give the soldiers money for their silence and invent a lie. They also want to placate their Roman superiors (Matt 28:11ff.). The high council shows itself deceitful once more. They know the truth, but invent a lie: "You must say, 'His disciples came by night and stole him away while we were asleep'" (28:13). The soldiers agree, taking the money, and then the narrator comments, "And this story is still told among the Jews to this day" (28:15b).

This narrative not only protects the disciples from the accusation of deception for the sake of apologetics. Much more meaningfully, it shows that even the angelophany and the empty tomb do not lead to faith in the resurrected Crucified One on the basis of the power of facticity. The Roman guard decides for mammon instead of the truth, and the high council decides, against its better knowledge, to invent an intentional lie.

The resurrection message is clearly displayed as an experience of reality that needs to be interpreted when some of the disciples see the risen Jesus and still doubt. As Jesus had announced beforehand (cf. Matt 26:32), as the angel at the tomb said, and then as the Resurrected One himself declared, Jesus went ahead of his disciples "to Galilee, to the mountain" (28:16b). By naming the place in this way, the text points intratextually to the Sermon on the Mount and confers upon it the character of revelation. "When they saw him, they worshiped him; but some[40] doubted" (28:17). Even seeing the resurrected Crucified One on the mountain of revelation does not automatically lead to the kind of acceptance that factual evidence induces by the overwhelming binary logic of the factual—an acceptance that requires no decision. The closing episode of the gospel of Matthew shows that faith in the Resurrected One does not follow from the power of facts. Such a state of affairs would remove the decision from the recipient. "This is no event in the sense of an actuality that knows no doubt. Rather, this is an event of the action of God, which permits every doubt."[41]

The plausibility of the resurrection is not accessible through the power of the factual. Rather, the resurrection becomes plausible only through trust in the immeasurable might of the royal rule of God and the concomitant conviction that this has been brought to effective expression in the words and deeds of Jesus. The resurrection of the crucified Jesus and thus his presence even to the end of the age are credible only for the one who turns, as in the "Our Father," in complete trust to the merciful and righteous God, just as Jesus urged.

The Power of the Resurrected Crucified One

Just as Jesus did not exclude Judas from table fellowship, and just as Peter remains a disciple of Jesus in spite of his betrayal, Jesus also refuses to banish the doubting disciples. He directs his word to all when he commissions them: "All authority in heaven and on earth has been given to me. Go therefore and make disciples of all nations, baptizing them in the name of the Father and of the Son and of the Holy Spirit, and teaching them to obey everything that I have commanded you. And remember, I am with you always, to the end of the age" (Matt 28:18-20).

Before the commissioning of the disciples, the resurrected Crucified One names the immeasurable ability of the one giving the commission and thus the ground of the ability to obey him. The gospel of Matthew poses the question of authority and answers it unambiguously. It is neither the deceitful values of the high council, nor Herod's arrogant claims to rule, nor the *imperium Romanum*, nor mammon, nor Satan that is to be obeyed, but Jesus, the Emmanuel, who through his resurrection from the dead was endowed with the fullness of the authority of God. This fullness transforms the one who is "God with us" into the one who says "I am with you." The experience of the presence of the Resurrected One becomes an experience of singular authority. The cosmic message of the resurrection rejects the validity of all other claims to universal authority. The message of the resurrection in the gospel of Matthew concerns the cosmological determination of reality as a whole, "on earth as it is in heaven."

Every believer becomes a sign of this authority when he or she orders his or her life around the message of Jesus. The message of the resurrected Crucified One is to be obeyed, and, in its directives for action, this message is identical with the teachings of Jesus of Nazareth before his crucifixion. What is required of the disciple is not simply to hold some sayings as true, nor to quote certain words of Jesus, nor to memorize formulas of faith. Rather, the message demands that one deal mercifully with one's neighbor. The one who merely believes that the tomb is empty is not the one who bears witness to the truth of the Resurrected One. Rather, the one who helps the needy and who engages in the quest for justice and righteousness, which the Sermon on the Mount formulates in decisive ways in order to orient Christian living, is the true disciple.

This way of discipleship leads to just as little a pain-free and happy-go-lucky existence as the way of Jesus did. Orientation to the will of God led Jesus to the cross. He could have fled. He could have annihilated his opponents with angelic violence. He did not do it. He died on the cross. He lost his life—and: he received it anew as a gift. Still more: he received eternal life and a body not able to be confined by any tombstone. The resurrected Crucified One is the proof of the fullness of the authority of God, who not only made all things but once again makes all things new.

Those, however, who follow him, share in the authority of the resurrected crucified one: "Truly I tell you, at the renewal of all things, when the Son of Man is seated on the throne of his glory, you who have followed me will also sit on twelve thrones, judging the twelve tribes of Israel. And everyone who has left houses or brothers or sisters or father or mother or children or fields, for my name's sake, will receive a hundredfold, and will inherit eternal life" (Matt 19:28b-29).

Jesus' unlimited orientation to the will of God, which even lets God call him into the feeling that God had forsaken him so that he cried out in despair with a psalm verse (cf. Matt 27:46), enables him to become "a ransom for many," namely, for those who orient themselves to the way of Jesus and who want to do the will of God just as much as he did. Through his resurrection, God confirms the encouragement given by Jesus: "But the one who endures to the end will be saved" (24:13).

This hopeful endurance does not express itself in obstinately holding fast to ideological formulations, or in taking the name of Jesus or God on one's lips. Rather, this endurance is something shown in the decisive praxis of merciful solidarity:

> Then the king will say to those at his right hand, "Come, you that are blessed by my Father, inherit the kingdom prepared for you from the foundation of the world; for I was hungry and you gave me food, I was thirsty and you gave me something to drink, I was a stranger and you welcomed me, I was naked and you gave me clothing, I was sick and you took care of me, I was in prison and you visited me." Then the righteous will answer him, "Lord, when was it that we saw you hungry and gave you food, or thirsty and gave you something to drink? And when was it that we saw you a stranger and welcomed you, or naked and gave you clothing? And when was it that we saw you sick or in prison and visited you?" And the king will answer them, "Truly I tell you, just as you did it to one of the least of these who are members of my family, you did it to me." (Matt 25:40)

The Presence of the Resurrected Crucified One

The promise of the resurrected Crucified One to be with his disciples holds true for all those who follow his way of mercy. They see the Crucified One in the needy, in the victims of unjust and merciless rule and who act in the conviction that his resurrection has confirmed his way of service to neighbors as the will of God. By becoming witnesses to the gospel in these ways, they themselves become signs of the resurrected Crucified One.

The gospel of Matthew is just such a sign itself. It recalls the words and deeds of Jesus as a book of history that narrates the royal rule of God as it was made manifest through the covenant with Abraham and through God's promise to David, a promise that remains in force throughout the exile. Matthew recalls that Jesus is the Emmanuel promised by Isaiah, who, on the basis of his steadfast orientation to the will of God, is killed by the arrogant and self-ruling domination of earthly authorities and who, through his resurrection, becomes the one who has the authority to be with them always.

They experience his presence in manifold ways. The prime place for this experience is the community of those who follow the way of mercy. The ἐκκλεσία (church) of Jesus is the community of those who deal mercifully with others and who strive for righteousness. No institution determines who belongs to this community in the present, but rather membership is determined by the coming judgment of God.

In the Last Supper (cf. Matt 26:26-29), communion with the resurrected crucified one in bread and wine becomes an embodied experience. With these elements and the remembered words of Jesus the community turns in full confidence to the God whom Jesus proclaimed as the merciful and righteous God of Israel. They know his goodness. They know his authority, which bestows eternal life with God upon the sorrowful, the meek, those thirsting for righteousness, the merciful, the peacemakers, and those persecuted for righteousness' sake. With the same power he will annihilate all destructive powers. According to the gospel of Matthew, the resurrection of the Crucified One and the eschatological resurrection of the dead stand as signs of the mercy and righteousness of the almighty God.

Those who follow Jesus perceive his presence and at the same time know him to be somewhere else. The plausibility of this ubiquitous presence does not depend upon empirical proof. Rather, it depends upon the faith that trusts what Jesus said about God. They expect his return from this other place and along with it the justice of the merciful God: "Then the sign of the Son of Man will appear in heaven, and then all the tribes of the earth will mourn, and they will see 'the Son of Man coming on the clouds of heaven' with power and great glory" (Matt 24:30).

The Gospel of Luke

The Proemium

Unlike the other Gospels, the gospel of Luke does not jump right into the narrative, but rather states its intentions and fundamental ways of working in its opening verses (Luke 1:1-4). With this proemium, the gospel of Luke locates itself within the tradition of Hellenistic-Roman historiography. A cascade of errors results, however, if one attributes to Luke the European Enlightenment's understanding of history or even the positivistic historiography in the tradition of Leopold von Ranke.[42] Historiography in antiquity is not first of all interested in the cogency of facts. Rather, it is much more concerned with the meaningful depiction of events and destinies that both entertain and instruct readers. Given this purpose it was sometimes necessary to invent speeches when fiction could shed light on the contexts being narrated. In the service of an aesthetically appropriate depiction of history in accord with the truth, fictionality and facticity are not opposed to each other, but rather legitimate means that instruct readers about a given topic in ways that are pleasant and pedagogically useful. In this sense, the gospel of Luke and, by the same token, the Acts of the Apostles are historiography.[43]

In the very first verse Luke shows his familiarity with earlier writings that narrated the events surrounding Jesus Christ. It is highly likely that the gospel of Mark was among these writings. Perhaps Luke knew the gospel of Matthew[44] as well, along with other texts that, however, were not handed down and with which therefore we are not familiar. It is certain, however, that Luke composed his gospel because he regarded the others that he knew as insufficient. According to him, it is precisely his own writing that offers a well-researched, appropriately arranged and stylized depiction, which presents "the certainty of the things you have been taught" (Luke 1:4; self-translation).

That Luke follows a reader-oriented conception in his entire depiction can be seen clearly in his address to Theophilus. Whether he has a real reader in view, or whether the name "friend of God" serves as a metaphorical designation for his intended reader, is a matter often neglected in reception-oriented approaches to Luke's work. According to the logic of the proemium, those who engage Luke's depiction and trust it reveal themselves to be friends—indeed, friends of God. The proemium thus lays out a kind of reading contract that establishes a mutual estimation between author and reader. Readers can regard themselves as friends of God when they ascribe to Luke's gospel the qualities described by the author in the proemium. Thus they will at the same time find themselves instructed by the work in a comprehensive and credible manner.

The Power of God and the Work of the Holy Spirit According to Luke 1 and 2

Luke considerably reshapes the gospel of Mark in numerous places, not only in terms of semantics, but also at the level of the syntagmatics of the Jesus-Christ-Story. The syntagmatic changes are effected, for example, by prefixing certain events before the public appearance of the Baptist at the beginning of chapter 3, as well as through the considerable care taken in depicting the journey of Jesus and his companions to Jerusalem, and not least through the appearance narratives at the end of the gospel.

It is precisely with the theology of the resurrection in view that something decisive happens. With the stories right at the beginning of the gospel, Luke supplies a framework for understanding the miracles to be recounted, as well as the resurrection of the Crucified One. In this way Luke's gospel removes from readers much of the theological work that Mark expects them to do.

Luke begins his narrative with the miraculous pregnancy of Elizabeth (cf. Luke 1:7, 13). He thus makes intertextual links to the stories of barren women in the sacred Scriptures of Israel, of which the most powerful is the miraculous conception of Isaac granted to Sarah (cf. Gen 11:30; 21:2). This conception is announced to Elizabeth's husband Zechariah by an angel. The angel's words weave stories about the prophet Elijah into this story. Moreover, this prophet's power and spirit will endow the son whom the angel announces that Elizabeth and Zechariah will have. Thus the power of raising the dead is already inscribed intertextually here, for the story of the revivification of the son of the widow of Zarephath, through the prayers and works of Elijah, belongs to the treasury of stories with which Elijah is connected.

The son the angel told Zechariah about "will be filled with the Holy Spirit, even from his mother's womb" (Luke 1:15b) and work "in the spirit and power of Elijah" (1:17a). Zechariah, a temple priest advanced in years, doubts the angel's announcement, and experiences in his own body a miraculous punishment that serves at the same time as a sign.

The doubt of the old, experienced priest Zechariah stands in direct contrast to the believing confidence that the young Mary displays in the face of the angel's announcement of her virginal conception. Thus at the very beginning of his gospel, Luke presents two different ways that the gospel can be encountered and received. The miraculous punishment of the doubting priest warns against underestimating the power of God, while the faith of Mary in the boundless creative power of God, in spite of the way this contradicts the plain facts, presents readers with an example to emulate. Mary's Magnificat also becomes readers' own song of praise when they read or hear the gospel with the kind of confidence in God's miraculous creative power that Mary expressed when she heard the angel's words: "And blessed is she who believed that there would be a fulfillment of what was spoken to her from the Lord" (Luke 1:45).

Luke further explains Mary's miraculous conception. She becomes pregnant through the direct action of the Holy Spirit, even without intercourse (cf. Luke 1:31, 34-35). This makes it clear from the beginning that the Jesus-Christ-Story concerns the immeasurable creative power and the saving mercy of God. The words of the angel Gabriel, who announces this miraculous conception to Mary, remove all doubt that this child is gifted with even greater power than Elizabeth's: "The Holy Spirit will come upon you, and the power of the Most High will overshadow you; therefore the child to be born will be called holy, the Son of God" (1:35). The angel then refers both of these pregnancies, impossible by any human account, back to the boundless creative power of God. These events establish the principle that makes plausible all of the miracles done by Jesus and his companions, as well as the miraculous resurrection and ascension of the Crucified One: "For with God nothing will be impossible" (1:37).

The plausibility of the conception and resurrection of Jesus depends in similar ways on the power of God, power that the Holy Ghost can share with chosen men and women. It is no accident that the Holy Spirit plays a decisive role not only in the gospel of Luke but also in the Acts of the Apostles. In his writings Luke offers a theology of the Holy Spirit that shows that God's Holy Spirit was at work from the beginning of the Jesus-Christ-Story. His power also makes the resurrection of the Crucified One conceivable. The same Holy Spirit also works within the present community of believers.[45]

On this basis, the first two chapters establish the gospel of Luke's universe of discourse. Thus the world in which the narrative develops enables its reader to view the meaning of the narrative in a plausible way. Luke here introduces more than simply God, Jesus as the Son of God, and the Spirit. He also provides the values that are bound up with God, his Son, and his Spirit. The merciful power of God reverses the self-centered values of the powers of this world. Mary's Magnificat develops this theme in a programmatic way (cf. Luke 1:49-54), and Zechariah's song of praise confirms it (cf. 1:67-79). In the latter text one finds even the terminology of resurrection being used, for, as Zechariah foretells, God "has raised up (ἤγειρεν) a horn of salvation for us." When the angel at the tomb announces to the women that the crucified Jesus has been raised by God he uses the very same word. The promise has been fulfilled.

Simeon, who is filled with the Spirit and speaks Spirit-inspired words, also alludes to the passion of Jesus in Luke 2:25-34 when he prophesies to Mary that "a sword will pierce through your own soul also." Simeon perceives in Jesus the salvation promised of old (cf. 2:30). He also prophesies, however, that not all will participate in that salvation. Thus with this difference Luke inscribes the dysphoric element of "fall" into the euphoric expectation of "salvation." Salvation is therefore again expressed with resurrection terminology: Jesus is "set for the fall (πτῶσις) and rising (ἀνάστασις) of many in Israel, and for a sign (σημεῖον) that is spoken against" (2:34b). The sign that will be spoken against will be Jesus' resurrection from the dead. Thus, both the gospel of Luke and also the Acts of the Apostles will devote their narratival efforts to the task of countering objections to the miraculous sign of Jesus' resurrection by making the event plausible.

Both of the opening two chapters establish the universe of discourse and the structure of the Jesus-Christ-Story in concentrated ways. They also introduce the decisive protagonists of the gospel, and, by means of a theology of the Holy Spirit, suggest what power works in and through those protagonists. After the first two chapters, readers are instructed whose friend they must be if they would follow the values of divine mercy. They are also told who, through an appropriate reading of the gospel, will receive salvation. But readers are also primed to expect a narrative with dysphoric elements in which the protagonists of the gospel, whom they have already met, will experience suffering. Nevertheless, it is clear from the beginning that the immeasurable power of God will annihilate every opposing power. Thus this irresistible power of God stands as a sign of his mercy, the value to which all readers of the gospel of Luke are obligated: "Be merciful, even as your Father is merciful" (Luke 6:36).

The Sign of God's Messiah

The main story thus opens in chapter 3: the word of God comes to John, the son of Zechariah and Elizabeth, and he thereupon begins his preaching of repentance and work of baptism. His decisive message is, "All flesh shall see the salvation of God" (Luke 3:6). To prepare oneself rightly for this saving encounter it is necessary to recognize one's errors and repent. Attentive readers already know from the preceding chapters that none other than Jesus, the Son of Mary, embodies this divine salvation. John's words demand that they prepare for an encounter with Jesus, the "salvation of God," by admitting their sins and repenting.

In connection with the summary depiction of John's activities, his arrest at Herod's hands is recounted (Luke 3:19-20). After that follows a retrospective note that Jesus had been baptized along with the people (3:21-22). As with Mark and Matthew, the heavens are opened, the Spirit descends upon Jesus, and the heavenly voice addresses Jesus and declares his Sonship to him. Only Luke remarks that the Spirit came down upon Jesus "in bodily form, like a dove" (3:22b). Through the introduction of the words "in bodily form (σωματικῷ ἔιδει)" the comparison of the Sprit and a dove (as Luke had found it in Mark) is made materially concrete.

This concretizing tendency shapes the entire gospel of Luke. It raises the impression that Luke wanted to avoid any and all spiritualizing dilution of the gospel. It motivates Luke's temporal ordering of events in Luke 3:1ff., as well as his formulation of the saying about the blessed poor, in the Sermon on the Plain (6:20b), who are poor in material terms, whereas Matthew in the Sermon on the Mount mentions the "poor in spirit." This tendency is also found just as much in the depiction of the resurrected Crucified One, an account that resonates with this emphasis still further.

First of all, however, it may be held that Luke makes the efficacy of the Holy Spirit, which he so impressively brings into play in the first two chapters, a supporting pillar of his portrayal in the main lines of the story. Jesus, to whom the Holy Spirit bore witness and who again at the baptism filled him, is led by the Holy Spirit into the wilderness and resists the temptation of the devil (Luke 4:1-13).

After this account of his endowment with power, Jesus begins his activities in Galilee. His message, which is developed with an intertextual reference to the prophecy of Isaiah, is wholly indebted to the concretization of mercy: "The Spirit of the Lord is upon me, because he has anointed me to preach good news to the poor. He has sent me to proclaim release to the captives and recovering of sight to the blind, to set at liberty those who are oppressed, to proclaim the acceptable year of the Lord" (Luke 4:18-19). In the synagogue of Nazareth, his hometown, he comments on this passage: "Today this Scripture has been fulfilled in your hearing" (4:21b). Jesus reacts to the protest and tumult of the crowd in Nazareth with an intertextual interplay involving Elijah and Elisha, the two prophets whose respective revivifications of the dead are recounted (cf. 1 Kgs 17:17-24; 2 Kgs 4:32-37). The infuriated crowd wants to kill Jesus, but he goes his way miraculously, "passing through the midst of them" (4:30).

In Capernaum he begins his ministry of miracles, which also includes the power of the revivification of a dead person in chapter 7. Just before that, Luke tells of the healing of the deathly ill servant of a centurion in Capernaum (Luke 7:1-10). The revivification of the young man in Nain that follows forces the boundaries of death before the eyes of the public. The crowd reacts to this raising of a dead man appropriately in terms of their encyclopedic knowledge: "Fear seized them all; and they glorified God, saying, 'A great prophet has arisen among us!' and 'God has visited his people!'" (7:16). In light of the many prior allusions to Elijah, the fact that the dead youth is explicitly identified as the son of a widow further supports the conclusion that Jesus is a greater prophet than even Elijah.

Nevertheless, the episode of the Baptist's query that follows the boy's resurrection (Luke 7:18-23) corrects any misunderstanding that Jesus is Elijah come again. Jesus' miracles, which include reviving the dead (cf. 7:22), have a sign function greater than even his proclamation of the gospel to the poor. They point to the fact that Jesus is the expected messiah, and with his response to John's question in 7:22-23 Jesus gives a definite answer to the Baptist's query.

Luke certainly wants to make sure that all his readers understand that Jesus is not Elijah come again. Rather, he is the expected messiah. Thus he has Jesus give voice to the unmistakable conclusion that the reader of the gospel of Mark must work out for himself: John is the messenger announced by the prophets. As such, he is even more than a prophet (cf. Luke 7:26ff.).

Just as the healing of the deathly ill servant of the centurion from Capernaum prepares the reader for the revivification of the young man from Nain, so too the story of the Gerasene demoniac living among the tombs prepares the reader for the revivification of the daughter of Jairus (cf. 8:26-56). This story answers the question asked by the disciples after the stilling of the storm: "Who then is this that he commands even wind and water, and they obey him?" (8:25). Luke lets no doubt arise that the power of Jesus, conceived and enabled by the Holy Spirit, is boundless because it is the power of God working in and through him. But Luke has as little interest in those whom Jesus revives as does the gospel of Mark, which he is correcting. Their revivifications have no cosmological or eschatological ramifications. Like his other miracles, they are signs of Jesus' messiahship and Sonship.

The interpretation that Jesus is a prophet, while ultimately insufficient, comes into conflict with other conceptions of Jesus' potential significance well before Herod has his say. Many regard Jesus as John the Baptist raised from the dead. Others say he is Elijah, and still others that he is one of the prophets (Luke 9:7ff.). The same pattern of potential interpretations of his identity is then recited by the disciples in answer to Jesus' question to them regarding his identity (9:18-19).

These interpretations are plausible within a Jewish context. Death sets no boundaries upon God's power. The eschatological dimension of the resurrection of the dead does not come into view in these individual cases of revivifications. In these cases the people who have been restored stand once again under earthly conditions and boundaries of space and time.

Peter recognizes that these interpretations of Jesus' identity are insufficient, and he answers, "You are the Christ of God" (Luke 9:20b). The first passion prediction follows this statement as well as the announcement of his resurrection. Luke leaves out Peter's objection to the passion of Christ and Jesus' harsh condemnation of him, details that Mark's gospel records. Luke mitigates to a considerable degree the conflict between Jesus and his disciples that is developed as a pillar of the Markan narrative.

In contrast to Mark's account, the disciples as depicted by Luke listen attentively to Jesus' words about the cross and discipleship (cf. Luke 8:23-27), nor are they devoid of understanding at Jesus' transfiguration. When they are taken into the cloud overshadowing the transfigured Jesus and the figures of Moses and Elijah who are speaking with him, they hear "from the cloud . . . a voice that said, 'This is my Son, my Chosen; listen to him!'" (9:35-36). In the gospel of Luke, the disciples' silence is not an expression of incomprehension. Rather it is an understanding silence, silent assent, whereas in the Markan parallel the disciples speak nonsense that reveals only their incomprehension (cf. Mark 9:2-10).

In addition, Luke has further changed the transfiguration scene in decisive ways through other components: While Mark simply maintains that Jesus, Elijah, and Moses speak with one another, Luke reports the content of their conversation, in particular Jesus' fate in Jerusalem. Thus he prepares the reader for the second passion prediction (Luke 9:43b-45) as well as the caesura in 9:51, which introduces the journey to Jerusalem. In 9:31 Moses and Elijah speak of "his departure, which he was about to accomplish at Jerusalem." In 9:51 Luke connects Jesus' fate with Jerusalem again with the verb "fulfill" (πληρόω): "When the days were fulfilled (συμπληρόω) for him to be taken up, he set his face to go to Jerusalem." In this way Luke invites the reader to join with Jesus on the way to his exaltation—that is, to his ascension. The way of the Son of God, who was generated by the divine Spirit and born miraculously by the Virgin, is fulfilled with his exaltation. Jesus accepts the suffering his opponents dole out because nothing and nobody can deflect him from the way of divine mercy. The words of Elijah and Moses strengthen him on this path, and indeed, he knows exactly where this path will lead him.

Finally, it becomes clear here that Luke—as with the authors of the other Gospels—shapes his narrative from the perspective of the death and resurrection of Jesus. In this way Luke seeks to explain why the death and resurrection of Jesus are events that have brought salvation to the entire cosmos.

On the Way to Jerusalem

In Luke 9:51 Jesus begins his final journey to Jerusalem, resolute and directed to his goal. Some of his disciples want to summon fire from heaven to annihilate a Samaritan village that, precisely because of his orientation to Jerusalem, did not receive him. They are certain of Jesus' power, but they have not yet fully realized the values of Jesus' proclamation about the kingdom of God. Jesus rebukes them—one of the few places in which Jesus criticizes his disciples in this gospel (9:51-56). Thus Luke leaves no doubt that the power of God at work in and through Jesus means that he could annihilate the city. He refrains from doing so because he has chosen the path of God's mercy.

Mercy, forgiveness, and joy over the one who repents are also central themes in the numerous parables that Luke has Jesus tell on his way to Jerusalem. Thus he tells the parable of the Good Samaritan in which mercy brought a man beaten half to death back to life (Luke 10:25-37). Another parabolic story of revivification is that of the Prodigal Son (15:11-32), the point of which is summarized in 15:32b as follows: "this brother of yours was dead and has come to life; he was lost and has been found."

Jesus' words on the way to Jerusalem further rework the theme of judgment, however. Thus he warns against living in an unmerciful way. Such a way of life leads to perdition and the forfeiture of eternal life in the Kingdom of God. Here belong the woes against the Galilean cities that rejected Jesus (cf. Luke 10:13-16), as also the interpretation of the sign of Jonah in 11:29-32. Jesus' interpretation of the sign of Jonah functions in Luke as an allegory of his death and resurrection. It is bound up with Jesus' warnings about the judgment of God and eternal damnation, consequences that hold for those who do not give themselves over to the way of God's mercy.

Both aspects—God's mercy and his annihilating power—are brought together in Luke 12:4-8. Jesus encourages those following him not to fear those who can inflict corporeal suffering, for they can injure only the body. They have no power over eternal life or eternal damnation. This power belongs to God alone, whose annihilating power consists in his "authority to cast into hell" (12:5b). Hell is thus not a separate realm belonging to the devil, but rather the place of the destructive power of God, which is a constant threat for those who do not walk the way of mercy.[46]

In the gospel of Luke, however, mercy is not an indeterminate concept. As was already mentioned, mercy has a definite effect in the corporeal world. In fact, this effect is determinative for the praxis of mercy: "He said also to the one who had invited him, 'When you give a luncheon or a dinner, do not invite your friends or your brothers or your relatives or rich neighbors, in case they may invite you in return, and you would be repaid. But when you give a banquet, invite the poor, the crippled, the lame, and the blind. And you will be blessed, because they cannot repay you, for you will be repaid at the resurrection of the righteous'" (14:12ff.).

Luke does not clarify what he means by the phrase "the resurrection of the righteous" (ἀνάστασις τῶν δικαίων). The context and semantic analysis show, however, that it concerns a future resurrection of a qualified number, an idea similar to the conception of resurrection one finds in the martyr theology of the book of Daniel. This conception, which conceives of the resurrection of the dead as a reward for bearing witness to God, is for Luke's theological and pragmatic concerns just as fruitful as other conceptions that assume a general resurrection of the dead for the purposes of judgment and punishment for those condemned, consisting either of eternal death or special agonies. The gospel of Luke does not offer a comparison between both conceptions. Luke is no systematic theologian. His resurrection scenarios differ in their conceptions,[47] but his message remains the same in terms of pragmatics. Only the one who practices mercy finds himself on the way of discipleship following the resurrected Crucified One. Only such a one will enter into the salvation of eternal life, just as he did.

In this way the parable of the Rich Man and Poor Lazarus (Luke 16:19-31) also thematizes the eternal consequences of a merciful or unmerciful way of life. The rich man shows no concern for Lazarus, the poor man, who longed to eat what fell from the rich man's table into the garbage, even as dogs licked his sores. Lazarus died "and was carried away by the angels to Abraham's bosom" (16:22b). The rich man also died and, after his burial, ended up in hell (cf. 16:22c-23).

As regards the reader's response to this Lukan story, in which the poor man is given a name and is thus encountered as an individual while the rich man lacks a name, the reader finds his sympathies directed wholly to Lazarus, the poor man, and his antipathies directed to the nameless rich man, who evinced no concern whatsoever for the needs of the poor and sick. The rich man, who can arrange for a burial befitting his rank, finds himself in hell directly after the ritual conclusion to his earthly life. But Lazarus, the poor man, is borne without burial by an angel directly into Abraham's bosom.

The metaphor of Abraham's bosom (κόλπος) signals a certain and secure rest for the dead Lazarus in communion with Abraham. Contrary to the concept of the underworld designated by the Greek concept of

"Hades" (ᾅδης), the parable signifies Hades as a place of torment in which flames and desiccation dominate. The bosom of Abraham is situated far above Hades but still within eyesight and earshot. There is no way to cross over from one place to the other. This setting is not to be misunderstood as a topography of the realm of the dead in a quasi-scientific way. Rather, it is an intentional element of the parable that makes possible the dialogue between Abraham and the rich inhabitant of hell.

The rich man now recognizes his error, which consisted in his unmerciful ignoring of the suffering of poor Lazarus. He asks Abraham to send "someone . . . from the dead" to his brothers to warn them, for the rich man thinks this will cause them to rethink their ways. The point of the parable lies in its conclusion when Abraham answers: "If they do not listen to Moses and the prophets, neither will they be convinced even if someone rises from the dead" (Luke 16:31).

Luke does not intend the parable of the Rich Man and Lazarus, the poor man, to be a speculative depiction of life after death, and he certainly does not seek to provide a topography of the world of the dead. Rather, he tells this parable in order to express his conviction that one's earthly way of life has consequences for one's life after death. Above all, Luke makes it unmistakably clear that Moses and the prophets provide the necessary knowledge concerning the shape of that life after death.

The final phrase can also be referred to the resurrection of Jesus and then read as ironic commentary about the synagogue at the time of the composition of the gospel of Luke. The Jews at the time of Luke, who place no faith in the Jesus-Christ-Story narrated by Luke and his predecessors, conduct themselves as Abraham predicted of the relatives of the rich inhabitant of hell.

This parable, then, introduces the idea that judgment is not fully postponed to the end of time. Rather, the consequences for how one has lived come into effect immediately after death. Even so, one must remember that this is a parable, a similitude that points to its own fictionality. Therefore, it should not be assumed to be a factual report about events after death, the bosom of Abraham, hell, and their distance from one another.

Luke's Depiction of Jesus' Death

Luke dramatically sharpens the conflict between Jesus and his opponents, a conflict that will result in Jesus' death, at the triumphal entry (cf. Luke 19:37-40). After Jesus' prophecy of the destruction of Jerusalem and the enacted prophecy of driving the moneychangers from the temple, which disrupts the temples cultic operations, "The chief priests, the scribes, and the leaders of the people kept looking for a way to kill him" (19:47).

The opponents of Jesus then justly bring down upon themselves the parable of the Wicked Tenants (Luke 20:9-19). Indeed, only their fear of the people prevents them from killing Jesus immediately (20:19). This parable not only suggests that Jesus' opponents kill him knowingly and with intent, and therefore offers no mitigating circumstances for their guilt for his death. Even more, it ranks Jesus among and above those prophets of God who were murdered unjustly. Just as the owner of the vineyard in the parable does not desire the deaths of his messengers, and certainly not of his son, so also God does not desire the deaths of his prophets, and especially not of the One conceived by his own Spirit.

Luke then narrates Jesus' argument with the Sadducees about the resurrection of the dead (Luke 20:27-40). He thus takes from Mark the point of departure and argumentation of the Sadducees. In Jesus' answer, however, he introduces some interesting additions. Jesus limits the circle of the resurrected. He says, "[B]ut those who are considered worthy of a place in that age and in the resurrection from the dead neither marry nor are given in marriage. Indeed they cannot die anymore, because they are like angels and are children of God, being children of the resurrection" (20:35-36). The resurrection of the dead according to Luke is not the rule, but a reward. Also here, as in 14:14, Luke draws upon a conception of resurrection operative in martyr theology.

Luke makes it clear that those raised at the eschaton are not revivified dead who will one day die again. Rather, they can never die again because the resurrection has given them angelic forms. Those so raised are called the children of God, as Jesus is the Son of God, because the same power of God's Holy Spirit will create them new and angelic, even as it conceived Jesus himself. And finally, Luke adds verse 38: "for to him all of them are alive." Abraham, Isaac, and Jacob are meant here first of all, but then also all others raised by God's power. All of them live their divine life for their creator.

Jesus' opponents' deadly intent toward him is then taken up anew in Luke 22:1. They gain a powerful ally who had left the scene in chapter 4 after the recounting of Jesus' temptation by the devil, the opponent of God. Now Satan enters Judas. In this way, Judas, and thus also the in-group as a whole, are freed from the burden of self-determined error, while Jesus' opponents are all the more guilty of the accusation that they stand in league with the devil.

Satan is also made responsible for Peter's denial, which Jesus predicted to him beforehand: "Simon, Simon, listen! Satan has demanded to sift all of you like wheat, but I have prayed for you that your own faith may not fail; and you, when once you have turned back, strengthen your brothers" (Luke 22:31-32). Again and again Jesus presses the point that the events of his suffering and resurrection must happen, so that what the Scriptures say about him may be fulfilled: "For I tell you, this scripture must be fulfilled in me, 'And he was counted among the lawless'; and indeed what is written about me is being fulfilled" (22:37).

Nevertheless, as in the other Gospels, Luke makes it clear that Jesus does not desire death. He prays in Gethsemane, "'Father, if you are willing, remove this cup from me; yet, not my will but yours be done.' Then an angel from heaven appeared to him and gave him strength. In his anguish he prayed more earnestly, and his sweat became like great drops of blood falling down on the ground" (22:42-44). The disciples drowse during this agony of Jesus, but even here they are exculpated by Luke. They do not sleep for reasons of incomprehension or a lack of solidarity; rather, sorrow has overcome them.

Jesus is then taken prisoner. A brawl erupts, in the course of which an ear of the servant of the high priest is cut off. At that point Jesus rebukes his pugnacious disciples, heals the ear of the servant, and with his interpretation of events qualifies the time and thus also his opponents: "But this is your hour, and the power of darkness!" (Luke 22:53b).

Luke not only mitigates the guilt of the Roman administration, but also releases its client, King Herod, of any and all complicity in Jesus' death. Neither Herod nor Pontius Pilate wants to execute Jesus. In fact, these men of state even become fast friends over the affair (Luke 23:12-15). But "the high priests and the elders and the people" collectively demand Jesus' execution and the release of the murderer Barabbas. Pilate gives in to their desires and has Jesus crucified (Luke 23:18-25).

Two criminals are crucified with Jesus. One of the two mocks him. The other, however, rebukes him and says, "'Do you not fear God, since you are under the same sentence of condemnation? And we indeed have been condemned justly, for we are getting what we deserve for our deeds, but this man has done nothing wrong.' Then he said, 'Jesus, remember me when you come into your kingdom.' He replied, 'Truly I tell you, today you will be with me in Paradise'" (Luke 23:40b-43).

Just as the poor man Lazarus was borne by angels directly after his death to Abraham's bosom, and just as the unmerciful rich man goes to hell immediately after his burial, so too does the penitent thief receive the promise that he will come into paradise (παράδεισος) immediately after his death. Here also it is a question of an exception and not the eschatological rule of the resurrection of the dead at the end of time, as expressed in Jesus' debate with the Sadducees over the question of the resurrection of the dead. The penitent thief asks of Jesus only that Jesus remember him when he comes into his kingdom, perhaps hoping that Jesus would be his advocate at the final judgment, something he probably needs because of his crimes. Jesus, however, promises him more than that. He has the power to take individuals with him into his kingdom even now, and thus he already has the power to forgive sin forever.

Luke pays a high price for this episode, however, for he introduces an inconsistency in his own narration: Not only will the penitent thief be in paradise on that very day, but he will be with Jesus in paradise. His resurrection will occur three days later, however, according to the passion predictions—a breach in the narrative logic that nevertheless makes clear that Luke does not pursue any systematization regarding events occurring after death. Rather, Luke's narrative is meant to serve as encouragement for readers to walk the way of mercy as well as the way of discipleship and solidarity with Jesus in the certainty that this decision for God's values will pay off after death.

Wholly according to his theology of God's Holy Spirit, Luke also changes Jesus' last words. In Luke's presentation, Jesus does not say, "My God, my God, why have you forsaken me?" (Mark 15:34c/Matt 27:46b). Rather, Luke makes a connection to the conception of Jesus by the Holy Spirit when he has him say, "Father, into your hands I commend my spirit" (Luke 23:46). The spirit of Jesus returns from whence it came: to God.

The Presentation of the Resurrected Crucified One
in Luke 24

In the gospel of Luke's presentation, the women go to the tomb on the third day with the intention of anointing the corpse of Jesus. The stone is already rolled away, the tomb is empty. Suddenly two angels announce the resurrection of the Crucified One to them (cf. Luke 24:1-8). The Resurrected One does not encounter them, however. They believe without seeing. Without being told to, they go and announce the news to the disciples, who regard it as an "idle tale" (24:11). Only Peter, for whose conversion after his denial Jesus had especially prayed, goes to the tomb and is "amazed at what had happened" (24:12b).

A change of scene: Two of the unbelieving disciples are on their way to Emmaus, a village about two hours from Jerusalem. They speak of recent events and while doing so the resurrected Jesus joins them on the way. But according to Luke, "their eyes were kept from recognizing him" (Luke 24:16). This shutting of their eyes, effected by God, assumes that Jesus otherwise would have been recognized. The same story is found in a shorter version in the longer ending of Mark: "After this he appeared in another form to two of them, as they were walking into the country" (Mark 16:12). According to Luke, Jesus' visible form is not changed by his death and resurrection.

Jesus asks the two of them what they are talking about, and they summarize the events as follows:

> The things about Jesus of Nazareth, who was a prophet mighty in deed and word before God and all the people, and how our chief priests and leaders handed him over to be condemned to death and crucified him. But we had hoped that he was the one to redeem Israel. Yes, and besides all this, it is now the third day since these things took place. Moreover, some women of our group astounded us. They were at the tomb early this morning, and when they did not find his body there, they came back and told us that they had indeed seen a vision of angels who said that he was alive. Some of those who were with us went to the tomb and found it just as the women had said; but they did not see him. (24:19b-24)

The two disciples' summary of events shows that they have not yet perceived that Jesus is the Son of God, conceived by the Holy Spirit. They still regard him as an especially mighty prophet whom they mistakenly hoped would bring salvation to Israel. With his death, however, their hopes, which were inspired by his works, are extinguished. The numerous passion predictions, which again and again prophesied the necessity of Jesus' suffering but then also his resurrection, do not enter their thinking. They are shocked by the women's report, however, especially as the examination of the tomb by some of the disciples revealed that the tomb was in fact empty, just as the women maintained. No one, however, has seen the Resurrected One to this point. The disciples on the way to Emmaus are not yet finished with their story, but in any event they lack the hermeneutical key for understanding the events.

Jesus then gives them this key when he responds, "'Oh how foolish you are, and how slow of heart to believe all that the prophets have declared! Was it not necessary that the Messiah should suffer these things and then enter into his glory?' Then beginning with Moses and all the prophets, he interpreted to them the things about himself in all the scriptures" (24:25-27).

The hermeneutical key that Jesus offers his confused disciples is a reading of the sacred Scriptures of Israel with real understanding, and indeed a reading that interprets the Scriptures wholly in light of the Jesus-Christ-Story. The necessity of the Christ's suffering is owed to the Scriptures, which have foreseen this suffering, because they know of the unbelief and faithlessness of Israel, God's people. God's Son had to suffer, not because God demanded the suffering of his Son for atonement, but rather because of the way that Israel had conducted itself with respect to his prophets. Not for an instant does the unfaithfulness of Israel, the misconduct of the chosen people, make the Son of God, conceived by the Holy Spirit, halt what the parable of the Wicked Tenants has already expressed. Indeed, Luke's clear ascription of blame to the high priests, the scribes, and the whole people of Israel confirms it. Luke thus inscribes into his gospel the study of the sacred Scriptures of Israel with reference to the Jesus-Christ-Story as the necessary horizon for understanding the Christian faith, and at the same time brings along a necessary program of Christian formation. Faith must understand, and understanding is possible only through formation in the sacred Scriptures of Israel.

Because their eyes are still kept shut by God, however, the disciples still do not recognize Jesus. Only when he breaks bread, give thanks for it, and begins to give it to them are their eyes opened. But, in the very moment they recognize him, he disappears from their sight. He does not take leave of them. He does not walk out the door. In one instant he is simply no longer there. His resurrected body is outwardly identical to that of his earthly life, but it no longer obeys the bounds of space and time. It now belongs to the world of the divine and is similar to the angels, just as was stated in the debate between Jesus and Sadducees about the resurrection of the dead.

The reaction of the disciples to his vanishing offers a pragmatic truth criterion: "Were not our hearts burning within us while he was talking to us on the road, while he was opening the scriptures to us?" (Luke 24:32). The presence of the resurrected crucified one as well as the revealing, truth-opening interpretation of the Scriptures is felt by the heart. The dullness of the heart and its incomprehension are now overcome, and the feeling of their burning hearts motivates them to go back to Jerusalem to report their encounter with the resurrected crucified one to the other disciples.

They find the eleven disciples gathered, and before they can speak, the others say to them, "The Lord has risen indeed (ὄντως), and he has appeared (ὤφθη) to Simon!" (Luke 24:34). Only now can the two disciples who were on the road to Emmaus tell their story.

That the resurrected Crucified One was seen by Simon Peter is formulated in the exact same way as Paul hands it down in 1 Corinthians 15. It is amazing that Luke does not develop this story.

While the two disciples are recounting their story, the resurrected Jesus appears among them suddenly and in a way transcending the bounds of space and time, just as earlier he had suddenly disappeared before the eyes of the two disciples he met on the way to Emmaus (cf. Luke 24:36).

The disciples not only are shocked but also misinterpret the presence of the Resurrected One, and this in spite of their already-expressed conviction that Jesus had been truly raised from the dead, and in spite of the confirmation of this conviction through the two disciples' story: "They were startled and terrified, and thought that they were seeing a ghost" (Luke 24:37).

Clearly Luke wants with this story to guard against the misunderstanding that the appearance of the Resurrected One involves the perception of a phantasm. Thus, Luke's concretizing and materializing tendencies play a significant role in this episode: "He said to them, 'Why are you frightened, and why do doubts arise in your hearts? Look at my hands and my feet; see that it is I myself. Touch me and see; for a ghost does not have flesh and bones as you see that I have.' And when he had said this, he showed them his hands and his feet" (24:38-40). The existence of ghosts in Luke's world is just as uncontroversial as the existence of the subconscious is today for moderns who have been raised in the West. But, just as we today do not think of the subconscious as something fleshly, or investigate its skeletal structure, the ancients knew that ghosts have neither flesh nor bones. Luke is here guarding against the potential misunderstanding that Jesus was not really raised from the dead, but was only a ghost hovering in the air and producing false visions.[48]

How strongly Luke believes he has to proceed against this potential misunderstanding is shown by the reaction of the disciples there present: "While in their joy they were disbelieving and still wondering, he said to them, 'Have you anything here to eat?' They gave him a piece of broiled fish, and he took it and ate in their presence" (Luke 24:41-43).

By way of contrast to Mark and Matthew, Luke allows no room for doubt within faith. He wishes to make faith certain, as he explains at the beginning of his gospel. In the face of so much evidence, the disciples can only remain silent. The resurrected Jesus again impresses upon them and upon readers of Luke the fitting, certain, and doubt-free interpretation of events:

"These are my words that I spoke to you while I was still with you—that every-thing written about me in the law of Moses, the prophets, and the psalms must be fulfilled." Then he opened their minds to understand the scriptures, and he said to them, "Thus it is written, that the Messiah is to suffer and to rise from the dead on the third day, and that repentance and forgiveness of sins is to be proclaimed in his name to all nations, beginning from Jerusalem. You are witnesses of these things. And see, I am sending upon you what my Father promised; so stay here in the city until you have been clothed with power from on high." (Luke 24:44b-49)

In Luke, unlike Mark and Matthew, Jesus does not go ahead of the disciples to Galilee, to the place where everything began. He shows him-self to his disciples in Jerusalem, and it is there that they are now supposed to wait for the Holy Spirit, the wondrous power from heaven, that will empower them in their mission to the world. Luke's Acts of the Apostles will go on to narrate these events. The message here is simple: repent and walk the path of divine mercy; then your past trespasses will be forgiven. The social message of mercy is also deeply inscribed in the sacred Scrip-tures of Israel, and even there one can find all one must know about the suffering of the Christ.

The cross does not nullify the truth of Jesus of Nazareth's proclama-tion; rather, it confirms it. To live out mercy and to demand justice for the poor and weak do not lead to riches and may even lead to deadly conflict. The one who walked this way consistently had to die on the cross as the Scriptures had foreseen. But this death did not have the final word. God's power is greater than death. The way of mercy may lead to the cross, but it is the only way into the kingdom of God, into eternal life with God and his Son.

After Jesus has instructed the disciples one final time, he ascends into heaven before their very eyes on the same day as his resurrection and appearances to them. Here again the resurrected body, which Luke represents in materially correct ways, no longer obeys the bounds of space and time.

The Acts of the Apostles

The first verses of the Acts of the Apostles look back to the close of the gospel of Luke and mark the narrative that follows as its continuation. Acts will advance the story by showing how the work of the Holy Spirit effected the spread of the gospel from Jerusalem to Rome and thus to the center of power of the world at the time of the gospel writer. In the center of the apostles' proclamation stands the message of the resurrection of the crucified Jesus of Nazareth. Numerous passages in the Acts of the Apos-tles make explicit reference to the gospel of Luke's resurrection theology, with its palpable tendencies not only to make its resurrection theology plausible but also to provide apologetic details to ensure it, expand it, and even prove it (cf. Acts 1:3a).

The Resurrection of the Crucified One as the Basis of the Gospel in Jerusalem

If the gospel of Luke already distinguishes between the resurrection and exaltation of the crucified one through the story of Jesus' ascension, then the Acts of the Apostles only increases this separation and even accepts an irreconcilable contradiction with the gospel. According to the gospel of Luke, the resurrection, appearances, and ascension of Jesus all occur on the same day, but Acts widens the time frame for the appearances to forty days (Acts 1:3). Only then does Jesus ascend on a cloud to heaven. Luke makes explicit mention of the fact that the ascension took place before the apostles' very eyes and that they therefore are to be counted as eyewitnesses of the bodily resurrection and ascension of Jesus.

It is perhaps from this perspective that one ought to conceive of the significance of Jesus' appearance before the eleven. The resurrected body may at times be visible, but it is clearly no longer bound by space and time. By the same token, the exalted body is fully in tune with the divine life. As such, the exalted one becomes visible only when the heavens are opened, just as Acts 7:56 and 9:3 recount.[49]

After Jesus' ascension his apostles return to Jerusalem as Jesus had instructed them, in order to wait for the Spirit, which will empower them for their mission to the world. On Peter's initiative a new apostle is chosen to replace Judas, who died cruelly by means of a miraculous punishment (cf. Acts 1:18). The criterion for the choice indicates that only someone who was with the apostles "during all the time that the Lord Jesus went in and out among us, beginning from the baptism of John until the day when he was taken up from us" (1:21-22) can exercise the office of apostle in the circle of the twelve. In this context his decisive task is "to become a witness with us to his resurrection" (1:22b). Thus for Luke, the apostles are above all witnesses to the resurrection of the crucified Jesus of Nazareth and thereby fulfill the commission given to them immediately before the ascension (cf. 1:8).

Immediately after the selection of Matthias as the successor to Judas, the Pentecost event is recounted (Acts 2:1-13), which is the fulfillment of the promise (cf. 1:8) of the miraculous gift of the Spirit,[50] who begins to work immediately: "All of them were filled with the Holy Spirit and began to speak in other languages, as the Spirit gave them ability" (2:4).

Although all the apostles preach, only Peter's sermon, sparked by his reaction to the accusation that the apostles are drunk, is recounted in detail (2:14-36).

Peter begins his Pentecost sermon with the proof text of Joel's prophecy. The outpouring of the Spirit the apostles have just experienced is the fulfillment of Joel's prophecy. In this way the eschatological and the cosmological dimensions of this event are coming to fruition. Only those who "call on the name of the Lord" (Acts 2:21b) are saved in this situation, which can be understood as the end time because of the outpouring of the Spirit. This name of the Lord is now identified with the name of Jesus through the reference to the death and resurrection of Jesus of Nazareth. Therefore, only those who call upon Jesus as Lord are saved. This identification, however, can be made only by those who come to know the true identity of Jesus by recognizing how God ultimately vindicated him. Calling upon the name of Jesus Christ thus becomes a soteriological criterion that decides between eternal life and death.

God attested to Jesus of Nazareth "with deeds of power, wonders, and signs that God did through him among you, as you yourselves know—this man, handed over to you according to the definite plan and foreknowledge of God, you crucified and killed by the hands of those outside the law" (2:22-23). With this formulation Luke specifies that the sovereign subject of the Jesus-Christ-Story is God. Through his divine and miraculous act, he has made it possible for all to know who Jesus of Nazareth truly is. Every Jew must have perceived that God was at work in God's dealing with Jesus. But by vindicating Jesus, God has more clearly marked him as the one who stands in covenant with him and lives and teaches his will. The Jews, however, have not received him as the messiah sent by God. They follow neither him nor his teaching. On the contrary: they had him cruelly killed by those who were without the law, and thus treated him as one who did not belong to the chosen people of Israel.

Although they therefore became the subjects who perpetrated the murder of God's authentic messiah and thus bear all guilt for his death, they are nevertheless not sovereign, almighty agents in this event. Only because God had already decided not to intervene were they able to carry out their evil act. God remains the sovereign subject of the event even in view of this wicked act performed by his people. God has deliberately allowed it. Thus becomes manifest what according to the Scriptures God already knew: even his chosen people do not act in accord with his merciful will, although his will in Jesus' teaching, attested to by signs and wonders, was made known again and again in striking fashion. The signature of men failing to do the will of God is not mercy, but merciless violence. Yet, God's mercy does not permit itself to be influenced by that. If men dole out death to the One sent by God, God reverses the result of that action not simply by restoring him to life. Rather, he snatches him away from the pains of death forever and turns his name into the almighty name of salvation.

While God's power knows no bounds and everything is possible for him, the power of death is limited by God's action. Therefore it was "impossible" for the Crucified One "to be held in its power" (Acts 2:24b). This thought is grounded in and ensured by the intertextual reference to Psalm 15:8-11. Luke interprets verses 8-11 of this psalm to the effect that the hope expressed there that God "will not . . . let [his] Holy One experience corruption" refers to the crucified and buried Jesus. Luke's Peter continues, "Since he was a prophet, he knew that God had sworn with an oath to him that he would put one of his descendants on his throne. Foreseeing this, David spoke of the resurrection of the Messiah, saying, 'He was not abandoned to Hades, nor did his flesh experience corruption.' This Jesus God raised up, and of that all of us are witnesses" (Acts 2:30-32). The fleshly depiction of the Resurrected One in the gospel of Luke is made plausible as a singular mark and distinction through the application of the words of this psalm to the resurrection of the crucified Jesus. David's prophecy as expressed in Psalm 15 is fulfilled in the fleshly resurrection of Jesus. The incorruption of the flesh of the Crucified One is thus shown to be a special case and not the rule regarding the resurrection of the dead. Jesus is distinguished by the fact that his flesh did not rot although he spent three days in Hades. The depiction of the resurrected crucified one in the gospel of Luke is indebted to this interpretation of Psalm 15. The uniqueness of the one conceived by God through his Holy Spirit persists also in his death and resurrection. If the dead experience corruption as a rule, then the power of death, which expresses itself in the process of bodily corruption, cannot harm the resurrected Crucified One. Even Luke, the writer of Hellenistic history, refrains from offering an empirical-historical investigation of the resurrection event, but rather interprets faith in the resurrection of the crucified by selectively applying passages from the sacred Scriptures of Israel in order to make the incomprehensible and inconceivable resurrection of the Crucified One conceivable and plausible.

Through the act of resurrection, "God has made him both Lord and Messiah, this Jesus whom you crucified" (Acts 2:36b). Peter's entire Pentecost sermon flows from this conviction. The resurrected Jesus has entered into divine life. He has gone up into heaven and sits at the right hand of God. Exalted in this way, he has received the Holy Spirit, which he now shares with his disciples in the Pentecost event (cf. 2:33-34). The effective binding of the Holy Spirit[51] ties together the conception, resurrection, and exaltation of Jesus of Nazareth, who through these events has become Kyrios and Christ. The Holy Spirit now also binds the exalted Kyrios and Christ to his apostles, and each is invited to call on the name of the exalted one in order to enter into this connection. Whoever calls upon the name of the exalted one receives his Holy Spirit and is saved through integration into this communion, which was founded by the Holy Spirit. If one asks how one is to do that, Peter responds, "Repent, and be baptized every one of you in the name of Jesus Christ so that your sins may be forgiven; and you will receive the gift of the Holy Spirit" (2:38).

The miracle story of the healing of a lame man in the Jerusalem temple that immediately follows demonstrates the efficacy of the name of Jesus Christ (cf. Acts 3:6-8). Peter guards against the potential misunderstanding that he worked this wonder of healing in his own power. In his speech explaining the healing miracle, he says, "But you rejected the Holy and Righteous One and asked to have a murderer given to you, and you killed the Author of life, whom God raised from the dead. To this we are witnesses. And by faith in his name, his name itself has made this man strong, whom you see and know; and the faith that is through Jesus has given him this perfect health in the presence of all of you" (3:14-17). The healing miracle, which happened before their very eyes, functions as proof of the resurrection of the Crucified One and, at the same time, as motivation to call upon the name of Jesus Christ.

Peter implores the Jews to whom he speaks, whom he himself makes responsible for the death of the "Author of life," to repent and to enter into the community of faith. In a way different from the parable of the Wicked Tenants (cf. Luke 20:9-19), Peter highlights mitigating circumstances for the crime against the Holy One of God: "And now, friends, I know that you acted in ignorance, as did also your rulers" (Acts 3:17). But it is not enough: in order to achieve his pragmatic aim of moving the erstwhile opponents of Jesus to repentance and baptism in the name of Jesus Christ, he again plays the card of divine sovereignty. But his formulation comes near the misunderstanding that God willed the death of Jesus of Nazareth: "In this way God fulfilled what he had foretold through all the prophets, that his Messiah would suffer" (3:18). At the same time he points out the urgency of the situation: Whoever does not repent will not have his sins forgiven and will be "utterly rooted out." Salvation and perdition, eternal life and eternal extinction depend on one's reception or rejection of the gospel of the resurrection of the Crucified One. Everyone, even the opponents of Jesus responsible for his death, can now repent: "When God raised up his servant, he sent him first to you, to bless you by turning each of you from your wicked ways" (3:26).

The high council shows that it lacks insight in spite of this offer, however. The priests and Sadducees disapprove of this talk of Jesus' resurrection. They have the apostles confined and thus incriminate themselves even more (cf. Acts 4:1-3). But they can indeed do nothing against the power of the word of the resurrection of Jesus Christ (cf. 4:4); again and again this refrain is sounded (cf. 4:33; 5:30ff.).

Many Jews in Jerusalem are deeply moved by the gospel of the resurrection. The community there grows, and even some of the temple priests enter it. The high council, however, persists in its denial. Stephen's speech finally accounts for these "stiff-necked" opponents. He weaves the Jesus-Christ-Story into the plot of Israel's story and illustrates the continuity of Israel's failures. He accuses them of the murder of the prophets and the murder of the Righteous One the prophets announced. He then summarizes, "You are the ones that received the law as ordained by angels, and yet you have not kept it" (7:53). Those being accused fall into a rage (cf. 7:54). Stephen, however, "filled with the Holy Spirit . . . gazed into heaven and saw the glory of God and Jesus standing at the right hand of God. 'Look,' he said, 'I see the heavens opened and the Son of Man standing at the right hand of God!'" (7:56). Upon finishing these words, he is stoned to death. He prays to Jesus to receive his spirit and, like Jesus on the cross, prays for his tormentors in the hour of his death (7:60).

Stephen's vision shows that the Resurrected One who has gone into heaven can still be seen only if heaven is opened. According to Luke, the resurrected Jesus is therefore not deprived of the customary perception of the world after his resurrection. Rather, this only happens after his exaltation. He is, however, present through the work of the Holy Spirit if one calls upon his name.[52]

The Gospel of the Resurrection among the Nations

After the stoning of Stephen, the new community, with the exception of the apostles, flees Jerusalem. Thus the gospel begins its triumphal procession to Rome. Philip preaches in Samaria, while Saul (Paul), the latter apostle to the Gentiles, to whose works more than half of Acts is dedicated, becomes a preacher of the gospel through a heavenly revelation of the Kyrios Jesus Christ (cf. Acts 9:1-31). This revelation makes his experience of the resurrected and exalted Jesus certain and indubitable.

The continuity between the resurrection message in Jerusalem and the resurrection message among the Gentiles is demonstrated in Peter's speech at Caesarea in the house of the Roman centurion Cornelius (Acts 10). Peter delivers this speech on the occasion of his discovery that "God shows no partiality, but in every nation anyone who fears him and does what is right is acceptable to him" (10:34b-35). In order to bring Cornelius up to speed on the Jesus-Christ-Story, Peter summarizes the fundamental events and their decisive significance (cf. 10:37-43). He begins with John the Baptist's preaching of baptism and the anointing of Jesus as the Messiah (Christ) through the divine gift of the Holy Spirit. Thereafter Jesus' salvific deeds, to which the apostles bear witness, are recounted. The next element of the Jesus-Christ-Story is Jesus' crucifixion. His resurrection by God's power on the third day follows. God then becomes the subject of the appearances: God "allowed him to appear." The appearances, however, did not take place in public, but rather before the apostles exclusively.

That Luke in Acts continues to focus on the resurrection of Jesus as a matter of flesh and bone is clear from the depiction in Luke's gospel that the apostles ate and drank with Jesus after his resurrection. The resurrected Jesus commissioned the apostles "to preach to the people and to testify that he is the one ordained by God as judge of the living and the dead. All the prophets testify about him that everyone who believes in him receives forgiveness of sins through his name" (Acts 10:42-43).

According to Luke, his death thus possesses no soteriological function. First and foremost, God appointed the resurrected Christ as judge. The forgiveness of sins was not effected through his death. Rather, whoever now calls on his name receives the gift of the forgiveness of sins at the judgment.

After the common apostolic conviction is expressed by relating the basic structure of the Jesus-Christ-Story in their proclamation of the gospel, everyone receives the Holy Spirit, even those who are not Jews. Thus God confirms Peter's recognition that the gospel of the resurrection of Jesus Christ and the forgiveness of sins through his exalted, mighty name holds for all people from all nations (cf. 10:44-48).

With this divine confirmation of the integration of the Gentiles[53] into the intended addressees of the gospel, the narrative foundation for Paul's mission to the Gentiles is also laid. That Paul becomes a powerful messenger of God is impressively shown by the miraculous punishment he metes out on the magician Elymas. This story depicts the first action of his nascent world mission (cf. 13:4-12). His first speech, which he delivers in Pisidian Antioch, confirms the agreement of his message with that of the other apostles, especially that of Peter but also that of Stephen as presented in chapter 7. The Lukan Paul orders the Jesus-Christ-Story within the story of Israel and interprets the events of the death and resurrection as the fulfillment of the messianic promise that God inscripturated through his prophets (cf. 13:32-33). The sacred Scriptures of Israel thus function as the script for the events of the death and resurrection of Jesus Christ. That holds especially for the conviction that Jesus was raised bodily. As a result, in contrast to David and all other dead, he did not see corruption, just as the Scriptures had predicted (cf. 13:32-37). The intertextual reference to Psalm 16:10 and not any empirico-historical argument motivates this conviction of the author of the Acts of the Apostles and the gospel of Luke. The conviction concerning the fleshly resurrection of Jesus helps to distinguish this special resurrection (that is, this unique Resurrected One in his cosmological and soteriological significance). Through this Resurrected One and not through any theologically significant sacrifice, the "forgiveness of sins is proclaimed to you [the addressees of the Gospel]; by this Jesus everyone who believes is set free from all those sins from which you could not be freed by the law of Moses" (13:38b-39). This Lukan simplification of Paul's message of justification stands in full concord with the sermons of Peter. It thus serves to demonstrate the agreement of Peter and Paul, the two preachers who are, in the account of Acts, the most significant.

The summary of Paul's preaching in Thessalonica also makes the death and resurrection the central theme (cf. Acts 17:2-3). And the narrator's commentary thematically summarizing Paul's speeches in Athens explains that Paul "was telling the good news about Jesus and the resurrection" (17:18b). In the famous speech at the Areopagus[54] that follows, Paul attempts to provide reasons rooted in creation theology for why the resurrection of the dead is indeed conceivable (cf. 17:24; 17:31). The message meets with a divided response. Some laugh at the idea of the resurrection of the dead, but others wish to hear more from Paul (cf. 17:32).

Luke also thematizes the topic of the resurrection of the dead again and again in the detailed depiction of Paul's arrest in Jerusalem and his journey as a prisoner to Rome. Paul exploits the controversy about the resurrection between the Pharisees and Sadducees and thus achieves the splitting of the high council (cf. Acts 23:6-9). Before the governor Felix he states that his fundamental conviction concerns his belief in the prophets and their promises: "I have a hope in God—a hope that they themselves also accept—that there will be a resurrection of both the righteous and the unrighteous" (24:15; cf. 24:21b). Before Agrippa, Paul maintains that he is being accused by the Jews because he hopes for the fulfillment of the promises of the prophets, and asks, "Why is it thought incredible by any of you that God raises the dead?" (26:8).

Finally, in the third description of Christ's appearing to him, he explicitly connects the resurrection of the dead to the resurrection of Jesus Christ in the same way as 1 Corinthians 15 is to be read.[55] Above all, he refers this connection back to the predictions of Moses and the prophets "that the Messiah must suffer, and that, by being the first to rise from the dead, he would proclaim light both to our people and to the Gentiles" (26:23).[56]

The Coherence of Resurrection Discourse in Luke–Acts

The theme of the resurrection of the crucified one not only runs like a red thread through Luke–Acts, it is the fundamental idea undergirding the narrative form of both the gospel of Luke and the Acts of the Apostles. Luke's plausibility strategy consists in showing that the Jesus-Christ-Story has brought to completion that which the sacred Scriptures of Israel foresaw. On the basis of his mercy, God has conceived the promised savior in a most wonderful way through his Holy Spirit. This savior has lived and announced the merciful will of God. But the reception of this savior on the part of God's chosen people went exactly as the Scriptures would lead one to expect. Their hard hearts led to the suffering and death of God's messiah. God, however, raised him as the first fruits of the resurrection of the dead. Moreover, he has especially marked Jesus in that this savior did not experience the corruption that the corpses of all other dead do.

His disciples were convinced of his special resurrection by seeing him, speaking with him, and eating with him. Indeed, his fleshly resurrected body was not subject to the bounds of space and time. Thus, it was not a question of a mere revivification of a dead man, but rather of the beginning of the eschatological resurrection of the dead at God's final judgment.

According to the gospel of Luke, the Resurrected One was taken into heaven on the very day of his resurrection. According to the Acts of the Apostles, however, the event happens some forty days later. God has thus appointed Jesus to be the mighty eschatological judge. Only calling on his name, which is able even in one's present earthly life to motivate the miraculous deeds of the Holy Spirit, makes the forgiveness of sins possible. Moreover, this forgiveness is necessitated by people's failure to follow the path of mercy, which is the will of God, in the manner that Moses and the prophets present it. Although Luke does borrow from the concept of resurrection that he finds in the martyr theology of his day, to show that part of following the path of mercy involves following Jesus, the Crucified One raised by God, it is nevertheless the case that the conception of the collective resurrection of the dead at the eschatological judgment dominates his resurrection theology. The dead will be raised at the end of the world, on the great day of judgment. Then Jesus Christ, the resurrected Crucified One, will judge them. Luke–Acts proclaims this as "the good news about Jesus and the resurrection" (cf. Acts 17:18b).

Chapter 4

The Johannine Writings

The Gospel of John

The gospel of John shows its readers the soteriological meaning of the eschatological-cosmological dimension of the resurrection of the crucified man Jesus of Nazareth. Its prologue provides an intertextual directive for a reading oriented to creation theology. Thus the beginning of the gospel organizes the narrative from the perspective of the context of the death and resurrection on this hermeneutical and theological basis in a consistent manner. In the man Jesus, who went to the cross out of love for his fellow creatures, John sees the same love at work with which the God of Israel created all things, chose Israel, and miraculously led them out of Egypt. This creative love of God effects not only the raising of the crucified one as his own resurrection, as the gospel of John presents it. Rather, this love also affirms all those who confidently await their own resurrection. Such people, who have remembered and taken comfort through the Spirit of the gospel, now know themselves to be united in the covenant of life with the resurrected Crucified One and with his Father.

The gospel of John complicates any linear conception of time.[1] Its depiction of the Jesus-Christ-Story is borne along by the conviction that this man Jesus is the communication of God himself become flesh. After his resurrection the cosmos as a whole and the life of Jesus Christ in particular cannot be conceived of in terms of a linear conception of time. Above all, the story of the resurrected Jesus of Nazareth, which at the same time relates the story of the resurrected Crucified One, shows that the cosmos is, from the ground up, God's own beloved creation.

This means, however, that a consecutive sequence of the depiction of the man Jesus of Nazareth before the event of the cross, that is then followed by the depiction of the resurrected Crucified One, is no longer possible for the gospel of John. Such a sequence is simply inappropriate for its content. In a way different from the Synoptic Gospels, the gospel of John generates its tension not so much by means of a dramatic plot, but rather through the construction of cognitive dissonances that readers are supposed to solve in ingenious ways with the help of the episodic narrative[2] of the gospel and its intertextual disposition.

As an intertextual rereading of the Synoptic Gospels[3] and the sacred Scriptures of Israel, the gospel of John develops a paradoxical theology of the single event of the cross and resurrection. Above all this theology makes possible the unfolding of the gospel's plausibility under the conditions of the acceptance of the universe of discourse established within it and its intertextually produced encyclopedic connections. Hartwig Thyen writes,

> [F]rom the sentences of the prologue concerning the light shining in the darkness, which cannot be extinguished in spite of all efforts thereunto (1:5), and concerning the expression "the Word became flesh" (1:14), which includes the death of Jesus, our Gospel is no longer like that of Mark, a "passion narrative with an extended introduction" (M. Kähler). Rather this is from the beginning a passion-Gospel, unique as such a witness to the glory of Jesus. John has made Jesus' passion, which paradoxically is Jesus' own divine act, his entire Gospel's principle of presentation in a wholly programmatic way.[4]

The gospel of John wants to be read as a paracletic witness to the love of God that has become flesh in the man Jesus, and that, co-originating in the single event of the cross and resurrection, has overcome all that threatens in the cosmos. The gospel of John itself thus becomes a sign of the Word of God whose ingenious view sees the love of God at work as the effective consolation in all times in the cosmos. On the basis of the gospel's peculiar Jesus-Christ-Story, John permits hope in the resurrection of the dead and eternal life in the community grounded in the love of God (cf. 20:31).

The Prologue

The very first words of the gospel of John bring the creation narrative as they are found in Genesis 1:1–2:4a into intertextual play. Through his reality-generating Word, God creates the cosmos and all that is to be found therein. Nothing has come into being without this powerful, creating Word. Everything owes its existence to God's Word. God is so very much in his Word that God and his Word cannot be separated. There is also no need for an additional purpose for God's creation through the Word, for his reason lies not on some external purpose but rather alone in the Word of God and thus in God himself. Because the Word of God cannot be separated from God, life itself is grounded in this Word and this divine life is the "light of all people," a light that neither is understood by the darkness, nor can ever be extinguished (cf. John 1:4-5).

After the first four verses have brought to mind and reinterpreted in an intertextual fashion the connections among God, his Word, his creation and life as the light of all people grounded in God, and his Word itself, verse 6 binds the Jesus-Christ-Story that the gospel of John then narrates with the man whom God sent, John the Baptist. This link is forged by way of the proper name of John, which functions as *pars pro toto* of this story with the creative act of God. This binding is semantically strengthened through John's function as a witness to the light that is in turn the light of all people—and this light is at the same time life grounded in God himself. To this light, to this life, John bears witness, and the reader of the gospel is thus instructed to believe the witness of John. That to which or to whom John testifies is the light—"The true light, which enlightens everyone, was coming into the world" (John 1:9)—*all* people, and thus also and not least all readers of the gospel of John.

This light was in the world, but although the world was created by this light, the world did not recognize this light when it was in the world (cf. John 1:10). Thus the dysphoric element necessary for the dramaturgy of the episodic narrative of the gospel, which was already sounded in 1:4-5, is felt even here in verse 10. This nonrecognition inscribes into the narrative a disturbing distance between creation and creator, a divine distance that will be the actual reason for the murder of Jesus, the one sent by God and indeed who is one with him, and thus of that very flesh that evinces no disturbing distance from God.

Neither the cosmos as a whole, nor "his own" (John 1:11b), the chosen people of God, receive him. Without any hint of transition, verse 12 then speaks of those who have received him. Unconditionally and without any consideration for societal and cultural location he gives to all who have received him "power (ἐξουσία) to become children of God, who were born, not of blood or of the will of the flesh or of the will of man, but of God" (1:12b-13). Eternal life or death depends on the reception or rejection of the light of creation come into the world. This logic is not linear, and every dogma of predestination that understands the doctrine in a causal way errs by introducing the logic of measurable linear time, the binary logic of the causality of empirical reality, into the gospel of John's paradoxical theology of the cross. Whoever receives Jesus Christ as the light, as the Word of God, and believes in his name is a child of God in an equiprimordial way. Such a one is, in other words, born from the divine Word of the gospel. Whoever on the other hand rejects Jesus remains trapped within the natural limitations of cause and effect and misses out on eternal life, which is grounded without limits in God.

The phrases contained in the first thirteen verses direct themselves to verse 14, the pivot of the prologue and perhaps even of the entire Gospel: "And the Word became flesh and lived among us, and we have seen his glory, the glory as of a father's only son, full of grace and truth." No other Word, no other logos than that from verse 1 is intended: the Word of the beginning, the reality-creating Word without which nothing was made, the Word in which God is so very much present that there is no difference between God and this Word. This Word has entered into the human life-limiting, empirically verifiable, vulnerable, mortal, interpretable realm of materiality, so that the glory of the divine Word of creation, which is one with God, became perceptible as the glory of the only begotten Son of God. His glory consists exactly in his being one with God and indeed precisely as a human being, who lives in solidarity with mortals in the cosmos that God created, who shows the cosmos to be a dwelling place of creaturely life. His life and death, which occur under the conditions of fleshly existence, is a life and death for others and indeed for the cosmos, God's beloved creation. It is not primarily in his miraculous deeds but rather precisely in his "pro-existence,"[5] inclusive of the passion, that the glory of the Son is shown in concord with the glory of the love of God as the purpose-free grounding of creation. Jesus Christ is one (ἕν) with God in this love (cf. 10:30). "Thus the unity of that which is *dissimilar* is expressed by the neuter ἕν; it does not perhaps mean that the heavenly God and the earthly man Jesus as his λόγος become flesh were one and the same."[6]

Verse 15 now fulfills what verse 6 announced: John bears witness to the one become flesh: "John testified to him and cried out, 'This was he of whom I said, "He who comes after me ranks ahead of me because he was before me."'"

Admittedly John says this nowhere in the course of this gospel. In Matthew 3:11 John speaks of the one who will come after him. The intertextual allusions to the Synoptic Gospels discussed in such detail by Thyen in his commentary on John begin here at the very latest. As Thyen has impressively demonstrated, it is a question not simply of the reworking of a source but rather of an interpretive process in its own right. This process therefore decentralizes the meaning of the text and thus interprets both the gospel of John through the Synoptic Gospels as well as the Synoptic Gospels through the gospel of John. The process thereby establishes new realms of meaning. This is shown in an exemplary fashion in the Johannine addition to the phrase "one who is more powerful" than John, announced by John in Matthew 3:11, that "He who comes after me ranks ahead of me because he was before me" (John 1:15). Thus a new approach to reading the gospel of Matthew is generated and at the same time the "one who is more powerful" of Matthew's gospel is integrated into John's gospel.

The reader of the gospel of John is therefore expected not only to know the Synoptic Gospels, but also to make links to them again and again in reading the gospel of John. Through the writing's texture, readers are also given the task of reflecting upon paradoxes with the help of the worlds generated in the gospel of John and with the help of the intertextually produced universe of discourse. In reflecting upon the paradoxes and metaphors as well as in clarifying narrative misunderstanding, they are supposed to think in new ways and learn to see, and thus do, precisely that which John the Evangelist, John the Baptist, and Jesus of Nazareth require in the Synoptic Gospels: "Repent, and believe in the good news" (Mark 1:15b; cf. Mark 1:4).

The paradox in John 1:15b can then be considered, guided by the import of the prologue: The man Jesus is the Word of creation become flesh and as such is the true light and life of men. His flesh did not exist before John, but indeed the Word of creation that became flesh at a determinate historical point in time. The flesh, and thus the man Jesus, stands under the empirical conditions of the material existence of every man. Thus he is born at a determinate historical point in time and then also killed. Jesus is no mythical figure invulnerable to suffering. Therefore his story is open to historical research in principle. That it was precisely this man who was one with God, however, and that through his story the glory of God itself becomes perceptible, and that both God and also his creation are to be freshly seen and considered through his story, have their material grounding in the single event of the cross and resurrection, interpreted on the basis of Old Testament creation theology. This event shatters the empirical-historical boundaries of fleshly existence. The man Jesus can be interpreted as the preexistent Son of God and his raising (that is, his resurrection) representable by means of the illumination provided by the resurrection of the Crucified One, for in it the creative power of divine life itself is operative.

Verse 17 finally identifies the logos who became flesh with Jesus Christ, and verse 18 denominates his decisive function: Jesus Christ, the

Word of creation become flesh and as such the only begotten Son of God, has revealed God finally and truly. Through his words and through his story God himself is revealed as the loving and merciful creator. At the same time, readers who agree with the message of the gospel of John experience the cosmos, humanity, and themselves as God's creatures: wanted, loved, and saved.

The Preexistence of Jesus as the Ground of His Passion and Glory

The plot of the gospel begins in John 1:19. The Jews send priests and Levites to John in order to establish his identity and function. With a reference to Isaiah he makes himself known as the forerunner of the messiah (cf. 1:23). That same day Jesus comes to him and John says, "Here is the Lamb of God who takes away the sin of the world" (1:29b).

The giving of the Spirit to Jesus is then retrospectively depicted from the perspective of the Baptist and employed as a valid and abiding mark that grounds the identification of Jesus as the expected messiah and as the "Son of God" (John 1:34b) through John the Baptist.

The metaphorical designation of Jesus as the Lamb of God who takes away the sins of the world has suffered a misunderstanding of sacrificial theology in the communion liturgy. Accordingly, God is often assumed to be a displeased tyrant who has his Son slaughtered in order to become merciful once more.[7] This hateful and idolatrous effigy wants to see blood in order to quench his thirst for revenge. That may indeed appear fitting again and again to many people, but a concept of revenge worthy of an idol is not compatible with the creative, loving, and merciful God as encountered in the Jesus-Christ-Story in the gospel of John.

In a way quite other than this sacrificial-theological constraining of a questionable metaphor, the composition of the gospel of John frustrates any "unambiguous determination of the significance of the Lamb," preferring instead "the openness of metaphorical language in order precisely to thus achieve new possibilities of language and broadenings of meaning for its message."[9]

This broadening of meaning is produced not least by the gospel's intertextual predisposition, which the prologue already prescribed as a directive for reading. The syntagm "Lamb of God, who takes away the sins of the world" reveals its potential for meaning primarily as a complex intertextual reference, which connects at very least Exodus 12, Genesis 22, and Isaiah 53 and their interpretations in the Targumim and other Jewish writings with the Jesus-Christ-Story. With the allusion to Exodus 12, the semantic marking of the Passover lamb from Exodus 12:5 is brought in. The Passover lamb must be spotless and free from defect. Its blood serves as the mark of the people of Israel as the people of God, protecting them from death through the Angel of Death.[10] In the framework of the gospel of John's universe of discourse, this means that whoever calls upon the name of Jesus Christ and is thus marked as belonging to him, by him who was executed bloodily, will be saved.

The memory in the Christian tradition of the "sacrifice of Isaac," known fittingly in the Jewish tradition as the "binding of Isaac" and intensively reflected upon in early Judaism before and during the composition of the gospel of John, shows that God is in no way pleased by human sacrifice. Its reception in early Judaism expresses the idea of Isaac's free cooperation, for Isaac is ready to die for Abraham's well-being. In Targum Pseudo-Jonathan at Genesis 22:14, the prayer for the forgiveness of sins also comes into play. There it reads, "When the children of Isaac come into a time of oppression, then for their favor remember the binding of Isaac their father, forgive them their sins, and free them from all distress."[11] It is thus not the blood of Isaac poured out but rather his free willingness to lose his life for the welfare of the community that is here brought to mind as the ground for the forgiveness of sins. By means of this intertextual association Jesus is thus designated as the one who is prepared to lose his life freely for the welfare of his community. John 15:13 will later explicitly formulate this precise point.

The association with Isaiah 53 is obvious because then not only can the brutal cruciform death of Jesus be interpreted, but also Isaiah 53:5 expressly says, "But he was wounded for our transgressions, crushed for our iniquities." The horrifying death of the servant of God, about whom Isaiah 53 speaks, was just as little the will of God as was the death of Jesus, the Lamb of God, about whom the gospel of John speaks. The cause of the cruciform death of Jesus is sin, which falls short of life lived in accord with creation in solidarity with creatures and in communion with the creator.

The sin of which the gospel of John speaks is no longer directed to the failings of Israel alone, however. Rather, the gospel brings the cosmological dimension of sin into play. The cosmos as a whole stands under the sign of sin, because, as a whole, it is no longer recognizable as God's beloved creation. Rather, through the rejection of the free love of God, it appears disfigured as a threatening battlefield of destruction. Jesus is therefore the Lamb *of God*, because God, by sending this Lamb, overcame the threatening nature of the cosmos and thereby revealed it again to be his beloved creation. The man Jesus, whose love is one with the love of God, goes his way motivated by the love of God unflinching and unforced, without being dissuaded from the way of love by the horrors and temptations of the cosmos. Even his cruel death on the cross does not make possible the ending of this way of love. The love with which God sent him into the cosmos, and the love with which he freely let himself be sent, also conquers the horrors, the violence, and the finality of death without trivializing its horrors. The resurrection of Jesus Christ is consummated through the power of the creative love of God.

Jesus is the free, unflinching, loving, powerful Lamb of God. He overcomes the alarming insanity, lovelessness, and derailing of the cosmos through the creative love of God. Thus he saves all those who, through the comforting Spirit of the Jesus-Christ-Story, can see, think of, and act with respect to themselves and the cosmos as a whole, as creatures who are beloved, wanted, and pure: "For God so loved the world that he gave his only Son, so that everyone who believes in him may not perish but may have eternal life. Indeed, God did not send the Son into the world to condemn the world, but in order that the world might be saved through him. Those who believe in him are not condemned; but those who do not believe are condemned already, because they have not believed in the name of the only Son of God" (John 3:16-18). These verses comment fittingly upon the symbolic designation of Jesus as the "Lamb of God, who takes away the sins of the world" and introduce Jesus' readiness to give his life for others as a willingness that is in accord with the love of God. Jesus' life and then also his death happen for the good of God's beloved world.

Jesus' preexistence determines the gospel of John to a large extent. In impressive ways John 10 shows, through intertextual allusions to Ezekiel 34:11-16 and other texts such as Psalm 23, that Jesus is the Good Shepherd who has the well-being of his entire flock in view.[12] The metaphor of the Good Shepherd is adumbrated no further, however.[13] Jesus is the Good Shepherd who lays down his life for the sheep (John 10:11). It is not the wish of the shepherd to die, but the Good Shepherd's care for his sheep is limitless. Even the danger of his own death does not stop it. Death is not the meaning of his life.[14] He lives his life as an interpreter of God (cf. 1:18) in order to reveal the world as the beloved creation of God. He lives his life for the life of all who find themselves called by him into the unity of life with him and his Father (cf. 10:16).

The hallmark of this community is again nothing other than love (cf. John 13:34-35). It is the God-grounded bond among God, the Son, creation, and all who are obedient to the mission of the Son. It is impossible for death to sever this bond. The story of Lazarus sets the stage for this insight with its dialogue.

But it is precisely this insight that is barred to antagonists of the Johannine narrative. While the authority of the Son of God overcomes death, Jesus' opponents are in league with death. After the story of Lazarus in chapter 11, some of the eyewitnesses tell the Pharisees "what [Jesus] had done" (John 11:46). "So the chief priests and the Pharisees called a meeting of the council, and said, 'What are we to do? This man is performing many signs. If we let him go on like this, everyone will believe in him, and the Romans will come and destroy both our holy place and our nation.' But one of them . . . said to them, 'You know nothing at all! You do not understand that it is better for you to have one man die for the people than to have the whole nation destroyed'" (11:47-50).

Even Jesus' opponents can no longer contest the wondrous signs worked by Jesus, as they attempted to do after the healing of the man born blind (John 9:18ff.). Their concern is not for their people, however. They are much more afraid of the Romans taking their land and people from them when Jesus' triumphal entry occurs. The advice of Caiaphas, the high priest, is that it would thus be better to kill Jesus than to risk armed conflict with the occupiers, which would further weaken the powerful position of the high council. The narrator's commentary, on the other hand, refers the high priest's utterance wholly to the proexistence of Jesus, who, with his whole life and then also with his death for all people, lives ever more for the cosmos. In this sense Jesus gives his life for the well-being and salvation of God's beloved creation (cf. 11:51-52). "The concept of 'offering one's life' [*Lebenshingabe*] means the *entire existence* of Jesus, that is, that *life* that Jesus lived in loving devotion to others, *and* that *death* that was the consequence of this life."[15]

This self-offering of one's life is not the action of a tired hero who longs for death. It is wholly and totally determined by love: "No one has greater love than this, to lay down one's life for one's friends" (John 15:13). Because Jesus lived his life consistently, free of constraint (cf. 12:27), and because he knows fully the risks that result, he is himself the "light" of the word (cf. 12:46). His proexistence, which does not seek suffering, but which also does not flinch in the face of suffering in the course of living his life for others, is his glory. "In John 12:23, the 'hour' is announced in which the Son of Man shall be glorified. . . . The motif of the 'hour of Jesus' pervades the entire Gospel like a red thread (John 2:4; 4:21, 23; 5:25, 28; 7:30; 8:20; 13:1; 16:2, 4, 25, 32; 17:1 . . .). The hour of the death of Jesus is hereby meant . . . , which in any event cannot be regarded as a catastrophe but rather as the hour of 'glorification.'"[16]

In light of Jesus' proexistence, death loses its ultimate power and is even brought into the service of life: "Very truly, I tell you, unless a grain of wheat falls into the earth and dies, it remains just a single grain; but if it dies, it bears much fruit" (John 12:24). This parable can be read as a commentary on the last words of Jesus on the cross in the gospel of John's depiction: "It is finished" (19:30b). The violent cosmos has employed murder as the final weapon against life and it cannot win. Jesus' crucifixion bears much fruit, for the Spirit of his story shows the undisguised face of the cosmos as God's beloved creation. In light of his way, his truth, and his life, the terrifying cosmos is overcome by its spiritual [*geistreich*] revelation as the beloved creation and through that revelation is itself saved (cf. 12:47b). Through his way of life formed by love, Jesus conquers the world insofar as it shows itself to be not the creation formed by love but rather a place of tribulation (cf. 16:33).

Therefore, the Johannine Jesus can say of himself, "I am the way, and the truth, and the life. No one comes to the Father except through me" (John 14:6). "Whoever has seen me has seen the Father" (14:9). That holds not only for the disciples addressed in the narrative, but also for the readers of the gospel of John. Whoever reads the gospel of John spiritually [*geistreich*] as the story of the light sent by God, as the story of the Word of creation become flesh, whose way of proexistence is at the same time his glory, will see the Father as the merciful ground of all being, even of his own. In spite of all the dangers and injustices in this world, he will understand himself and the world from the perspective of the love of God.

The Authority of the Son

In the gospel of John, Jesus is no powerless victim of human or cosmic violence. He has authority, limitless authority, but out of love he refrains from using this power to annihilate his enemies (cf. John 18:11). As Jesus' way from the beginning of the gospel of John is shaped by his passion, in equal measure it is also shaped by his authority.

After Jesus' divine power became manifest, through his overwhelming knowledge, which surpassed all human possibilities (cf. John 1:43-51; 4:17ff.), and above all through his miraculous signs (cf. 2:1–12:23; 3:2; 4:43-54; 5:1-9), which were openly equated with the wonder-working power of God (5:17), "the Jews were seeking all the more to kill him, because he was not only breaking the sabbath, but was also calling God his own Father, thereby making himself equal to God" (5:18). The accusation of Jesus' opponents therefore touches on the identity of the narrative's protagonist, but they do not accept that Jesus marks himself as the Son of

God. They do not perceive that Jesus is truly the Son of the Father and as such one with God (cf. 10:30).

In John 5:19-47, Jesus reacts to this accusation by explaining his full divine authority. The authority of the Son therefore has its ground not in him himself, but rather in the authority of the Father. He shows the Son everything, and the unity between Father and Son, of which 10:30 expressly speaks, is grounded in the Son's doing that which the Father shows him (cf. 5:19-20).

The authority of the Son reaches as far as the authority of the Father. That includes the power to raise the dead: "Indeed, just as the Father raises the dead (ἐγείρει) and gives them life, so also the Son gives life (ζῳοποιεῖ) to whomever he wishes" (John 5:21). The parallel construction reveals that no terminological difference should be introduced. Even in the gospel of John the metaphorics of the resurrection can hardly be unlocked through verbal semantics.

More illuminating, on the other hand, is the syntagmatic compression of the theme of resurrection by means of thoughts about judgment. The eschatological judgment occurs already through the sending of the Son, but this judgment is not absorbed by it. The gospel of John compresses the times into one another without absorbing the future into the present. Whoever now confesses the Son sent by the Father "has eternal life, and does not come under judgment, but has passed from death to life" (John 5:24b). In this sense the Son has already done in an eschatological, effective, and living fashion that which will be revealed in the events of the final judgment. The Father "has given [the Son] authority to execute judgment, because he is the Son of Man. Do not be astonished at this; for the hour is coming when all who are in their graves will hear his voice and will come out—those who have done good, to the resurrection of life, and those who have done evil, to the resurrection of condemnation" (5:27-30).

The eschatological judgment takes place primarily at the end of the world, in which the dead are also involved. They are raised up for this. But it has already taken place for those who encounter the Son and therefore conduct themselves in a certain way with respect to him, be it by rejecting him or by praising his glory: "Very truly, I tell you, the hour is coming, and is now here, when the dead will hear the voice of the Son of God, and those who hear will live" (John 5:25). The dead who already hear the voice of the Son of God are, first, those whom Jesus healed in the course of the gospel of John and who lived again: the deathly ill son of the royal official (cf. 4:43-54) and even more Lazarus (cf. 11:1-44), and with them the deathly ill and revivified of the Synoptic Gospels, who play intertextual roles in the gospel of John through these stories.[17] They are above all, however, all the recipients of the Jesus-Christ-Story who see the glory of the Father and of the Son in the Word of the gospel. Reading the gospel of John thus becomes itself an apocalyptic-eschatological event, which decides the future of its readers and hearers, because judgment already occurs based on their rejection or acceptance, without, however, replacing the future of the futuristic-eschatological final judgment. Whoever finds himself already pulled by the Father to the Son through the logos of the gospel (cf. 6:44) can expect his own resurrection to eternal life with confidence: "And this is the will of him who sent me, that I should lose nothing of all that he has given me, but raise it up on the last day. This is indeed the will of my Father, that all who see the Son and believe in him may have eternal life; and I will raise them up on the last day" (6:39-40). Thus the gospel of John regards this faith not as a human achievement that brings salvation but rather as "the work of God" (ἔργον τοῦ θεοῦ; cf. 6:29b).

The authority of the son thematized in chapter 5 comes sufficiently into view first when the import of 5:26 is grasped: "For just as the Father has life in himself, so he has granted the Son also to have life in himself." Only God, the creative maker of everything, has life in himself. Therefore he can make life and also make the dead live. Only to the Son has God given the gift of inherent life. Only because he carries this divine life within himself can he be regarded as the one who was created before all things (cf. 8:58b).

Because he carries this life within himself as the gift of God, he can speak of his death and resurrection as follows: "For this reason the Father loves me, because I lay down my life in order to take it up again. No one takes it from me, but I lay it down of my own accord. I have power to lay it down, and I have power to take it up again. I have received this command from my Father" (John 10:17-18).

What the narrative depicts syntagmatically as a sequence is to be understood as an equiprimordial [*gleichurspruenglich*] event by means of the interpretive speeches. The man Jesus, raised from the dead by God, receives divine eternal life as a gift in the act of resurrection and through this gift receives a share in the all-encompassing and all-pervading life of God at all times. The Jesus who even interprets himself in the gospel of John thus interprets God and thus completes the task ascribed to him in the prologue (cf. John 1:18)

The Revivification of Lazarus as Sign of the Eschatological Resurrection

The revivification of Lazarus is the final sign that Jesus accomplishes before his execution.[18] All the miracles Jesus works in the gospel of John are retold as divine works exceeding all human possibility. These, however, have no meaning in and of themselves. Rather, they reveal the man Jesus to be the Son sent by God out of love for the salvation of the cosmos and especially for the salvation of the human race.

The sort of faith that grows out of the miraculous works of Jesus is not disparaged in the gospel of John. The first miraculous deed, the transformation of water into wine in John 2:1-10, is, without any irony, described in 2:11 as follows: "Jesus did this, the first of his signs, in Cana of Galilee, and revealed his glory; and his disciples believed in him." The second sign recounts the healing of the son of a royal official (4:43-54). It too leads to the official and his whole household having faith. Nowhere does the narrator criticize this sort of faith, produced as it was by witnessing a miracle (cf. 4:52-53). Following the third miracle story, the healing of a lame man at the pool of Bethesda (5:1-18), Jesus is persecuted because the healing took place on a Sabbath (cf. 5:16ff.). After the demonstration of his authority already thematized above, Jesus brings his miraculous signs forth without any distancing from it, as a witness to his divine sending: "But I have a testimony greater than John's. The works that the Father has given me to complete, the very works that I am doing, testify on my behalf that the Father has sent me" (5:36).

The reaction to the Feeding of the Five Thousand (John 6:1-15) is as follows: "When the people saw the sign that he had done, they began to say, 'This is indeed the prophet who is to come into the world'" (6:14). Here also Jesus does not criticize the conclusion arising from the miracle, but rather he evades the attempt of the crowd to install him as an earthly king. Jesus retreats immediately to the mountain and then walks his way upon the water to his disciples' boat, which had gone out ahead of him (6:16-21). In his "bread of life" discourse that follows (6:22-58) he criticizes not the faith issuing forth from the sign but rather the attitude of the crowd, oriented to material things (6:26).

It is precisely the miraculous signs of Jesus that prompt some from the people, and also the Pharisee Nicodemus, "a leader of the Jews" (John 3:1b), to recognize Jesus as the Christ, the Son sent by God (cf. 3:2; 7:31). Among some of the people, the healing of the man born blind leads to Jesus' desired reaction (9:16b, 33). The man who was healed himself says,

"'Lord, I believe.' And he worshiped him" (9:38). And finally, in the confrontation at the temple dedication, Jesus says to his opponents, "I have told you, and you do not believe. The works that I do in my Father's name testify to me; but you do not believe, because you do not belong to my sheep" (10:25-26). To the accusation that he is guilty of blasphemy because he makes himself out to be God (cf. 10:33), he responds, "If I am not doing the works of my Father, then do not believe me. But if I do them, even though you do not believe me, believe the works, so that you may know and understand that the Father is in me and I am in the Father" (10:37-38).

The miracles Jesus works as God's works are introduced in the course of the narrative as signs of his divine sending not only without any irony but also as means of generating faith. The narrator's commentary resumes in 20:30-31, directed squarely at the readers of the gospel: "Now Jesus did many other signs in the presence of his disciples, which are not written in this book. But these are written so that you may come to believe that Jesus is the Messiah, the Son of God, and that through believing you may have life in his name." Indeed, this commentary refers immediately to the stories of Jesus' resurrection appearances in chapter 20, but according to the material content the same can be said about the miraculous signs before the crucifixion. The gospel of John narrates Jesus' miracles as signs of his divine sending. It thereby seeks to awaken faith by means of its very inscripturation. This holds just as much for the resurrection of Jesus, which still remains to be discussed.

The revivification of Lazarus possesses especial significance as the last miracle before the passion of Jesus. This story confirms not only Jesus' claim made in his presentation of his authority in John 5:21: "Indeed, just as the Father raises the dead and gives them life, so also the Son gives life to whomever he wishes." By way of Jesus' miraculous actions, chapter 11 presents a telescoping of the eschatological resurrection of the dead, as the Pharisees and probably also the majority of Jews at the time of Jesus expected it to happen. The sequence of these miraculous events reaches its apex in the following words: "I am the resurrection and the life. Those who believe in me, even though they die, will live, and everyone who lives and believes in me will never die" (11:25-26). And finally the story of Lazarus foreshadows the death and resurrection of Jesus.

The opening of the Lazarus story already shows that Jesus wishes to employ the revivification of Lazarus as a sign of his divine Sonship in order to awaken faith. Lazarus falls ill, and his sisters Mary and Martha inform Jesus about it. The numerous intratextual connections with other stories in the gospel of John, as well as the intertextual references to the

Synoptic Gospels, indicate the rich and complex layers of meaning that are present in the Lazarus story.[19]

Jesus' reaction to the message prefigures the significance of the entire event: "This illness does not lead to death; rather it is for God's glory, so that the Son of God may be glorified through it" (John 11:4). The narrator's commentary that follows, however, guards against the potential misunderstandings that Jesus used Lazarus and that the fear and sorrow of Mary and Martha for their brother were no concern of his. Rather, as 11:5 reads, "Jesus loved Martha and her sister and Lazarus." The following event would be repulsive if this statement were ignored. Jesus is in solidarity with the sorrowful sisters in this story. He lets things run their course only because he has the foreknowledge that Lazarus' sickness will not end in death. Indeed, it will contribute to the marking of his glory, which will awaken faith.

Only after two days does he depart for Judea, although he made his disciples aware of the danger that he risked in going there (cf. John 11:6-10). Jesus replied to his disciples, "Our friend Lazarus has fallen asleep, but I am going there to awaken (ἐξυπνίσω) him." The double metaphor of this saying escapes the disciples and they misunderstand Lazarus' sleep as the sleep that restores health (11:12-13). And indeed Jesus abandons metaphorical speech and explains to them that the death of Lazarus is cause for joy: "Lazarus is dead. For your sake I am glad I was not there, so that you may believe. But let us go to him" (11:14b-15). The reaction of the disciples, verbalized by Thomas, leaves no trace of Jesus' joy and demonstrates that even the disciples are not yet filled with the fullness of faith, which would permit them to recognize the whole glory of Jesus without signs. Rather, they simply see that Jesus is in danger of death, but also that they themselves are too. If they go to Judea and again expose themselves to the danger of conflict with Jesus' opponents (cf. 11:16), they might be killed.

Verse 17 tells of the arrival of Jesus and challenges Jesus' words that Lazarus' sickness would not be unto death with the fact that Lazarus has already been in the tomb for four days. Jesus' words in 11:4b and the fact of the corpse in the tomb represent a contradiction that human possibility cannot overcome. The progress of the narrative, however, resolves this tension in the highest dramatic fashion.

That Bethany is only a half hour's distance from Jerusalem makes plausible the statement in verse 19 that many of the Jews from even Jerusalem had come to visit Mary and Martha to mourn with them. The miracle thus takes place before the citizens of Jerusalem. The event is visible to all those present.

Martha pulls Jesus aside, alone. Mary remains with the mourners. Martha then expresses her conviction that Jesus could have healed Lazarus had he been there. As her speech progresses, however, the supposed accusation becomes a plea expressing her boundless confidence in the total power of Jesus: "But even now I know that God will give you whatever you ask of him" (John 11:22). Jesus' answer announces the fulfillment of Martha's implicit request: "Your brother will rise again (ἀναστήσεται)" (11:23b). Martha now mentions what was for her, Jesus, the Pharisees, and probably most Jews the shared and uncontroverted eschatological knowledge, which, as such, would not touch on her implicit request: "I know that he will rise again in the resurrection on the last day" (11:24). Jesus' answer does not yet address Martha's implicit request, that Jesus might yet revivify Lazarus by the power of God. Rather, Jesus' answer confronts the futuristic-eschatological expectation of the resurrection of the dead on judgment day with his own apocalyptic-eschatological identity: "I am the resurrection and the life. Those who believe in me, even though they die, will live, and everyone who lives and believes in me will never die. Do you believe this?" (11:25-26).

Jesus' self-predication as the resurrection and the life does not reduce the Jewish futuristic-eschatological hope in the resurrection to a spiritually narrowed presentist eschatology. Such a notion would have nothing more to do with the cumbersome materiality of a corpse. The Johannine theology of resurrection does not amount to a new self-understanding, although it naturally also aims at it. The Johannine Jesus can predicate himself as the resurrection and the life because he is marked in his entirety as the resurrected Crucified One whose bloody body stops every dematerializing, spiritualizing evacuation cold in its tracks. He *is* the resurrection and the life because his presence, which the gospel of John itself signifies, is wholly determined by loving creative power, by the very life of God. Jesus is the resurrection because one can speak of him truly only as the resurrected Crucified One, whose resurrection and divine life are offered to all who let themselves be shown God and the world anew by the Spirit of the Jesus-Christ-Story. Whoever perceives the murdered Jesus as the resurrected Crucified One will find that the futuristic hope in the resurrection of the dead, and thus also the hope for one's own resurrection, makes sense. Such a one will also find at the same time that this future reaches into the present of one's life, and permits the world, one's fellow men, and oneself to be seen as beloved and saved creatures of the merciful creator.

The ground of Martha's "yes" is to be understood in this connection: "Yes, Lord, I believe that you are the Messiah, the Son of God, the one coming into the world" (John 11:27). Jesus' self-predication as the resurrection and the life as well as his marking as Christ and as the Son of God come into the world interpret each other mutually.

Then Martha brings Mary into play and with her the entire company of mourners. Mary falls crying at Jesus' feet, and although she speaks the same words as Martha spoke at the outset, she formulates the exact same accusation that Martha transformed into a confident request: "Lord, if you had been here, my brother would not have died" (11:32b). Jesus reacts fiercely to this accusation (cf. 11:33, 37-38) and goes to the tomb. He has the stone rolled away from the tomb. The doubts now rising also in Martha once again function to reinforce the difficulty of Jesus' task: "Lord, already there is a stench because he has been dead four days" (11:39). But Jesus reminds her of his promise: "Did I not tell you that if you believed, you would see the glory of God?" (11:40). Then Jesus directs his eyes to the heavens to make visible contact with his Father and speaks an explanatory prayer of thanksgiving: "Father, I thank you for having heard me. I knew that you always hear me, but I have said this for the sake of the crowd standing here, so that they may believe that you sent me" (11:41b-42). For Jesus, therefore, neither words nor eye contact with heaven would have been necessary, but he wants to demonstrate to those present that his power, which will presently effect the unbelievable, is the power of God working through him. With this demonstration it is shown that Jesus is the Christ, the Son of God, sent by God.

It is precisely that, however, which is the declared goal of the gospel of John's entire presentation. The gospel as a whole and especially with the miracle stories wants to paint a picture of the murdered Jesus as the Word of God become flesh by virtue of his resurrection. The signs of the gospel bear witness to that by representing him. The gospel's intention is congruent with the intention of the miraculous actions of its protagonist. This intention finds its exemplary recipients in 11:45: "Many of the Jews therefore, who had come with Mary and had seen what Jesus did, believed in him."

The Sign of the Resurrection and the Sign of the Resurrected One

Like the Synoptic Gospels, the gospel of John leaves no doubt that Jesus died on the cross (John 19:30b). But like Luke, over against Mark, John also changes the last words of Jesus on the cross. In John's presentation the dying Jesus says immediately before his death, "It is finished (τετέλεσται)." With his death on the cross what the Scriptures predicted is also fulfilled, which is pointed out several times (cf. 19:24, 28, 36-37). His way of suffering has come to its end with his death, but not the Jesus-Christ-Story, as the gospel of John narrates it. The eschatological power of the Jesus-Christ-Story, which overcomes the threatened and thus threatening the distance of the cosmos from God, is grounded in the conviction that the crucifixion is not the final word. And thus the implied author steps out from his hiding place after his depiction of Jesus' death. He turns to the readers in order to bring before their attention the conviction that the gospel of John continues the ranks of witnesses that began with John the Baptist in the prologue. He testifies that after Jesus' death at the hands of the soldiers, none of his bones were broken, unlike the others. Rather, they pierced his side with a lance and "blood and water" came out (19:34b). However one might interpret this symbolism,[20] it is in any case clear that the progression of the narrative after Jesus' death expresses something unusual that does not correspond to the experience of this world.

Jesus is buried by Joseph of Arimathea and Nicodemus in an unused tomb. He is already embalmed and wrapped in linen. Everything happens "according to the burial custom of the Jews" (John 19:40c). Mary Magdalene goes to the tomb very early on the first day of the week, alone, and—in contrast to the women in the Synoptic Gospels—without any intention of anointing Jesus, for that was already taken care of at the burial. She "saw that the stone had been removed from the tomb" (20:1c). She did not enter the grave, for she is spontaneously convinced that Jesus' corpse was stolen. In spite of all of Jesus' proclamations, in spite of the sign of the revivification of Lazarus, Mary Magdalene thinks and acts wholly in accord with the logic of death.[21] The tomb is opened, the dead cannot themselves open tombs, and thus others must have opened it to make away with Jesus' corpse.

She runs in her perplexed rage "to Simon Peter and the other disciple, the one whom Jesus loved, and said to them, 'They have taken the Lord out of the tomb, and we do not know where they have laid him'" (John 20:2). Both disciples run to the tomb, and the one whom Jesus loved arrives first, looks into the tomb without entering it, and sees the linen wrappings. Simon Peter enters the tomb, also sees the linen wrappings, as well as the cloth that had been wrapped around Jesus' head, lying in another place in the tomb. Now the first disciple to arrive also enters the tomb, sees, and believes (20:10). The narrator's commentary explains why they did not immediately understand what had happened: "for as yet they did not understand the scripture, that he must rise from the dead" (20:9). For the gospel of John, the Scriptures are the condition for understanding the resurrection of the Crucified One. It therefore makes sense that its prologue begins with the intertextual reference to the very beginning of the Scriptures.

While both disciples are in the tomb, Mary Magdalene weeps before the tomb. While weeping, "she bent over to look into the tomb" and sees not the disciples but rather "two angels in white, sitting" (cf. John 20:11-12). The angels say to her, "Woman, why are you weeping?" Although she sees the empty tomb, although she can even see the linen wrappings, although she is addressed by two angels from the tomb, she still thinks according to the logic of death: "They have taken away my Lord, and I do not know where they have laid him" (20:13).

While she is saying this, she turns around and sees Jesus but does not recognize him. Rather, she thinks he is the gardener and perhaps even one of those who has made off with the corpse of Jesus. Therefore she addresses him as follows: "Sir, if you have carried him away, tell me where you have laid him, and I will take him away" (20:15b). The body of the resurrected Crucified One is no longer a dead corpse, but also something other than what it was prior to the resurrection. When Mary turns away from the tomb, she sees the Resurrected One and when she hears the voice calling her by name she recognizes him as the resurrected crucified one. She answers him in Hebrew, calling him "'Rabbouni!' (which means Teacher)" (20:17). The resurrected Crucified One then speaks to her as a teacher and charges her: "Do not hold on to me, because I have not yet ascended to the Father. But go to my brothers and say to them, 'I am ascending to my Father and your Father, to my God and your God'" (20:17). Mary complies with the commission, finally departs from the tomb, and informs the disciples, whose reaction is not recounted, however. The empty tomb is no unmistakable proof of the resurrection of the Crucified One, but rather an eerie place of misunderstanding.

On the evening of the same day, Jesus comes through the locked doors, shows himself to his disciples, and speaks to them: "Peace be with you" (John 20:19). His resurrected body no longer obeys the laws of space and time. After showing them the scars that remain, the disciples are overjoyed, for now they recognize their Lord (20:20). Jesus once more wishes them peace and charges them, "As the Father has sent me, so I send you" (20:21b). The disciples need power for their sending, for their way will be accompanied by conflict and suffering. They too are entering into a way of life that demands their lives under the sign of love. The resurrected Crucified One breathes upon them, giving them the promised power of the Holy Spirit (cf. 20:22) and gives them full authority to forgive sins (20:23).

In this scene Thomas, "who was called the Twin" (John 20:24), is absent. He cannot believe the disciples' report, but rather demands, "Unless I see the mark of the nails in his hands, and put my finger in the mark of the nails and my hand in his side, I will not believe" (20:25b). In any event Thomas must live with his uncertainty for eight days, for after eight days Jesus comes again to his disciples through locked doors (cf. 20:26). He invites Thomas to do what Thomas demanded and to believe, not to be the unbelieving one (20:27). Without touching him to prove the matter, however, Thomas responds, "My Lord and my God!" (20:28). "Jesus said to him, 'Have you believed because you have seen me? Blessed are those who have not seen and yet have come to believe'" (20:29).

This Thomas has unjustly been named "Doubting Thomas," for (with one exception) like all the other disciples he comes to faith by seeing the resurrected Crucified One and by hearing his voice. Only the disciple whom Jesus loved believed without seeing the resurrected Crucified One and without understanding from the Scriptures that Jesus must be raised (John 20:8c). The conclusion of the gospel, which necessarily belongs to the entire gospel (cf. 21:24-25), identifies this individual who believes without visual proof as the author of the gospel and as an example for all believers.

The gospel of John would therefore have itself read as a witness of those who believe without seeing. Its witness, however, becomes a sign of the resurrection of the Crucified One, which portrays the signs of the resurrected Crucified One before its readers eyes in order to enable them to come to common faith (cf. John 20:31). The disciple who believed without seeing becomes a guarantor of that seeing that the gospel of John communicates. It invites one to a faith that experiences the absence of Jesus' corpse no longer as a fear-generating catastrophe (cf. 20:11-14) but rather as the unavailability of Jesus Christ killed and raised. This latter point is an essential characteristic of his exaltation:

> The Johannine Christ manifests himself where and when he will (vv. 20, 26). He is no longer subject to the contingency of historical existence. This narrative line of unavailability expresses the *new identity* of the Christ who has returned to the Father. Certainly the resurrected one is none other than the crucified one—as the scene with Thomas shows, the marks of crucifixion are the only signs which identify the Lord— the resurrected one lives as the crucified one, but no longer as a historical human being. The disciples are invited to this Christ, who in spite of their familiarity with him has become another, who lives with God and is unavailable in the world (v. 17), in order to establish a new relationship.[22]

Real readers of the gospel of John are invited to this perspective of faith along with the disciples. By showing the unavailability of the resurrected

Crucified One as his victory over the violence and the deadly threat of the cosmos at its remove from God, the gospel of John invites one to a confident faith that supplies those who so believe with the power, as children of God, to learn to see anew (cf. John 1:12) and to find themselves thus already receiving consolation in communion with the resurrected Crucified One, of whom the gospel tells.

The Gospel of John's Consolation

The resurrected Crucified One shows himself to his disciples a third time (cf. John 21:1). Again they fail to recognize him (cf. 21:4). It is right after they catch an amazing amount of fish at Jesus' instruction that Peter concludes, "It is the Lord!" (21:7b). Even the breathing in of the Holy Spirit (cf. 20:22) does not give them the capability to recognize the resurrected Crucified One in his resurrected form.

Jesus prepares a meal for them and gives them bread and fish without himself eating (cf. John 21:12-13). After the meal he asks Peter three times whether he loves him and entrusts his sheep to him. The resurrected crucified one prophesies Peter's death to him and finally calls him to follow him (21:18-19). Peter then asks him about the fate of the disciple "whom Jesus loved" (21:20). Jesus answers, "If it is my will that he remain until I come, what is that to you?" The answer then precipitates a misunderstanding among the disciples that "this disciple would not die" (21:23a). The narrator's commentary, however, declares, "Yet Jesus did not say to him that he would not die, but, 'If it is my will that he remain until I come, what is that to you?'" (21:23b). The interpretation of the saying "this disciple would not die" is rejected. The blowing in of the Holy Spirit does not protect the disciples from misunderstanding the Resurrected One's words. Only the narrator of the gospel knows that it is indeed a misunderstanding, although he offers no interpretation of his own, simply repeating Jesus' saying.

The conclusion of the gospel identifies the narrator of the Jesus-Christ-Story as the disciple whom Jesus loved, who believed at the tomb without seeing the Resurrected One, and to whom will fall the special fate of remaining until the resurrected Crucified One comes again. There cannot be a more trustworthy author for relating what has been told (cf. 21:24). Writing further gospels would therefore be totally useless (cf. 21:25).[23]

Every reading of the gospel of John confirms Jesus' prophecy: The narrator of the gospel abides. He is present in every reading, even if its author lies long dead. And what remains with this conclusion of the gospel is the expectation of the return of the resurrected Crucified One.

The resurrection appearances in the gospel of John in the two concluding chapters clarify that the resurrected Crucified One gave his disciples the gift of the Spirit, but this Spirit will protect them neither from suffering nor from misunderstanding. The true witness, who alone remains, is the narrator of the gospel. He does not remain, however, because he does not die. Rather, he remains as the narrator of the gospel, as an actor in this gospel and as the guarantor of the truth of the gospel. The gospel of John would have itself read as the reliable, authenticated sign that tells the Jesus-Christ-Story and thus stands for the absent Son in a representative manner. Whoever sees the Son with the help of this gospel, however, sees the Father, and whoever lets himself see the cosmos as the beloved creation of God, in confidence and faith in the Spirit of this narrative, will be taken up into the communion of the Father and the Son. Such a one thus already has a share in the bond of divine love and indeed lives even if he dies, and will not remain in death but rather will be raised by the Son on judgment day.

The gospel of John itself takes over the function of the Paraclete, which Jesus, as depicted in the gospel, has promised: "I have said these things to you while I am still with you. But the Advocate, the Holy Spirit, whom the Father will send in my name, will teach you everything, and remind you of all that I have said to you" (John 14:25-26). The Spirit of the Jesus-Christ-Story that the gospel tells provides effective consolation. The Spirit is the one who gives readers new birth and teaches them to see the kingdom of God in spiritual ways (cf. 3:3-8) and empowers them to be called children of God thereby (cf. 1:12-13). The Spirit does not pull a veil over the dangers, the violence, the brutality of a world that does not understand itself as God's beloved creation. The Spirit also does not make its receivers infallible, understanding and knowing everything. Rather, its consolation consists much more in its vision of Jesus' way of life—which is also no longer limited by death—as the victory of creative love over the obsessively brutal distance from God, and calls all to see by this vision of things.

Whoever hears this call will thankfully and confidently look into the face of his fellow creatures and see also in his own mirror one of God's beloved and saved people. The Paraclete bestows effective consolation upon him who sees anew and also expects his own resurrection, grounded in the creative love of God, which in Jesus' story has shown itself stronger than death.

The Letters of John

The letters of John further the gospel of John's intertextually oriented theological work of interpretation. Their concern is to define the Spirit of the Jesus-Christ-Story, as the gospel of John tells it, as the Spirit of truth. This Spirit stands against other spirits that do not spring up from the ground of the gospel of John. The letters seek to challenge their readers to remain in the love of God revealed in the Jesus-Christ-Story.

While 1 John is most likely an epistolary tractate, with 2 and 3 John we are dealing with real letters. Their common concern of remaining in the creative love of God, to which the gospel of John testifies, demonstrates at the same time that even the Johannine community was no conflict-free zone of love, but rather that the interpretation of the Jesus-Christ-Story was disputed. While 1 John assumes the gospel of John as a well-known point of reference for its argumentation, 2 John refers to 1 John and 3 John refers to 2 John.[24]

First John offers a clear criterion for discerning the spirits. When discussing this criterion 1 John 1:1-4 already plays intertextually with the prologue of the gospel, and claims the authority to judge every interpretation of the Jesus-Christ-Story. The criterion is this: "By this you know the Spirit of God: every spirit that confesses that Jesus Christ has come in the flesh is from God" (1 John 4:2). This criterion is then mentioned again in 2 John 7.

On this basis the meaning of the incarnation is signified. The love of God can be perceived in the Son's way of life, oriented as it was to the love of God, who steadily went his way to death: "We know love by this, that he laid down his life for us—and we ought to lay down our lives for one another" (1 John 3:16). This love is so very much the love of God that it must be understood as a predicate of God: "God is love" (1 John 4:8b). God sent his Son into the world out of love in order to save it.

From this love, grounded in God and flowing out from him, all who experience and conduct themselves as God's beloved receive the gift of life and at the same time find forgiveness of their sins, understood as failures of love: "God's love was revealed among us in this way: God sent his only Son into the world so that we might live through him. In this is love, not that we loved God but that he loved us and sent his Son to be the atoning sacrifice for our sins" (1 John 4:9-10).

The letters of John refuse reduction to a presentist eschatology. In the Spirit-effected, unifying bond of love, which always occurs as the love of God, the Johannine community experiences itself as the real effect of the same creative love that was also effective in Jesus' way of life and that also overcame his death. They are the "fruit" of his death and his resurrection (cf. John 12:24). The community created by this love is the eschatological work of the Father, and of the Son, and of their Holy Spirit. Therefore only those who remain in this love are the children of God, recognizable in their faith in the resurrected crucified one and in their love truly lived: "And this is his commandment, that we should believe in the name of his Son Jesus Christ and love one another, just as he has commanded us" (1 John 3:23).

These who love, being beloved by God, have already "passed from death to life," for the love of God is creative, effective, reality-creating love. "Whoever does not love abides in death" (1 John 3:14). The community must remain in this love and life, however, for the community of love experienced in the here and now transcends its present existence.

Just as the body of the resurrected Crucified One became another no longer bound to the limits of space and time, so will the community of love now also be conformed to the resurrected Crucified One: "Beloved, we are God's children now; what we will be has not yet been revealed. What we do know is this: when he is revealed, we will be like him, for we will see him as he is" (1 John 3:2).

Spiritual [*geistreich*] seeing sees everything in order to be certain that God's creative love and his creative Spirit will not abandon God's children to death. Rather, the Spirit will create them anew in wondrous ways just like the resurrected Crucified One. How the form of the new creature will appear, however, remains hidden even to spiritual seeing until "the firstborn of the dead" (Rev 1:5b) returns.

The Revelation to John

While the gospel of John presents the life and death of the human Jesus from the perspective of the resurrection of the Crucified One and thus reveals the threatening cosmos as the good creation of God in a new way, the Revelation to John addresses the present[25] threats to the communities in Asia Minor. It also addresses their final victory through the power of the resurrected and raised Crucified One on the common basis of their conviction of the cosmological power of the resurrection of the Crucified One. His testimony for God is the model of their suffering, and as the eschatological victor over every affliction the resurrected and exalted Crucified One is at the same time the ground of their own hope for resurrection to a new, untroubled life in communion with God and Jesus Christ.

With this soteriologically and cosmologically oriented Christology, the Revelation to John as a prophetic book like the gospel takes up the paracletic function of effective consolation. Its prophetic encouragement says that neither affliction, nor suffering, nor violent death shall have the final word, but rather God and his new creation, "for the Lamb at the center of the throne will be their shepherd, and he will guide them to springs of the water of life, and God will wipe away every tear from their eyes" (Rev 7:17).

That the Revelation to John comes not from the quill of the author of the gospel of John can likely be regarded as an assured scholarly conclusion, for the linguistic and stylistic peculiarities of the two writings simply differ to too great a degree. Jörg Frey[26] has identified significant commonalities among the gospel of John, the letters of John, and the Revelation to John, however, which point to a common encyclopedic horizon, which probably can be located in Asia Minor on the basis of the sending of the Revelation to John into Asia Minor. The soteriological interest in the eschatological-cosmological dimensions of the resurrection of the Crucified One stands out as a common concern of the Johannine writings precisely when one considers the question of resurrection discourse.

The Revelation to John was a severely contested writing already in the time of the ancient Church. Its canonical status was precarious until well into the tenth century, especially in the Eastern Church. It is precisely this writing, however, that shapes the enduring conception of the resurrection of the dead and their destiny in heaven and hell in Christianity. "Until the Enlightenment of the eighteenth century, it was the most beloved, most read, most illustrated book of the Bible; its influence upon the Christian conception of the beyond (heaven; hell) as well as upon ecclesial art and architecture . . . cannot be estimated highly enough."[27]

The Contract for Reading the Proemium

Before the Revelation to John presents itself in 1:4 as a letter to the seven churches in the Roman province of Asia, the first three verses install a reading contract [*Lektürevertrag*] that transcends this particular epistolary communication situation. The reader of the Apocalypse and its hearers are pronounced blessed for keeping what they hear and aligning their lives with it. The words read aloud are designated as "words of the prophecy" (1:3). What they contain is designated as the "revelation of Jesus Christ" in verse 1. Jesus Christ himself has received this from God, so that he can show those who serve him what will and must soon happen. This revelation was disclosed to John through an angel. Verse 2 designates John as the one who testified to the Word of God and the witness of Jesus Christ precisely as he saw it. It is nothing other than the living nature and effectual power of the crucified, raised and exalted Jesus Christ, whose story the Revelation to John assumes is known. The readers and hearers read and hear what John wrote down as that which it claims in the first two lines to be, and thus at the same time confirm the testimony of John and count themselves in the ranks of witnesses.

The reading contract proves to be a reciprocal recognition of the readers and the author of the writing, to which every reader and hearer in all times and places can agree. In this way the Revelation to John is in the final analysis identified as a prophecy proceeding from God. This reading contract, open to all readers, breaks the boundaries of the epistolary reading situation between John and the churches he addresses, set in place from 1:4. It thus opens the book up for an undetermined, much broader readership.

The text first introduces the epistolary communication in 1:4, which in 1:4-20 presents an introductory address to the seven churches in Asia Minor and then in 2:1–3:22 presents seven localized open letters. Each letter is indeed addressed to a church, but through the letters' integration into the document as a whole each letter is also made accessible to every church. The reader finds a transition in 4:1, which introduces the actual book of visions, in which John has inscribed his ethereal visions according to his commission. This book too is a component part of the letter introduced in 1:4, which ends only with the final verse of the writing (22:21). Thus the Revelation to John can collectively be designated as a letter[28] to the churches in Asia Minor, a letter that contains a book of visions in itself, whose readership, however, is delimited by the prior proemium.[29]

The proemium thus provides the reading of the Revelation to John with several parameters:

- The text should be read as a prophetic writing, which was indeed written down by a man named John at a particular point in time in earthly history. According to the text, however, the content derives from God and thus claims the highest authority.
- The text presents itself as a letter written first and foremost at a particular point in time in earthly history to the churches in Asia Minor, but it is also a book of prophetic words that ultimately derive from God. Thus the text is directed to an unlimited readership from the middle of the proemium on.
- The text provides not only a share in the knowledge of John about the near future (1:3c), but also prophetic words aimed at the conduct of the recipients.

- The intended conduct is already outlined by the semantics of witness, which verbally (ἐμαρτύρησεν) refer to John and substantively (μαρτυρία) refer to Jesus Christ, and by the demand to keep the prophetic words. It involves remaining a witness to the resurrected and powerfully exalted crucified Jesus Christ, even while accepting conflicts marked by suffering, and thus giving God honor.[30]

The Resurrection and Exaltation of the Crucified One as a Theological Basis

The proemium (Rev 1:4-8) of the introductory letter (1:4-20), directed to the seven churches in Asia Minor, outlines in a compressed manner the connections among the theology, pneumatology, Christology, and soteriology of the Revelation to John and thus designates the cornerstones that lend the argumentation, visions, and stories of the book plausibility.

John first identifies himself as the sender of the letter in a most modest manner without any title or further designation but only with his proper name. He then names his addressees very soberly, solely as "the seven churches that are in Asia" (Rev 1:4), without any *captatio benevolentiae*. The accompanying tripartite wish of grace and peace then designates God, "the seven spirits," and Jesus Christ as the givers of grace and peace.

In an instance of syntax that breaks grammatical rules, God is designated first and foremost as the one "who is and who was and who is to come," the word "God" lacks explicit mention (Rev 1:4c). In an instructive contribution to the language of the Revelation to John, Traugott Holtz presents the thesis that the violations of the rules of grammar do not point to a lack of linguistic competence on the part of the author of the Apocalypse. Rather, the language itself is used metaphorically in a highly reflective way, which brings to expression the inadequacy of human language to designate God.[31] In any case, the syntagm that is repeated in Revelation 1:8 and introduced with the phrase, "I am the Alpha and the Omega, says the Lord God," refers to the creative, encompassing for all time, power of God who then at the end of verse 8 is also titled comprehensively as the ruler of all (παντοκράτωρ).

The God of the Revelation to John is the powerful creator God, who encompasses all time and rules everything (cf. Rev 1:8, 4:11). His power is limitless and precisely therein is founded the hope for the ultimate victory over the limited but nevertheless dreadful havoc-wreaking power of evil. The God of the Revelation to John is a cosmological *Pantokrator* whose power knows no bounds. The plausibility of the talk of the resurrection in the Revelation to John lies grounded in this unlimited power of the creator. The final writing of the New Testament permits no god to be compared with this creator and permits not even one opponent to stand independent of him, in spite of the numerous powers of evil, which the Revelation to John depicts in drastic visions. The Pantokrator allows no dualistic theology, as some gnostic systems would have it. Even the destroyers ultimately receive their power from God (cf., e.g., 13:15).

The Pantokrator is, however, none other than the wonderfully creative creator God of Israel (cf. Rev 4:11), whose works of creation in 15:3 are sung with the "song of Moses," which is at the same time the "song of the Lamb." Although the Revelation to John employs no direct citations of the Holy Scriptures of Israel, it is intertextually bound up with them inseparably.[32]

The "seven spirits who are before his throne" (Rev 1:4d) are closely connected through their ordering with God and his witness Jesus Christ. In the throne vision in chapter 4 they are depicted as the seven "torches" burning before the throne of God (cf. 4:5) and in 3:1 the seven spirits belong to the exalted Christ.

The syntagm "Spirit of God" is found in the Revelation to John just as little as the syntagm "Spirit of Christ." If, however, the seven spirits are expressly embedded in the proemium with God and with Jesus Christ and are identified together with them as those who offer grace and peace , then this prominent role in connection with its semantic underdetermination encourages one to understand them as working in every way and manner as the "Spirit of God," and also as the "Spirit of Christ."

This interpretation is suggested through the use of the absolute singular "the Spirit," which is always encountered as the closing of the individual letters to the seven churches in the form: "Let anyone who has an ear listen to what the Spirit is saying to the churches" (Rev 2:7, 11, 17, 29; 3:6, 13, 22). In 3:1b the seven spirits belong to the speaker of the letters, the exalted Jesus Christ. The seven spirits are thus the way with which God (or Christ) communes with his churches and effectively communicates grace and peace to them.

Finally one finds several genitive constructions in the singular as well as in the plural, such as "spirit of life" and "spirit of prophecy," or "spirits of the prophets" but also "spirits of demons." The significance of the Spirit who works in various and different ways and who takes up his visionary place as the sevenfold burning torch before the throne of God is well summarized by Ferdinand Hahn:

> The reality of the Spirit, proceeding from God himself, in which the heavenly Christ participates, is, as the power of creation and new creation, the condition for the salvific work of the Exalted One, communicated through the prophets. The living

power of salvation, grounded in the death, resurrection and exaltation, is experienced in the full power of the prophetic witnesses.[33]

The christological expressions in Revelation 1:5-6 are also inscribed in this soteriological connection of creation and new creation. Jesus Christ is designated first and foremost as "the faithful witness" (ὁ μάρτυς ὁ πιστός). Thus the "testimony (μαρτυρία) of Jesus Christ" from verse 2 is taken up again and strengthened. Jesus Christ is the witness of God par excellence. His witness was and is without limit and no power could or can hinder him from laying aside the absolutely valid and therefore convincing testimony about God, the creator and ruler of all. His true and effective witness, in which he took upon himself suffering to the point of death on a cross (cf. 1:7b, 11:8b), is the paradigm for all who like John make themselves servants of the resurrected Crucified One in his domain and thus become witnesses themselves (cf. 1:2).

This witness does not protect one from suffering and death. Jesus Christ, the "faithful and true witness" (Rev 3:14b), was cruelly killed (cf. 1:7b). But the power of the violence directed at him did not have the final word. The "pierced" witness (cf. 1:7b), the lamb who was slain (cf. 5:6), received from God, the Pantokrator, new life given by God's creative Spirit and also power that overcomes all earthly rulers. As the Resurrected One, he who was killed by earthly kingdoms is established "the ruler of the kings of the earth" (1:5).

Because the witness who was killed, Jesus Christ, is the "firstborn of the dead" (Rev 1:5), he is at the same time himself the testimony to God's unlimited creative power. He therefore gives all following witnesses confidence, that their testimony, even when it leads to death, is true. The witnesses themselves are not ultimately devoured by the power of death, but rather receive new life through the Spirit of God (cf. 11:11). The proemium presents Jesus Christ as God's witness who was killed, raised, and exalted. He is the paradigm for all witnesses who follow him. This complex of death, resurrection, and power offers effective consolation as well as the hermeneutical key for the interpretation of the suffering of those who have given themselves over to discipleship but who in that discipleship also experience violence and disaster. "As firstborn 'of the dead' Christ vouches for and guarantees the future resurrection of believers."[34] In being a disciple of Jesus Christ, the complex of witness, suffering, and participation in the power of God becomes a model of every one's world- and self-understanding.

Because this salvific complex has come about via the fate of Jesus, who can be communicated through the witness of this complex, his death has redemptive power. The witness to God that Jesus Christ himself has provided, in his life and death, becomes through his witnessalso a witness to the resurrection and exaltation of other faithful and true witnesses, a witness to which his followers testify.

What Paul expresses with the syntagm "word of the cross" (1 Cor 1:18; NRSV: "the message about the cross"), the Revelation to John designates as "the witness of Jesus Christ" (cf. Rev 1:2, 9). In spite of the diversity of theological approaches and ways of thinking, the phrases come together in this: that the eschatological complex of the events of Jesus' death, resurrection, and exaltation, which lays a new foundation, unfolds its soteriological power through the Word that testifies spiritually to this event. The relationship between the first witness and his followers that comes about through this is to be understood as a relationship of ruler to ruled. This relationship is not marked by the violent exercise of power, however, but rather by the love that the new ruler feels toward his own, and even his making of them "kings and priests" (1:6). The new ruler loves his own and gives them a share in his power.

At the time of the composition of the Revelation to John, however, the crucified, resurrected, and exalted witness to God has not yet become visible to all. The "kings of the earth" still exercise their violence, but he will come soon: "Look! He is coming with the clouds; every eye will see him, even those who pierced him; and on his account all the tribes of the earth will wail. So it is to be. Amen" (Rev 1:7). The time of composition is a paradoxical in-between time. The resurrected Crucified One is already ruler over the kings of the earth, but they still exercise their dominion of violence. Those who bear witness to Jesus Christ are already "kings and priests before God" (1:6), but they still endure the violence of the "kings of the earth" (1:5). God, the ruler of all, himself guarantees that the hope for the speedy coming of Jesus Christ and the concomitant hope for the end of injustice and the beginning of the indestructible new life is no cheap empty promise but rather God's potent comfort: "'I am the Alpha and the Omega,' says the Lord God, who is and who was and who is to come, the Almighty" (1:8).

The Persecution of John, the Persecution of the Churches, and Endurance in Jesus

The witness of John, which was already introduced in Revelation 1:2 as an essential identity marker, is made concrete in 1:9. John finds himself in grievous trouble (θλῖψις) on the island of Patmos, "because of the word of

God and the testimony of Jesus" (1:9). But trouble is not the only characteristic of his situation. He is at the same time much more a member in the kingdom of God and in "endurance in Jesus." He characterizes himself in precisely this way when writing to the "brothers" in Asia Minor. "The series of concepts is noteworthy. The suffering Christians already have a share in God's rule."[35] Their communal sharing in the kingdom of God does not protect them from grievous oppression. They can persevere in this paradoxical situation only "in the endurance of Jesus." This endurance of Jesus is, however, nothing other than the persistence with which Jesus went his way of witness to the cross, as the gospel of John tells it. In the same way God has answered the faithfulness and perseverance of his witness Jesus with his resurrection from the dead, so Jesus' followers in their witness can also hope in confidence that they will receive new life as a gift from God. The resurrection of the Crucified One is a paradigm for them and a hermeneutical key for the meaning of their own experiences of oppression and for their bearing up under the terrors caused thereby.

We are not told what oppression John had to suffer on Patmos. The semantic indeterminacy permits its identification with every sort of trouble, which then can indeed also be understood in each and every way in the letters. What is more, all other readers who are brought into the readership through the prophetic words of the proemium in 1:1-3 can also now feel that they are integrated into the community of oppressed witnesses and thus likewise are connected with those in the community who have a share in the kingdom of God.

The individual letters fully evince the paracletic concern of the Revelation to John. All the churches in Asia Minor stand under oppressive trials, which could drag them away from the way of witness to Christ. In this situation the resurrected, cosmically empowered, exalted Crucified One speaks through the prophetic words of the letter in both warning and comforting terms in order to strengthen them. The letters, each constructed similarly, are addressed to the angel of each church and as regards content open with the self-introduction of the resurrected and exalted Crucified One (Rev 2:1, 8, 12, 18; 3:1, 7, 14). Thereafter follows praise and criticism of the churches, to each of whom the reward for holding fast as witnesses is attached. The phrase regarding the speaking Spirit, "Let anyone who has an ear listen to what the Spirit is saying to the churches," which marks the content of the letter as a message of the Spirit and demands attentive hearing, closes each individual letter (2:7, 11, 17, 29; 3:6, 13, 22).

*The Cosmic Power of the Resurrected Crucified as the Ground of Hope
and Perseverance in Discipleship after the Witness of Jesus Christ*

The particular self-presentation of the resurrected and exalted Crucified
One found preceding the individual letters is his same self-presentation
found in John's vision, which in the introductory letter John imparts to all
the churches to which he writes, "Do not be afraid; I am the first and the
last, and the living one. I was dead, and see, I am alive forever and ever;
and I have the keys of Death and of Hades" (Rev 1:17b-18). Through the
power of his resurrection from the dead the resurrected Crucified One
receives a share in the eternal life of God and now in a transformed way
can refer the self-predication of God as the Alpha and the Omega in 1:8
to himself. His essential identity marker is therefore the expression, "I was
dead, and see, I am alive forever and ever" (Rev 1:18b). With the help of
the aorist the state of death is marked as a closed act lying in the past. Jesus
was dead, totally dead, but he did not remain in this death. He became
living in a way which in the breaching of the temporal earthly order shows
him to be living forever and ever. He was thus not made alive again simply
within the timeline of earthly time in order to die again according to the
laws of earthly time, but rather he was gifted with a life that endures forever and ever. This life, however, is the life of God alone, God the creator,
the Pantokrator, who introduced himself in 1:8. Jesus was resurrected into
the eternal life of God and was at the same time endowed with cosmic
power (cf. 1:6).

To that also corresponds his fear-inspiring form, which is barely recognizable as human, and whose unconquerable strength is visualized with
"eyes like a flame of fire" and "feet . . . like burnished bronze, refined as
in a furnace" (Rev 1:14b-15a): "his face was like the sun shining with full
force. When I saw him, I fell at his feet as though dead" (1:16b-17), John
says of the effect which this terror-inducing form had upon him.

An essential component of this power consists in the giving of the
"keys of Death and of Hades" (1:18b). The resurrected Crucifie One,
endowed with power, is deemed judge of death and life, of heaven and
hell. He assumes God's eschatological office of judge. Even the churches,
symbolized by the seven lampstands, are subject to his judicial office, symbolized by the two-edged sword in his mouth (cf. 1:16, 20).

The self-expressions at the beginning of the letter to the seven
churches take up individual aspects as *pars pro toto* of the picture of the
cosmic Christ depicted in Revelation 1:12-20 and thus mark the authority
of the sender. "These are the words of him who holds the seven stars in
his right hand, who walks among the seven golden lampstands" (2:1b; cf.

1:16a, 20). With these words the resurrected Crucified One presents himself as the cosmic Christ who participates in the cosmic power of God, to whom the churches as well as their angels listen. He praises the church in Ephesus for its readiness to endure suffering, its exposure of false apostles and its rejection of the Nicolaitans. He rebukes it, however, because it has abandoned its "first love." He threatens the church of Ephesus with the penalty of repudiation if it does not return to its original way of love (cf. 2:2-6). In an intertextual recollection of the paradisal Tree of Life (cf. Gen 3:22ff.) he promises it eternal life, if it overcomes its trials (cf. 2:7).

"These are the words of the first and the last, who was dead and came to life" (Rev 2:8b; cf. 1:18). The exalted Christ presents himself to the church in Smyrna with the memory of his death on the cross and his resurrection. He names a persecution by Jews, who actually are not really Jews, and prophesies that some members of the church will even go to prison for a certain time. He adjures them to remain faithful, even in the face of the danger of death. For this faithfulness, he promises them eternal life (cf. 2:9-10), for the "second death" (2:11), thus the death administered by the cosmic Christ as a punishment at the eschatological judgment (cf. chap. 20), will not overtake them.

"These are the words of him who has the sharp two-edged sword" (Rev 2:12b, cf. 1:16b). With these words the resurrected Crucified One presents himself to the church in Pergamum as the eschatological judge. He praises them for their faithfulness, although there is already a death in the church to be mourned. He rebukes them, however, for some members of the church sympathize with the Nicolaitans. He threatens judgment if no change of mind occurs (cf. 2:13-16) and promises them heavenly food which in turn will lead to eternal life, if they overcomes their trials (cf. 2:17). At the same time they receive a white stone, which in an emblematic way bears a new name "that no one knows except the one who receives it" (2:17d).

"These are the words of the Son of God, who has eyes like a flame of fire, and whose feet are like burnished bronze" (Rev 2:18b; cf. 1:14b-15). To the church in Thyatira the exalted Christ represents himself as the cosmic Christ in powerful form. After praising the church, criticism follows: it tolerates Jezebel, a prophetess, who incites the church to idolatry. He announces the punishment of Jezebel, her children, and all who involve themselves with her (cf. 2:19-25). To those who overcome this trial, however, he promises a share in his judicial power, just as God has given him a share in his power (cf. 2:26-29).

"These are the words of him who has the seven spirits of God and the seven stars" (Rev 3:1b; cf. 1:16a, 20; 2:1b). To the church in Sardis the resurrected and exalted Crucified One presents himself in a similar way to how he presented himself in the letter to the church in Ephesus. Even though they know the name of Jesus Christ and thus belong to those to whom is accorded divine life, he accuses the members of the church of acting like those who do not know the name and are dead. He announces his coming in terms of a surprise (cf. 3:2-3). The somnolent church will then be judged, but some among them are faithful, and these will "walk with me, dressed in white, for they are worthy" (3:4b). Those who persevere in communion with Jesus Christ will receive the gift of eternal life, for their names will not be blotted "out of the book of life" (3:5). What is more, the resurrected and exalted Christ will confess their names before God and the angels as belonging to him.

"These are the words of the holy one, the true one, who has the key of David, who opens and no one will shut, who shuts and no one opens" (Rev 3:7b). The resurrected and exalted Crucified One presents himself to the church in Philadelphia with a second use of the allusion to his eschatological office as judge. This church is especially praised and designated as one that he loves (cf. 3:9d). For overcoming its trials it will be granted the special designation of an eternal "pillar in the temple of my God" (3:12), which he himself will inscribe with the name of God and with his own new name. This church is thus marked in an especial way as belonging to God and to Christ.

"The words of the Amen, the faithful and true witness, the origin of God's creation" (Rev 3:14b). This final self-predication of Jesus Christ, which is addressed to the church in Laodicea, presents at the same time the conclusion of the christological self-expressions of the resurrected and exalted Crucified One. He is the Amen, the final Word of God, because he was, is, and remains the faithful and true witness of God. As the one resurrected and taken into eternal divine life by God, he is the new creation and as such he is freed from the temporality of the first creation. Consequently he is also at the same time the beginning of the new creation and the beginning of the creation of God in general. The true witness criticizes the church in Laodicea, because it has not clearly decided either for or against the testimony of Christ (cf. 3:15-19). To those who overcome their trials and confess themselves clearly as witnesses of God is now offered the opportunity of a communion meal with the resurrected and exalted Crucified One (3:20). Finally, however, they will rule together with Christ, in the same way as also Jesus Christ received a share in the power of God, after he had overcome the trial of the threat of death.

Together the letters in Revelation 1:9–3:22 show that the resurrected and exalted Crucified One communicates with his churches through the Spirit and reveals to them his own fate as the hermeneutical key to their own situations. Just as he lived his witness to God, accepted the consequence of suffering violent death, and lived out his unlimited faithfulness to God therein, so also should the persecuted churches persevere in their witness for Jesus Christ, even if they must suffer violence. Just as the murdered Jesus was repaid for his faithfulness with new, eternal life and with a share in the cosmic power of God, so also can those who stand in discipleship to Jesus Christ be assured that violence and physical death will not have the last word. Even more, their patient abiding in witness for Jesus Christ leads to eternal life in communion with Jesus Christ, the "firstborn of the dead" (1:5), and with God, the cosmic creator God, who is able to give the dead the gift of new life.

The Annihilation of Powers Opposed to God through the Ram Who Was Slain, the Twofold Resurrection, and Eternal Life in the Golden City

If the letters of the resurrected and exalted Crucified One are directed to the seven churches at the time of the composition of the Revelation to John, then we encounter the future fully at Revelation 4:1. Present and future are in no way strictly separated realms of reality, however. Rather, the book of visions is supposed to comfort the churches in the present time of John the writer and beyond that to comfort all readers in their respective times and strengthen them in the troubles they suffer in bearing witness to Christ so that they might overcome the trials that could lead to their abandoning their following of the paradigmatic Witness. Because the future will bring the ultimate victory over the enemies of God and will bring eternal life for the witnesses of Jesus Christ, it is therefore worth enduring in the present. In essence, the visions display in multifold ways the ultimate destruction of the powers opposed to God, achieved through the ram[36] who was slain, and the eternal life of those who are resurrected in the golden city. The visions are thus nourishment in the form of a prophetic word of well-founded hope in the midst of an oppressive present.

That in which the churches to which the letters are addressed can hope is not necessarily an immediate end to their threatening situation: "If you are to be taken captive, into captivity you go; if anyone is to be slain with the sword, with the sword he must be slain" (Rev 13:10). The Revelation to John paints an ugly picture of calamity. It does not blur the danger that comes from the enemies of God. It is aware of the tears caused by injustice and violence. It does not call for retaliation, however, and does not meet injustice with new injustice. Rather, it trusts in the confidence that the wrath of God and the wrath of the resurrected and exalted Crucified One, whose commission involves judgment, will annihilate all injustice and violence (cf. 6:17), and those who identify with the "blood of the ram," with the innocent Victim's violent death on the cross, and thus become his witnesses, will be led "to the springs of the water of life," and "God will wipe away every tear from their eyes" (7:17). The Revelation to John does not block out the violence of this world, but it surrenders violence to the just divine wrath, because it is oriented toward the witness Jesus Christ. The hope of receiving the gift of eternal life after suffering and death is created out of the certainty that results from discipleship in the way of the witness of Christ. The linchpin of this interpretation of reality is its soteriological construal of Christology, in whose center stands the resurrection and exaltation of the Crucified One.

In the first vision in chapter 4 John sees God on his throne with his royal court. The scene, depicted with images especially from Ezekiel 1 and Isaiah 6, culminates in the praise of the twenty-four elders: "You are worthy, our Lord and God, to receive glory and honor and power, for you created all things, and by your will they existed and were created" (Rev 4:11). The God of the Revelation to John is above all the wonderful creator God, as he appears in the Holy Scriptures of Israel. Chapter 5 brings into play the book that opens the eschatological battle against all evil that overruns God's creation with suffering and violence, but no one in God's royal court is worthy to open the book. Only the ram who was slain, "the Lion of the tribe of Judah, the Root of David," is found worthy to open the book with its seven seals, because he has conquered (ἐνίκησεν) (cf. 5:5) by overcoming the temptation to turn from the way of witness to God, even though he was threatened with death and torture and suffered both.

The ram appears in the vision "as though it had been slaughtered" and with "seven horns and seven eyes, which are the seven spirits of God sent out into all the earth" (Rev 5:6), which are endowed with immeasurable might. The ram is thus enabled to win the battle before him. This mighty ram, which nevertheless still bears the traces of violence on his body, is none other than the resurrected and exalted Crucified One. To him in 5:9b is it said that he as the slaughtered one has "by his blood . . . ransomed for God saints from every tribe and language and people and nation" and has made them "a kingdom and priests" for God (5:10), and "they will reign on earth" (5:10). Therefore, in 5:11-13 the resurrected Crucified One is enthroned: "Then I heard every creature in heaven and on earth and under the earth and in the sea, and all that is in them, singing, 'To the one seated on the throne and to the Ram be blessing and honor and glory and might forever and ever!'" (5:13).

The battle in chapter 6 can begin after the throne scene in chapters 4 and 5 has made clear that God the creator has found in the resurrected Crucified One, the one who by reason of his faithfulness is worthy to be praised by all creatures, like God himself, and is therefore also worthy to be given the power of God, which will empower him to achieve the cosmic victory over all powers opposed to God. This battle, transpiring through the scenes of the seven seals and the seven trumpets and bowls of wrath as a structured event in which God appears as the sovereign of all courses of events precisely through its structure, is depicted in ever-new spectacular scenes of horror.

The victims of this battle are also witnesses to Christ. After the opening of the fifth seal, John sees

> under the altar the souls of those who had been slaughtered for the word of God and for the testimony they had given; they cried out with a loud voice, "Sovereign Lord, holy and true, how long will it be before you judge and avenge our blood on the inhabitants of the earth?" They were each given a white robe and told to rest a little longer, until the number would be complete both of their fellow servants and of their brothers and sisters, who were soon to be killed as they themselves had been killed. (Rev 6:9-11)

The vision of the fifth seal assumes that it will not remain a matter of the letters telling of individual cases of witnesses killed by the sword, but rather that many more victims of violence will come as well. In no way is this threatening situation celebrated, and neither is the fate of the martyrs glorified. Those martyred cry out for vengeance, but they themselves do not take the matter into their own hands. Rather, they leave vengeance to God. They indeed keep at this point their white garments as the clothing of the heavenly world, but they must repose until the battle is ended and all the victims are gathered so that they might enter into eternal divine life together. It is only at the end of the battle that all the living and the dead are judged (cf. 11:18). The dead rest until the end of the cosmic battle.

That the times and worlds are compressed together, and therefore that the futuristic eschatology already affects the present and that the present also influences the future, becomes clear when one observes that Jesus has through his death on the cross effected the battle against the adversary as *pars pro toto* for all powers opposed to God. The witnesses to Jesus also contribute to this battle through the "word of their testimony":

> Now have come the salvation and the power and the kingdom of our God and the
> authority of his Messiah, for the accuser of our comrades has been thrown down,
> who accuses them day and night before our God. But they have conquered him by
> the blood of the Ram and by the word of their testimony, for they did not cling to
> life even in the face of death. (Rev 12:10-11)

The witnesses, both the churches addressed in Asia Minor as well as all
readers of the Revelation to John who, according to the reading contract
of 1:1-3, commit themselves to their words and who align themselves with
them in their lives, are not merely pawns in the cosmic battle. Rather,
their faithfulness to the word of testimony is the way in which they
participate as witnesses in the struggle on the battlefield of the earth.

And this battle is hard. Because the devil knows that his time is short,
he lashes out mercilessly (Rev 12:12). Faithfulness to the word of testimony does not shield one from the violence of the adversary and those who
stand in league with him, consciously or unconsciously. Even witnesses
suffer death. But they can be certain that they will receive new life from
God, the wonderful ruler of all, who accomplishes his justice: "'Blessed
are the dead who from now on die in the Lord.' 'Yes,' says the Spirit, 'they
will rest from their labors, for their deeds follow them'" (14:13). The living, however, receive a challenge: "'Fear God and give him glory, for the
hour of his judgment has come; and worship him who made heaven and
earth, the sea and the springs of water'" (14:7).

In the midst of the cosmic battle, whose events play out on earth, are
those holy ones who "die in the Lord," who do not in gross impatience take
up weapons or even go over to the side of earthly perpetrators of violence:
"Here is a call for the endurance of the saints, those who keep the commandments of God and hold fast to the faith of Jesus" (Rev 14:12). The
battle of the witnesses at all places and at all times, who will be rewarded
with the "first resurrection" (cf. 20:5), consists in three things: (1) to live in
trust in the Jesus-Christ-Story, which reveals Jesus as God's outstanding
witness, in whose destiny one's own destiny can be read; (2) to remain firm
against the fact of injustice and violence themselves, in the solidarity of
creaturely life; and (3) to give God honor thereby, that he might be praised
as the creator of all life and that earthly life might be shaped in recognition of the way which God's commands prescribe.

The twentieth chapter of the Revelation to John differentiates
between two resurrections and takes up again the language of the second
death, employed already in Revelation 2:11b. After the multifold visions
of battle, an angel binds the devil: "he bound him for a thousand years,
and threw him into the pit, and locked and sealed it over him, so that he

would deceive the nations no more, until the thousand years were ended. After that he must be let out for a little while" (20:2b-3). The power of the devil, bringing violence and horror over God's creation, is experienced so strongly in John's visions that he is rendered harmless only for a limited time after all the battles that are depicted in chapters 6–19. Those who are resurrected during this peaceful time of one thousand years[37] are they

> who had been beheaded for their testimony to Jesus and for the word of God. They had not worshiped the beast or its image and had not received its mark on their foreheads or their hands. They came to life and reigned with Christ a thousand years. (The rest of the dead did not come to life until the thousand years were ended.) This is the first resurrection. (20:4b-5)

The first resurrection is indeed already an eschatological resurrection, but it is valid only for faithful witnesses. They are now granted dominion on earth with Christ. This resurrection to eternal life is permanent. The resurrected need no second resurrection, for, "Blessed and holy are those who share in the first resurrection. Over these the second death has no power, but they will be priests of God and of Christ, and they will reign with him a thousand years" (20:6). Thereafter, however, the devil will be released once more and will rage terribly for a short time. Immediately after this he will finally be thrown into the lake of fire, "where the beast and the false prophet were, and they will be tormented day and night forever and ever" (20:10). Immediately after the devil has been thrown in the lake of fire for all eternity, all the dead are raised who did not take part in the first resurrection. Many also of them receive eternal life in communion with those already raised as kings and priests. But all others will go into the lake of fire with the devil, and "[t]his is the second death" (20:14b), from which there is no more escape.

After justice is done in this way and God's creatures are divided, some with eternal damnation if their deeds are to be punished, and others to whom eternal life is given, the holy, golden city, the new Jerusalem, comes down from heaven. It needs no temple any longer, for God lives with Jesus Christ together with those raised to eternal life:

> Nothing accursed will be found there any more. But the throne of God and of the Lamb will be in it, and his servants will worship him; they will see his face, and his name will be on their foreheads. And there will be no more night; they need no light of lamp or sun, for the Lord God will be their light, and they will reign forever and ever. (Rev 22:3-5)

The book of visions ends with these verses.

Revelation 22:6-21 forms the conclusion to the Revelation to John and takes up again the reading contract from 1:1-3:

> And he said to me, "These words are trustworthy and true, for the Lord, the God of the spirits of the prophets, has sent his angel to show his servants what must soon take place." "See, I am coming soon! Blessed is the one who keeps the words of the prophecy of this book." (Rev 22:6-7)

The section of 22:8-21 underscores the reading compact once more and ends finally with the grace wish that ends the letter: "The grace of the Lord Jesus be with all the saints. Amen" (Rev 22:21).

This open grace wish corresponds to the opening addressed to the hearers and readers of the Revelation to John in Revelation 1:1-3 and is thus of particular soteriological moment. In no way does the Revelation to John assume a limited number of those who will be raised to life. It wishes this salvific future for everyone. It is precisely the partition of the resurrection into a first resurrection, which remains reserved for faithful witnesses, and into a second, in which judgment is delivered to all the other dead, that shows that the Revelation to John even counts on the fact that it is not only the publicly faithful witnesses to the resurrection who enter into eternal life. The grace of Jesus Christ, who indeed himself will function as judge, is open for all, but this grace is no license for all conceivable misdeeds. The presentation of judgment in the Revelation to John does not distinguish itself in this respect from that of Paul, of the synoptic evangelists, or of the other Johannine writings. They all reckon with the possibility that on the ground of one's own sins, understood as unjust acts against God and his creatures, one will reap not eternal life but rather eternal death. It is precisely the possibility of a double outcome of judgment that makes one aware of the seriousness of the orientation of one's life. That there is salvation at all, however, in view of the sinful reality of the cosmos, which shows itself ever again not as a wanted and beloved creation of God but rather as his creatures' battlefield, is due to divine grace alone, which through the witness of Jesus Christ is offered to all creatures who take their place alongside the resurrected Crucified Oneand who follow his witness in their own testimony.

A Question of Power

The Revelation to John was and is a controverted book. Again and again loud voices were and are raised calling for it to be struck from the New Testament canon because of its revenge fantasies. A humanistically enlightened Christianity especially wishes that this book, with its horrifying,

violent visions, had never been included in the canon. That potentially violent Christian fundamentalists and the churches they inhabit have divided
the world into an empire of evil and an empire of the good, and thus have
even justified war and torture, blocks access to the cosmological Christology and soteriology of the Revelation to John for many contemporary,
peace-loving men and women.

Keeping in mind the theme of the present investigation, it should
first of all be remembered that the Revelation to John sheds light on the
fact that the visionary experience of the resurrected Crucified One in no
way ends with the witnesses of 1 Corinthians 15, but rather persists in
the tradition of prophecy. John sees the resurrected Crucified One during
his exile on Patmos and sees him in a form not identical with the human
Jesus prior to his resurrection. The resurrected and exalted Crucified One
appears in the visions of John first and foremost as a mighty, fear-inspiring
figure (cf. Rev 1:10-20), which recalls very much the visions of Isaiah 6
and Ezekiel 1, and then as a ram, which at the same time appears as slain
and fights endowed with unimaginable might. The different images of
the Revelation to John prevent one from exchanging their depicted signs
for that which is signified by them. The visions do not depict, but rather
symbolize, that which will happen. They are born of the confidence that
the death and resurrection of Jesus Christ do not form a special eschatological case, but rather represent the model and ground of the destiny of
those who are convinced of the truth of the Jesus-Christ-Story in spite
of their experience of catastrophe and who orient their lives accordingly,
even if that brings with it violent death for them. In this situation, be
it under Nero, Domitian, Trajan, or Hadrian, the violent vision relo-
cates the desire for revenge to the God who judges and his Christ. The
Revelation to John thus legitimates feelings of aggression and the desire
for revenge, but it pleads that one not let these destructive feelings take
charge. Rather, one should hold fast to the commands of God and to
faith in his resurrected witness Jesus Christ, even if it puts one at a dis-
advantage. Vengeance should be left to God and to his mighty ram. They
did not themselves become mighty, but rather God will demand his justice with the assistance of Jesus Christ, and all who decide against God
and his creatures, even indeed inflicting immeasurable suffering on them,
will be held accountable. Faithfulness, however, will be repaid with the
first resurrection, which already leads ultimately to eternal life with God
and Christ. The powers and violence opposed to God and his creatures
will experience God's vengeance to such a degree that they will not be

annihilated in one stroke but rather will first be imprisoned for a thousand years and only then ultimately deprived of power.

The Revelation to John shows that the resurrection of the dead, wholly bound up with the conviction of the resurrection and exaltation of Jesus Christ, is woven inseparably into the hope for the end of injustice. In uncomfortable and therefore precisely unavoidable ways the Revelation to John brings to expression that the question of power and the concomitant question of God's justice are posed when one talks about the resurrection of the Crucified One and the resurrection of the dead. In the final analysis, which power effects and determines the destiny of this world and those who live on it? The answer of the Revelation to John is shockingly clear. It is the power of the almighty creator God, of whom also the Holy Scriptures of Israel rightly speak.

The Revelation to John does not ultimately shy away from the consequences of speaking the theological language of the creator God as the ruler of all, which involves understanding that the destructive violence in the cosmos and thus also such violence on earth is at least tolerated by God for a determined time. Note well: tolerated, not willed. God permits his creatures the choice and in this freedom lies the ground of the possibility and the reality of all injustice and of every lapse from the life willed by God and lived in solidarity with divine creatures. God himself is thus involved in sin. His eschatological judgment is necessary to render his justice ultimate and eternal. Therefore the eschatological resurrection of the dead is no selfless act of mercy on the part of an uninvolved creator, but rather the pledge [*Erweis*] of theodicy, of the justice of God. The Revelation to John makes this connection more clearly than any other writing of the New Testament, and therefore it must remain in the canon as an uncomfortable book, in order to keep Christian thinking alert.

Chapter 5

The Catholic Letters

Already in the early Church, several letters that were not directed to any particular communities but rather to the universal company of believers were designated as *catholic* letters. Since the Synod of Laodicaea (ca. A.D. 360), James, both letters of Peter, and Jude were numbered among them.[1] One cannot make out any common theological line in these so-called catholic letters, even if there are obvious points of contact between James and 1 Peter and between Jude and 2 Peter. Therefore in the discipline of New Testament introduction at present, the three letters of John, which stand much closer to the gospel of John than to the catholic letters, are numbered among the *corpus Johanneum*, and only the two letters of Peter, the letter of James, and the letter of Jude are summarized as catholic letters.[2] The outline of the monograph at hand also follows this decision. The fact that 2 Peter stands in a much closer literary connection with Jude than with 1 Peter grounds the determination below to deal with the letters of Jude and 2 Peter together in a common section.

Although the resurrection of the Crucified One and the resurrection of the dead are not dealt with in a thematic fashion in the catholic letters (with the exception of 1 Peter)—indeed, even resurrection terminology is thoroughly lacking—the catholic letters will nevertheless be here examined from this perspective. It will be argued that even the catholic letters, which are animated by concerns other than the resurrection of the dead, assume the resurrection of Jesus Christ as the foundation of their eschatological construal.

The Letter of James

That James, Jude, and 2 Peter make neither the resurrection of the dead in general nor the resurrection of the Crucified One a major theme does not lead to the conclusion that resurrection theology would have been of no significance for them. The language of the Kyrios Jesus Christ in James 1:1 in its syntagmatic connection with God makes sense only if the resurrection of the Crucified One and his exaltation are assumed. James, the explicit author, is presented as a servant both of God and of the Kyrios Jesus Christ, and no differentiation is here made. His particular qualifications to write this letter are bound up with his relationship to God and the Lord Jesus.[3] The title of *kyrios* is first employed for Jesus Christ (1:1), while God is designated as *Theos*. In the further course of the letter both God (1:7, 12; 3:9; 4:10; 5:4, 10, 11) and also Jesus Christ (2:1; 5:7, 8, 14-15) are designated as Kyrios. Sometimes it is not clear whether God or Jesus Christ is in view when Kyrios is employed (cf. 4:15). Both, however, appear as eschatological judges. This latter point makes sense only with reference to Jesus Christ, whose violent death in 5:6 is remembered, if his resurrection through the miracle-working creator God is also assumed (cf. 5:13-18).

Only a few exegetes accept the position that the letter of James was written by the flesh-and-blood brother of Jesus. If this is correct, the letter must then be dated sometime before A.D. 62, the year that saw the execution of the brother of the Lord at the instigation of the high priest of Jerusalem. The overwhelming majority assumes a pseudonymous author whose concern was to oblige believers to obey God's word not only in their thoughts but also in their deeds by means of his "letter of admonition [*Mahnbrief*]."[4] The letter of James stands much closer to Jewish wisdom literature.[5] "The decisive reason that the authority of the letter was placed under the authority of James could have been James' enduring reputation as an ethical example, a reputation soon consolidated in his byname of 'the just' (*Gosp. Thomas* 12), which would then permit him to appear a fitting authority for a letter of ethical correction such as James."[6] Perhaps James 5:6 has to do with not only the crucifixion of Jesus but also the stoning of James.

The ethical impulse of James is not only indebted to its Jewish tradition; rather, it stands much more in direct connection with its eschatological expectation, which already appears in the first section of the letter (James 1:2-12). The trials mentioned in 1:2 should be understood as probationary possibilities for the believer who in this way gains "endurance" (1:3), appropriately throughout life (1:4), and then receives from the Kyrios

(1:7b) what the beatitude toward which the whole section drives designates as "the crown of life that the Lord has promised to those who love him" (1:12b). This "crown of life" will hardly be any other eschatological gift than that which other early Christian writings name: eternal life in peaceful communion with God and Jesus Christ.

Even the binding of resurrection theology and creation theology can be made out in James 1:17-18, whereby a decided theology of the word of God brings both together. As in Paul, faith is here understood not as one's own work but rather as the gift of God, which comes into being through the creative word of God. Just as according to the first creation account in Genesis 1:1–2:4a God created everything through his Word, so also have believers been newly given "birth" as "a kind of first fruits of his creatures" through the word of God, the "word of truth" (James 1:18). God, who is designated as "the Father of lights," creates continuously through his word. The fitting answers to this word that creates anew are deeds in everyday life befitting the mercy of God (cf. 5:11) and the grandeur of the divine image of God in humanity (cf. 3:9b).

This theology of the creative word of God does not amount to a presentist eschatology. Rather, it is much more a matter of those now born anew through the word living in accord with their newly given existence in order to receive the "crown of life," eternal life, at the end. This word is not the fulfillment of the promise already in the here and now but, in a way very similar to Pauline theology, is rather the power of God which is able to save (cf. James 1:21b; Rom 1:16b).

The content of the faith created through the word is "our glorious Lord Jesus Christ" (James 2:1). This can hardly mean anything other than the Crucified One raised from the dead and exalted. He proclaimed the kingdom of God before his death on the cross and, according to the gospels and according to the letter of James, greatly valued the expression of true faith in acts of love (cf. Matt 25:31-46). In agreement with the Torah and with the Jesus tradition the double command of love becomes the fundamental orientation for action and conversion (cf. James 1:12, 2:8; Matt 22:37ff.; Lev 19:18).

If James' polemic against a so-called faith that feeds the needy with pious words and does not meet the bodily needs of the other with active love (cf. 2:15ff.) is actually directed against the Pauline conviction "that a person is justified by faith apart from works prescribed by the law" (Rom 3:28b), then the author of the letter of James would have deeply misunderstood Paul. Even Paul wants to impress upon his hearers that faith is active in and through love (Gal 5:6) and believers too will be measured by their deeds at the eschatological judgment (cf. Gal 5:13-26; 1 Cor 3:13ff.).

Whoever ascribes to the letter of James a sort of works-righteousness against which Paul polemicizes, like Martin Luther and with him the overwhelming majority of Protestant exegetes,[7] greatly misunderstands James' word-of-God theology. According to James, works do not replace faith but rather complete it (cf. James 2:22-26). The word creates faith in Jesus Christ and at the same time [*gleichursprünglich*] effects the new creation of believers. This faith expresses itself in acts of love. Whoever lets faith in Jesus Christ work in himself will endeavor to live accordingly in the day to day, even though he fails again and again. Endurance, which in spite of all trials attempts again and again to live in active love and meet the needs of the needy and weak and declare itself to stand in solidarity with the victims of the logic of exploitation, is founded on the eschatological certainty of receiving "the crown of life," eternal life, from the crucified, resurrected, and exalted Kyrios at the end (1:12).

This endurance expects "the coming of the Lord" (James 5:7) and with his coming the great day of judgment, the ultimate reestablishment of justice. The sort of social responsibility that the letter of James demands rests upon the eschatological conviction that "the Judge is standing at the doors" (5:9b). "[T]he coming of the Lord is near" (5:8c). In endurance, the letter of James expects none other than the crucified, resurrected, and exalted Kyrios Jesus Christ, whose passion is recalled in 5:6, and with his coming the completion of the eschatological act of God.

The First Letter of Peter

The numerous intertextual connections with the Pauline letters,[8] but also with the letter of James[9] and even more the elevated Greek style of 1 Peter, make it appear impossible to accept Simon Peter as the epistle's author.[10] With the vast majority of researchers, I believe 1 Peter is to be regarded as a pseudepigraphic writing by an anonymous author, which addresses itself to Christianity in Asia Minor at the end of the first century in order to strengthen those communities in their difficult social situation. Specifically, they bear an outsider status, and this follows directly from their confession of the crucified, resurrected, and exalted Jesus Christ and the God who raised him.

Reinhard Feldmeier has demonstrated in his monograph *Die Christen als Fremde* and in his commentary on 1 Peter that in 1 Peter the positively overcoded metaphor of the stranger serves as a leitmotif for the meaning of Christian existence in an overwhelmingly non-Christian society. This metaphor is no longer understood from the valid plausibility structures of society as it exists, but rather from its connection, made possible by the proclamation of the death and resurrection of Jesus Christ, to the eschatological reality that God has opened up with the resurrection of Jesus Christ for those who so believe. "According to 1 Peter, believing existence is eschatological existence."[11]

This eschatological existence is not indebted to any empirical experience of or visionary gaze upon the resurrected Crucified One, however, and absolutely not to any empirical examination of the tomb of Jesus: "Although you have not seen him, you love him; and even though you do not see him now, you believe in him" (1 Pet 1:8a). The eschatological existence of faith is indebted only to the creative power of the word of God. It understands itself as "born anew, not of perishable but of imperishable seed, through the living and enduring word of God" (1:23).

The content of this word is the gospel, in whose center stands the narrative of the death, resurrection, and exaltation of Jesus Christ. God has "raised him from the dead and gave him glory, so that your faith and hope are set on God" (1 Pet 1:21b). This faith, effected by means of the gospel of the resurrected and exalted Crucified One, serves final salvation, which was already prepared for believers through the eschatological act of power that was the resurrection of Jesus Christ through God's wondrous creative power, but which will first be revealed at the end of time (cf. 1:3ff.). "The Christ-event as an act of God structures and qualifies the entirety of human time and makes ultimate time out of present time."[12] Those who understand themselves as grounded in faith in the eschatological resurrection of the Crucified One therefore experience themselves as having received "new birth into a living hope" (1:3), because with this new connection to the ultimate future not only is their view of their own lives changed from the ground up, but also the cosmos is perceived as something wholly and fully new. From this new perspective, filled with eschatological hope, the conflicts and sufferings that the confession of God and Jesus Christ bring with them can also be borne without losing the eschatologically grounded joy over the promise of eternal life with God and Jesus Christ.

This gospel of Jesus Christ was "announced to you through those who brought you good news by the Holy Spirit sent from heaven" (1 Pet 1:12d). It reveals Jesus Christ, the Crucified One, as the Christ raised and exalted by God. With this revelation, the grace of God is offered at the same time [*gleichursprünglich*], grace that alone in view of the coming eschatological judgment is in a position to ground hope of salvation (cf. 1:13).

Rebirth through the creative and powerful word of God is not to be identified with the eschatological resurrection of the dead, however, for it is a rebirth "into a living hope" (1 Pet 1:3b). This hope expects to receive eternal life at the end of time as "the crown of glory that never fades away" (5:4b), as the gracious gift of God. The language of rebirth does not stand precisely under the sign of an eschatology operative in the present. Rather, it is much more a matter of an apocalyptic eschatology that ascribes its perception of the Crucified One, who is also the resurrected and exalted Kyrios, not to itself, but to the work of the Holy Spirit. Thus this language conceives of the capacity for such a renewed perception as being born again into a new hope. The rebirth is not the resurrection. Such a view of things is made possible when the Holy Spirit opens up the perception of the Crucified One as the resurrected and exalted Kyrios and, at the same time [*gleichursprünglich*], reveals hope as hope in the resurrection of the dead and salvation from the eschatological judgment of God.

This hope for salvation stands in the apocalyptic expectation of the imminent coming of universal judgment (cf. 1 Pet 4:7), which also involves the dead: "For this is the reason the gospel was proclaimed even to the dead, so that, though they had been judged in the flesh as everyone is judged, they might live in the spirit as God does" (4:6).[13]

The parenetic concern of the letter, to give grounded encouragement to the "survival of the communities under oppression and persecution,"[14] is based on the creation-theological foundation of this apocalyptic eschatology, which assumes the resurrection of the Crucified One as an eschatologically effective salvific event worked by God. This eschatological hope describes the capacity for such saving faith as a rebirth. With this perspective on things one can now also hope in one's own resurrection, the resurrection of the dead, and the inheritance of eternal life. The empirical experience that the letter makes known is the suffering of believers, which threatens to block their joy in the gospel. It is primarily the letter's setting of their own suffering in parallel with the suffering of Jesus Christ that permits them to reject their own suffering as the deadly power of reality. "The saying of the gospel, that suffering flows over into glory, is credible. Thereupon an arduous existence (which will be described later) can be endured without fear of annihilation or illusion."[15]

The Letter of Jude and the Second Letter of Peter

Neither the letter of Jude nor its "concerted new interpretation"[16] in the form of the letter of 2 Peter makes the resurrection of Jesus Christ a major theme. Although both writings display a decided interest in the still-outstanding end-time judgment of God, they do not mention the resurrection of the dead. They could therefore be wholly left out of the present investigation, given its concerns. If, nevertheless, they are briefly examined, then it is only to guard against the erroneous impression that the resurrection of the dead and the resurrection of Jesus Christ are without significance for these two letters.

Already from the outset in the prescript the letter of Jude operates with the connection of theology, Christology, and futurist eschatology. The latter assumes conviction of the resurrection and exaltation of Jesus Christ. Jude, supposedly the brother of James, is named as the sender. Thus, the letter claims to be composed by Jude, the brother of Jesus of Nazareth. In designating himself at the same time as "a servant of Jesus Christ," he assumes that Jesus Christ is alive, for no one serves a dead brother.

He names the addressees as "those who are called." These are then more precisely qualified through their connection to God and their connection to Jesus Christ. They are beloved by God, the Father, and they are kept safe for Jesus Christ (Jude 1b). Their call is grounded in the love of God, and they will find their purpose in a common "eternal life" with the resurrected and exalted Jesus Christ. This fundamental conviction is then taken up again in verses 20-21 in an admonitory and encouraging way that at the same time reinforces it: "But you, beloved, build yourselves up on your most holy faith; pray in the Holy Spirit; keep yourselves in the love of God; look forward to the mercy of our Lord Jesus Christ that leads to eternal life." This merciful love is supposed to be on the part of those who are called, the addressees of the letter, even for their opponents, who are heavily chastised and threatened with eschatological punishment in the main body of the letter (vv. 22-23).

The giving of the Spirit is claimed as a mark of distinction between those who are called and their opponents. The chief accusation against their opponents consists in their causing divisions (cf. Jude 19). As Henning Paulsen points out, the material conflict can be seen in the letter's mention of teaching about angels: "The opponents do not accept the high estimation of angels, which is precisely an essential component of the theology of Jude."[17] The angelology of Jude, which is seen clearly in the letter's reference to the archangel Michael (v. 9) and also in its calling upon the book of Enoch in verse 14, sets Jude's entire cosmological interpretation of the world in the thought horizon of Jewish apocalyptic, in which angelology plays a decisive role. It can be assumed that the resurrection of the dead is a self-understood fundamental assumption in need of no further emphasis, as it is necessary for the universality of the eschatological judgment of God, as in all apocalyptic writings.

The same holds for 2 Peter as well, which is probably the latest writing in the collection of the New Testament. Although 2 Peter claims the authority of the apostle Peter with its reference to him as the sender and its reference to the first letter of Peter (2 Peter 3:1), its references to the letters of Paul, to the gospel of Matthew, and to the letter of Jude (references that are more literarily obvious) are more substantive than references to the first letter of Peter. As decisive authorities for its theology, 2 Peter calls upon "a certain understanding of the Scriptures . . . of the revelation of Christ, and of the Pauline letters."[18] The recourse to Peter serves on one hand to anchor the *euaggelion* (gospel) in the works of Jesus of Nazareth before his crucifixion and resurrection. As its guarantor, Peter is employed as an eyewitness (cf. 1:16ff.), who now himself sets down his testament of the gospel in the form of 2 Peter, shortly before his death. On the other hand, with the emphasis on the certain parousia, this epistle binds together origin and eschatological goal of the *euaggelion*.

Thus, the revision of the eschatological problem of the delay of the connected parousia plays here a heavy role also in connection to the question of the New Testament's resurrection discourse. The argumentation of 2 Peter stresses the fact that divine reality cannot be defined by human perception (cf. 2 Pet 3:8) and designates the supposed delay of the parousia as a delay only if one imagines it within the empirical limits of the capabilities of human perception. At the same time, the addressees are led back to the "patience" of God, whose mercy gives all men sufficient opportunity for "repentance" (cf. 3:8ff.). When the entire context is seen, the resurrection of Jesus Christ and the eschatological resurrection of the dead for universal judgment are thus beyond all question.

Like Jude, 2 Peter shifts the understanding of judgment—that is, that the opponents only will meet with judgment—and thus paints judgment in more horrible images than does Jude, his source. Granted all necessary criticism of this one-sided use of presentation of judgment for the opponents only, the extensive admonition in Jude and 2 Peter to believers to keep watch, in view of the still-outstanding eschatological events of the return of the resurrected and exalted Jesus Christ and in view of the universal judgment, preserves their apocalyptic eschatology and thus opens the hope of a future marked by the merciful and just action of God. The letters therefore also guard against mere piety ensconced comfortably in the unjust structures of present reality. The conviction of the overwhelming majority of New Testament writings that such judgment is coming for all, and not only for the opponents, stands in contradiction to the position of Jude and 2 Peter, which seem to proclaim that there will be no judgment for the believers in the gospel.[19] The eschatological opening of Christian existence, however, cannot be had without the fundamental acceptance of the resurrection of the Crucified One, or without the hope in the resurrection of the dead for the purposes of universal judgment.

PART II

Resurrection and the New Testament
Systematic Interpretations

Chapter 6

The Fundamental Structure of Resurrection Discourse in the Writings of the New Testament and the Problem Posed for the Second Part of the Investigation

The first part of this monograph attempted to show how the resurrection of the dead and the resurrection of Jesus Christ are communicated in the writings of the New Testament. The exegetical investigations described resurrection discourse within the universe of discourse of each text or complex of texts. This was done for two reasons. First, the intensity, complexity, disunity, as well as the partially contradictory nature of resurrection discourse in the New Testament was shown. This was done in order to break through the reduction(ism) of exegetical research into the question of the resurrection of Jesus Christ and its connection to the resurrection of the dead in 1 Corinthians 15 and the endings of the Gospels. The hope is that this approach will help avoid the fixation on historical concerns about the character of the appearances of the Resurrected One and about the condition of Jesus' tomb (empty or not) in service of perceiving the entirety of New Testament resurrection discourse. Second, however, inquiries about the precise syntagmatic, semantic, and pragmatic connections that make talk of the resurrection of the dead in the writings of the New Testament appear plausible, conceivable, comprehensible, and relevant for one's own life must also be made, without burdening the presentation with further inquiries concerning other conceptions of reality. How do the fundamental assumptions about reality, assumptions that permit New Testament discourse in all its variety to speak of the resurrection of Jesus Christ and of the dead seriously and with conviction, actually look?

The chief point of New Testament resurrection discourse may be given briefly: The basic conviction is that the God of Israel, as the sacred Scriptures of Israel bear witness to him, is the merciful and just creator

God, who with his creative power has created everything lovingly and purely for his own sake. This creation theology, which understands the cosmos together with all creatures as coming from the pure love of God, is carried forth by the authors of the New Testament writings. Only this creator God, as the creative God testified to in the sacred Scriptures of Israel, is in a position to raise the dead.[1]

The resurrection of the dead is no end in itself, but rather serves to establish the justice of God, which has been impaired by the violence of godless powers and men. The resurrection of the dead is narrowly bound up with sin on the creation's side of the relationship and with the question of theodicy on the divine side of the relationship. It is answered with the conviction that God will ultimately judge both the living and the dead and thus will heal even the damage done to justice. The reestablishment of justice therefore serves creatures who become once again capable of unlimited relationships. It is only under this assumption that creatures can enter into eternal life as an enduring relationship with God and the resurrected Crucified One. It also, however, serves as a proof of God's relational capacity when he will have revealed himself as the just and merciful God in not forgetting acts of violence and above all the victims thereof. He will thereby have achieved his divine justice for the salvation of the entire cosmos and his creatures, ultimately and without any limitations whatsoever.

Resurrection discourse in the New Testament weaves a new thread that changes the cloth from the ground up into the web of creation theology, reflection on sin, questions of theodicy, and apocalyptic eschatology: the resurrection of the crucified Jesus Christ. It is not brought in as a powerful miracle of the revivification of a dead man, as one finds in, say, 1 Kings 17 or John 11. Rather, the claim is that the eschatological resurrection of the dead that will take place at the end of time has already definitively begun with the resurrection of the Crucified One. The Crucified One who was raised from the dead was not brought back into his old fleshly life, but rather was taken into divine life that cannot be limited whatsoever by space and time. This exaltation into the life of God made it necessary, however, for the Resurrected One to receive a new body that did not assume the laws of space and time and thus also was no longer subject to decay and death. But for his new life he also requires a body that can be perceived by the eyes of the first creation in analogy to the bodies of angels as an appearance of light.

His new body permits the resurrected crucified one to retain the ability to be perceived in spite of his exaltation as the crucified one, a reception with which the continuity of the first body with the second is inscribed.

It also marks out the exalted one who is Kyrios to believers as a creature of God, for the signature of all creatures is their bodily nature. The difference between creator and creature thus remains preserved as a difference between God the Father and his Kyrios Jesus Christ. Only God, the creator, requires no body for his own eternal life.

The resurrected Crucified One exalted to Kyrios communicates with believers not only by means of a few revelatory appearances, which Galatians 1 and 1 Corinthians 15 but also the visions of the Johannine Apocalypse make known. Rather, in the writings of the New Testament the basal proof of the resurrection consists much more in the fact that the Jesus who died on the cross can be experienced in believers' present time as living and active. The fundamental confession—Kyrios Jesus Christ—expresses in formal terms the conviction that Jesus did not remain in death, but rather was raised by God and installed as Lord of all who believe and now actually lives, reigns, acts, and will act as Kyrios. He communicates himself, will even take part in the resurrection of the dead, and above all will cooperate decisively with God the Father as the Judge at the eschatological judgment. In the Lord's Supper he is present and can be experienced.

Other proofs of the resurrection of the Crucified One are simply not found. Outside of the Gospels, the empty tomb is never made to serve as a sign of the resurrection of Jesus. Not once in Acts does Luke employ the story of the absence of Jesus' corpse from the tomb as a means of proof. Neither the empty tomb nor any other empirical, materially representable data whatsoever are put forth as proofs of the resurrection, for one's own experience of communion with the crucified, resurrected, and exalted Kyrios Jesus Christ makes for plausible, sufficient proof of the truthfulness of his all-changing resurrection, to which those who are convinced bear witness.

The resurrection of the Crucified One is thus not presented as a unique eschatological event, but rather is woven into the expectation that the eschatological resurrection of the dead is coming soon. Even now those who believe the gospel of the resurrection of the dead are taken up into the eschatological quality of the new creation. They are situated in a paradoxical intermediate state of already being new creatures but still living in their fragile, fleshly bodies.

Even if several letters like Colossians and probably still more like Ephesians threaten to undermine this paradoxical tension by speaking of an already-completed resurrection, it can be said of the New Testament writings as a whole that they carry forward apocalyptic eschatology with its futuristic expectation of the resurrection of the dead for judgment.

Those who believe the gospel of the resurrected crucified one expect eschatological judgment confident of escaping the righteous wrath of God on the basis of their communion with the Kyrios. But several writings, especially Jude and 2 Peter, do not preserve a radical understanding of sin as regards believers themselves. They employ the eschatological judgment much more as a rhetorical means of intimidating opponents without evincing any awareness that all, including themselves, have earned God's judgment.

The resurrection of Jesus is thus interpreted as the eschatological inbreaking of divine eternity into the empirical, temporal world and thus as the beginning of the end of the temporal world, which runs its course to the eschatological judgment of God. The resurrection of the dead is therefore no end in itself. It serves to reckon with the cruelties and transgressions of creaturely life in the temporal world and thus aims at the reestablishment of God's justice and at the same time the healing of the victims of the temporal world. By dispensing his justice to the living and the dead at the end, God shows himself to be the merciful and just creator God. By taking those who rely upon the word of the cross which is the gospel into his own divine life, however, as he has thus already done in the case of the resurrected Crucified One, he surpasses the first creation with the second creation. In the kingdom of God, which has broken in with the resurrection of the Crucified One and which will be eternal without disruption after the completion of eschatological judgment, those who are raised up live in glorious new bodies in eternal communion with the Kyrios Jesus Christ and with God himself.

Without creation theology, without an understanding of sin, without questions of theodicy, and without apocalyptic eschatology, the coherence of the plausibility structures of New Testament discourse about the resurrection of the dead would collapse. The universe of discourse the New Testament writings present, however, no longer corresponds in an unbroken fashion to the conceptions of reality assumed by post-Enlightenment societies. Angelic bodies of light are now at home in fantasy films. Apocalyptic scenarios are understood as natural catastrophes based on the law of cause and effect. The resurrection of the dead is hardly looked upon as a serious question in the discourse of the humanities. The question of sin is dismissed as moralizing ecclesial ideology removed from real life.

At the same time, however, the reduction of reality to empirically measurable and principally repeatable data no longer convinces, but rather is felt to be an inappropriate limitation in view of the complexity and the diversity of humankind's perception of reality. A would-be leap back into the time before the Enlightenment opens up no sound alternative, but indeed leads to a religious fundamentalism that in turn could come about only under the conditions of the Enlightenment and under unreflective acceptance and improper use of its reductionistic binary conception of reality.[2] The flight from the difficult theological work of thinking, attempted by parapsychology, depth psychology, or the psychology of death, remains trapped by an empirical conception of reality and does not solve the theological problem involved in conceiving of the resurrection. Neither does trying to cut the Gordian knot through radical constructivism—which solves the question of truth instrumentally, and in conjunction with present brain research empirically, as an adaptation to the requirements of the environment necessary for survival, and thus relegates all assumptions about reality to the realm of mind game—solve the theological problem involved in speaking of the resurrection of the dead in biblically grounded ways that are conceivable today.[3]

The question of the reality of the resurrection is moreover not only a theoretical but also precisely an existential problem: On what can I rely in death? What can I say to the dying and those left behind that is theologically responsible? What provides real comfort, and what only puts someone off? This question of the resurrection is not primarily a historical question. Rather, it is an eschatological question in the midst of our present: it concerns the ultimate truth of our reality, out of which everything will experience its ultimate determination. The faithful answer of the New Testament writings to these decisive questions about the future is that God shall make everything well. But—so asks doubt standing close by— is this not only a pious wish, a construction of those who do not want the brutal reality of bloody history and of one's impending, ultimate death to be true? The question of the reality of the resurrection is not merely one question among many. Rather, the entirety of the biblical understanding of the world, of God, and of the self is here at stake.

How can one speak plausibly of the resurrection of Jesus Christ and the resurrection of the dead in the thinking of our time and, at the same time, offer a philosophically and theologically grounded rebuttal to fundamentalist ignorance and the mind games of radical constructivism? The thesis that will be presented in what follows is this: the reality of the resurrection, as it is found in the New Testament writings, can also be expressed under contemporary conditions of the production of knowledge if it involves itself in pluralistic discourse of society as a theological hypothesis about the disclosure [*Erschließung*] of reality. This necessary critical hypothesis has to explain how the content of the precritical, emotional confidence of faith in the truth of the Jesus-Christ-Story can become conceivable. It cannot demonstrate the truth of that faith. That is no defect of the Christian hypothesis but a constitutive part of it. Therefore it is above all necessary to adumbrate a conception of reality according to categorical semiotics and with its help to interpret resurrection discourse in the New Testament within the framework of contemporary encyclopedic knowledge.

Chapter 7

The Conception of Reality According to Categorical Semiotics

Categorical semiotics is no radical constructivism. Thus Charles Sanders Peirce, the founder of categorical semiotics, can explain reality precisely as a corrective to subjective opinion when he conceptualizes reality as "what is true of something, independent of whether someone regards it as true or not."[1] This holds even for perception of oneself. When I dream, then I have dreamed, even if I can no longer remember it. The dreaming was real, even if I am no longer conscious of it and perhaps no one will ever know of it, and even if this dream does not repeat itself, but rather remains a unique, contingent event.

If someone is unhappy, then he is still unhappy even if he denies it. His unhappiness is real, even if he tries the whole time to convince himself and all others that he is happy. Perhaps he is able to override his true feelings so well that everyone regards him as a happy person, but his true feelings remain real, even if no one perceives them, not even he himself.

Let us leave behind the plane of self-perception and choose an example from the hard, objective world that Wilfried Härle depicts:

> I go through a room and do not notice that it is divided by a glass wall that resists most strongly and painfully my attempt to cross the room. All that which I have just said about this experience has already been communicated through our conventional linguistic signs and through my interpretations. But at the base of all these interpretations lies the unarticulated perception of "something," which confronted me—painfully—with a reality that in any case we have *not construed*, that indeed we have not yet once *interpreted*. I repeat: Every interpretation of this perception—e.g., as "blow" or "pain" or "glass wall"—takes place on the plane of Thirdness, thus in the medium of conventional signs and our interpretation, but that *through which* this communication and interpretation is activated lies *underneath*, or *before*, this plane of Thirdness.[2]

Even signs cannot be construed or interpreted in an arbitrary way, however. When something stands for something else in a certain aspect and thus takes on the function of a sign, then that for which the sign stands cannot be construed in any arbitrary way. Only in this way can unfounded utterances be falsified. Whoever maintains that Jesus' last words in the Gospels are "Let us eat, drink, and be merry, for tomorrow we die" passes by the reality given for the condition of the signs as handed down and speaks nonsense, even if he quotes from one of the most important chapters pertaining to the biblical theology of the resurrection, namely from 1 Corinthians 15:32b. The reality of the given signs possesses a quality that enables them to be the criterion of their interpretations.

But it is not only measurable and primarily repeatable configurations that possess this quality. The example of the dream shows that the forgotten dream possesses reality and perhaps even a reality that determines the entire life of the dreamer more strongly than his empirically demonstrable environment.

In the conception of categorical semiotics, reality is understood as a network consisting of the phenomena of Firstness, Secondness, and Thirdness. Reality is not construed independent of these phenomena in a self-making way with sovereign creativity. Rather, it is much more a revealing of the interweaving of various phenomena by means of signs. Reality is prior not only to thinking and feeling, but also to every perception of phenomena, for something is always perceived that is not completely absorbed in a given act of perception, be it a phenomenon of Firstness, like an indeterminate, precritical feeling, a phenomenon of Secondness, like the collision of two objects, or a complex phenomenon of Thirdness, like perhaps the emerging collection of the writings of the Old and New Testaments.

Reality can be disclosed only by means of signs in acts of sign interpretation. In the conception of reality in categorical semiotics, signs are not deficient means of access to some unreachable *Ding an sich*. Rather, they are the way in which the phenomena of perception appear.

According to Peirce's doctrine of categorical semiotics,[3] all phenomena can be subsumed under three possible relations: Firstness, secondness, and Thirdness. "Firstness is that which is as it is, simply and without any connection to anything else." The dream dreamed as such, forgotten, unrecounted, uninterpreted, is a phenomenon of firstness. It is what it is, precritically, uncensored, unanalyzed. "Secondness is that which is as it is, because a second entity is as it is, without relation to some third." The resistance that the glass wall offers to my body is a phenomenon of Secondness. Something reacts to something. The phenomena of Secondness exist. They step outside themselves and can therefore react to one another. "What we understand under existence consists in how every existing thing reacts with all other existing things of the same universe in a broad sense (which reveals its relative position in space)."[4] Existence is a mode of being on the level of Secondness. Existence is empirically perceptible, measurable, embodied: " *'to exist'* means on the basis of the *ex* in *existere* to affect/effect something, to work back against other things that exist in the psycho-physical Universe."[5]

"Thirdness is mediation."[6] It discloses the relationship of phenomena reacting to each other and brings them to expression. Thirdness binds and discloses contexts, rules, and laws.

Any higher relation contains the relations standing under it, so that in a Thirdness are contained a Firstness and Secondness, in a Secondness is Firstness, but in a Firstness no Secondness and in a Secondness no Thirdness. "Reality as experienced and reality that can be experienced in general—understood as real universals—present themselves as 1. pure possibility; 2. the 'raw reality of things and actualities'; and 3. the ability to be bound in the production of connections, which is precisely what the establishment of a sign constitutes: as such it binds an object with one of these designating interpretations. Semiotics not only gives a structural description of the processes of perception, recognition, or language, but also represents reality as a three-tiered structure—just as we experience and reproduce it. Reality is a sign process."[7]

Semiotics receives its name on the basis of its endeavor to provide a theoretical conceptualization of the sign process, of semiosis. "Semiosis, the sign process, never means 'only' signs (in opposition to or removed from a wholly other or 'deeper' reality), but rather reality as mediated by signs, as they arise in the thought of the time."[8]

Categorical semiotics works out its sign model on the basis of the triadic phenomenology sketched above: "A Sign, or Representamen, is a First which stands in such a genuine triadic relation to a Second, called its Object, as to be capable of determining a Third, called its Interpretant, to assume the same triadic relation to its Object in which it stands itself to the same Object. This means that the Interpretant itself is a Sign that determines a Sign of the same Object and so forth without end."[9] In distinction to structuralist semiology,[10] *categorical semiotics*[11] speaks of signs as a triadic relation with the relata of *Sign, Object,* and *Interpretant.* The individual relata receive their sign function only within the framework of this sign relation. The Sign can only be a Sign when it represents an Object and is interpreted by an Interpretant as a Sign of this Object.

An Object can only be an Object when it is represented by a Sign and is interpreted by an Interpretant. An Interpretant can be an Interpretant only when it binds an Object and a Sign as Sign and Object together. The perception-theoretical point of categorical semiotics is therefore this: without Signs and Interpretants, speaking of an Object is meaningless. The same holds, however, going in the other direction: without an Object and Sign, speaking of an Interpretant is meaningless, since the Interpretant would have nothing which it could interpret. And the last follows: without an Object and Interpretant, speaking of a Sign is meaningless.

The Sign represents the Object *in a certain respect*. No Sign is therefore in a position to represent its Object in every respect. It chooses a certain point of view. This Object, represented in the sign relation through the selection of a certain respect, Peirce calls the *immediate* Object. The immediate Object has its place inside the sign relation and indeed *only* inside this triad. The *dynamic* Object on the other hand is the Object that motivates the production of a Sign and of this Sign the immediate Object represents only one respect. The connection between the dynamic and the immediate Object is preserved through the *ground* of the dynamic Object. Speaking of the *respect* of the immediate Object thus means that the dynamic Object cannot be represented as the whole by a Sign, but rather only with a view to one characteristic, which, however, in turn not only attributes to this (Sign) a specific dynamic Object. A dynamic Object can be fictive, real, dreamed or even belong to some other mode of being. It is not semiotic grammar but rather semiotic rhetoric—which investigates the ambit of Signs in concrete sign complexes on the basis of their ordering to the universe of discourse, to the encyclopedia—that clarifies the ordering of the Object to one of these modes of being.

Sign events are not only formally relational structures. A Sign functions first through its use in sign complexes such as writings, church services, texts, images, buildings, concerts, academic congresses, and so forth. These contemporary sign complexes in turn form the totality of a given culture. Cultures are based upon the societally conventionalized, creative, and controverted use of Signs—cultures are sign complexes.

A Sign therefore needs at least two correlations in order to function: it must belong to a presently perceptible sign complex and at the same time to a culture as the totality of its virtual sign complexes. In reliance on and modification of Peirce's conceptualization, I name the concretely perceptible sign complex the *universe of discourse*. With Umberto Eco, I name the comprehensive cultural sign complex the *encyclopedia*.[12]

The universe of discourse of a given sign complex, for example, a text, is then the world that this text sets forth and assumes, so that that which the text recounts or maintains can function plausibly. The concept of the universe of discourse always refers to a concrete sign complex, be it a text, an archeological excavation, an image, or a coin. On the other hand the encyclopedia, necessarily virtual because it cannot be grasped in its full complexity, encompasses the conventionalized knowledge of a given society and thus transcends the boundaries of individual sign complexes set by the concept of the universe of discourse. Every instance of sign production and sign reception must reach back to an encyclopedia of culturally conventionalized knowledge.

Let us return to semiotic grammar, which delineates a formal theory of Signs. It is responsible for a differentiated understanding of the Interpretant. Peirce distinguishes among the *immediate*, the *dynamic*, and the *final Interpretant*.[13] The *immediate Interpretant* is the indeterminate, vague connection between two relata, which determine these as Sign and Object, so that generally a process of semiosis is set in motion.[14] "The Dynamic Interpretant is just what is drawn from the Sign by a given Individual Interpreter."[15] "The Final Interpretant is the ultimate effect of the Sign, so far as it is intended or destined from the character of the Sign, being more or less of a habitual and formal nature."[16] While the immediate and the dynamic Interpretant are given in every semiosis, the final Interpretant is the regulative idea of a true interpretation in the most comprehensive meaning of the word. Its truth consists in the fact that it represents the dynamic Object in every respect. Peirce shows himself here to be a representative of the correspondence theory of truth. The point of Peirce's semiotic theory lies in the fact that it teaches one to conceive of the multiplicity of interpretations as necessary stations on the way to truth without propagating arbitrariness. *In the short run*, however, no interpretation can claim to be the absolute interpretation. It cannot even show itself to be adequate to the dynamic Object. Only an interpretive community can achieve an approach to the final Interpretant *in the long run*.

The regulative idea of the final Interpretant guards against every absolute claim. That is its ideological-critical component. It also requires, however, respect for the object of interpretation as an Other to be differentiated from the interpreter. That is its ethical component.[17] Finally, it issues an invitation to a common search for truth. Semiotics shows itself to be a "theory of a world disclosed in communication."[18]

The interpretation of phenomena is thus understood formally as a sign process that is propelled by a dynamic Object and at the same time forms a first Interpretant that perceives something as a sign of this dynamic Object and by means of this Sign brings a determinate aspect of the dynamic Object as an immediate sign object into the sign relation (to be ontologically differentiated from the dynamic Object) on the basis of a common ground postulated between the dynamic Object and the immediate Object.

The act of sign formation itself can be conceived of as an act of conclusion, wherefore semiotic logic enters the picture next to semiotic grammar and semiotic rhetoric. Peirce sets abduction next to deduction and induction: "The *abductive* conclusion represents (instinctively) the appearance of something new, the realm of possibility for the following disclosure of regularities and habits of behavior . . . the *deductive* conclusion explicate and orders that which is found, . . . the *inductive* conclusion methodologically reviews the given world of experience."[19]

If something is perceived as a Sign of something, then we have a single case at hand, which hypothetically can be the basis for a rule. Peirce names this line of reasoning abduction. Interpretation can then be described as an abductive line of reasoning, for the formation of an Interpretant causes something to become a Sign of something else. Interpretation is an abductive act of reasoning, "in which we encounter some very strange conditions that one could explain through the assumption that it is a question of a single case of a certain rule, wherefore we accept this assumption."[20] "Abduction allows us not only to interpret messages which refer to uncoded contexts or situations. It also helps us to determine the correct code or subcode for an imprecise message. . . . In view of the fact that in principle we must decide which code to refer to every time we hear a word, abduction appears to be part of every act of decoding."[21]

Inductive and deductive closure are found also, again, in the act of interpretation, but abduction represents the universal process of reasoning for the formation of every Interpretant, and also permits conceptualization of the necessary creativity in interpretation, without narrowing it in a constructivist manner.

Chapter 8

Semiotic Interpretation of the Phenomena of Resurrection Discourse in the Writings of the New Testament

Keeping in mind the results of the investigating the narrative and rhetorical strategies of texts that were examined in the first part of the present inquiry within the framework of their universe of discourse, the textual data under examination will now be interpreted and classified within the framework of the encyclopedia of our present knowledge, by means of the semiotic categories of Firstness, Secondness, and Thirdness.

It should once more be recalled that the concept of phenomenon here simply means that which appears to perception. One can only make interpretive decisions about the category and ontological status of a particular phenomenon in consideration of the universes of discourse and encyclopedias involved. The famous dictum of Charles Sanders Peirce— "All thought is in signs"[1]—means precisely this: only Signs, which are themselves the genuine phenomena of Thirdness, make possible the representation of the phenomena of Firstness and Secondness *as* the phenomena of Firstness and Secondness. The same holds for the phenomena of the category of Thirdness. It also can be represented only by means of signs because there can be no phenomena of Fourthness. That does not in any way mean, however, that access to the phenomena of Firstness and Secondness let alone to Thirdness as such is barred to us. Rather, they are disclosed [*erschlossen*] through their interpretive representation by means of signs.

The results of the investigation conducted in the first part will now be interpreted by placing them in the categories of Firstness, Secondness, and Thirdness. It will thus be shown that the high level of plausibility of New Testament resurrection discourse comes about through the interplay of all three categories and therefore the understanding of reality that New Testament resurrection discourse puts forth comes into view.

The results of the first part are not completely classified and interpreted here, however. That would go beyond the bounds of the scope and intention of the present study. Here the New Testament understanding of reality in view of its resurrection discourse will simply be disclosed [*erschlossen*].

Appearances: Doubt, Fear, Tears, Joy, and Burning Hearts (Phenomena of Firstness)

Recalling the New Testament depiction of the transformation of Paul from a persecutor of the Christian communities to an apostle of Jesus Christ, we observe that the depictions in Galatians 1 agree with those in Acts 9:22 in that Paul was in no way prepared for this event. The experience arose spontaneously, without any warning, and Paul reacted just as spontaneously, as is especially clear in his own presentation in Galatians. Neither in the depiction in Acts nor in his autobiographical narrative in Galatians 1 does Paul check in an empirical manner whether the tomb of Jesus in Jerusalem is empty. Moreover, he engages in no scriptural argumentation to help him evaluate his perception. Rather, the perception of the appearance, and his reaction to it as the perception of his commission, collapse into each other co-originally [*gleichursprünglich*] and precritically. This spontaneous act of perception with Paul's spontaneous reaction is to be evaluated as a phenomenon of Firstness. This event—however we may interpret and categorize it today, be it as an objective vision of the resurrected and exalted Kyrios, be it as a psychological projection of a disturbed Paul—forms the basis of the Pauline conviction of the resurrection of the crucified Jesus Christ. No tradition, no argumentation, no empirically repeatable proofs, but rather the contingent evidence of his own experience forms the emotional foundation of Pauline theology.

In placing his own experience in the memory of such experiences of others in 1 Corinthians 15, Paul shows that he would not wish to understand his vision as a singular individual experience but rather precisely as the foundation for those convinced of the resurrection of Jesus before him. Whether the witnesses named in 1 Corinthians 15 understood their own experiences in the same way as Paul we cannot say,[2] for we are familiar only with Paul's autobiographical depiction. Being depictions of such experiences at a certain remove, the gospels and Acts cannot be investigated as authentic witnesses of the appearances. It is even possible that in the Acts of the Apostles Luke has written out in narrative fashion what he found before him in Galatians 1, 1 Corinthians 9:1, and 1 Corinthians 15.

In the experience indicated in 1 Corinthians 15 with ὤφθε lies the precritical foundation of the conviction that Jesus Christ, killed on the cross, lives again. The origin of Easter faith therefore lies in the precritical feeling of having seen Jesus alive after his execution.

That which precipitates this feeling is to be understood in the theoretical terminology of signs as the dynamic Object, which already gives the first precritical reaction to it to be understood as the immediate Interpretant, which then denotes the resurrected Crucified One as the immediate Object of the first sign-formation process of Easter. This semiotic reconstruction of the formation of Easter faith thus represents the hypothesis that the foundation of all speech about the resurrection of Jesus Christ lies in a spontaneous experience that was precipitated by something that is not completely absorbed in this experience.[3]

In order to avoid misunderstandings, this semiotic hypothesis does not involve a positivistic view of revelation on the level of Secondness and thus does not maintain that the dynamic Object, which precipitates semiosis, was the resurrected and exalted Crucified One, but rather that the resurrected Crucified One was conceived, at least by Paul as one who had such an experience and expressed it in general as the final Interpretant. Thus, as a consequence of this interpretation of Paul, two things are to be maintained: (1) The conviction concerning the resurrection of the Crucified One rests precritically on an experience that precipitated a sign process, and is emotionally anchored in this experience. (2) The conviction concerning the resurrection of the Crucified One is a conclusion of an abductive act, which co-originally [*gleichursprünglich*] assigns an immediate Interpretant to the perception of the experience of a Something and then determines that Interpretant with the dynamic Interpretant, "Jesus lives."

This reconstruction of the formation of Easter faith is strengthened through the observation that the secondary narrative depictions of the gospels and Acts portray the spontaneity of the experience of the Resurrected One (or the message of his resurrection) for all their significant differences.

The gospel of Mark, which through its depiction prepares readers on the way to the empty tomb, step-by-step, and by means of the multiple predictions of the passion, death, and resurrection of Jesus also has the disciples of Jesus come to this knowledge. The gospel impressively portrays all the disciples failing to anticipate the resurrection. The same holds for the women who were driven to the tomb by the logic of death and the burial rites, not the expectation of the Resurrected One. The signs of his resurrection, the empty tomb and the message of the angel, generate paralyzing fear, flight, and silence as spontaneous reactions. The reaction of the women may be read as a foil standing in contrast with the spontaneous reaction the gospel desires of its readers, which is written into the resurrection discourse of the New Testament positively with the spontaneous conduct of Paul. While the women refrain from speaking further out of spontaneous fear, Paul is the one who reacts appropriately not by investigating the matter either neutrally or even skeptically on the level of Secondness or Thirdness, but rather by immediately beginning to announce the good news of the resurrection of the Crucified One without any hesitation.

No one shows himself or herself to be appropriately prepared for an encounter with the Resurrected One or with the message of his resurrection in the gospel of Matthew either. Here too the women go to the tomb because of the logic of death and burial rites. Ironically, only the opponents of Jesus think about the prediction of his resurrection. They therefore place a guard at the tomb so that the disciples cannot steal the corpse and maintain that the prophecy of his own resurrection was fulfilled (cf. Matt 27:62-66). The guards also thus fail to reckon with a resurrection event, and they suffer deadly fright when the tomb is opened with a loud roar and the angel appears in terrifying form. The women, to whom the message of the resurrection is now being shared, react spontaneously with both fright and great joy. As with the soldiers, the fright paralyzes them, but the women's joy, which is so great that it conquers their fear, makes them want to spread the news. In this way, already emotionally convinced of the message of the resurrection of the Crucified One, they encounter him and fall at his feet to pay homage. The disciples first react with their journey to the mountain in accord with the resurrection message. But then some of them paradoxically doubt precisely when they see him (Matt 28:16-17).

Luke, who like his predecessors also motivates the journey of the women to the tomb by the logic of death and burial rites, has the women fall into confusion at the empty tomb. They can make no rhyme or reason of their perception of the absent corpse, a perception that disturbs the logic of death. The resurrection message, which is made plausible in the memory of the passion predictions and thus the announcement of the resurrection bound up with them, precipitates a cognitive reaction first of all and not an emotional reaction: "Then they remembered his words" (Luke 24:8).

In any event the departure from the tomb and the retelling of the message to the disciples can be considered as thoroughgoing agreement with the resurrection message. The disciples in any case regard this message as "an idle tale, and they did not believe them" (24:11). Peter, however, investigates the women's words by going to the tomb. But for Peter the empty tomb is no proof of the resurrection, but it is at least a sign that causes him to wonder. Even Luke, who as was shown in the first part of the present investigation is the one who is most strongly interested in an empirically verifiable proof of the resurrection, and again and again depicts the materially somatic dimension of the gospel and also of the resurrection of Jesus, regards the rational acceptance of the message of the resurrection as an occasion to examine it empirically. But even the empirical indices do not achieve the plane of Firstness. They do not convince one emotionally of the truth of what was said and they can supply no interpretive framework on the level of Thirdness, which could lead from mere wonder into an interpretive understanding in which the empirical indices and the emotional condition of conviction would be bound together plausibly in a way that can be depicted. On that point, even Luke requires an emotional reaction and a hermeneutical key. These are encountered, however, precisely in the "burning hearts" of the disciples on the road to Emmaus, who burn precisely in the moment when the Resurrected One speaks with them and "opened the Scriptures" to them (24:32). They recognize him in the breaking of the bread, because their eyes are there opened by God (24:31b): They feel the truth through his words and they understand what has happened through the interpretation of the Scriptures. In the moment in which they recognize their companion on the way as the resurrected Crucified One, the body of the Resurrected One vanishes from their sight. Luke is so very interested in the empirical-material dimension, thus in the phenomenon of Secondness, that he very much precludes the misunderstanding of a hermeneutical automatism of empirical phenomena. The empty tomb can be understood at best as a sign of an event given to provoke thought, which breaks through the limits of the phenomena of Secondness. Even in Luke the body of the Resurrected One no longer obeys the laws of bodies of flesh, blood, and bone. The truth of the message of the resurrection, however, according also to Luke, is to be felt and then interpreted only within the framework of the Scripture. In any case, in his Acts of the Apostles Luke will employ the tomb no more as proof, indeed not once more, even for the sake of stimulating thought.

In the gospel of John, the open tomb leads to a spontaneous misunderstanding: "Early on the first day of the week, while it was still dark,

Mary Magdalene came to the tomb and saw that the stone had been removed from the tomb. So she ran and went to Simon Peter and the other disciple, the one whom Jesus loved, and said to them, 'They have taken the Lord out of the tomb, and we do not know where they have laid him'" (John 20:1-3). The open tomb is introduced wholly into the experience of the conflict that led to Jesus' execution. Subsequently Mary offers the hypothesis that the opponents of Jesus continued their enmity now even to the point of stealing a lifeless corpse, not wanting it to take part in its ritual rest.

Peter and the beloved disciple run to the tomb in order to examine the matter. Only the beloved disciple comes to believe spontaneously in light of the clues of the open tomb and carefully arranged grave clothes. He, who probably as the author of the gospel should be portrayed as especially reliable, concludes from the open tomb, in syntagmatic connection with the order of the clothes, that no violent grave robbery could have taken place here. Without any further aids to understanding he "saw and believed" (John 20:8). His faith arises spontaneously and not once needs any framework of understanding to feel the truth. All that was needed was some impetus, the perception of a sign, to make possible his spontaneous reaction of faith. Its exceptional exemplary function lies in the spontaneity of his faith as the dynamic Interpretant of the perception of decoded clues.

Peter, on the other hand, does not come to faith here, for he still lacks the hermeneutical key that John takes over from Luke: "for as yet they did not understand the scripture, that he must rise from the dead" (20:9).

Even Mary remains stubbornly stuck in her misunderstanding and does not recognize the Resurrected One through her tears over the continued injustice done to her Lord. She identifies him as the "gardener" and even regards him as one of the grave robbers. Only when he calls her by name does she perceive the truth and retells the events to the disciples (John 20:18).

Finally, the disciples, who sit in a locked room "for fear of the Jews" and see that the resurrected Crucified One can force his way into the room without opening the doors, "rejoiced when they saw the Lord" (John 20:20). The appropriate emotional reaction to the perception of the resurrected Crucified One is joy.

According to the Scriptures of the New Testament, the foundation of Easter faith consists in a spontaneous feeling of truth driven by phenomena that cannot be reduced to the perception of the recipients. Easter faith is fundamental and is a phenomenon of Firstness, a precritical feeling of truth, before any critical examination and before any reflective encyclopedic connections, which is established [*sich einstellen*] as the dynamic Interpretant of a perception of something. According to the Scriptures of the New Testament, Easter faith is not to be explained as an interior psychological construction that compensates for the cognitive dissonance between the experience of saving communion with Jesus in the Jesus movement before his death and then the experience of his horrific end through Jesus' execution.[4] Easter faith is first and foremost the spontaneous answer to an overwhelming phenomenon.

Cross, Tomb, and Visions
(Phenomena of Secondness)

The experiences lying at the root of Easter faith as a phenomenon of Firstness are viewed as visions[5] within the framework of empirical-historical investigation. Historical research does not therefore possess the means to examine whether the question concerns interior psychic processes, as the subjective vision hypothesis of David Friedrich Strauss maintains, or whether something objective was seen in the visions by those seeing them, as the so-called objective vision hypothesis requires.[6] On the level of Secondness it can only be determined that the Scriptures of the New Testament present those who saw the resurrected Crucified One or something else concluding he was alive and convinced that it was not a product of pious imagination. Without doubt the relevant New Testament Scriptures stand on the side of the objective vision hypothesis. That does not speak for their validity on the level of their historical quality under the conditions of our contemporary knowledge of the world, however.

The understanding of ὤφθη in 1 Corinthians 15:3-8 is highly controverted between the representatives of the subjective and the objective vision hypotheses. In her historical analysis Gudrun Guttenberger rightly asks that the meaning of ὤφθη not be overburdened, as one sees again and again in exegetical treatments of 1 Corinthians 15. In a sober manner, she determines the following:

1. "The use of the term ὤφθη is therefore not very wide: The expression is encountered in the formulas in 1 Cor 15:3-5 and Luke 24:34 as well as Acts 9:17, 13:31, and 26:16; Paul employs it freely (1 Cor 15:8) in reliance on its linguistic usage in the formula in 1 Cor 15:5. It does not appear in the narratives of the Gospels."[7]

2. "More likely" than its use as technical term referring to revelation "is thus a profane use ('he was seen') or its use referring to a religiously relevant event without further specificity, as in Tob 12:22 or in Josephus, *War*, 6:293-298. Therefore the assumption that the

very use of the term leads to the conclusion that the texts that identify the appearance of the Resurrected One with ὤφθη determine him as the exalted one in a position equal to God is rather uncertain. On the basis of the word's usage there is no reason to doubt that ὤφθη indicates visually perceptible events—even if one assumes a terminological usage."[8]

It is thus not historically reasonable to contest the claim that the visions, of which 1 Corinthians 15 speaks prominently, relate actual experiences of historical individuals that lead them to the conclusion that the Crucified One lives. *This* "cognitive dissonance,"[9] between empirical-historical knowledge of the crucifixion of Jesus and his burial on one hand and the perception of the truth of having experienced him as living, is the historically tangible catalyst corresponding to the depictions in the New Testament that precipitates discourse about God's resurrection of the Crucified One. But the claim that this could function as historical proof or at least suggest that the visionaries actually saw the resurrected Crucified One must be categorically denied.

While the overwhelming majority of exegetes conceive of the Easter experience as the historical origin of the conviction of the resurrection of the Crucified One, in his study *Der Ablauf der Osterereignisse und das leere Grab*, Hans von Campenhausen presents the following thesis: "The decisive impetus that set everything in motion was the discovery of the empty tomb."[10] This thesis has not proven plausible in historical research, even if it is formulated again and again.

In a weaker way, Wolfhart Pannenberg used the historical hypothesis of the empty tomb to support the weight of his argument for an objective vision hypothesis. Recently, however, Dale C. Allison, on whom Pannenberg's writings area significant influence, has renewed the hypothesis of the empty tomb in his study "An Opened Tomb and a Missing Body?"[11] Allison's perceptive investigations work out two strong arguments against the empty tomb, and present two stronger arguments from him for the assumption that the tomb of Jesus had been found empty.

Although Allison comes to the conclusion that it is historically more likely that the tomb was empty, his analysis shows the limitations of every one-sided self-certainty of one or another position, and also here emphasizes the appropriate insight mentioned above that ultimately an overarching view will decide the interpretation of the data. Against the empty tomb he discusses the fact that the early Christians were demonstrably in the position of generating fictional narratives and that a whole series of legends of vanished bodies can be demonstrated in the history of religions. On the other hand, two things speak for the empty tomb: (1) The appearances of Jesus without the knowledge of the empty tomb would not have led to the acceptance of his resurrection but rather to his exaltation. (2) The discovery of the empty tomb by Mary Magdalene and the other women do not leave the impression of fiction.[12] Allison, however, avoids the categorical conclusion of basing the greater probability of the acceptance of the empty tomb on the actuality of the resurrection of Jesus. Rather, he speaks here of a "dead end"[13] for historical argumentation, for the empty tomb says nothing about the reason for its void.

Indeed, Allison lists the decisive arguments for and against the empty tomb in an appropriate manner, but it appears to me the issue of sources speaks in favor of a narrative fiction. The gospel of Mark is the only source that presents a story in which the corpse of the dead Jesus is no longer to be found in the tomb after his burial. Matthew, Luke, and John are dependent on Mark. No other New Testament writing calls upon the empty tomb. There is therefore only one enduring witness, and he has a strong motive to invent a story of an empty tomb. Mark 16:1-8 forms the brilliant conclusion of the entire composition, as I analyzed it in part I of the present investigation. The empty tomb symbolizes the absence of the corpse and therefore depicts a double negation: (1) The corpse is not where the logic of death assumes it must be. (2) The tomb of Jesus is therefore no longer the empirically verifiable sign of his death, but rather evidence that his body does not obey the laws of death, the interpretation of which decides belief or unbelief. The story of the empty tomb can therefore be regarded as a composition of the narrative theology of the gospel of Mark. Indeed, the limits Allison maintained for his own historical hypothesis hold also for this hypothesis: it is one of the two plausible possibilities for the formation of a historical hypothesis concerning the evangelists' stories of the absence of Jesus' corpse from the tomb.

A third historical hypothesis that to this point has hardly found mention in German-speaking scholarship is represented by John Dominic Crossan,[14] who points to the fact that those crucified usually received no burial. The question may thus be raised whether Jesus, executed as a criminal, would have had an orderly burial at all. Since, however, the tradition of the burial is encountered not only in the Gospels but also in 1 Corinthians 15, and since it is not certain whether Jewish practice was to entomb criminals, this hypothesis is to be accorded little historical probability.

In no case, however, can the tomb, whether full or empty, be regarded as empirical proof of the resurrection of Jesus,[15] for there are many historically conceivable possibilities that could account for the empty tomb:

the theft of the corpse, confusion about the location of the tomb, and so on.

It is of especial importance, however, to call to mind once more the historicity of the crucifixion of Jesus of Nazareth. The existence of Jesus of Nazareth and his execution on the cross, testified to by diverse sources also outside the New Testament, cannot be controverted with plausible arguments grounded in historical reason. Of course that is no proof of his resurrection, but it locates the Jesus-Christ-Story told by the New Testament Scriptures in the categorical realm of existence, of Secondness, of reality approachable in empirical-historical terms. With the existence of Jesus and the fact of his crucifixion, the Jesus-Christ-Story receives its grounding in the midst of the hard world of facts. It is not to be located in the mythical realm of religious phantasms. It tells the wretched story of the cruel execution of an existing human being liable to suffering who deserves our pity. The cross on which he died in agony, however, is not suited for religious kitsch, being as it is an instrument of torture. The bloody body of Jesus nailed to the cross is a victim of human brutality. On the categorical level of Secondness, the cross mocks every religious romanticism. The cross without the word of the cross "is and makes mute."[16] The cross in the framework of the Jesus-Christ-Story, however, binds the word of the cross to the empirically and historically approachable reality and locates the gospel in the midst of the reality of its historical existence. Therefore one ought to agree with Andreas Lindemann: "What would happen if one day someone were to find the remains of Jesus' corpse and were able to identify it without a doubt? Faith in Jesus' resurrection—more precisely, *my* faith—would not be affected. *I* could no longer believe in Jesus' resurrection if it were to be shown that Jesus did not die on the cross."[17] This important insight, which Lindemann here expresses modestly as his own confession of faith, can certainly be formulated in supraindividual, general ways. The historical analysis of the New Testament Scriptures shows that resurrection discourse arises overwhelmingly without reference to the empty tomb, but not, however, without the importance of the actuality of the crucifixion of Jesus. And even those Scriptures that depict stories of the empty tomb have the logic of the factual break through their portrayals: "The evangelists' narratives show with all clarity that the empty tomb lacks the character of a proof for the evangelists themselves."[18]

Cross, tomb, and visions are to be approached in historical research as phenomena of Secondness. The reality to which the word of the cross bears witness does not come into view, however, precisely because it breaks through the logic of the factual and lets something new be seen, something contingent, unique, without analogue, that lets everything, even the phenomena of Secondness, become something else: the resurrection of the Crucified One as the eschatological act of God. The cross serves as a reminder that this eschatological event took place not in utopia but rather in the midst of reality as experienced by the human body, in the midst of the world that God's creatures inhabit.

The Great Story of the Scripture(s) as Epistemological Framework for Resurrection Discourse (Phenomena of Thirdness)

The New Testament Scriptures not only make claims about the eschatological resurrection, but they also make it conceivable by locating the emotional conviction about the life and work of the resurrected Crucified One in the midst of the world of hard facts and by binding both in a coherent manner by means of discourse about the resurrected Crucified One by the merciful and just creator God of Israel. It is not only the overwhelmingly discursive texts of the letters but also the narrative texts of the gospels and the Acts of the Apostles as well as the visionary composition of the Apocalypse of John that appeal to the reasoning powers of their readers in order to express the reality of the resurrection in a comprehensible manner. The New Testament Scriptures aim for a critical and understanding faith that knows enough to shut out religious romanticism, bloodless formulations of abstract worldviews, and constructivist phantasms. The "burning hearts" feel the effective truth that the silent cross does not signify the end of the Jesus-Christ-Story. Rather, in reliance on God's creativity and with understanding provided by the lenses of Israel's sacred Scriptures, they let the good news of the eschatological resurrection of the Crucified One shine forth as the breaking in of the ultimate, salvific, eternal reign of God in the midst of the present time, which signifies nothing less than the beginning of the saving of the entire creation through its new creation.

The plausibility of resurrection discourse is generated by the narrative framework of the creation to the new creation, which the Bible presents as a whole. The texts of the Bible are held together by a grand narrative that runs from the beginning to the end of this world. The books of the Old Testament are determined by the (his)story of God with his chosen people Israel. The New Testament books make reference to this (his)story and interpret it anew in light of the Jesus-Christ-Story, whose fundamental story and driving power are the crucifixion of Jesus and the eschatological event of his resurrection. If the Old Testament books present the narrative, epistemological, and theological assumptions of the New Testament books, then the word of the cross of the New Testament books discloses the proper Christian understanding of the Old Testament Scriptures. It is chiefly the word of the cross as the narrative of the all-changing eschatological event of the resurrection of the Crucified One that reads the sacred Scriptures of Israel as the Scriptures of the Old Testament.[19]

The Story the Old Testament Tells—A Narrative Sketch

The Old Testament tells a story arising out of the many local narratives of the sacred Scriptures of Israel. From the beginning on it tells of the creatively loving, just, and merciful God of Israel: *creation*. It begins by telling how God created everything. God pursued no purpose nor profit when he created the world through his creative word. Neither did God need the world. It simply pleases him to create it, and everything he created pleases him. He loves his creation. A good beginning. This world, these plants, these animals, and not least of all also human beings are wanted and loved for their own sake, simply as ends in themselves. Human beings are especially near to their creator. The creator has created them after his own image precisely in that which especially marks him out. They also have the capacity for creativity in linguistic acts and can call things by name with their language, a special task entrusted to them as an especial responsibility for God's creation.

But soon God's confidence and trust in humankind is disappointed. Humankind is led astray by the promise of no longer being created after the image of God but rather to become like him at any price and with guile and spite. Thus is the intimate, blessed relationship between creator and creature disturbed with the most serious consequences, which immediately leads to unmerciful decisions: fratricide, exploitation, and depriving the weak are all signatures of this way of life that fails to live in accord with one's own nature as creature and thus with the creator. God ultimately reacts most severely and kills his flesh-and-blood creatures by means of the great flood. But he risks a new beginning with Noah, his family, and the animals on the ark. God even repents of his severity and binding himself in a first covenant he promises never to act in such a way again.

But humanity proceeds with its failed way of life. Instead of living lives rich with blessing on earth, they desire to storm heaven and so build the Tower of Babel. God defends himself and confuses their communicative acts through a multitude of different languages. In spite of this attack on heaven, God does not abandon humankind.

Covenant with Abraham

God chooses Abraham, makes a covenant with him, and in wondrous ways makes him the father of many nations, above all the father of Israel, the nation chosen by God.

God is a faithful God. He stands by his word and when his people Israel become enslaved in Egypt, God liberates them. He tells Moses what he has planned and Moses relates it to the Israelites. Pharaoh, however, does not wish to do without his slaves. Through ten terrible plagues that God visits upon the Egyptians, he backs down and lets them go.

Exodus

God delivers his people from Egyptian subjection and thereby reveals who he is: he is the one who leads his people from servitude and leads them into the promised land. He also thus gives them what they actually need to know in written form: he communicates his Torah to them, his instructions for a good and ever more just life in accord with their creaturely nature and his unlimited creativity. But while he gives Moses the tables with the Ten Commandments for those created by God for the living of a communal life, on their own initiative they make other gods for themselves and dance around the golden calf. God is indeed a faithful God and does not prescind from his promises. He is also a just God whose wrath punishes. And thus these faithless people are not punished with death, but they must spend forty years wandering in the wilderness, and it is the next generation that will first enter into the promised land.

Israel settles in Canaan and establishes themselves in the way of other peoples. They set up a state, choose kings, run after the gods of other nations, forget again and again their God and his salvific instructions for a peaceful life. Again and again the justice due the weak is trampled underfoot. Their actions are not directed by love for its own sake and the recognition of their own nature as creatures, but rather it is the logic of human power over other humans that determines their thinking, feeling, and behavior. The ends justify the means. Even the first kings chosen by God's anointing do not remain in the path of communal life. They shatter justice and brutally exploit their power to their own advantage. David, for whom God ensures the existence of his house, has Uriah, husband of beautiful Bathsheba, sent to his death in combat so that David can take Bathsheba for his own. The house of David is no guarantor of justice and righteousness. Wise Solomon is more the exception than the rule. After his death Israel is divided by conflict and distances itself from God again and again.

But God does not give up reminding them what his justice and righteousness require for their actions. He commissions his prophets in both north and south: Elijah, Amos, Isaiah, Jeremiah, Ezekiel, and many others. But even the messengers of God are persecuted by their own people. Sometimes the prophets even break through with their message, but enduring repentance seldom results. What God's prophets had announced happens. First the northern kingdom falls and then also the southern kingdom. Even the temple of Jerusalem is destroyed. The rich and powerful of Jerusalem are carried off to Babylon: *Exile*.

But God is a faithful God, and his covenant with Israel will stand to the end of the world. He comforts his people and heals their wounds. When the Persian king Cyrus conquers the Babylonians, he permits the Jews to return to Israel. Some remain, many return. They build a new temple in Jerusalem and write down many of their stories of their relationship with God.

For a little while Israel is once again independent, a time of which Daniel speaks in code and the books of the Maccabees speak openly. But the new kings of Israel are no less obsessed with power and devoid of piety than other rulers who rule themselves. The hope for an Israel that would build a kingdom of peace through its kings, in accord with the picture Isaiah had so beautifully painted, is shattered. The prophetic promises remain, however: God's bringer of peace, the Messiah, will establish God's kingdom of peace in Israel: "Look, the young woman is with child and shall bear a son, and shall name him Immanuel" (Isa 7:14).

The grand story of the sacred Scriptures of Israel ends here. The hopeful expectation that this story sets forth transcends itself. The Messiah will come. A new covenant (Jer 31:31-34) will be written in hearts and the Spirit of God will be poured out (Joel 3:1-5). Jews wait to this very day for the fulfillment of this promise. Christians believe it was fulfilled long ago. Christians and Jews live in two different narrative worlds and therefore interpret reality in differing ways. Jews are situated in the time before the fulfillment of the messianic promise. Christians live in another time: they live after the fulfillment of these promises. The Jesus-Christ-Story tells of this. Its core is the resurrection of the Crucified One.

The Word of the Cross as Continuation and Transformative Interpretation of Israel's Grand Narrative

The books of the New Testament narrate the Jesus-Christ-Story as the fulfillment of the messianic promises of the Old Testament Scriptures. Thus they assume the constancy of God and the validity of the sacred

Scriptures of Israel as his word. They even maintain the special position of Israel. They are convinced, however, that the turning of the ages has taken place with the resurrection of the Crucified One and therefore now—as indeed the prophets also promised—all nations are called to accept God's saving invitation. The eschatological time has broken into the present and by this everything is changed, even if it has not yet become visible to all.

Because the narrative complex of the death and resurrection of the crucified Jesus of Nazareth shapes the narrative and theological dynamic of the Jesus-Christ-Story, this complex is narrated in the Gospels in differing ways: who the Crucified One was, how he worked, what he taught, how he came to his execution, and on what the certainty of his eschatological and thus ages-turning resurrection is grounded.

Interpretants are embedded in the narratives of the Gospels as meta-commentaries that derive their depiction from their faith that the Crucified One was raised by God and that he is the Messiah awaited by Israel, whom God attests to be such through the resurrection, and whom God has installed as the mighty Kyrios of those who follow him. The Gospels are no antiquarian reports that tell of a life come to an end in a closed-off past. Rather, they tell of the living Kyrios, who as the resurrected crucified one bears the signature of human sin on his body forever. They narrate his story in such a way that they contrast his way of mercy rooted in the love of God for its own sake with the merciless power of exploitation, which knows no bounds and which even brutally assaulted the Son of God. They make the gravity of the situation clear precisely by not saying that all manner of things will be well because God is the God of love. Rather, they continue the Old Testament portrayal of God precisely in all its complexity. God, as Jesus also proclaims him in the Gospels, is a merciful and just God, and his wrath smites those who follow the values of those earthly and heavenly powers abusing creation, who do not establish themselves on the way of loving mercy for its own sake.

The gospel relates good news, namely that forgiveness is offered to all if they establish themselves on the way of mercy established by God and his Son. This offer, however, can also be rejected. Everything depends on it, death or life. The gospel calls for decision.

The Acts of the Apostles then narrates how the work of the Holy Spirit founded the church of Jesus Christ and its spread to the center of the world. The Holy Spirit is the way that the exalted, resurrected Crucified One communicates and works, and thus is also in the present of contemporary readers. The church owes itself to no human hierarchies and reforms but rather to the working of the Holy Spirit.

The letters interpret the death and resurrection of the Crucified One in very different ways and reflect from there onward upon the consequences for the various concrete situations in the respective communities to which they are addressed. Thus we find statements that are not only sensible for their original situations but also still plausible and valid today.

The Apocalypse at the end of the Bible provides a meaningful conclusion, because this book illustrates the cosmological battle that the entire Bible assumes. In multiple images it depicts the brutality of the power of the wicked in the certainty that the resurrected Crucified One, empowered with the might of God, will annihilate evil. The Apocalypse takes the brutality and violence of evil seriously, thinking of evil in general terms. In the Bible's estimation, the experiences of suffering, violence, injustice, and death are also indeed matters of individual guilt, but not only matters of individual guilt. The anthropology of the Bible and especially the anthropology of the Apocalypse do not regard human beings as subjects sovereign over themselves but rather as beings bound up in the real power of supraindividual powers, independent of which one cannot act. The Apocalypse is no dark denial of the world. It is a book of hope, indeed of confidence, and therefore its promise of the new heaven and the new earth as the place and time where all tears are wiped away for all Christians should give hope for a good end in the same way as the creation stories tell them of a good beginning.

Summary: The Understanding of Reality in New Testament Resurrection Discourse

There is no other way to reconstruct the emergence of Easter faith than by interpreting the Scriptures of the New Testament as an Interpretant of the event that led to Easter faith. Every psychologizing explanation stands in the unavoidable danger of prematurely importing one's own worldview into the Scriptures of the New Testament and reducing everything to an analogy-laden complex of cause and effect. The purpose of Easter faith would then consist in "holding fast to the special significance of Jesus even after his crucifixion."[20] This interpretation arises not from the witness of the Scriptures, however, but rather from thinking in terms of empiricism that Easter faith should be explained on the level of Secondness, and therefore employing a psychological complex of cause and effect as an interpretive pattern in order to avoid coming into conflict with the binary rationality of scientific thinking after Newton. Therefore the categorical levels are no longer properly distinguished, but rather are blended together into an opaque muddled mass, something the incisive epistemological analysis of

Georg Essen already clearly pointed out in 1993: such an approach leads back "to the virulent and unsettled problem of a conceptually inadequate and categorically imprecise determination of the nature of the reality of the Easter event."[21]

But also those who like Wolfhart Pannenberg wish to interpret the resurrection of the Crucified One as a historical event overdetermine the New Testament texts and especially the semantics of ὤφθη in 1 Corinthians 15:3-8. Rather, the resurrection discourse of the New Testament binds the emotional certainty of the active and effective life of the Crucified One in their own present with their own contemporary experience and with the remembrance of the Jesus-Christ-Story as handed down to them, and in connecting these realms of phenomena with the sacred Scriptures of Israel concludes that the all-encompassing eschatological act of God, the resurrection and exaltation of the Crucified One, is the beginning of the new creation. These concentrations of phenomena generate the reality of the language of the resurrection of the Crucified One and the expected resurrection of the dead on the day of final judgment. Only those who are influenced emotionally, daily, and rationally by this language, by the word of the cross, by the gospel of the Jesus-Christ-Story, can see the world in the spirit of this story as New Testament resurrection discourse gives it to be seen. Thus, however, the experience of the Jesus-Christ-Story itself becomes a phenomenon of Firstness. The spirit of this story convinces one on an emotional level. Or it does not. But can this emotional, precritical acceptance generated by the spirit of the biblical story withstand the critical examination of hard facts? And is it possible to bring reflection upon the fundamental epistemological decisions of the biblical texts into conversation with an understanding of reality operative in today's scientific discourse? Or is Christian faith with its central story of the resurrection of the Crucified One a relic of a bygone era, which at best can still be looked upon as a great poetic work in Goethe's sense, but which no longer belongs within the realm of the disclosure of the entirety of reality?

Chapter 9

Semiotic Interpretation of Protestant Resurrection Discourse Today

The fundamental decision of Protestant theology consists of the Reformation principle of *sola scriptura*. Only the interpreted Scriptures can be the norm and measure of Christian faith, precisely because only then will the fantasies of enthusiasts, reduction of reality, and ungrounded dogma and philosophical ideas receive a critical evaluation that is based on the power of the signifiers. This Protestant scripture principle knows all about the necessity of interpretation and criticism of the scripture and even furthers them. If the scriptural signs are interpreted appropriately so that the world is seen with the eyes of the Spirit, then they have achieved their spiritually revelatory power. Scripture's purpose is neither the spiritless citing of the scripture nor any credos but rather the effective coming of the spirit of the scripture into one's own existence, and only in this way does it become Holy Scripture, the Word of God. Protestant Christians do not believe in a dogma of the resurrection. Rather, in their brokenness and doubt they experience the resurrected Crucified One as living because the Scripture illuminates them with trust in God's loving, uncreated creativity.

Keeping in mind the question of a sustainable Christian way of speaking of the resurrection of the dead, this means, only in an discerning interpretation of the biblical scriptures, anchored in one's own life in the thought forms of one's respective time, does the language of the resurrection of the dead become Protestant discourse about the resurrection.

Therefore in the following I shall ask how the three levels of phenomena may come to bear upon an understanding of the reality of the resurrection indebted to the Protestant concept of *sola scriptura*, and how on this basis one can speak plausibly about the resurrection of Jesus Christ and the resurrection of the dead.

"He Is Risen." "He Is Risen Indeed!"
(Phenomena of Firstness)

The category of Firstness possesses foundational power not only for New Testament resurrection discourse, but also for contemporary resurrection language. When one hears in the Easter Sunday service the call "He is risen" and the response according to Luke 24:34 "He is risen indeed," then one is dealing with the phenomenon of Firstness if those responding with the Lukan citation perceive the feeling of saying something that affects their salvation fundamentally. This feeling can express itself in a happy facial expression, a reverent posture, an indescribable feeling in one's stomach, or even a "burning heart." It maintains its revelatory power precisely as a phenomenon of Firstness, that is, as precritical perception that does not distinguish this feeling and the one feeling it. Neither does it inquire analytically into the origin of this feeling, and nor does it differentiate between one's own utterance and the citation. Neither does it undertake any critical investigation into its conceivability or coherence with other experiences and insights. The spontaneous, precritical feeling that expresses itself in various ways in the speaker's body is the basis of any perception of reality. Whoever does not perceive the truth of the Easter call in such a diffuse way will not have the Easter message revealed to him emotionally. One can then perhaps become a professor of religious studies and describe from the perspective of an outsider how those who hear the Easter call—as a reality that immediately affects them and the entire cosmos—conduct themselves. But in the terms used by religious studies, the reality of the resurrection is not revealed as the reality that makes it possible to perceive the world and oneself in this light.

But it is not only the acceptance of but rather also the rejection of or indifference to the Easter message that is grounded in the level of Firstness. Every conception of reality that shows itself active in thinking, feeling, and living can be located precritically in bodily perceptions. Even the "no" to the Easter message is felt, even indifference is perceived bodily (for example) as boredom and lethargy in the Sunday service.

Events and the Boundaries of Empirical
and Historical Research (Phenomena of Secondness)

Feeling is not everything! Whoever thinks that his own feeling of truth must be separated from all others, and must be immunized not only against other feelings of truth but also even against other insights that can only be achieved on the categorical level of Secondness and Thirdness, turns into a strange, pigheaded companion in the best case scenario. Whoever then decides to change the world politically in such a way that it must be organized according to one's own feeling of truth as binding upon all becomes in the worst case scenario a fundamentalist ready to do violence. Acting this way means one will never arrive at a biblically grounded attitude toward faith.

The examination of one's own feeling of truth through the critical perception of the phenomena of Secondness and the reflection of Thirdness belongs to a critical faith, as it is presented in the biblical texts.

On the level of Secondness it is of fundamental significance to perceive that historical research situates the Jesus-Christ-Story remembered in the Scriptures of the New Testament in the empirical-historical environment of the Levant, above all in Galilee, Samaria, and Judea in the time of Roman rule. The man Jesus depicted in the Gospels is shown by historical-critical research to be a man of flesh and blood, whose biography can no longer be sketched in any detail, whose self-understanding and significance are highly controverted,[1] but whose existence is not seriously or plausibly debatable. The Jesus-Christ-Story is thus no myth or a fairytale that shares a nature with *Alice in Wonderland*. It is first of all a question of the history of a man who lived at a certain time in a certain land and in a certain culture that, in spite of all difficulties that historical Jesus research shares with every other field of history writing, is principally approachable through historical research. On the level of Secondness it can be maintained that Jesus was a Jewish man from Galilee who learned a manual trade and who as an adult was an itinerant preacher proclaiming as the theme of his preaching the coming kingdom of God. His preaching met with some success, he engaged in works of healing that can be explained psychosomatically, and partly through the actions of an individual from his circle he was executed on the cross by Jewish and Roman authorities. This man suffered horrifying agonies at his death. Jesus died a terrible death, and all those dreaming romantics and those seeking the sensational who in an unspeakable manner portray the crucified Jesus as only half dead, the Jesus who after his crucifixion went to India or somewhere else, commit an offense not only against the plausibilities of historical reason but also, worse still, against the agony and suffering of the man Jesus of Nazareth, executed most violently.[2]

On the level of Secondness it can be said that after the death of Jesus some were convinced that they had seen the Crucified One alive and powerful in another form with which the eschatological resurrection of the dead had begun, and this feeling of truth on the level of Firstness was so strong for them that they interpreted this perception as the appearance of the resurrected Crucified One, under the conditions of the knowledge of the sacred Scriptures of Israel within the encyclopedic framework of their apocalyptic worldview.

On the level of Secondness it can be historically debated whether the tomb of Jesus after his burial retained his corpse, or whether it was found empty by his adherents. Historical-critical investigation of this question has not to this point come to a certain historical result. On the level of empirical-historical research, however—and it matters not how the question about the empty tomb is answered—one can only proceed from the assumption that Jesus' corpse rotted like every other corpse, and it matters not whether that happened in the tomb or somewhere else. On the level of Secondness it is unthinkable under the biological, physical, and climactic conditions of Judea that a body of flesh and blood would not rot.

Since the books by R. A. Moody[3] and Elisabeth Kübler-Ross,[4] near-death experiences and appearances of those who have died have again and again been evaluated as quasi-analogical proofs of a life after death. This estimation must be categorically denied. Near-death experiences are experiences in the dying process. But dying belongs to the experience of life before death, and as such the experiences are approachable by empirical research. By means of an investigation of experiences before death, empirical knowledge of a life after death on the level of Secondness can in no way be achieved. Indeed, neither Moody nor Kübler-Ross remains on the level of empirical research when they exploit their empirical results as proofs of a life after death and thus esoterically soften the reality of death. On the other hand, Thiede makes clear that

> precisely there where one would like to count on divine transcendence of the barrier of death, there can be no talk of proof of the divinity of such transcendence either on scientific-theoretical or on theological grounds. It is only evident that there is an interculturally verifiable "humanum" that becomes especially apparent in the structure of the child psyche: the capability of spiritual-psychic transcendence in somatic-psychic boundary situations.[5]

In his investigation and interpretation of the appearances of the Resurrected One recounted in the Gospels, Dale C. Allison[6] also comes to the negative result that the tools of historical criticism do not allow one to determine how far the individual narratives preserve authentic memory. Nothing historical can be said about the reports in 1 Corinthians 15:3-8 either. It is not at all possible to investigate the "feelings" and "emotions" of the first Christians, as Gerd Lüdemann claimed.[7] Allison then however holds to two "facts" as the positive result of his investigation: (1) Different persons reported Christophanies. (2) Jesus appeared several times to more than one person at the same time.[8]

In the section that follows, titled "Seeing Things,"[9] Allison attempts to explain these two "facts" by means of an analogy: reports of appearances of the dead. While with the help of this analogy Gerd Lüdemann attempted to debunk the conviction of guilt-plagued Peter who saw the resurrected Jesus psychologically or as self-deception, Allison employs it in a wholly different way. In particular, Allison assumes actual contact between the living and the dead and underscores his conception not only by adverting to serious empirical investigations of such reports of appearances but also—in analogy with the rhetoric of Paul (!)—with an autobiographical argument. Not only he himself but also other members of his family have experienced appearances of the dead.[10] It is a question of "a regular part of cross-cultural experience." Our present cultural prejudices that deny contact between the living and the dead, that relegate them to the realm of superstition or mental illness, may not deny the realities of human experience.[11] On this basis, then, the appearances recounted in the New Testament literature are indeed to be regarded as authentic memories of real events. The deceased Jesus appeared to them.[12]

What, however, is happening here by means of this analogical approach to the resurrected Crucified One? As in all analogical models, it is robbed of its absolutely unique specificity. The resurrected Crucified One turns into a dead man who makes contact with the living, like millions and millions of other dead men and women before and after him as well. It is precisely Allison's openness to other realities, as a historian of the New Testament thinking in terms of analogies—which rightly warns against cultural prejudices—that overlooks the eschatological uniqueness of and impossibility of analogy to the resurrection of the crucified Jesus of Nazareth and the cosmological dynamic bound up with it. By means of Allison's well-intended analogical approach, the Crucified One becomes a dead man among other dead men and women and the event of the resurrection thus loses its cosmological meaning and its soteriological power. Allison's sympathetic lack of prejudice once again shows where a historical criticism that has forgotten theology leads: to the theological evacuation of the cosmological event complex of the death and resurrection of Jesus of Nazareth. While Lüdemann and Allison argue on different grounds, the neglect of theological thinking leads both into the subjective situation of an idiosyncratic metaphysic.

In the further course of Allison's book this becomes ever more clear. He reflects the altogether fitting insight that the individual data are to be evaluated by the entire setting of a respective worldview.[13] Unlike Hermann Deuser, Ingolf Dalferth, Heiko Schulz, Hans Kessler, Georg Essen, Michael Welker, and Robert C. Neville, Allison does not come to the conclusion that a metaphysical debate about the foundation of reality or conceptions of reality is the order of the hour in order to work out ways of thinking and criteria just as appropriate to the reality of religious experience as to the reality of empirical facts and to the reality of the significance of events. Rather, he throws the choice of the encyclopedic frame of interpretation to the random desire of the subject, according to the slogan: let's not fight about worldviews.[14] But it is precisely the phenomena of religious experience woven into each other, the existence of things, and the plurality of interpretations of the world that set this task before us.

Allison's empiricizing of the New Testament appearance narratives by means of his particular analogical approach, comparing them to reports of appearances of the dead, misinterprets the resurrected crucified Jesus Christ of Nazareth as a dead man come back and overlooks the cosmological theologic of the event complex of the death and resurrection of the biblical Jesus-Christ-Story.

Finally, the biblical writings in their enduring material character are phenomena of Secondness before any interpretation. We possess no originals, but rather copies of copies and their translations down to editions of the Bible in the present day. The visually and tangibly perceptible material of textual criticism are empirical data that can be viewed in contemporary museums in their respective material conditions. The materials of written signs are the awkward given of every interpretation. They supply the data that then on the level of the phenomenon of Thirdness lead to the formation of Interpretants, which also today permit one to speak plausibly of a theology of the resurrection. It is not the materiality of the rotted corpse, or the materiality of the empty tomb hypothetically asserted, but rather the materiality of the written signs that forms the empirically perceptible foundation of Christian faith. The materiality of the written signs replaces the materiality of the absent body of the historical Jesus as well as the absence of his corpse.

Empirical scientific and historical knowledge investigates phenomena of Secondness. On this level it can be shown that the one of whom the New Testament Scriptures speak was crucified, and after his death was perceived as alive by several people, that he was a man who can be investigated principally by historical research, whose corpse after his death rotted in accord with expectations. Hermann Deuser writes,

Our picture of the "historical Jesus" necessarily ends with his death and the Easter witness of the first community as it has been handed down to us. There cannot be any bare "fact" of the resurrection on the same historical level and in some sort of empirical-material sense, because therein God in his world-transcending creativity would become an object bound within time and space.[15]

As C. S. Peirce put it, "What is not a question of a possible experience is not a question of fact."[16]

If we were only concerned with the phenomena of reality that exist, then our investigation would end here. The reality of the resurrection, of which the New Testament scriptures speak in conjunction with the Old Testament scriptures, cannot be considered within the limits of empirical experience, although the Jesus-Christ-Story, on which Christian discourse about the resurrection decisively depends, also exhibits the phenomena of Secondness and thus cannot be classified as a product of a utopian imagination. The feeling of truth tied to the Easter message and the critical classification of the insights of historical research can be bound together in a coherent way only when the materially perceptible written signs of the Bible that make it possible to read about the reality of the resurrection are interpreted theologically. The reality of the resurrection can primarily be conceived on the phenomenal level of Thirdness, which encompasses both the phenomena of Secondness as well as the phenomena of Firstness.

Creation and New Creation as Hypotheses of a Protestant Conception of Reality

The question of the resurrection of the dead as well as the question of the resurrection of the crucified Jesus Christ cannot be treated as an isolated theme if one wishes to answer in terms of its entire reality-disclosing power according to the Scriptures of the New Testament, and Protestant theology cannot make its task anything other than this. The issue does not concern whether one regards life after death as somehow possible or not. The issue does not concern whether one intends to contact the dead using supernatural or even magical power. The issue does not concern what everybody regards as possible. The resurrection of the dead according to the scriptures of the New Testament is not suited for a television program like *X-Files* or something similar that investigates supernatural phenomena in the quasi-empirical manner of an Uri Geller.

The resurrection of Jesus Christ is just as little a dogmatic formula that one must regard as true in order to rightly receive an entrance card for the "Sunday services" as is the hope in the resurrection of the dead, however. According to the scriptures of the New Testament, the reality of the resurrection is disclosed exclusively in the New Testament's canonical connections with the scriptures of the Old Testament, involving a personal relationship with God, namely the God who acts in the scriptures of the Old Testament as the merciful, just, and almighty creator God and to whom therefore praises are sung because of the goodness of his works of creation. Only the one who can sing psalms of creation will be able to perceive the truth of the reality of the resurrection according to the Scriptures of the New Testament.

Subjecting contemporary expressions of faith to a critical examination by binding it again and again to the interpretation of the Scripture as the norming hermeneutical and critical authority is not the only task of Protestant theology, however. Rather, Protestant theology must endeavor to explain also to such people for whom the truth of the faith according to the scriptures is not enlightening how one may understand the world as a whole with the eyes of Protestant faith.

For this task, and precisely with an eye to making the question of the resurrection plausible, creation theology plays a decisive role. The resurrection of Jesus Christ and the hope in the resurrection of the dead are impossible without a strong theology of creation. The theology of creation is the foundation upon which stands resurrection discourse, understood as the new creation.

In the 1980s, speaking of the world as the good creation of God experienced renewed plausibility thanks to the peace movement and thanks to the new sensitivity to the natural world inhabited by humans, of which "environment" is an insufficient description. One can here discover again a phenomenon of Firstness, namely the feeling that the purely instrumental and mechanistic conception of nature as environment does not sufficiently correspond to the perception of life in this world. Speaking of creation as something to preserve is a criticism of a mechanistic and exploitative way of thinking that conceives of nature only as consumable resources.

This impulse, which arose from the experience of the world, was then taken up by Protestant theology. With his two-volume study of creation theology, Christian Link[17] gave an important impulse to the systematic-theological clarification of the phenomenon of Firstness discussed above that broke through the individualistic narrowing of Protestant faith and which profoundly reconsidered cosmological questions by means of a theology of creation, to the end of providing a nonreductive understanding of faith and the world under the conditions of our contemporary knowledge of the world.

In his monograph *Gott: Geist und Natur. Theologische Konsequenzen aus Charles Sanders Peirce' Religionsphilosophie*, Hermann Deuser employed the conception of reality bound up with categorical semiotics as an alternative to the reductionism of empiricist and historicist conceptions of reality, and has been able to show in numerous publications that the Protestant faith that would like to be no longer misunderstood as a private religion for the salvation of one's own personal soul not only must welcome an encounter with the natural sciences but also needs a metaphysical model, in order both to be able to differentiate appropriately and also to bring together the phenomena of which faith speaks and the phenomena of which the natural sciences speak. The goal is thus not some peaceful coexistence of the natural and human sciences side by side. Rather, the goal is to be able to contribute discursively to a common understanding [*Erschliessung*] of the world within the necessary and irreversible differentiation of knowledge: "The formation of empirical theories and life-oriented contexts [complexes] of meaning are neither wholly congruent nor independent of one another."[18]

Pointing to the "limited range of causal explanations," Deuser allots to theology and the natural sciences different realms of competence, for "the natural sciences, that is, empirically and theoretically responsible developmental explanations of the universe, are one thing, while a personal relationship with God in view of creation, the 'what for' of life, and 'preservation' of creation are *another*."[19] Creationism, on the other hand, as an underage child of the Enlightenment, confuses the truth of the theology of creation with the cogency of an empirical explanatory model of the world as a consequence of its unreflective empiricist model of reality.

Deuser does not simply stop at this clarifying distinction, but rather in comparing evolutionary theory after Darwin with the biblical theology of creation sees in the Darwinian concept of chance precisely the "creative postulate" of creation theology as well as evolutionary theory: "Out of the anti-teleological and anti-metaphysical concept of chance, the modal concept of the *possibility* [*Möglichkeit*] of development thus comes about, as well as a cosmological-ontological concept of *making possible* [*Ermöglichung*]."[20] From this he concludes, "This—otherwise inscrutable—cooperation of chaotically indeterminate Nothing of that which can be made possible [*Ermöglichung*] with that which is becoming in life can not otherwise be explained except by *understanding* it as creation."[21] Religious language about creation is thereby conceived of as an irreplaceable disclosure of the "hermeneutical situation" of human beings in the world, which gives them occasion "not only to analyze the priority of the universe of experience empirically but also to trust its unconditionality and to work out and interpret this relationship of trust as such, as religions as far back as human memory can remember have taught and lived." It is precisely therein, however, that Deuser sees the "*commission* of human culture."[22]

With these considerations from the realm of the philosophy of religion the biblical theology of creation becomes comprehensible as a disclosure of the cosmos as the creation coming to an appropriate self-understanding, wanted by God, intended by God, made possible creatively and only in relation to him. According to the hypothesis of Protestant theology, the world, all life, and also one's own life spring not from blind chance but rather from the intentional creativity of the God who establishes relationships in love, as he is portrayed in the Bible. Whoever does not share this hypothesis cannot speak of the resurrection of Jesus Christ and the hope in the resurrection of the dead, with the scriptures of the New Testament in their canonical connection with the Old Testament scriptures.

But this hypothesis also already contains the understanding of sin as the breach of humanity's creaturely self-understanding, having been made in the image of God, with dramatic consequences for one's relationship to God, violent consequences for one's relationship to one's fellow men, one's exploitative relationship to the rest of nonhuman creation, and one's own mistaken self-understanding. God's creative act of creation is even the ground of possibility for one's own creative self-formation and shaping of one's life given as a gift. The image of God in humanity, marking humans out from all other creatures and calling them to a relationship of responsibility for their fellow creatures (cf. Gen 1:27), consists in humanity's creativity, in humanity's own capability to work creatively and to bring forth new things, a capability that is given to humanity in large measure through his capacity for symbolization as semiotic competence. Humanity has the ability to disclose itself, others, and its environment as creature, fellow creature, and component of its environment. Therein, however, also lies the capability for exploitation of power, grounded in authority, with which the *dominium terrae* in Genesis 1:26 and 1:28 deals. The creativity of humanity that the image of God gives to it can also be used to act in accordance to God's good creation and to employ one's own power for it. It can—and will—also be used to accomplish one's own interests, however, with other creatures bearing the burden.

The biblical explanation of injustice and violence means that everything wicked has its roots in the fact that humanity does not live in the solidarity of the creature nor thank God with the singing of psalms of thanksgiving for the gift of life. Rather, humanity sets itself in the place of God, and thus withdraws from solidarity with its fellow creatures and subjects them to its own self-ruling purposes. Creation is and remains God's good creation, but it becomes warped through the purpose-driven alienation of the creature by means of its creative power. The creation thereby becomes a dangerous outside realm, a battlefield of self-seeking and conflicting interests that demands its victims day by day. The profit-maximizing strategy of the stock exchange is not interested in the millions of children suffering from hunger. They do not appear in this purpose-oriented way of thinking. The shape of the political realm would look different if human beings understood themselves as creatures in solidarity with one another who have received the God-given gift of powerful creativity and the power of formative life.

In the creative creation of creative beings, however, also lies God's own responsibility for the evil in the world. God creates creaturely beings that can also employ the power of creativity for self-seeking, destructive, and unmerciful ends. God is also responsible, and he discerns his responsibility as a just God. He communicates his will in the form of the Torah, the proper directions for living life in solidarity with one's fellow creatures. Through his prophets he turns again and again to his people Israel.

The eschatologically decisive act of God with which he breaks through the power of sin and thus the breach of creaturely life is the resurrection of the Crucified One. By thus breaking the power of sin, he establishes his justice as creator. By depicting this resurrection not as a single case but rather as the beginning of a rule that transforms creation as a whole and is determined as the new creation wholly by the righteousness of God, he ultimately and eternally establishes his justice and thus answers the question of theodicy.

Within the framework of biblical thinking the resurrection of the dead is no miraculous shake-up, and it does not belong in the realm of the paranormal or the esoteric. The event of the resurrection of the Crucified One understood as the beginning of the eschatological resurrection of the dead answers the question of theodicy in such a way that God has broken the power of sin and will again establish his justice universally at the End for all eternity. Protestant faith does not believe in the resurrection of the dead as a miraculous feat but rather in the power of the creativity of God that overcomes even sin and death, which the sacred Scriptures of Israel and Jesus of Nazareth's proclamation of the kingdom of God have made known. Protestant faith does not believe in the facticity of the revivification of dead corpses but rather in the merciful and just God who does not forget the victims and therefore will bring perpetrators to account. Protestant faith believes in the God who through the Jesus-Christ-Story has taken sides openly and comprehensibly with the victims and for their sake answered the question of his justice with the new creation in which flesh and blood cannot dwell but rather into which new glorious bodies will enter. The word of the cross is the gospel, the power of God that saves the one who through the spirit of the Jesus-Christ-Story sees the resurrected Crucified One as a sign of the living, merciful, and just creator God, and henceforth recognizes his or her own delinquency in solidarity with this victim of human violence, and thus recognizes God's justiceat the same time and can thus perceive himself as a new creation by means of God's declaration of justification, in the hope of entering into wondrous glory at judgment day, the glory that the spirit of the Jesus-Christ-Story now makes known.

PART III

Resurrection and the New Testament
Ecclesial and Educational Praxis

Chapter 10

Protestant Discourse about Death and Resurrection in Funeral Services

This third and final section of the present investigation offers no detailed pedagogical program for religious education or practical theology. Rather, the relevance of Protestant discourse about the reality of the resurrection in and according to the scriptures of the New Testament in their connection with the Old Testament scriptures worked out in the first two parts will be shown in a fragmentary but exemplary way with the help of three fields of praxis. This third section of the present investigation will have achieved its purpose if it provides impetus by which practical theology and the pedagogy of religious education as well as every concrete theological praxis in church, school, university, and society may have a more intensive encounter with the theology of the resurrection, and bring it into Protestant praxis.

What can a Protestant funeral sermon say to provide well-justified comfort, and by what makes it recognizable as a particularly Protestant funeral sermon? How can one thus speak of the resurrection in accord with the biblical scriptures in religious instruction in schools, so that students do not encounter dogma irrelevant for their everyday lives, but rather a fundamental question of human life necessitating real consideration for the entire formation of their identity? And finally, what must be borne in mind in celebrating the Lord's Supper so that it is not dragged around as the dead ritual of a dying form of worship but rather so that it is celebrated worthily and joyfully, because it contributes to believers' assurance of community with their Lord and therefore also strengthensone's own life?

Death makes one silent and stiff. It is a break that wholly ends empirically perceptible life. Death robs the body of every possibility of action. It turns the living, perceiving body into a stiff, unfeeling corpse unable to do anything else by itself. It draws a line that neither the living nor the dead can overcome.

But even a corpse, which can do nothing more, which has served its purpose, which has become useless, and which is rotting or reduced to ashes, remains God's creature and therefore rests in God's hand. From this fact the burial service receives its value and meaning. "Ashes to ashes, dust to dust." With this phrase Christians give thanks for the gift of the enlivened body and remind themselves that the body is not their possession that they can rule over autocratically. The body is a gift of God for a time, enlivened material that is given back again to the continuum of the material after the expiration of the breath of life.

The corpse rests in the hand of God. Even the dead belong to the unlimited realm of his reign. It rests in God's hand even if its organs are removed in order to enable others to live longer on earth. It also rests in the hand of God if it is cremated or torn to pieces by bombs even when pieces are altogether missing. There is no condition of matter, and there is no place, that lies outside the realm of God's reign. Nothing can escape the almighty creator and the continuum of his creation. There is nothing outside God's creation.

Death is an unconquerable boundary for creaturely existence, but not for God. Therefore, from a Protestant perspective, there is no anthropology of resurrection, and indeed not even the supposition of a soul that lives on. Nothing, and especially nothing in the creature, is able to halt death. Human beings have nothing that they can contribute to their resurrection. They are radically dependent on the power of the creator.

The soul that lives on is a supposition of Greek mythology and philosophy. It is not to be found in the Bible.[1] The idea of the immortality of the soul trivializes the reality of death and sets aside the radical reliance of the creature on the creator. Seen from Protestant perspective, continuity between living existence and life after death is a self-serving construction with regard to creatures. Rather, death creates a distinction, a difference that cannot be overcome by creaturely existence.

In the Protestant perspective there is therefore no anthropology but rather exclusively a theology of resurrection. Protestant Christians trust exclusively in the promise of God and with Paul in the fact that God can also do what he has promised (Rom 4:21). Thus stands and falls the Protestant hope in eternal life in the community of the resurrected with

God and his Son. Human beings can therefore contribute nothing to their resurrection. They can rise again only if God wakes them and creates for them a new body that is no longer subject to the conditions of existence pertaining to the first creation. The continuity between the first and second creation lies solely in the mind and in the creativity of God. God maintains all in his eternal memory. No one dead in his or her individuality is forgotten by God. God's memory is no mass grave. It is not only corpses that rest in the realm of the almighty creator's reign but also the entire earthly existence of each individual that is kept in God's memory. Nothing is lost, for at the Last Day, Judgment Day, God and his Son will raise the dead by creating them anew from God's memory.

The new body is not only an ensouled body. It also totally indebted to the power of the Holy Spirit, the Spirit of God, which has already effected the resurrection of the Crucified One and given him a new spiritual body. This new spiritual body should not be imagined as spiritualistic, however, in such a way that the concept of spirit excludes that of corporality. The new body will remain a body even as a spiritual body. The second creation will be a bodily creation as well, for corporality is and remains the signature of God's creation. This signature differentiates it from the creator. The difference between creator and creature is maintained in the second creation as well, but this eternal difference does not prevent the qualitatively greater closeness between the creator and his new creation. If human beings are already made in God's image in the first creation, then the new body makes eternal dwelling with God and his Son possible. In terms of the Bible's figurative language, one can conceive of this new body as a body of light if it remains absolutely clear that such is no empirical expression but rather an attempt to speak about something transcending all experience.

The resurrection of the dead is not an end in itself. It serves theodicy, the ultimate proof of God's justice and the continuity of his being as creator. It is the resurrection at the last judgment that deals with the sins of the first creation so that they have no entry into the new creation. Sin is thereby understood as failure in proper creaturely life with regard to the creature's thankful connection to God and solidarity in community with fellow creatures. The last judgment is the place where every injustice, every crime, every pain is brought forth for the sake of the victims. God forgets nothing and no one. God will pronounce justice upon all creatures, powers, and acts of violence. The victims of human violence will receive their justice just as the victims of natural disasters, accidents, and illnesses, because God will provide them with justice.

And the offenders are named and judged—and indeed by God and his Son. In view of their insight into their own failings as regards life in the solidarity of community with their fellow creatures, Protestant Christians trust in the conviction that God will reckon to them as justice their solidarity with the Crucified One, the victim of individual and structural injustice, a solidarity made possible by the Jesus-Christ-Story, and therefore have mercy on them. No one has earned eternal life in communion with God and his Son; it can only be received with thanks on the basis of the merciful grace and goodness of God.

In view of the silence-making experience of death, Protestant Christians hope that the rigor of death will not have the last word, for then all victims throughout time remain forgotten and the offenses of the offenders without atonement. But in this case God would be an unjust God. Protestant Christians believe in the merciful and just God, the Almighty, of whom the Bible tells and who has identified himself with the picture of God presented by the Jesus-Christ-Story.

The funeral belongs to the most complex tasks of pastoral care and theology given to pastors. It is precisely the biblical understanding of death, knowing as it does the radicality of death and whitewashing nothing, that makes it possible to understand the unspeakable grief that death produces in those left behind. The corpse is robbed of its ability to stand in a living relationship with the living. Even the deaths of people old and full of life make for sorrow, for they can no longer participate in life. The dead break out of the relational structure of the living. Death is a break that those left behind experience in pain.

A memorial service becomes a Protestant funeral service when with the Bible not only the radicality of death and the pain of those left behind finds mention but also (formulated and delivered appropriately according to the needs of the mourners) the promise of the resurrection of the dead is proclaimed by the pastor with joy and certainty, because it is grounded in the reality of the resurrection of the Crucified One . A memorial service becomes a Protestant funeral precisely through the proclamation of the gospel of the resurrection of the Crucified One.

In view of the mourners it is still more difficult to speak of the last judgment before which all stand, even the deceased being mourned. Language about the last judgment at a funeral will unleash its comforting power if the positive meaning of judgment is expressed. Everything that vitiates proper creaturely life, or perhaps even has hindered or destroyed it, will come to expression. Even those things in which those left behind have wronged the deceased will have their day there. Nothing remains forever unredeemed because God will judge it with his justice. The last judgment, which produces ultimate justice, comprises the last chapter of the first creation and at the same time opens the door to eternal life in the new creation, which is marked by unmediated communion with God and Jesus Christ.

The *Agenda* (a liturgical manual) for the Union of Protestant Churches in the Protestant Church in Germany (EKD, Evangelische Kirche in Deutschland) from the year 2004 was fundamentally fair to this complexity when it explained,

> Ecclesial burial is an act of Christian worship, in which the congregation leads its deceased members to their final rest, tells of the grace of God, and testifies to the fact that God's might is greater than death. In the encounter with death and mourning the congregation considers life and death in light of the Gospel and proclaims the resurrection of the dead. The congregation accompanies the dead mourns with those left behind. It comforts them with God's Word and accompanies them with pastoral care and prayer.[2]

With an eye to typical situations of mourning, it is especially the task of pastoral care that the *Agenda* provides for in its different liturgical provisions for the conduct of and texts worthy of worship services. Its strengths lie in the sensitive articulation of mourning. The phases of mourning that Yorick Spiegel[3] has worked out are considered just as much as the necessity of sounding cautious tones with respect to the age of the deceased and the circumstances of death, something that several texts succeeded impressively in doing in poetic ways.

For all the *Agenda*'s good, it is conspicuous that its emphasis falls upon the articulation of suffering, of mourning, of pain, of anger, of open questions, of lamentation. The joyful hope in the future resurrection of the dead and the liberating purification of all injustice at the last judgment is by and large not to be found in the new texts of this *Agenda*. It remains to the greatest extent a component of received liturgical tradition.

This observation should not detract from one's evaluation of the *Agenda*, but precisely in view of its qualities in regard to theology and pastoral care it can be read as an indication that resurrection hope hardly represents a deeply felt and therefore deeply loved core of Christian faith in the present time. Even more seldom does the eschatological judgment find mention. Has Protestant theology taken leave of our eschatological hope?

If the funeral service is only a eulogy and if the only connection to God is found in mourning, then we are not dealing with a Protestant funeral service. Certainly there are situations such as the unspeakable event of the death of a child, the death of a murder victim in the prime of life, or the innumerable victims of natural disasters that threaten to extinguish joyful eschatological hope and for which, therefore, it appears to be impossible to articulate. But for contemporary Christians, language about the *Deus absconditus*, about the hidden God, appears to proceed from the lips faster than language about the almighty, creative, and just God. In the course of the anthropologizing of theology "God" has become a powerless metaphor, an impotent God, who can no longer be trusted to bring about the new creation.

Whoever wishes to speak theologically in accord with the Bible—and precisely that is the mark of Protestant theology—will articulate the good news even in the most difficult situations, namely the gospel of the almighty mercy of the creator, who has even ultimately overcome death and who has established new, eternal life in a nearness never known before with God and his Son. Precisely this is the task of Protestant theological language in all situations. Not only must the pastor be compassionate with the mourners and empathetic in every individual, unique situation; keeping an appropriate distance from the situation of bereavement, the pastor can say something that those in mourning are not able to say themselves. The pastor should articulate the unspeakable pain and therefore help its processing. The indispensable Protestant task consists in articulating in any given situation the powerful and effective comfort of the gospel of the overcoming of injustice and death, as the Spirit of the Jesus-Christ-Story would have it understood.

Whoever wishes to speak of the promise of the resurrection of the dead must employ poetic language. With its numerous metaphors, like that of the resurrection itself, or that of the new creation, the Bible provides numerous mental images of the new heavens and the new earth and so forth, images that guard against treating them as quasi-empirical data precisely by means of their multiplicity. Whoever thinks that we can dispense with these long-standing figurative ways of speaking because they no longer suffice may discover or even invent new ways of speaking, but the new metaphors must fit to the language of the Bible in their expression and range of association. Biblical metaphors are no end in themselves, but not every new image, not every contemporary metaphor permits the gospel to be repeated fittingly. Whoever speaks of the immortality of the soul sets himself in contradiction to biblical theology. Whoever speaks of reincarnation has left the realm of Christian hope and thinking behind. Whoever cannot speak in any way of the eternal life that God will create anew should not preach in Protestant worship services.

Whoever is entrusted with the task of delivering a Protestant funeral sermon should be clear about his own hope, find his own courage and strength, and depict images of eternal life in the kingdom of God in keeping with the Spirit of the Jesus-Christ-Story that are definitive for his own existence. Whoever finds such images for himself will be able to portray them with empathy and gentleness before the weeping eyes of mourners as well, and choose the colors according to the circumstances.

One could say the following with well-grounded hope in a funeral sermon: The dead rest in the hand of God. He keeps every individual, each, all, and everything in his memory. God forgets no one until the day on which he will raise them and with his Son will bring all that has happened to expression. The merciful and just God pronounces justice, and there will be justice. He wipes away every tear and makes a new heaven and a new earth. Mercifully he creates new, spiritual bodies prepared for eternal life in the creature's communion of love with God and his Son. And death will be no more. And injustice will be no more. And pain will be no more. Healing, joy, justice, peace, and love are the signatures of the new creation. No one sings songs of mourning any longer. Heavenly music praises God's goodness and creativity. Life. Eternal life!

Chapter 11

Resurrection as a Theme in Religious School Instruction

In his substantive essay on "Dying, Death, and Resurrection as Themes for Children and Youth," Werner Thiede rightly calls for more attention to be paid to the pedagogy and praxis of religious instruction in schools, for the complex of themes his title adumbrates. Thiede shows that with their level of language acquisition children not only encounter the empirical experience of death but also endeavor to find meaningful answers to the question of death with the development of their cognitive categories, as Piaget more or less described them. Elementary school students already "require the most meaningful answer possible to questions about the 'last things,' after they become aware of the finality of life and the world as a whole."[1] This requirement occurs throughout the entirety of childhood and continues into adolescence—and beyond—because the question about their own identity as a question about the possibilities and limits of their own lives is expressed in this way. Thus is promised the question of meaning arising from life itself, "which is generated by knowledge of one's mortality and works itself out on all levels of human thought and action."[2] Thiede also sets forth the significance of this complex of questions for dealing with dying children and those children and youth at risk of suicide. Even if the complex addressed last can be proven only through empirical investigation, and with difficulty, the developmental and social-psychological fact of the increasing suicide fantasies among children and youth in our time sets before us the task of clarifying in our religious pedagogy how consideration of biblical language about the resurrection of the dead can further children and youth on their way in the development of their own self-understanding and world-understanding.

On the other hand it appears strange that the theme of the resurrection of the dead is so rarely found in schoolbooks. In view of the fundamental significance of resurrection theology for Protestant and Catholic religious instruction, one can comprehend Hubertus Halbfas' irritation when he writes,

> In all available religion books, one checks for examples in their chapters about the resurrection and ascension of Christ: There one finds a beautiful Easter picture (but what is "beautiful," really? What didactic relevance does an individual picture from the high middle ages have?), texts from the Gospels and 1 Corinthians, a liturgical hymn and some practical application, reasons why the resurrection depicted by these means brings Christendom joy and fills it with hope, but the word "resurrection" for its part finds no elaboration, nor does the motif of the "three days," nor the difference between resurrection and appearance stories, nor the relevance of the "empty tomb." Such an omission can only regarded as a refusal to provide information, and society suffers altogether from this deficit.[3]

Certainly Halbfas' call for more "material yield [*Sachhaltigkeit*]" in religious instruction as well as in society hardly suffices to solve the problem of finding a fitting depiction and life-promoting reflection on biblical language about the resurrection of Jesus Christ and the resurrection of the dead in a comprehensive way, for Halbfas' religion-pedagogical concept comes much too close to the danger of copying religious instruction at the university level, of setting too much emphasis on the transmission of knowledge, and of not sufficiently taking into account the emotional and social realities of students as a whole. Nevertheless, with Halbfas we must emphasize the duty to transmit information in religious instruction, when for example in a book of religious instruction one finds only two pages on the topic of the resurrection that then only consist of pictures without introducing the material issues of this difficult topic. The homework assignment[4] paired sensibly with the pictures burdens the students with reflecting upon the theology of the resurrection on their own; nothing is laid before them to aid their consideration of the material. They themselves are already supposed to know the significance of "Good Friday" and "Easter." Sowelcome is the approach of this schoolbook *Mitten ins Leben* (*In the Midst of Life*) for its use of the emotional and creative capacities of students as an entry into religion, thus taking up and employing the phenomenon of the category of Firstness, that the theological silence of these two pages on the theme of "Death and Resurrection" is perplexing. Finding nothing to aid their consideration of the material, students are left alone with the problems of resurrection theology and overburdened thereby. But that can hardly be laid at the feet of the editors' and authors' lack of didactic competence in this book on religion and therefore dismissed as an instance of individual failure. Rather, the silence regarding the complex of the cross and resurrection of Jesus we see here openly is a deep and wide-ranging theological problem—and indeed not a problem of the students' making, as the Thiede essay cited above makes plain, but rather a problem of contemporary Protestant theology in church, school, society, and university. "The cross as such is silent and makes for silence," writes Ingolf Dalferth,[5] and it seems that as regards praxis in the universities, schools, and churches, and especially in society, the silence-making cross has triumphed, and not the new life made possible by the word of the cross.

If the theme of the resurrection of Jesus Christ or the theme of the resurrection of the dead is to be presented appropriately in Protestant religious instruction in schools, then both of these themes must always be attended to in their biblical connections and with consideration of the three categories that reveal reality as a semiotic process.

With Thiede, we can understand the facticity of death as something awkward, as a fundamental problem of human existence, as a phenomenon of the category of Secondness that calls one's own wholeness into question and that limits one's own identity, for which biblical discourse about the resurrection provides an answer. Note well: *one* answer among many. Religious instruction in schools will also inform students about other solutions, such as reincarnation, esoteric ideas, or the ancient Egyptian books of the dead. Protestant religious instruction will sharpen its theological profile if more attention is dedicated to biblical discourse about the resurrection and its effective power in contemporary Protestant faith and thought.

Therefore the Protestant faith of people currently living should be expressed first of all on the level of Secondness, and thus as an empirically describable phenomenon, a faith that permits them in the Easter service to respond to the proclamation of the resurrection with an immediate, unmediated feeling of truth: "He is risen indeed." What makes people today speak this phrase with existential involvement and to experience it as relevant to their own lives? Whatever lets contemporary people perceive the resurrected Crucified One when they celebrate the Lord's Supper. One approaches the complexity of biblical discourse about the resurrection when contemporary Easter experiences are viewed in their fragmentary nature, emotional nature, and precritical existential relevance. Neither the historical question about the tomb nor the character of the visions nor the complex questions of the presentation of resurrection theology in the biblical writings, and probably least of all dogmatic formulas, suffice for an introduction into the theme. People are convinced even today of the effects and the approachability of the resurrected Crucified One. This fact shows the convincing power of biblical language about the resurrection even under the conditions of pluralistic scientific societies. Why can people still believe in such ways today? That would be an interesting, candid, and ideologically impartial introductory question into the theme of the resurrection of Jesus Christ and the resurrection of the dead. Moreover, students who stand at a distance from Christian faith could at least learn respect for others' perceptions of truth, and precisely this is an indispensable educational goal of all curricular and extracurricular formation in pluralistic societies, which are no longer indebted only to one religious tradition and no longer only to one model of explaining the world.

The contemporary experiences of Protestant Christians of the living reality of the resurrected Crucified One lead inexorably to the biblical witness as the decisive source for their faith tradition. Here one can now bring the complexity of biblical discourse about the resurrection of Jesus Christ and the resurrection of the dead into conversation, with the help of well-chosen examples, in order to compare them with the expressions of faith of contemporary Christians. For example, one can contrast passages from Romans with corresponding passages from Colossians, or—even more simply—compare the depiction of the empty tomb in the gospel of Mark with that of the gospel of Luke. Precisely because harmonization is not being attempted here, a realistic entry into the Bible opens up that does not misunderstand its writings as quasi-empirical reports but that rather understands them as metaphorical language about ultimate questions of one's own existence and its significance in connection with the entirety of perceptible and desired worlds. When students thus experience a hint of a suspicion that nothing else is being said about all these decisive fundamental questions than something metaphorical, then religious instruction has achieved its goal in forming the religious sensibilities of students. Religious formation is a lifelong project that is then integrated into life when its relevance for its entirety is opened emotionally, and is formulated with regard to one's own linguistic and intellectual capabilities.

Biblical language about the resurrection is not to be depicted in an isolated manner, however, as if the resurrection were a phrase that one must regard as true. Rather, it is a question of bringing all biblical themes, in their connections with the entire biblical picture of God, humanity, and the world, into conversation again and again, in at least a rudimentary fashion, so that the plausibility structures of the great biblical story are engraved in students in an enduring way. As a feature of Protestant religious instruction, resurrection cannot be presented and reflected upon without appropriately incorporating creation theology, hamartology, soteriology, and questions of theodicy. This holds fully independently of the existential ability of teachers and students to assent to it.

Protestant religious instruction is no esoteric mix of religion, but rather an interpretation of God, humanity, and the world oriented and normed through the interpretation of the Scriptures, which in its ideological structure can be researched, taught, learned, and criticized. Knowledge thereof can be examined in tests, in-class work, homework, reports, and so forth. This critical and reproducible knowledge is in no sense exchangeable with faith.

Faith according to the Good News of the New Testament scriptures is this knowledge of religion when the emotional, precritical assent to still so fragmentary and perhaps even naive occurs, so that Protestant knowledge becomes the certainty of one's own sheltered position in the hand of God, whom Jesus Christ proclaimed and who raised him from the dead. Religious instruction in schools would be overburdened and its purpose misunderstood, however, if its task was supposed to be awakening faith. It would have achieved much, however, if religious instruction in schools cleared away the obstacles—not seldom misinformation—that block persons on their way to developing their own religious sensibilities. Religious instruction in schools should lead to a critical knowledge of one's own religion, and above all introduce creatively the phenomena of religiosity and empower students to develop their own religiosity emotionally and critically for the entirety of their lives.

Chapter 12

The Lord's Supper as a Gift of the Resurrected Crucified One

The life lived with and in the great story that the Bible narrates is even today no longer self-understood in many Protestant congregations. This concerns not only familiarity with biblical stories and knowledge of ecclesial holy days. Even the knowledge of ritual already evinces considerable decline, because attendance at the celebration of the worship service on Sundays represents more the exception than the rule for the majority of church members.

But even among many loyal churchgoers and among not a few pastors, an emotional and cognitive distance from the Christian tradition and even from the celebration of the Lord's Supper is growing.

The consolidation of congregations, the sale of church buildings, the closing of church-run kindergartens, the dismantling of sacred spaces are hardly experienced as an opportunity for new breakthroughs in the everyday life of congregations, but rather as obvious signs of the downfall of Christian churches. Not a few congregations and whole church circles are so very much engaged in the bureaucratic, organizational, and also human conflicts of these restructuring processes that they hardly ever engage in theological reflection upon their own experiences. The experience of the reality of congregational life hardly encourages anyone to confront such a shocking and complex issue as the *theologia crucis*. On the contrary: the frustration of many engaged church members and also many pastors leads not seldom to the judgment that the central contents of Christian faith itself are outmoded. The dark message of the cross, the obsolete understanding of sin, the depressing liturgy of Holy Communion—all this is supposedly at fault for the waning attractiveness of the Christian message in the midst of the hip events of the more attractive counterculture. One thus avoids the language of the cross, of sin, of the wrath of God, of the power of God, of the judgment of God, and speaks rather in contemporary platitudes about love, security, community, and the "loving God."[1]

What, however, gets lost is a framework for understanding in which the themes and narrative connections adumbrated just now can develop their plausibility structures. This framework for understanding is the great story from creation to new creation, which is not merely an arbitrary sequence pulled out of the canonical collection of books. Rather, it opens up a great narrative framework in which not only the individual pericopes of the Sunday sermon but also the crucial Christian holy days and also the Lord's Supper can unleash their salvific narrative power.[2]

The Great Narrative of the Bible and the Misunderstanding of Salvation-Historical Conceptions

When the French philosopher and sociologist of knowledge Jean-François Lyotard proclaimed the end of the "grand narratives" in his epoch-making work *The Postmodern Condition* at the end of the 1970s, he hardly had the mythical stories of antiquity and certainly not the grand narratives of Judaism and Christianity in mind. These were long ago by the time Lyotard conceived of the epistemology of modernity as the rationality of real knowledge in direct opposition to established fictional constructs:

> The scientist questions the validity of narrative statements and concludes that they are never subject to argumentation or proof. He classifies them as belonging to a different mentality: savage, primitive, underdeveloped, backward, alienated, composed of opinions, customs, authority, prejudice, ignorance, ideology. Narratives are fables, myths, legends, fit only for women and children. At best, attempts are made to throw some rays of light into this obscurantism, to civilize, educate, develop.[3]

Not a few scientists of the present day indeed still share this estimation, without observing in Lyotard's rhetoric that this "scientific" rejection of narrative knowledge breaks through again and again as a caricature, and permits narratives thus to enjoy their limited, local rights.

Lyotard's point consists much more in the observation that even the grand conceptions of knowledge in modernity attempt to generate their legitimacy with the help of grand narratives, for even enlightened knowledge cannot produce this legitimacy through itself. Lyotard introduces as proof "two major versions of the narrative of legitimation. One is more political, the other more philosophical."[4] Regarding the political, Lyotard writes, "The subject of the first of these versions is humanity as the hero of liberty. All peoples have a right to science. If the social subject is not already the subject of scientific knowledge, it is because that has been forbidden by priests and tyrants."[5] "With the second narrative of legitimation, the relation between science, the nation, and the State develops quite differently."[6] The question concerns the fundamental narrative of German idealism, which sought to legitimize the freedom of science with a story of the Spirit, as for example Hegel construed it.[7]

According to Lyotard, however, in the production of knowledge in the Western world both the state-political and the philosophical-speculative metanarratives forfeited their plausibility, and thus he states,

> In contemporary society and culture—postindustrial society, postmodern culture—the question of the legitimation of knowledge is formulated in different terms. The grand narrative has lost its credibility, regardless of what mode of unification it uses, regardless of whether it is a speculative narrative or a narrative of emancipation.[8]

This assessment conceptualizes the grand narrative as a construct that always totalizes and thus always terrorizes, a construct that permits the political imperialism of the Western world to spread into its production of knowledge as well. Lyotard's scientific-ethical admonition regarding contemporary scientific discourse is grounded on the thesis that the thinking of the one always excludes the other. Whoever would like to consider all things together in one universal unity on the basis of some grand narrative is already well along on the way of terror, even if this unity is presented as a grand "consensus" achieved discursively, as for example in Jürgen Habermas' theory of communicative action. According to Lyotard, the universal condition of the consensus is precisely not in any situation where it can consider the other in his own validity and let him be,[9] and thus make an accountable pluralistic society possible.

In theological discourse, the grand narrative of the Bible then becomes a totalizing dogmatism when it is no longer regarded as a narrative interpreting God and the world but instead steps outside the boundaries of its semiotic nature. Wolfhart Pannenberg is undoubtedly right when he emphasizes that the Bible does not require thinking to be turned off, and one to commit oneself to an authoritarian or enthusiastic irrationalism. Faith, according to the Bible, not only is accessible to unprejudiced thinking but also challenges thinking not to rely on its prejudices but rather to rethink and abandon them and to think otherwise, to think absolutely in the new terms that the Bible provides for thinking with the event of the resurrection of the Crucified One.[10]

These important and fruitful insights into Pannenberg's conception of universal history are narrowed in the momentum toward a Christian ideology, however, in which the semiotic nature of text and thus their

polyvalence are referentially bypassed. The strength of a narrative conception, on the other hand, consists in being able to avoid this narrow ontol-
ogy, from one's knowledge of the semiotic conditions of every production
of meaning, without surrendering the truth claim and the reality-reveal-
ing power of the biblical writings, by introducing into the world of the
stories and how to live these stories in the political and individual world
of the everyday. Semiotic theology works in the texts and in interaction
with texts and their dynamics and thus encounters the danger of building
a rigid ideology out of the grand narrative of the Bible that would simply
not fit the paradoxical movement of the theology of the cross.

Thinking about this event, however, causes everything—God, the
world, and also oneself—to be seen differently. Thinking about this all-
changing event makes thinking itself participate in this event and in its
process. Or, said in other ways: thinking without prejudice about the
event of the resurrection of the Crucified One becomes a significant way
in which the Spirit works. This thinking thinks wittily: creatively, dis-
tinctively, presently, free, realistically, self-consciously, self-critically, in
solidarity, politically, kindly, confidently, with discernment, thankfully.
Witty rethinking perceives things, thinkers and one's own self plainly and
thus acts in salutary and promising ways. Such thinking sees that it cannot ground itself but also that it in no way needs to, because it is already
indebted to the gift of the event. Witty thinking keeps the whole in view
in incarnate, located ways, without having to dominate it.

Paul therefore connects the word of the cross to the story of his own
experiences and to the narrative complexes from the sacred scriptures of
Israel and therein binds together Jewish and Hellenistic world knowledge,
Greek philosophy, and rhetoric in order to give form to the "word of the
cross." He persuades through interweaving arguments and located stories
whose connection is grounded in a grand narrative that is restructured
ingeniously through a small, particular narrative.

The paradoxical dynamic of the Jesus-Christ-Story forms the restructuring of a grand narrative through a small, particular story that is
developed in narrative, discursive, and argumentative ways. The epistemological achievement of the "word of the cross" consists in organizing a
coherent narrative of world knowledge in such a way that this grand story
does not initiate any totalizing and thus terrorizing insularity, but rather
provides an occasion for its recipients to think wisely about that which is
and those who are other, that which is surprising, that which is irrupting,
and that which is new. Thus narration and knowledge are not exclusive.
The narrative foundation opens up a space for thinking that in its manner

of interpreting the narrative generates "diverse ultimate lines of meta-argumentation, that is, lines of argumentation limited by space-time that have metaprescriptions as an object."[11] In this sense the partial and even contradictory depictions of the gospels, as well as those of all the other books comprising the Bible, can be conceptualized with Lyotard's concept of paralogy. The terror of the ideal of a unifying consensus disappears in the Bible through the productive power of dissent. This "paralogy"[12] does not aim any longer at an unanimity of world knowledge. Rather, it furthers discourses that encounter the possibility of conflict but also in peaceful ways a plurality of interpretations of reality, and conceives of them programmatically above all as the appropriate means of the production of human knowledge. Paralogy, as Lyotard predicted in the manner of a clear-seeing prophet, is distinguished precisely in fundamentally distrusting every strategy of legitimization that grand narratives use referentially so that their semiotically conditioned ambiguity is obscured, in order to thus construe a totality of knowledge.

The Lord's Supper as Part of the Great Story

When Christians celebrate the Lord's Supper, then the question concerns everything: they celebrate the victory of life over death. However fitting this general saying may be, and however appealing, contemporary, and politically noncommittal it may sound in its comforting generality, it receives its Christian face chiefly in its being embedded in a story, and indeed not in any general human history or history of a religion, but rather in a wholly particular story that is specifically Christian, namely the "Jesus-Christ-Story,"[13] which receives its most felicitous designation from Paul, as the "word of the cross" (1 Cor 1:18a). The Lord's Supper itself is a part of this story, and whenever it is celebrated, it narrates and proclaims the word of the cross in its celebration. The Jesus-Christ-Story in turn receives its plausibility through its embedding in the grand narrative of creation and new creation, whose logic is not one of means and ends, but rather one determined by the contingent, creative love of God. God creates and maintains his creation and creatures not as means to any end but rather because it pleases him because they please him, because he simply loves them—the earth, the stars, the plants, the animals, human beings.

Indeed human beings of flesh and blood shed blood for their own purposes. They do not share the goods of creation in pure, fraternal love, but rather use creation for their own desires and accept that God's creatures become victims of their wishes and purposes. But nothing, neither powers nor violence and certainly not we ourselves, can separate us from the love of God, the wanton love of God spiting all powers (cf. Rom 8). The Lord's Supper narrates this: from a victim of human violence and from the creative love of God that made a story with a good ending out of a human tragedy, whose humor and spirit gives the gift of a loving, liberated, and liberating laugh to all who live in light of this story, without any conditions.

More than anything else, the word of the cross narrates the story of a betrayal and a judicial murder, in which the highest domestic and Roman officials in Judea and thus two different systems of justice took part. The weighty words of institution recall this: "In the night in which he was betrayed" (cf. 1 Cor 11:23b).

Jesus was not betrayed from the outside but from the inside. Judas, one of his closest companions, one from the circle of the twelve, betrayed him and made him known with a kiss at his arrest (cf. Matt 26:47ff.). According to the Gospels, at the Last Supper with his disciples Jesus knows about Judas' betrayal, but he does not expel him from his table (cf. Matt 26:20-30). The Last Supper, in which the Lord's Supper is grounded, is not a meal of some conflict-free, harmonious community, no happening of a nonviolent in-group, no closed society of moralistic heroes. Judas, the traitor, and Peter, the denier, are both guests at the table of the Lord, and no one doubts their belonging there.

This community of the meal does not allot good and evil according to the principles of inside and outside. The power of sin and of violence-ready misunderstanding works on the inside as well. The Last Supper does not divide neatly into a kingdom of men of good will and a kingdom of evil. The Last Supper knows of the boundless nature of the power of sin and thus casts a critical eye to inside and outside.

The Jesus depicted in the Gospels knows that his way leads to the cross. Several times he announces his suffering but also his resurrection (cf. Matt 16:21; 17:9; 17:22; 20:17-18; 20:28; 26:32). The scene in the garden of Gethsemane makes it impressively clear that Jesus does not want to die (cf. Matt 26:38ff.). The Gospels portray Jesus not as a hero weary of life and certainly not as a mythical figure unmoved by suffering. He is not, however, deemed a powerless victim, which the cursing of the fig tree (Matt 21:19) expresses, as do his words at his arrest: "Do you think that I cannot appeal to my Father, and he will at once send me more than twelve legions of angels?" (Matt 26:53). He deliberately refrains from calling upon his cosmic host. He goes his way of unconditional love and thus follows the wanton, loving will of God. From this arises the astounding impression that generates Jesus' action: He does not only speak the words of the Our Father, but also lives it: "Thy will be done" (Matt 6:10b) holds for him also in full view of the looming crucifixion (cf. Matt 26:36-42).

But it is not the arbitrary will of God that kills Jesus but rather the treacherous exploitation of human power. It is not the royal rule of God that nails the innocent one to the cross, but rather the conscious tolerance of injustice. No divine plan requires a bloody human sacrifice, but rather the human intrigue that devises lies in the service of killing.

Judas, one of the disciples, betrayed him with a treacherous kiss (cf. Matt 26:48ff.). The high council does not seek the truth but rather seeks false witnesses to pin a crime on Jesus that will serve as the rationale for his intended execution (cf. Matt 26:59). When this plan fails, the high priest intervenes and misuses the power of his venerable office to interpret Jesus' words as blasphemy and demand the death penalty (Matt 26:65-66). Jesus is spat upon, beaten, and mocked (Matt 26:67-68). Even Peter makes himself guilty of deceit. He denies Jesus three times (Matt 26:69-75).

On the next morning the high council decides upon the death penalty, and because only the Roman government can pronounce a capital sentence, Jesus is sent to Pontius Pilate (Matt 27:1-2). Judas hears of it and kills himself (Matt 27:3-10).

Pilate, warned through his wife's dream, first attempts to get the Jews to agree to let Jesus go free, for he knows through his wife's dream that Jesus is innocent, and he knows moreover that Jesus is a just man (cf. Matt 27:11-23). But he knowingly permits this injustice to pass (cf. Matt 27:24ff.). Now Jesus is also tortured by the Roman soldiers and mocked and then nailed to the cross (Matt 27:27-36). An inscription affixed over Jesus' head gives the reason for his execution: "This is Jesus, the King of the Jews" (Matt 27:37b).

Jesus, bleeding, nailed to the cross, is mocked by his own people's elites and even by the robbers crucified with him, according to Matthew. Jesus dies an agonizing death. With his last words, a verse from a psalm, he turns to God: "My God, my God, why have you forsaken me?" (Matt 27:46b/Psalm 22:2).

If the story ended here, then we would have little more than the tragic story of a good man who died as a victim of human violence, or, read more cynically: with the confirmation of the power of human rule and the powerlessness of justice. The ends-oriented power relations of the factual would once more have the last word. The cross without the word of the cross "is silent and makes silent."[14]

The word of the cross, however, narrates the story further and presents a wonderful twist.[15] God pulls Jesus, the victim of human violence, up from death into his own divine life. God identifies with the Crucified One and lets himself be found on the cross thereby. The significance of the cross is thus recoded from a death-dealing martyr's stake to a place of encounter with God in which eternal life is revealed. God inscribes himself in the story of the Crucified One and thus declares from the place of the cross the way of life and the proclamation of the Crucified One to be his own affair.

With the identification of God with the Crucified One and the resurrection of the Crucified One into that divine life determined by wanton love, the event of the cross becomes an eschatological event of salvation that ultimately breaks the power of sin. The last word does not go to power of sin over its victim executed on the cross, but rather to the word of the cross as the word of God, the God who gives the gift of new, eternal life, who identifies himself in love with the victim, and who thus establishes his justice.

The word of the cross concerning God's merciful offer of participation in the Jesus-Christ-Story, to all who through the Spirit of this story identify themselves with this victim of human violence and thus make his death and his life their own, becomes the eschatological and cosmological event of salvation. They therefore trust that God's just and merciful creative power will be vindicated and not the merciless and pitiless power of sin.

Baptism and the Lord's Supper are two ways in which this offer of participation can be experienced and grasped. It is not any organizational form or reform of the church—however necessary they otherwise may be—but rather the word of God to which the Bible bears witness and these two sacraments that form the foundation from which the church lives, according to the Protestant understanding.[16]

The Lord's Supper offers participation in the Jesus-Christ-Story as an incarnational reminder.[17] The celebration of the Lord's Supper proclaims the death of the resurrected Crucified One in a narrative way that serves as a reminder. In 1 Corinthians 11:26 we read, "For as often as you eat this bread and drink this cup, you proclaim the death of the Lord until he comes." This remembrance incorporates the Jesus-Christ-Story through the consumption of bread and wine in such a way that it becomes one's own story. In 1 Corinthians 10:16 Paul writes, "The cup of blessing that we bless, is it not a sharing in the blood of Christ? The bread that we break, is it not a sharing in the body of Christ?" As God identifies with the victim of power and violence and thus declares his cause to be his own, the loving and creative spirit of the Jesus-Christ-Story grasps those participating in the Lord's Supper and makes it so that the fate of the victim Jesus becomes their own experience. Jesus does not die for guilty human beings according to the ends-oriented logic of substitutionary atonement. Rather, every individual who celebrates the Lord's Supper takes part in the death of the victim Jesus of Nazareth. Communion with the victim Jesus of Nazareth, a solidarity constituted by the Spirit of the Jesus-Christ-Story, leads into solidarity with all the victims of injustice and violence, into loving solidarity with all victims of exploitation and abuse.

The political message of the Lord's Supper consists in the appeal to give oneself over to this solidarity with victims. The Crucified One is the victim of an unjust act committed by individuals and institutions inside and outside. The political message of the Lord's Supper recalls the death of the Crucified One as a metonymy of injustice and violence in which all are ensnared, even the guests who are body and soul at the Lord's table, and it obligates those sharing the table of the Kyrios to take the side of the victims now and in everyday life, and therefore in all life decisions and political options to regard others as creatures of God loved just as much as they are, that they do not fall victim to human violence and political structures of power.

This ethical maxim of the Lord's Supper is grounded in the hope in the God who creates everything out of nothing and will create everything new. It is grounded in the loving creator of all life who will raise the dead and who has in fact already raised the Crucified One (cf. Rom 4:17). They hope that the merciful and just God has not raised the crucified Jesus into his divine life and given him a new body consisting no longer of flesh and blood (cf. 1 Cor 15) as a singular exception. Rather, they hope that the new creation of God has already been made with Jesus' resurrection, the new creation with which God establishes his justice and righteousness universally, piercing the entirety of creation. They do not hope in a mere revivification of the dead and thus the continuation of the status quo. They hope for a new world in which God's unconditional love works without limits and all find peace and righteousness thereby.

If the political message of the Lord's Supper does not remain bound up with this universal eschatological hope, it degenerates either into the paying of Sunday lip service, or into moralistic activism of the self-righteous, or into a malign desire for suffering that idolizes one's own suffering. Without the theology of resurrection, the community of the Lord's Supper does not celebrate the in-breaking of the kingdom of God, but rather situates itself in the hell of its own self-righteousness or self-pity for the duration.

If it is celebrated with biblical knowledge of incarnational communion with the resurrected Crucified One, then the Lord's Supper stands in continuity with Jesus' Last Supper with his disciples and becomes an event of the kingdom of God thereby. Celebrated this way, the Lord's Supper practices the righteousness of the kingdom of God. Everyone receives as much as one needs to live. There is no hierarchy any longer between rich and poor, men and women, office holders and laity.

This experience of communion on the part of those God has invited to his table will also show itself active in everyday life, and this phrase can be reversed. Only if this experience is productive in everyday life was the Lord's Supper celebrated worthily. Whoever experiences the death of Jesus the victim in his or her own body through the loving and creative Spirit of the Jesus-Christ-Story in the Lord's Supper, and tastes and incorporates into himself or herself the bread and the wine as a participation in the body of Christ through chewing and drinking, perceives in himself or herself the power of the new life given as a gift by the just and merciful God. Whoever experiences the power of sin and the greater power of the loving creativity of God in this deep and rich cultic event goes about everyday life attentively and critically inside and outside in both political and private spheres, strengthened through the communion experienced with the resurrected Crucified One in one's own body.

Whoever thus gives himself or herself over in faith to the Jesus-Christ-Story, and celebrates the Lord's Supper in the manner described, namely in a way worthy of this Jesus-Christ-Story, will have God reckon this faith as forgiveness of one's transgressions, one's own sins (cf. Rom 1:16-17). The crucified Jesus died "thus not for God and for God's sake, but rather . . . *for us men and women* and *for our sake.*"[18] His story thus becomes the place at which reconciliation is achieved (cf. Rom 3:25-26) by us recognizing our own transgressions in our Spirit-effected identification with the Crucified One, and by God forgiving our sins at the same time. Whomever the Jesus-Christ-Story seizes breathes its Spirit. Freed from the merciless logic of exploitation and self-abuse, freed from the pressure of one's own guilt, freed from the fear of the mercilessness of individual and structural violence, freed from one's own laming sloth, freed from the pressure of success in one's own achievements, our vision, our attitude, our actions become visibly and perceptibly changed, even now: "Where the Spirit of the Lord is, there is freedom. And all of us, with unveiled faces, seeing the glory of the Lord as though reflected in a mirror, are being transformed into the same image from one degree of glory to another; for this comes from the Lord, the Spirit" (2 Cor 3:17b-18). Even now, even today, and in all eternity.

The Lord's Supper invites one to let the loving and creative Spirit of the Jesus-Christ-Story work in oneself, to see the world and oneself through the eyes of this story, to be affected, to throw oneself into life, and to take a stand. That is the political message of the Lord's Supper. It has firm grounding in the theological message of the Lord's Supper: in his merciful wisdom, God has turned the unjust death of Jesus Christ on the cross into salvation for his entire creation.

Staurology

The grand story that the sacred scriptures of Israel narrate adumbrates an emotionally grounded mental framework for the interpretation of the entire cosmos. The cosmos and all life are ends in themselves and owe themselves only to a creative power that takes pleasure in its works. No name and no play on words can limit this creative power and its wanton love.

Employing metaphorical and narrative language is the appropriate way to depict the creative, loving, and just power that we name God in order to distinguish him from his creatures. This is the decisive alternative in the interpretation of the world: Is it a question of a loveless product of chance given by end-oriented powers that only allow for the regularity of cause and effect, or a desired event of creative love? Are we alone or "by good powers made wonderfully secure" (Dietrich Bonhoeffer)?

The grand story of Israel sees the world as God's creation and human beings as God's beloved and wanted children, as the creation of a merciful and just God, who is expressed through the stories of creation, covenant, exodus, exile and its end, the messianic hope in the reign of peace, and in the final establishment of the merciful righteousness of God.

The cross breaks through the logic of the temporal sequence and also through the political logic of the messianic hopes of the Scriptures of Israel. In the midst of now, the eschatological event breaks in and indeed in a way wholly other than expected. It changes everything and yet everything old seems to remain: the Romans remain.

But the word of the cross is effective. It creates reality. It changes knowledge and the ways of knowledge. Knowledge of the Jesus-Christ-Story permits ingenious new thinking. Out of the cross's story of death it makes the story of the beginning of eternal life. It speaks of God's limitless power without trivializing the power of death. It speaks of God's love in solidarity, which cedes no ground. On the cross, and not only in the cross, God encounters a particular place of cruelty and injustice. God is there, he was there, and he will be there. He shrinks before nothing and no one, for he lives.

The community in solidarity with the victim Jesus of Nazareth that is constituted by the Spirit of the Jesus-Christ-Story celebrates the common meal and goes consciously with all deliberation bodily into solidarity with all victims of injustice and violence, into loving solidarity with all victims of exploitation. It speaks clearly for both the great and the small, particular stories of fear and despair, exploitation and merciless abuse. It looks deeply and declares that knowledge of the victims is indispensable for life. Its knowledge brings the oppression of guilt and injustice into the light and makes them an object of public knowledge.

The Spirit of the Jesus-Christ-Story lets one breathe again and think anew. The grand narrative of Israel, which is narrated anew through staurology, the consideration of events from the place of the cross outward, breaks through the logic of terror, the merciless progression of violence and counterviolence, the merciless logic of the maximization of profit, the division of good and evil into the categories of inside and outside.

In the Lord's Supper, understood as a gift of the resurrected Crucified One, staurological knowledge becomes knowledge of others. It motivates one to live concretely in love with God's creatures and indeed precisely there where and how they encounter one.

Notes

Introduction

1   Dieter Zeller, "Religiongeschichtliche Erwägungen zur Auferstehung," *ZNT* 19 (2007): 15–23, here 21f.

2   Cf. Stefan Alkier, "Art. Semiotik—III. Bibelwissenschaftlich," *RGG* 7 (2004): 1194f.; Hermann Deuser, "Art. Semiotik—VII. Ethisch," *RGG* 7 (2004): 1196f. Cf. also in detail Stefan Alkier, "Neutestamentliche Wissenschaft—Ein semiotisches Konzept," in *Kontexte der Schrift II. Kultur, Politik, Religion, Sprache*, ed. Christian Strecker (Stuttgart: Kohlhammer, 2005), 343–60; Alkier, *Wunder und Wirklichkeit in den Briefen des Apostel Paulus: Ein Beitrag zu einem Wunderverständnis jenseits von Entmythologisierung und Rehistorisierung* (WUNT 134; Tübingen: Mohr, 2001); Hermann Deuser, *Gottesinstinkt. Semiotische Religionstheorie und Pragmatismus* (RPT 12; Tübingen: Mohr Siebeck, 2004).

Chapter 1

1   Cf. also François Vouga, "Ist die Kreuzestheologie das hermeneutische Zentrum des Neuen Testaments?" in *Kreuzestheologie im Neuen Testament*, ed. A. Dettwiler and J. Zumstein (WUNT 151; Tübingen: Mohr, 2002), 283–326.

2   The following observations draw on my *Wunder und Wirklichkeit in den Briefen des Apostel Paulus: Ein Beitrag zu einem Wunderverständnis jenseits von Entmythologisierung und Rehistorisierung* (WUNT 134; Tübingen: Mohr, 2001), 306: "From the standpoint of Pauline Christianity, miracles do not belong to the realm of that which is baffling, clouded in secrecy, or seeking the sensational. . . . They receive their plausibility from the knowledge of God, the creator, as the Hebrew Bible speaks of him. The Pauline Christians have experienced the miraculous power of God in their own lives, and they are possessed of the certainty that God will employ his immeasurable power as creator for the ultimate salvation of all believers; he has saved them through the death and resurrection of his Son Jesus Christ from his legitimate eschatological wrath and he will transform their frail and corruptible earthly bodies into radiant incorruptible spiritual bodies so that they might enjoy

eternal communion with their Lord Jesus Christ, who already was transformed as the firstfruits of the dead."

3 Richard B. Hays, *The Faith of Jesus Christ. An Investigation of the Narrative Substructure of Galatians 3:1–4:11* (SBLDS 56; Chico, Calif.: Scholars Press, 1983).

4 Ben Witherington III, *Paul's Narrative Thought World: The Tapestry of Tragedy and Triumph* (Louisville, Ky.: Westminster John Knox, 1994).

5 Eckart Reinmuth, "Narratio und argumentatio—zur Auslegung der Jesus-Christus-Geschichte im Ersten Korintherbrief. Ein Beitrag zur mimetischen Kompetenz des Paulus," *ZTK* 92 (1995): 3–27. Cf. also Reinmuth, "Historik und Exegese—zum Streit um die Auferstehung Jesu nach der Moderne," in *Exegese und Methodendiskussion*, ed. S. Alkier and R. Brucker (TANZ 23; Tübingen: Francke, 1998), 1–20; Reinmuth, "Erzählen und Begreifen. Ein Beitrag zum neutestamentlichen Verständnis eines theologischen Missverständnisses," in *Die Gleichnisreden Jesu 1899–1999. Beiträge zum Dialog mit Adolf Jülicher*, ed. U. Mell (BZNW 103; Berlin: de Gruyter, 1999), 237–56; Reinmuth, *Hermeneutik des Neuen Testaments. Eine Einführung in die Lektüre des Neuen Testaments* (Göttingen: Vandenhoeck & Ruprecht, 2002); Reinmuth, *Neutestamentliche Historik. Probleme und Perspektiven* (TLZ.F 8; Leipzig: Evangelische Verlagsanstalt, 2003); Reinmuth, *Paulus. Gott neu denken* (BG 9; Leipzig: Evangelische Verlagsanstalt, 2004).

6 Ian Scott, *Implicit Epistemology in the Letters of Paul. Story, Experience and the Spirit* (WUNT 2/105; Tübingen: Mohr, 2006). Cf. also my review of I. Mädler, "Transfigurationen. Materielle Kultur in praktisch-theologischer Perspektive," *THLZ* 132, no. 9 (2007): 368–70.

7 Cf. Willi Marxsen, *Der erste Brief an die Thessalonicher* (ZBK.NT 11.1; Zürich: Theologischer Verlag Zürich, 1979), 14f.

8 On the theology of election in 1 Thessalonians, cf. Jürgen Becker, "Die Erwählung der Völker durch das Evangelium. Theologiegeschichtliche Erwägungen zum 1Thess," in *Annäherungen zur Urchristlichen Theologiegeschichte und zum Umfang mit ihren Quellen*, ed. U. Mell (BZNW 76; Berlin: de Gruyter, 1995).

9 Udo Schnelle, *Einleitung in das Neue Testament* (UTB 1830; Göttingen: Mohr, 1999), 67.

10 Cf. Bruce C. Johanson, *To All the Brethren. A Text-Linguistic and Rhetorical Approach to I Thessalonians* (CB.NT 16; Stockholm: Almquist & Wiksell, 1987), 49f.: "Thus, the textual world is informed by the conceptual universe(s) of the Christian gospel of salvation, a salvation grounded in the death and resurrection of Jesus Christ and to be consummated at his parousia."

11 Cf. Jürgen Becker, *Auferstehung der Toten im Urchristentum* (SBS 82; Stuttgart: Katholisches Bibelwerk, 1976), 37: "The resurrection formula thus enables the community to look upon Jesus as the Son of Man, and at the same time legitimates hope as the proclamation of salvation to the addressees. As with the original proclamation of the resurrection, this signifies precisely that Jesus' resurrection is to be understood as something exceptional and unique."

12 Eckart Reinmuth, "Der zweite Brief an die Thessalonicher," in *Die Briefe an die Philipper, Thessalonicher und an Philemon*, ed. N. Walter, E. Reinmuth, and P. Lampe (NTD 8/2; 18th ed.; 1st rev. ed.; Göttingen: Vandenhoeck & Ruprecht, 1998), 121.

13 For a detailed exegetical grounding of the above, cf. Alkier, *Wunder und Wirklichkeit*, 98–106.

14 Cf. François Vouga, "Zur rhetorischen Gattung des Galaterbriefes," *ZNW* 79 (1988): 291: "The actual theme of the letter is no apology for Paul's academic office or his theology, but rather an admonition to remain loyal to this gospel." Cf. also Vouga, *An die Galater* (HNT 10; Tübingen: Mohr, 1998); Joop Smit, "The Letter of Paul to the Galatians: A Deliberative Speech," *NTS* 35 (1989): 1–26; Alkier, *Wunder und Wirklichkeit*, 124–53.

15 Cf. Alkier, *Wunder und Wirklichkeit*, 131–38. Cf. also Hans Dieter Betz, *Der Galaterbrief. Ein Kommentar zum Brief des Apostels Paulus an die Gemeinden in Galatien* (HERMENEIA; München: Kaiser, 1988), 139–40; Ulrich Luck, "Die Bekehrung des Paulus und das paulinische Evangelium. Zur Frage der Evidenz in Botschaft und Theologie des Apostels," *ZNW* 76 (1985): 187–208.

16 Cf. Betz, *Der Galaterbrief,* 139–40.

17 Cf. Karl-Wilhelm Niebuhr, *Heidenapostel aus Israel. Die jüdische Identität des Paulus nach ihrer Darstellung in seinen Briefen* (WUNT 62; Tübingen: Mohr, 1992).

18 Cf. Daniel Boyarin, *A Radical Jew: Paul and the Politics of Identity* (Contraversions I; Berkeley: University of California Press, 1994); Timo Laato, *Paul and Judaism: An Anthropological Approach* (Studies in the History of Judaism 115; Atlanta: Scholars Press, 1995); Ed Parish Sanders, *Paul and Palestinian Judaism* (Philadelphia: Fortress, 1977); James D. G. Dunn, "The New Perspective on Paul," *BJRL* 65 (1983): 95–122; Jörg Frey, "Das Judentum des Paulus," in *Paulus. Leben— Umwelt—Werk—Briefe,* ed. O. Wischmeyer (Tübingen: Mohr, 2006), 5–43.

19 Cf. Vouga, "Ist die Kreuzestheologie?"

20 Cf. Margaret M. Mitchell, *Paul and the Rhetoric of Reconciliation. An Exegetical Investigation of the Language and Composition of 1 Corinthians* (HUTh 28; Tübingen: Mohr, 1991).

21 On this point, cf. in detail Alkier, *Wunder und Wirklichkeit*, 155–59.

22 Cf. Mitchell, *Paul and the Rhetoric of Reconciliation.*

23 Ingolf U. Dalferth, *Der auferweckte Gekreuzigte. Zur Grammatik der Christologie* (Tübingen: Mohr, 1994), 44.

24 Jakob Kremer, *Der Erste Brief an die Korinther* (RNT; Regensburg: Pustet, 1997), 175.

25 Cf. David Moffitt, "Affirming the 'Creed': The Extent of an Early Christian Formula in 1 Cor 15,3b-7," *ZNW* 99 (2008): 49–73.

26 Richard B. Hays, *First Corinthians. Interpretation: A Bible Commentary for Teaching and Preaching* (Louisville, Ky.: Westminster John Knox, 1997), 254.

27 Since Adolf von Harnack, most historical-critical scholars have argued that only 15:3b-5 is an early Christian quote. With plausible arguments taken from the logic of the text, Moffitt, "Affirming the 'Creed,'" 49–73, proved that the longer version 15:3b-7 is a quote and only 15:6b is a Pauline addition.

28 [Translator: In German: "Durch dieses Evangelium werdet ihr gerettet, wenn ihr an dem Wortlaut festhaltet, den ich Euch verkündet habe." The *Einheitsübersetzung* (literally, "Unity Translation") has been a Catholic project that has involved significant Protestant cooperation, particularly in the area of the Psalms and New Testament. Begun in 1962, the translation received final approval of the German Catholic Bishops Conference in 1978. In 2005 the Protestant Church of Germany (EKD, Evangelische Kirche in Deutschland) withdrew from cooperation in the process of the translation's revision.]

29   Cf. Reinmuth, "Narratio und argumentatio," 24: "Thus one observes that the reproduction of σταυρὸς τοῦ Χριστοῦ (v. 17) through the similar λόγος τοῦ σταυροῦ (v. 18) forms a wholly decisive hinge. The cross of Christ is not merely a past historical event, but rather is thus comprehended in its significance as the act of God." The "narrative reference to the Jesus-Christ-Story in 1 Corinthians" (22) thus does not first begin in 1:20b, but rather is called up by the recipients through the sign σταυρὸς in 1:17-18. Moreover, if one goes further with Reinmuth and with Alexander J. M. Wedderburn ("Paul and the Story of Jesus," in *Paul and Jesus*, ed. Wedderburn [JSNT.S 37; Sheffield: JSOT Press, 1989], 161–91) and employs the concept of "story" or the syntagm "Jesus-Christ-Story" "in order to encompass that part of the Jesus-Christ-Story that can be designated as myth as well as that which perceives the historical events—and not indeed to separate that which for Paul belongs together" (Reinmuth, 5), then this narrative reference began already with the section of 1:1-9, which introduces Jesus Christ within the universe of discourse as a figure acting in the past, present, and future, and therefore implicitly narrates that the Jesus-Christ-Story did not end on the cross but rather belongs to the reality of the sender and the addressees for its continuance.

30   Fraunz Mußner, "Zur stilistischen und semantischen Struktur der Formel von 1Kor 15:3b-5," in *Die Kirche des Anfangs*, ed. R. Schnackenburg (Freiburg: Herder, 1978), 407: "It is abundantly clear that the old *credo*-formula is also constructed according to the stylistic device of the 'enumerative way of speaking,' with whose help the stages of a successive event are named consecutively: 'Christ died and he was buried and he has been raised and he appeared.' The enumerated consecutive 'stages' of this narrated event are strung together with the help of the paratactic καί."

31   Cf. Umberto Eco, *Lector in Fabula. Die Mitarbeit der Interpretation In erzählenden Texten* (trans. H. G. Held; München: Hanser, 1987).

32   Hays, *First Corinthians*, 255.

33   In his monograph *Der Streit um die Auferstehung der Toten. Eine religionsgeschicht-liche und exegetische Untersuchung von 1. Korinther 15* (FRLANT 138; Göttingen: Vandenhoeck & Ruprecht, 1986), Gerhard Sellin sheds light on the exemplary function of this autobiographical narrative passage with which Paul, the narrator, writes himself into the Jesus-Christ-Story: "In the person of Paul, in his conversion and call, God has made a dead man alive by divine grace. . . . The appearance of Christ before Paul is therefore an example of the life-creating, dead-raising, effectual power of God. . . . The effect of the creative grace of God consists in its widely-working activity . . . in the εὐαγγέλιον. The *kerygma* thus has even the power to create life" (250).

34   Cf. also Pierre Bühler, "Kreuzestheologie und die Frage nach dem Kanon. Einige hermeneutische Thesen—im Gespräch mit François Vouga," in Dettwiler and Zumstein, *Kreuzestheologie im Neuen Testament*, 327–32; François Vouga, "Crux probat omnia. Der oder ein Prüfstein der neutestamentlichen Hermeneutik? Dialog und Konsens mit Pierre Bühler," in Dettwiler and Zumstein, *Kreuzestheologie im Neuen Testament*, 333–39.

35   Dale B. Martin, *The Corinthian Body* (New Haven, Conn.: Yale University Press, 1995), 106.

36   Becker, *Auferstehung der Toten im Urchristentum*, 90. "Sun, moon and stars appear in series in Gen 1:14-19 and are arranged expressly according to their brilliance

(Paul interprets shine as a degree of glory). According to Gen 1:20ff., the animals on land, in the air and in the water are created in reverse sequence, with the man as the ultimate and as the crowning of creation (Gen 1:26ff). Paul thus reads—probably because of his desired orientation to man—the creation account as if from behind. The Apostle makes reference to the differences among the kinds of animals, which are deliberately emphasized (Gen 1:21). Finally one will also ask whether the mention of seeds and the differentiation among the seeds according to their kind is built upon Gen 1:11-12. Moreover, when Paul maintains that God does this 'as he has chosen' (1 Cor 15:38), it is an interpretation in accord with the creation command in Gen 1:11."

37   Sellin, *Der Streit um die Auferstehung der Toten,* 214.

38   Cf. Gudrun Guttenberger, "῎Ωφθη. Der visuelle Gehalt der frühchristlichen Erscheinungstradition und mögliche Folgerungen für die Entstehung und Entwicklung des frühchristlichen Glaubens an die Auferstehung Jesu (Teil 1)," *BZ* 52, no. 1 (2008): 40–63.

39   Cf. Ingolf U. Dalferth, ed., *The Presence and Absence of God,* Claremont Studies in the Philosophy of Religion, Conference 2008 (Religion in Philosophy and Theology 42; Tübingen: Mohr, 2009).

40   Cf. Alkier, *Wunder und Wirklichkeit,* 171–91, esp. 190–91.

41   Schnelle, *Einleitung in das Neue Testament,* 87.

42   Cf. Hans Windisch, *Der zweite Korintherbrief* (Göttingen: Vandenhoeck & Ruprecht, 1970), 36: "Among the thanksgiving sections at the beginning of a letter, the one in 2 Corinthians takes a special place. While otherwise the thanksgiving-filled view is turned immediately to the community of readers (also in 1 Corinthians), here the one praying speaks out of the fullness of his own experiences and draws the readers only so far in as they themselves will take part and will have part in the suffering and consolation of the Apostle. The introductory thanksgiving for the rich spiritual life is here lacking (as in Galatians)."

43   Otfried Hofius, "Der Gott allen Trostes. Paraklesis und parakalein in 2 Kor 1, 3–7," in *Paulusstudien,* ed. Hofius (WUNT 51; Tübingen: Mohr, 1989), 244–54.

44   Hofius, "Der Gott allen Trostes," 253.

45   Cf. Hofius, "Der Gott allen Trostes," 245–46.

46   Hofius, "Der Gott allen Trostes," 246, draws attention to the context of 2 Cor 1:3-7 as "Old Testament panegyric [*Lobsprüche*]."

47   Cf. Heinrich August Wilhelm Meyer and Georg Heinrici, *Kritisch exegetisches Handbuch über den zweiten Brief an die Korinther* (KEK 6; Göttingen: Vandenhoeck & Ruprecht, 1883), 20.

48   Windisch, *Der zweite Korintherbrief,* 47, observes the syntagm τῷ θεῷ τῷ ἐγείροντι τοὺς νεκρούς: and comments, "This formulation . . . is found . . . also in the Eighteen Benedictions, in the second Benediction as in the concluding Benediction. . . . That it was known much earlier in Israel can perhaps be seen on the basis of Deut 32:39, 1 Kgs 2:6, and 2 Kgs 5:7. . . . The manner of expression is thus old semitic and used in Judaism long before Paul. One observes that every connection to Jesus Christ is lacking: The Jewish formulation here is not yet Christianized. Its significance and use is double. According to the oriental way of speaking in the Old Testament, which already sees the danger of death as the condition of death, illness as a journey into the underworld, and correspondingly preservation from death as a

resurrection from death, it can point to an effective resurrection of the dead, as also to liberation from danger to one's life; with regard to Paul, both are conceivable."

49 Ulrich Heckel, *Kraft in Schwachheit. Untersuchungen zu 2 Kor 10–13* (WUNT 2/52; Tübingen: Mohr, 1993), 283: "Paul does not thus set his carefree, joyous, courageous and elevated condition over and against the external burden of suffering but rather his trust in God, who raises the dead (2 Cor 1:8-10)."

50 Friedrich Lang, *Die Briefe an die Korinther* (NTD 7; Göttingen: Vandenhoeck & Ruprecht, 1986), 254: "With his wonderful power, God has intervened and rescued him from the danger of death."

51 Hofius, "Der Gott allen Trostes," 246.

52 Heckel, *Kraft in Schwachheit*, 281.

53 Heckel, *Kraft in Schwachheit*, 282.

54 Relevant is the observation of Ulrich Brockhaus, *Charisma und Amt. Die paulinische Charismenlehre auf dem Hintergrund der frühchristlichen Gemeindefunktionen* (Wuppertal: Brockhaus, 1987), 138: "There is no ground for loading the word χάρισμα (2 Cor 1:11) with the purpose of service to the congregation; what is intended is much simpler: an intervention of God in the life of Paul, who experienced it as a gift and so designated it."

55 Victor Paul Furnish, *II Corinthians*, translated with introduction, notes, and commentary (AB 32A; Garden City, N.Y.: Doubleday, 1984), 125, writes, "[P]etition no less than thanksgiving is rooted in a profound trust in the power and goodness of God."

56 Cf. Heckel, *Kraft in Schwachheit*, 226.

57 Cf., e.g., Windisch, *Der zweite Korintherbrief*, 44–45; Christian Wolff, *Der zweite Brief des Paulus an die Korinther* (ThkNT 8; Berlin: Evangelische Verlagsanstalt, 1989), 25; Furnish, *II Corinthians*, 122–23; and Margaret Thrall, *A Critical and Exegetical Commentary on the Second Epistle to the Corinthians. Introduction and Commentary on II Corinthians I–VII* (ICC; Edinburgh: Clark, 1994), 115–17.

58 Furnish fittingly observes, "Paul's portrayal of the miserable state to which he had been reduced by the affliction in Asia, and of his reliance upon God who raises the dead, accords with one of the prominent themes in his letters to Corinth. While it may be too much to claim, . . . that 'power' (dynamis) was one of the catchwords of Paul's opponents in Corinth, it does appear that one of the fundamental charges being brought against Paul there concerned his 'weakness' (astheneia). There is evidence of this especially in chaps. 10–13 of 2Cor (e.g., 10:10), but it is probable that the apostle's consciousness of such charges lies behind certain passages in 1Cor as well (e.g., when Paul parodies the Corinthians in 4:8-13 and contrasts their 'strength' with the 'weakness' of the apostles; cf. 12:22). Instead of denying his weakness, Paul affirms it as a fact, and more than once catalogs the hardships he has experienced as an apostle (4:8-9, 6:4c-5; 11:23b-29; 12:10; cf. Rom 8:35; 1Cor 4:9-13). In these various afflictions, he says, he will dare to 'boast' (11:30; 12:5), because precisely in his endurance of them the divine power is revealed (12:9-10)" (*II Corinthians*, 122f.).

59 Heckel, *Kraft in Schwachheit*, 16. Cf. also the felicitous outline of chaps. 10–13.

60 Ernst Käsemann, *Die Legitimität des Apostels. Eine Untersuchung zu 2. Korinther 10–13* (Libelli 33; Darmstadt: Wissenschaftliche Buchgesellschaft, 1956), 510: "Paul has not excluded himself from such traditions creeping over his reputation:

The miracle actually belongs to the essence of apostleship and is thus employed by him also for himself."

61 Heckel, *Kraft in Schwachheit*, 75–76, emphasizes that "the passivum divinum ἐδόθη makes plain that this suffering along with the rapture of vv. 2-4 goes back to God as its cause." Cf. Heckel, *Kraft in Schwachheit*, 79.

62 Heckel, *Kraft in Schwachheit*, 88.

63 Heckel, *Kraft in Schwachheit*, 107, with 2 Cor 13:4 in view, emphasizes "that not only the speaker Paul, but also the one who commissions him, Christ, lives out of the full power of God and both ultimately owe their effectiveness to the one and the same divine power. This is it shown that it is precisely the human helplessness of Jesus that becomes for God an occasion to make his power perfect in weakness."

64 Cf. also Wolfgang Wiefel, "Die Hauptrichtung des Wandels im eschatologischen Denken des Paulus," *ThZ* 30 (1974): 65–84.

65 Thus the thesis of Hans Dieter Betz, *Der Apostel Paulus und die sokratische Tradition. Eine exegetische Untersuchung zu seiner "Apologie" 2. Korinther 10–13* (BhT 45; Tübingen: Mohr, 1972), 84, which Heckel refuted for good reasons in *Kraft in Schwachheit*, 64–65. On page 65 Heckel comes to a different conclusion: "Therefore he does not parody the depiction of such heavenly journeys, but rather the self-praise of his opponents on the ground of such revelatory experiences."

66 Heckel, *Kraft in Schwachheit*, 316.

67 With regard to the following discussion, see also Alkier, *Wunder und Wirklichkeit*, 259–81.

68 Cf. Rom 1:4, 4:17, 24-25; 5:10; 6:4-9; 7:4; 8:11, 34; 10:9; 11:15; and 14:9.

69 Charles E. B. Cranfield, *A Critical and Exegetical Commentary on the Epistle to the Romans. Introduction and Commentary on Romans I–VIII* (ICC; Edinburgh: Clark, 1977), 1:60, understands the significance of κατὰ σάρκα fittingly as "'as a man,' 'so far as his human nature is concerned.' By using it Paul implies that the fact of Christ's human nature, in respect of which what has just been said is true, is not the whole truth about him."

70 Otto Michel, *Der Brief an die Römer* (KEK 4; 14th ed.; 5th rev. ed.; Göttingen: Vandenhoeck & Ruprecht, 1978), 38: "κατὰ σάρκα designates the human, historical heritage (Rom 9:3, 5; 1 Cor 10:18), while κατὰ πνεῦμα ἁγιωσύνης paraphrases the eschatological new creation, the mystery of the wondrous act of God."

71 Peter Stuhlmacher, *Der Brief an die Römer* (NTD 6; 15th ed.; 2nd rev. ed.; Göttingen: Vandenhoeck & Ruprecht, 1998), 22: "Vv. 3 and 4 contain the Christ-story the gospel tells in short form, and they emphasize that the entire way of Jesus from his birth to his exaltation stands under the sign of the promises of God."

72 Dieter Zeller, *Der Brief an die Römer* (Regensburger NT; Regensburg: Pustet, 1985), 54: "The deadly wrath of God stands against every 'godlessness and injustice.'" On the syntagm "wrath of God," cf. 53–54; cf. also Hans-Joachim Eckstein, "Denn Gottes Zorn wird vom Himmel her offenbar werden. Exegetische Erwägungen zu Röm 1,18," *ZNW* 78 (1987): 74–89.

73 Cranfield, *Critical and Exegetical Commentary*, 1:211–12: "God's patiently holding back his wrath is familiar in Judaism. But for god [*sic*] simply to pass over sins would be altogether incompatible with His righteousness. He would not be the good and merciful god, had he been content to pass over sins indefinitely; for this would have been to condone evil—a denial of His own nature and a cruel betrayal of sinners."

74   Stuhlmacher, *Der Brief an die Römer*, 60: "In biblical thinking, justification is the
      creator God's act of justice and therefore at the same time an act of the new cre-
      ation, and those he justifies by his power attain before God participation in his
      glory and righteousness."
75   Beate Ego, "Abraham als Urbild der Treue Israels. Traditionsgeschichtliche Über-
      legungen zu einem Aspekt des biblischen Abrahambildes," in *Bund und Tora.
      Zur theologischen Begriffsgeschichte in alttestamentlicher, frühjüdischer und urchristli-
      cher Tradition*, ed. Friedrich Avemarie and Hermann Lichtenberger (WUNT 98;
      Tübingen: Mohr, 1996), 25–26, rightly emphasizes that the Pauline interpretation
      of Gen 15:6 and thus the interpretation of Abraham in Rom 4 "stands diametri-
      cally opposed" to the interpretation of Abraham in early Judaism.
76   Ernst Käsemann, *Paulinische Persepktiven* (Tübingen: Mohr, 1969), 159. Ernst
      Käsemann, *An die Römer* (HNT 3a; 3rd rev. ed.; Tübingen: Mohr, 1974), 115–17,
      offers further intertextual references on the topic; cf. also Walter Schmithals, *Der
      Römerbrief. Ein Kommentar* (Gütersloh: Mohn, 1988), 144; Zeller, *Der Brief an die
      Römer*, 102–3; and Ulrich Wilckens, *Der Brief an die Römer (Röm 1–5)* (EKK VI/1;
      2nd rev. ed.; Zürich: Benziger, 1987), 274–76.
77   The Christian picture of Abraham is formed by Romans 4. The Pauline interpreta-
      tion of Abraham neglects the doubting sides of Abraham and effaces the fact that
      he first laughs when he receives the promise of having his own child in Gen 17:17.
      The laughter of Abraham has been silenced and the laughter of Sarah has been
      displayed for all to see even up to the textual selections of contemporary children's
      Bibles.
78   Michel, *Der Brief an die Römer*, 127: "In the resurrection of Jesus Christ from the
      dead, God has confirmed his own creative power: the Easter event is thus nothing
      other than a manifestation of the creative power of God. Faith in the resurrection
      of 'our Lord Jesus' from the dead is therefore here ordered to faith in the promise,
      particularly as he connects it immediately with the promise of the 'seed of Abra-
      ham' (Gal 3:16)." Cf. also Cranfield, *Critical and Exegetical Commentary*, 1:251.
79   Cf. also Wolfgang Kraus, "Der Tod als Sühnetod bei Paulus. Überlegungen zur
      neueren Diskussion," *ZNT* 3 (1999): 20–30; on the religious-historical back-
      ground, cf. Bernd Janowski, *Sühne als Heilsgeschehen. Studien zur Sühnetheologie
      der Priesterschrift und zur Wurzel KPR im Alten Orient und im Alten Testament*
      (WMANT 55; Neukirchen-Vluyn: Neukirchener Verlag, 1982).
80   Cf. also Henning Paulsen, *Überlieferung und Auslegung in Römer 8* (WMANT 43;
      Neukirchen-Vluyn: Neukirchener Verlag, 1974).
81   *Bürgerrecht* ("citizenship" or "civil liberties") is the translation of πολίτευμα of
      Peter Pilhofer, *Philippi I* (WUNT 87; Tübingen: Mohr, 1995), 130; cf. Gerhard
      Friedrich, "Der Brief an die Philipper," in *Die Briefe an die Galater, Epheser, Phil-
      ipper, Kolosser, Thessalonicher und Philemon*, ed. G. Friedrich, H. Conzelmann, and
      J. Becker (NTD 8,15; 15th rev. and enl. ed.; Göttingen: Vandenhoeck & Ruprecht,
      1981), 165–66. On the proper understanding of Phil 3:20, cf. Pilhofer, *Philippi*,
      127–34.
82   Wayne A. Meeks, "The Man from Heaven in Paul's Letter to the Philippians," in
      The Future of Early Christianity, ed. B. A. Pearson et al. (Minneapolis: Fortress,
      1991), 335.
83   Cf. Ernst Lohmeyer, *Kyrios Jesus. Eine Untersuchung zu Phil 2,5–11* (Darmstadt:
      Wissenschaftliche Buchgesellschaft, 1961), 73.

84 Cf. Lohmeyer, *Kyrios Jesus*, 5–6.

85 Lohmeyer, *Kyrios Jesus*, 10–11.

86 Lohmeyer, *Kyrios Jesus*, 3.

87 Cf. also Ernst Käsemann, "Kritische Analyse von Phil 2:5-11," in *Exegetische Versuche und Besinnungen I*, ed. Ernst Käsemann, 6th ed., vol. 1; 3rd ed., vol. 2 (Göttingen: Vandenhoeck & Ruprecht, 1970), 52–53.

88 Käsemann, "Kritische Analyse," 76, 71.

89 Käsemann, "Kritische Analyse," 72.

90 The question of the authorship of Phil 2:6-11 has left its mark upon the research; cf. also Walter, Reinmuth, and Lampe, *Die Briefe an die Philipper, Thessalonicher und an Philemon*, 56ff. Ralph Brucker, *"Christushymnen" oder "epideiktische Passagen"? Studien zum Stilwechsel im Neuen Testament und seiner Umwelt* (FRLANT 176; Göttingen: Vandenhoeck & Ruprecht, 1997), 310–15, expresses a cogent argument for the hymn's Pauline authorship. Cf. also the literature that Brucker cites in notes 51, 67, and 69.

91 On the problem of the semantic determination of the denotation of this syntagm, cf. Joachim Gnilka, *Der Philipperbrief* (hTkNT 10; Freiburg: Herder, 1980), 112–14.

92 Nikolaus Walter, "Geschichte und Mythos in der urchristlichen Präexistenzchristologie," in *Praeparatio Evangelica. Studien zur Umwelt, Exegese und Hermeneutik des Neuen Testaments*, ed. Nikolaus Walter (WUNT 98; Tübingen: Mohr, 2002), 285.

93 Otfried Hofius, *Der Christushymnus Philipper 2,6-11. Untersuchungen zu Gestalt und Aussage eines urchristlichen Psalms* (Tübingen: Mohr, 1991), 63: "The cross as the most extreme sign of the most extreme powerlessness and sharpest shame makes Jesus' renunciation of his divine power and glory apparent in its full measure and thus at the same time the true dimension of his taking the 'form of a slave.'" Cf. Lohmeyer, *Kyrios Jesus*, 46; Lohmeyer, *Der Brief an die Philipper, and die Kolosser und an Philemon* (KEK 9, 13th ed.; Göttingen: Vandenhoeck & Ruprecht, 1964), 96.

94 Walter, "Geschichte und Mythos in der urchristlichen Präexistenzchristologie," 285.

95 Walter, "Geschichte und Mythos in der urchristlichen Präexistenzchristologie," 286. Cf. also idem, *Die Briefe an die Philipper*, 62–63.

96 Cf. Michael Theobald, "Der Kolosserbrief," in *Einleitung in das Neue Testament*, ed. M. Ebner and S. Schreiber (Stuttgart: Kohlhammer, 2008), 436.

97 Cf. Theobald, "Kolosserbrief."

98 Thus, e.g., Eduard Schweizer, *Der Brief an die Kolosser* (EKK XII; 3rd rev. ed.; Zürich: Benziger, 1989), 198.

99 Andreas Lindemann, "Gemeinde von 'Kolossä.' Erwägungen zum 'Sitz im Leben' eines pseudopaulinischen Briefes," *WD* 16 (1981), 111–34, repr. in *Paulus, Apostel und Lehrer der Kirche. Studien zu Paulus und zum frühen Paulusverständnis* (Tübingen: Mohr, 1991).

100 Theobald, "Kolosserbrief," 435–36.

101 Cf. Andreas Lindemann, *Der Kolosserbrief* (ZBk 10; Zürich: Theologischer Verlag, 1983), 22.

102 Cf. also the synoptic overview by Theobald, "Der Epheserbrief," in Ebner and Schreiber, *Einleitung in das Neue Testament*, 411–12.

103 Theobald, "Der Epheserbrief," 416.

104 Cf. Clinton E. Arnold, *Ephesians. Power and Magic: The Concept of Power in Ephesians in Light of Its Historical Setting* (SNTSMS 63; Cambridge: Cambridge University Press, 1989); Rainer Schwindt, *Das Weltbild des Epheserbriefes. Eine religionsgeschichtlich-exegetische Studie* (WUNT 148; Tübingen: Mohr, 2002); Gerhard Sellin, *Der Brief an die Epheser* (KEK 9; Göttingen: Vandenhoeck & Ruprecht, 2008), 59–62.

105 Sellin, *Der Brief an die Epheser*, 61.

106 Cf. also Stefan Alkier, "Leben in qualifizierter Zeit: Die präsentische Eschatologie des Evangeliums vom römischen Novum Saeculum und die apokalyptische Eschatologie des Evangeliums vom auferweckten Gekreuzigten," *ZNT* 22 (2008): 20–34.

107 Tae-Seong Roh concurs with this judgment in *Der zweite Thessanicherbrief als Erneuerung apokalyptischer Zeitdeutung* (NTOA 62; Göttingen: Vandenhoeck & Ruprecht, 2007).

108 As Andreas Lindemann contends in "Zum Abfassungszweck des zweiten Thessalonicherbriefes," *ZNW* 68 (1977): 35–47.

109 Reinmuth, "Der zweite Brief an die Thessalonicher," 165.

110 Cf. also Gerd Häfner, "Die Pastoralbriefe (1Tim/2Tim/Tit)," in Ebner and Schreiber, *Einleitung in das Neue Testament*, 454.

111 Michael Wolter, *Die Pastoralbreife als Paulustradition* (FRLANT 146; Göttingen: Vandenhoeck & Ruprecht, 1988), 196.

112 Alfons Weiser, "Freundschaftsbrief und Testament. Zur literarischen Gattung des zweiten Briefes an Timotheus," in *Zeit-Geschichte und Begegnungen*, ed. G. Riße (Paderborn: Bonifatius, 1998), 158–70.

113 Cf. Annette Merz, *Die fiktive Selbstauslegung des Paulus. Intertextuelle Studien zur Intention und Rezeption der Pastoralbriefe* (NTOA 52; Göttingen: Vandenhoeck & Ruprecht, 2003), 210ff.

114 Cf. Heinz Schürmann, "'Pro-Existenz' als christologischer Grundbegriff," in *Jesus—Gestalt und Geheimnis. Gesammelte Beiträge*, ed. H. Schürmann and K. Scholtissek; Paderborn: Bonifatius, 1994), 286–315 [Translator: Schürmann coined the term *Pro-Existenz*, which refers to Jesus' earthly life before the cross.]; cf. also Christfried Böttrich, "Proexistenz im Leben und Sterben. Jesu Tod bei Lukas," in *Deutungen des Todes Jesu im Neuen Testament*, ed. J. Frey and J. Schröter (Tübingen: Mohr, 2005), 415n15.

115 Trans. Wesley W. Isenberg, http://www.gnosis.org/naghamm/gop.html.

Chapter 2

1 Cf. Hans-Friedrich Weiß, *Der Brief an die Hebräer* (KEK 13; 15th ed.; 1st rev. ed.; Göttingen: Vandenhoeck & Ruprecht, 1991), 38ff.

2 Albert Vanhoye, "Hebräerbrief," *TRE* 14 (1985): 497. Cf. Vanhoye, *La structure littéraire de l'épître aux Hébreux* (StudNeot 1; Paris: Desclée de Brouwer, 1963); Vanhoye, "Literarische Struktur und theologische Botschaft des Hebräerbriefs," *SNTSU* 4 (1979): 119–47.

3 The outline of the writing that Vanhoye provides takes these facts into account. Cf. also Vanhoye, "Hebräerbrief," 498–99.

4 Cf. also Weiß, *Der Brief an die Hebräer*, 763: In Heb 13:23 there "follows a further personal observation by means of which the author sets himself obviously and consciously in continuity with the mission of the apostle." Cf. also Vanhoye, "Hebräerbrief," 495–96.

5 Ingo Broer, *Einleitung in das Neue Testament 2. Die Briefliteratur, die Offenbarung des Johannes und die Bildung des Kanons* (NEchtB; 2 vols.; Würzburg: Echter, 2001), 581: "In no writing of the New Testament does the Old Testament play a comparable role, for in none is there to be found anything approaching the number of citations and allusions, and no author understands himself as an interpreter of the Scriptures to the degree that the author of the Letter to the Hebrews does."

6 Weiß, *Der Brief an die Hebräer*, 769–70.

7 Since most scholars do not think Jesus' resurrection matters much (if at all) for Hebrews, David Moffitt, *Atonement and the Logic of Resurrection in the Epistle to the Hebrews* (SNT 141; Leiden: Brill, 2011), has shown the importance of the concept of resurrection for the argumentation in Hebrews. Moffitt's important point with regard to the Epistle to the Hebrews is that "the author's affirmation of Jesus' bodily resurrection unifies and drives the high-priestly Christology and the soteriology of his homily" (299). Cf. David Moffitt, "Der Hebräerbrief im Kontext der neueren englischen Forschung. Ein kurzer Überblick über die wichtigsten Forschungsprobleme," *ZNT 29* (2012): 2–13.

8 Moffitt, *Atonement and the Logic of Resurrection*, 299.

9 Weiß, *Der Brief an die Hebräer*, 754: "It is thus also a clue to the 'biblical theology' of the author of Hebrews when he very clearly formulates this expression in v. 20 in connection with the traditional Pauline 'resurrection formula.' This varies, however, when he 'refers it back' to Isa 63:11 and therefore in turn places his own accent upon it. This takes place in three concrete aspects: Once through the participial divine predication ὁ ἀναγαγὼν ἐκ νεκρῶν (instead of the traditional ὁ ἐγείρας ἐκ νεκρῶν) modelled after Isa 63:11; for another, through the predication of the 'resurrected one' as the 'shepherd of the sheep' (again in connection with Isa 63:11); and finally, third, in connection with the traditional 'resurrection formula,' through the wholly unusual use of the phrase ἐν αἵματι διαθήκης αἰωνίου, which is turned to refer to the cruciform death of Jesus (that is, his self-offering). This phrase—in distinction to the first two instances of 'accent setting' named above— clearly has its place in the author's own theological conception."

10 Broer, *Einleitung in das neue Testament*, 586.

Chapter 3

1 Martin Kähler, *Der sogenannte historische Jesus und der geschichtliche, biblische Christus* (TB 2, 3rd vol.; München: Kaiser, 1961), 60.

2 This supports the idea that Matthew and Luke also posed these questions to themselves and that their criticism of the gospel of Mark motivated the composition of their own gospels.

3 Eta Linnemann, "Der (wiedergefundene) Markusschluss," *ZTK* 66 (1969): 255–87, put forth the hypothesis that the original ending of Mark consisted of Matt 28:16-17 and Mark 16:15-20. In her analysis, Matt 28:16-17 is supposed to go back to an older edition of the gospel of Mark that lay before Matthew. For criticism of this hypothesis see in addition Kurt Aland, "Der wiedergefundene Markusschluss? Eine methodologische Bemerkung zur textkritischen Arbeit," *ZTK* 67 (1970): 3–13; Aland, "Der Schluss des Markusevangeliums," in *Neutestamentliche Entwürfe*, TB 63, ed. Aland (München: Kaiser, 1979), 246–83. The hypothesis of a lost ending to Mark can still be found today, even if lacking the early optimism

regarding its reconstruction; cf. Schnelle, *Einleitung in das Neue Testament* (UTB 1830; Göttingen: Mohr, 1999), 223–24.

4 Henning Paulsen, "Mk XVI 1-8," *NovT* 22 (1980): 138–75, repr. in Paulsen, *Zur Literatur und Geschichte des frühen Christentums* (WUNT 99; Tübingen: Mohr, 1997), 75–112.

5 Cf. Gen 2:7 (LXX): καὶ ἔπλασεν ὁ θεὸς τὸν ἄνθρωπον χοῦν ἀπὸ τῆς γῆς καὶ ἐνεφύσησεν εἰς τὸ πρόσωπον αὐτοῦ πνοὴν ζωῆς, καὶ ἐγένετο ὁ ἄνθρωπος εἰς ψυχὴν ζῶσαν.

6 ἐξεθαμβήθησαν is the third person plural aorist passive indicative of ἐκθαμβέω and should also be translated as a passive.

7 Second person plural imperative present middle passive.

8 Cf. Mark 4:10–13:41; 6:49-50; 8:16-21; 9:6, 10, 32; 10:32. On the interpretation of the disciples' incomprehension in the gospel of Mark, cf. William Wrede, *Das Messiasgeheimnis in den Evangelien. Zugleich ein Beitrag zum Verständnis des Markusevangeliums* (4th ed.; Göttingen: Vandenhoeck & Ruprecht, 1969); Robert C. Tannehill, "The Disciples in Mark: The Function of a Narrative Role," *JR* 57 (1977), 386–405.

9 The punctuation of the Nestle-Aland leads to error here. No main sentence begins with καθώς. Verse 1 is thus not to be read as a title.

10 Eve-Marie Becker, *Das Markus-Evangelium im Rahmen antiker Historiographie* (WUNT 194; Tübingen: Mohr, 2006), 245–56, comes to a similar conclusion, but on different grounds and with a different intention: "The *historiographical function* of the opening of this book, which begins neither with the appearance of Jesus, nor with the actions of the Baptist, but rather with a prophetic announcement, lies in placing the beginning of the history of events which Mark tells in what follows back in the time of Jesus." In her interpretation of the gospel of Mark as a historiographical writing, Becker overlooks the scriptural and theological function of the citation expressed by γέγραπται. Although she points out on page 247 that the conclusion in 16:8 is clearly directed to the beginning of the gospel, her thesis of historiography leads to the overall characterization of the gospel of Mark as "the history of the events of the work and death of Jesus" (410). Like the position of Rudolf Bultmann on the theological achievement of the Markan narrative, now shown to be entirely outdated by more recent research, Becker maintains: "In the literary conception of the Gospel as a whole, no theological coherence is achieved" (417). That Becker misjudges the theological achievement of the literary conception of the gospel of Mark as a whole is shown not least in her astounding ignorance of the gospel's resurrection theology. Therefore, in her work the connection of the deeds, acts, and death of Jesus of Nazareth formulated and narratively shaped by the gospel of Mark becomes "the history of the events of the work and death of Jesus" (410). Becker misunderstands the gospel of Mark's theology of the cross as a "theology of suffering," which supposedly shows itself as a "negative-panegyric element of the Gospel" (412).

11 The concept of the encyclopedia employed here comes from the semiotics of Umberto Eco. Cf. Eco, *Lector in Fabula*. Cf. also Alkier, *Wunder und Wirklichkeit*, 72ff.; Alkier, "Neutestamentliche Wissenschaft," 350ff.

12 Not until the crucifixion does a human beingarrive at the appropriate designation of the protagonist Jesus as the Son of God (Mark 15:39). This man is in no way designated as one of Jesus' followers, but rather is a Roman centurion.

13   I have taken the concept of the universe of discourse from Charles Sanders Peirce
      and reworked it for the needs of exegesis. Cf. Alkier, *Wunder und Wirklichkeit*;
      Alkier, "Neutestamentliche Wissenschaft," 350ff.
14   In the perspective of tradition history, the citations in vv. 2b and 3 admittedly
      derive from Isaiah 40:3 only in part. Exod 42:20 and Mic 3:1 are also pulled in.
      For the intratextual interpretation it is therefore of special significance that only
      the name of Isaiah appears in the text and thus that the book of Isaiah is espe-
      cially emphasized. Cf. Joel Marcus, *Mark 1–8* (Anchor Bible Commentaries; New
      Haven, Conn.: Yale University Press, 2002), 142–43.
15   *Euphoric* narrative elements contribute to the success of the intentions of the pro-
      tagonist, while *dysphoric* elements disturb them—that is, they lead to failure.
16   Willi Marxsen, *Der Evangelist Markus. Studien zur Redaktionsgeschichte des Evan-
      geliums* (FRLANT 67, 2nd ed.; Göttingen: Vandenhoeck & Ruprecht, 1959).
17   The encyclopedic ordering of this syntagm in the conventionalized knowledge of
      Judaism in the first century A.D. is still hotly contested. Among all the complexi-
      ties of the debate, one should not lose sight of the fact that it calls to mind inter-
      textually both prophetic (Ezekiel) and apocalyptic literature (Dan 7:13; 1 Enoch
      37–71), even if the double determination—*the* Son *of [the]* Man—is set down for
      the first time in the gospel of Mark and fits well with its emphatic use in the gospel
      of Mark. Jesus designates himself as "the Son of Man" in sixty-nine places in the
      Synoptic Gospels. In the gospel of John a further thirteen are to be found. Cf.
      Delbert Burkett, *The Son of Man Debate. A History and Evaluation* (SNTSMS 105;
      Cambridge: Cambridge University Press, 1999).
18   Cf. Mark 6:2, 10:26, 11:18.
19   Cf. Werner Kahl, "Zur Interpretation des Neuen Testaments im sozio-kulturellen
      Kontext Westafrikas," *ZNT* 5 (2000): 31. Cf. also Kahl, *New Testament Miracle
      Stories in their Religious-Historical Setting. A religionsgeschichtliche Comparison from
      a Structural Perspective* (FRLANT 163; Göttingen: Vandenhoeck & Ruprecht,
      1994).
20   I have investigated intertextual aspects of Mark 4 in other places: Cf. Stefan Alk-
      ier, "Die Bibel im Dialog der Schriften und das Problem der Verstockung in Mk 4.
      Intertextualität im Rahmen einer kategorialen Semiotik biblischer Texte," in *Die
      Bibel im Dialog der Schriften. Konzepte intertextueller Bibellektüre*, ed. Stefan Alkier,
      Richard B. Hays (NET 10; Tübingen: Francke, 2005), 1–22; cf. Alkier, "Intertex-
      tuality and the Semiotics of Biblical Texts," in *Reading the Bible Intertextually*, ed.
      R. B. Hays, S. Alkier, and L. A. Huizenga (Waco, Tex.: Baylor University Press,
      2009), 3–22.
21   Cf. in addition in greater detail Alkier, "Intertextuality and the Semiotics of Bibli-
      cal Texts."
22   Cf. in addition Jesper Svenbro, *Phrasikleia. Anthropologie de la lecture en Grèce anci-
      enne* (Textes à l'appui 188; Paris: Éditions la Découverte, 1988).
23   Kristina Dronsch, *Bedeutung als Grundbegriff neutestamentlicher Wissenschaft. Text-
      theoretische und semiotische Entwürfe zur Kritik der Semantik dargelegt anhand einer
      Analyse zu* ἀκούω *in Mk 4* (NET 15; Tübingen: Francke, 2010).
24   Here also is the shift from aorist to present to be observed.
25   Cf. Jakob Kremer, "ἀνάστασις κτλ," *EWNT* (2nd ed.; 1980), 1:210–21; Kremer,
      "ἐγείρω," *EWNT* 1:899–910.

26 Cf. Dale C. Allison, *Resurrecting Jesus. The Earliest Christian Tradition and Its Interpreters* (New York: Clark, 2005). The third essay of this volume, titled "The Problem of Gehenna" (56–110), counters in a first line of argumentation the conception that the historical Jesus would have known no eschatological punishment and said nothing about hell: "Maybe a Jesus who says nothing about hell is the artifact of interested historians who themselves have nothing to say about hell, or at least nothing good to say" (58). An overview of Jewish tradition and its sacred scriptures, in which the historical Jesus was anchored, speaks for the fact that Gehenna and eschatological punishments would have been self-evident to the Jew Jesus. Moreover, the theme of the final judgment appears in numerous and different forms in the gospels of the New Testament. Thus Allison considers it indeed impossible in most cases to prove individual words of Jesus authentic. He does not draw a pessimistic conclusion from this, however. On the contrary, he declares the overwhelming majority of Jesus' words in the synoptic gospels as "possibly authentic" (76), with which he expresses both the necessary critical caution of the historian as well as his confidence in the synoptic tradition. He adduces Mark 9:43-48 especially as an authentic piece of evidence for his thesis that as an eschatological prophet of the end time, Jesus reckoned with the final judgment and its punishments in the foreseeable future. Admittedly, Gehenna—that is, eschatological punishments—is never an independent theme of the historical Jesus. Much more do they belong to the entire setting of his apocalyptic prophesying (cf. 78ff.). Jesus used talk of hell rarely as a threat against outsiders, however, but rather much more for those who followed him. Regarding Jesus' words on the final judgment, the Jesus tradition and the evangelists set no new accent upon them (cf. 82). In the remaining twenty pages of the essay Allison pursues the question concerning whether and to what extent Jesus' words about hell and the final judgment could also be relevant for modern people for whom the Enlightenment has made it clear that the question of hell concerns a mythical place. According to Allison, mythological talk about hell points to responsibility for our actions. But the concept of heaven as a counterconcept to hell is also a mythological way of speaking. Allison's interpretation of these mythological beliefs does not lead him to any philosophical, secularized meaning, however. Instead, he conceives of heaven and hell as metaphorical language for the otherwise ineffable reality of life after death, which does not ignore deeds done before death.

27 Cf. in addition Stefan Alkier and Stefanie Karweick, "'So hab' ich Jesus ja noch nie erlebt!' Die sogenannte 'Tempelreinigung' in der sechsten Klasse einer Realschule," in *"Man hat immer ein Stück Gott in sich." Mit Kindern biblische Geschichten deuten* (Jahrbuch für Kindertheologie Sonderband, vol. 2; Stuttgart: Calwer, 2006), 150–67.

28 Cf. on this point the work by Jürgen Becker, *Die Auferstehung Jesu Christi nach dem Neuen Testament. Ostererfahrung und Osterverständnis im Urchristentum* (Tübingen: Mohr, 2007), 182–208.

29 Ernst-Joachim Waschke, "Auferstehung I. Auferstehung der Toten 2. Altes Testament," *RGG* 1, no. 4 (1998): 915.

30 Bernd Janowski, "Die Toten loben JHWH nicht. Psalm 88 und das alttestamentliche Todesverständnis," in *Auferstehung/Resurrection. The Fourth Durham–Tübingen Research Symposium: Resurrection, Transfiguration and Exaltation in Old Testament, Ancient Judaism and Early Christianity (Tübingen, September 1999)*, WUNT 135,

ed. Friedrich Avemarie and Hermann Lichtenberger (Tübingen: Mohr, 2001), 3–45, esp. 37, suggests that the conception of "deliverance from death" and the concept of "eternal life/immortality" are to be understood as prior stages on the way to later resurrection hope. On the OT discussion, see also Andrew Chester, "Resurrection and Transformation," in Avemarie and Lichtenberger, *Auferstehung/ Resurrection*, 44–77; Günter Stemberger, "Das Problem der Auferstehung im Alten Testament," *Kairos* 14 (1972): 273–90; Horst Dietrich Preuß, "'Auferstehung' in Texten alttestamentlicher Apokalyptik (Jes 26,7-19, Dan 12,1-4)," in *'Linguistische' Theologie. Biblische Texte, christliche Verkündigung und theologische Sprachtheorie*, FThL 3, ed. Uwe Gerber und Erhardt Güttgemanns (Bonn: Linguistica Biblica, 1972), 101–33.

31   Isa 26:14 and Isa 26:19 do not form a contradiction, however, for 26:14 is directed to enemy dead, while 26:19 has only Israel's dead in view. On this point cf. Dieter Zeller, "Religionsgeschichtliche Erwägungen zur Auferstehung," *ZNT* 19 (2007): 16–17.

32   Cf. Kristina Dronsch, "Text-Ma(h)le. Die skripturale Funktion des Abendmahls in Mk 14," in *Eine gewöhnliche und harmlose Speise? Von den Entwicklungen frühchristlicher Abendmahlstraditionen*, ed. Angelika Standhartinger (Gütersloh: Gütersloher Verlagshaus, 2008), 157–79.

33   Thomas Hieke, "Neue Horizonte. Biblische Auslegung als Weg zu ungewöhnlichen Perspektiven," *ZNT* 12 (2003): 66. Although I do not altogether agree with Hieke's designation here, I do agree with his fundamental literary-critical direction, and refer readers to his research-furthering *Habilitation, Die Genealogien der Genesis* (Herders Biblische Studien 39; Freiburg: Herder, 2003).

34   Cf. on this point Alkier, "From Text to Intertext: Intertextuality as a Paradigm for Reading Matthew," *HTS* 61, nos. 1–2 (2005): 1–18; Alkier, "Zeichen der Erinnerung—Die Genealogie in MT 1 als intertextuelle Disposition," in *Bekenntnis und Erinnerung*, RTS 16, ed. Klaus-Michael Bull and Eckart Reinmuth (Münster: Lit, 2004), 108–28. Cf. also Hays, Alkier, and Huizenga, *Reading the Bible Intertextually*. Cf. also Hartmut Stegemann, "Die des Uria," in *Tradition und Glaube. Das frühe Christentum in seiner Umwelt*, ed. Gert Jeremias (Göttingen: Vandenhoeck & Ruprecht, 1971), 246–76.

35   Cf. Alkier, "Zeichen der Erinnerung," 112–17.

36   Cf. on this point Warren Carter, *Matthew and Empire. Initial Explorations* (Harrisburg, Pa.: Trinity Press, 2001).

37   Cf. on this point Alkier, "Himmel und Hölle. Zur Kontextualität und Referenz gleichnishafter Rede unter besonderer Berücksichtigung des Gleichnisses vom Fischnetz (Mk 13,47-50)," in *Unter der Mitarb. v. Gabi Kern, Hermeneutik der Gleichnisse Jesu. Methodische Neuansätze zum Verstehen urchristlicher Parabeltexte*, WUNT 231, ed. Ruben Zimmermann (Tübingen: Mohr, 2008), 588–603.

38   Cf. on this point the detailed interpretation of Mark 12:18-27 in the present chapter, which also holds for the parallels in the gospel of Matthew.

39   Eckart Reinmuth, "Ostern—Ereignis und Erzählung. Die jüngste Diskussion und das Matthäusevangelium," *ZNT* 19 (2007): 5–6, points to the intratextual connection between the temptation narrative in Matt 4 and the crucifixion scene in 27:40 and interprets further, "Jesus never adduces 'proof' in the Gospel of Matthew for his possibilities. He does not leap; he summons no legions when he is

arrested (26:53)—although Matthew is convinced that he could do it—, he does not descend from the cross" (6).

40   Cf. on this point William D. Davies and Dale C. Allison, *A Critical and Exegetical Commentary on the Gospel According to Saint Matthew* (3 vols., ICC; Edinburgh: Continuum, 1988), 3:681–82. Cf. also Ulrich Luz, *Das Evangelium nach Matthäus* (4 vols., EKK I/4; Zürich: Neukirchen Vluyn, 2002), 4:438–39.

41   Reinmuth, "Ostern," 9. "Easter can be contested; Easter can be believed. That is the theologically reflective Matthean alternative" (8).

42   What Ernst Haenchen formulated in *Die Apostelgeschichte* (KEK 3, 12th rev. ed.; Göttingen: Vandenhoeck & Ruprecht, 1959), 465, with a view to Paul's Areopagus speech (Acts 17:16-34), can also be referred to the entirety of Luke–Acts: "If one deals with Luke as one would with a modern realist, then one ensnares oneself in contradictions."

43   Cf. Eckhard Plümacher, "Stichwort: Lukas, Historiker," *ZNT* 18 (2006): 2–8; Plümacher, *Lukas als hellenistischer Schriftsteller. Studien zur Apostelgeschichte* (SNT 9; Göttingen: Vandenhoeck & Ruprecht, 1972); Alexander Mittelstaedt, *Lukas als Historiker. Zur Datierung des lukanischen Doppelwerkes* (TANZ 43; Tübingen: Francke, 2006).

44   Cf. Werner Kahl, "Erhebliche matthäisch-lukanische Übereinstimmungen gegen das Markusevangelium der Triple-Tradition. Ein Beitrag zur Klärung der synoptischen Abhängigkeitsverhältnisse," *ZNW* 103 (2012): 20–46.

45   Cf. Schnelle, *Einleitung in das Neue Testament*, 270.

46   Cf. François Bovon, *Das Evangelium nach Lukas (9:51–14:35)* (3 vols., EKK III/2; Zürich: Benziger, 1996), 2:254: "Luke's God, who is stronger than death, is also more dangerous than death."

47   So also Bovon, *Das Evangelium nach Lukas (9:51–14:35)*, 2:495.

48   Cf. on this point Eduard Schweizer, *Das Evangelium nach Lukas* (NTD 3, 18th ed., 1st rev. ed.; Göttingen: Vandenhoeck & Ruprecht, 1982), 250; Jakob Kremer, *Lukasevangelium*, (Neue Echter Bibel 3; Würzburg: Echter, 1988), 243–44.

49   Cf. on this point Becker, *Die Auferstehung Jesu Christi nach dem Neuen Testament*, 47.

50   Jacob Jervell, *Die Apostelgeschichte* (KEK 3, 17th ed., 1st rev. ed.; Göttingen: Vandenhoeck & Ruprecht, 1998), 115: "The Spirit expresses itself as δύναμις, as miraculous power in wonder and word, wherefore for Luke proclamation is always accompanied by miracles. . . . The Spirit equips one for service as a witness, that is, for proclamation and working miracles. The eyewitness report of the Christ-event is to be understood in this way: Acts 1:22; 2:32-33; 3:15; 5:32; 10:39, 41; 13:31; 22:15; 26:16. Above all, the issue concerns Jesus' resurrection."

51   Cf. Wilfried Eckey, *Die Apostelgeschichte. Der Weg des Evangeliums von Jerusalem nach Rom*, 2 vols. (Neukirchen-Vluyn: Neukirchener, 2000), 2:622: "The Lukan designation of the Holy Spirit as the power of God at work largely follows the characterization of the Spirit as the motive and effective power of the God of Israel in the OT, especially in its Greek version (Septuagint, LXX)."

52   Cf. Eckey, *Die Apostelgeschichte*, 2:617–22.

53   Cf. on this point Ute E. Eisen, *Die Poetik der Apostelgeschichte. Eine narratologische Studie* (NTOA/SUNT 58; Göttingen: Vandenhoeck & Ruprecht, 2006), 169–87.

54   On this point, Haenchen's comment (*Die Apostelgeschichte*, 466) is fitting: "Paul speaks in principle to the whole of Athens, and Athens in turn represents the

entirety of Greek culture and piety. What we see here is an 'ideal scene' that flouts every attempt to understand it realistically."

55 Cf. Rudolf Pesch, *Die Apostelgeschichte*, 2 vols. (EKK V/2; Neukirchen-Vluyn: Neukirchener, 1986), 2:281.

56 Cf. Stanley Porter, *The Paul of Acts. Essays in Literary Criticism, Rhetoric and Theology* (WUNT 115; Tübingen: Mohr, 1999), 161. Cf. also Pesch, *Die Apostelgeschichte*, 2:274–75.

Chapter 4

1 On the complex conceptions of time in the gospel of John, cf. Jörg Frey, *Die johanneische Eschatologie II. Das johanneische Zeitverständnis* (WUNT 110; Tübingen: Mohr, 1998).

2 On this point, cf. Jean Zumstein, "Das Johannesevangelium: Eine Strategie des Glaubens," in *Kreative Erinnerung. Relecture und Auslegung im Johannesevangelium*, ed. Jean Zumstein (Zürich: Pano, 1999), 33–34.

3 In his epochal commentary on John, *Das Johannesevangelium* (HNT 6; Tübingen: Mohr, 2005), Hartwig Thyen has demonstrated the intertextual references of the gospel of John to the Synoptic Gospels with a masterful combination of precise textual work, textual theory informed in interdisciplinary ways, and congenial theological thinking.

4 Thyen, *Das Johannesevangelium*, 706. Thyen continues with the rationale: "Among other things, this is demonstrated by the Baptist's words about Jesus as the Lamb of God who takes away the sins of the world (1:29), the story of the cleansing of the temple with Jesus' words about the destruction of the temple of his body by the Jews already in the second chapter, John's playing on the synoptic versions of the words of institution of the Lord's Supper in John 6:51ff., the repeated attempts of the Jews from 5:18 on to kill Jesus or at least to arrest him, Jesus' speech about the Good Shepherd who gives his life for the sheep (10:11ff.), the scenes in 10:31ff. and 11:47ff., which play intertextually with the synoptic versions of the trial of Jesus before the Sanhedrin, the plan to kill not only Jesus but also Lazarus, who through his raising has become Jesus' witness (12:10), the words about the grain of wheat that must die so that it might bring much fruit (12:24), and finally the entire farewell address of Jesus centered on the last meal of Jesus with his disciples."

5 Cf. Schürmann, "'Pro-Existenz' als christologischer Grundbegriff."

6 Thyen, *Das Johannesevangelium*, 499.

7 Cf. on this point Michael Welker, *Was geht vor beim Abendmahl?* (3rd ed.; Gütersloh: Gütersloher Verlagshaus, 2005). This book is recommended to all who concern themselves with the theology of the Lord's Supper.

8 The sacrificial-theological conception does not here arise because, in its logic, the offered victim functions as a third figure who communicates between the giver of an offering and the receiver of an offering. The fundamental expression of the gospel of John, that the Father and the Son are one (cf. 10:30), leads this logic *ad absurdum*, for God would in this case be the giver of the offering, the receiver of the offering, and also the victim offered.

9 Ruben Zimmermann, *Christologie der Bilder im Johannesevangelium. Die Christopoetik des vierten Evangeliums unter besonderer Berücksichtigung von Joh 10* (WUNT 171; Tübingen: Mohr, 2004), 112.

10   Christine Schlund, "Deutungen des Todes Jesu im Rahmen der Pesach-Tradition," in *Deutungen des Todes Jesu im Neuen Testament*, WUNT 181, edited by Jörg Frey and Jens Schröter (Göttingen: Mohr, 2005), brings attention to the fact that the protection of the community stands in the foreground of the Passover tradition, and that this protecting is not bound up with conceptions of propitiation.

11   (My translation of Thyen's translation, *Das Johannesevangelium*, 122. Cf. also Thyen's interpretation of 1:29, 118–23.)

12   Cf. Bernd Janowski, "Das Leben für anderen hingeben. Alttestamentliche Voraussetzungen für die Deutung des Todes Jesu," in Frey and Schröter, *Deutungen des Todes Jesu im Neuen Testament*, 99–104.

13   On John 10, cf. Zimmermann, *Christologie der Bilder im Johannesevangelium*, 241–404.

14   Cf. Janowski, "Das Leben für anderen hingeben," 103.

15   Janowski, "Das Leben für anderen hingeben," 98, emphasis in original.

16   On this point, cf. Ruben Zimmermann, "Das Leben aus dem Tod. Vom sterbenden Weizenkorn—Joh 12,24," in *Kompendium der Gleichnisse Jesu*, ed. Ruben Zimmermann (Gütersloh: Gütersloher Verlagshaus, 2007), 805.

17   Cf. on this point Thyen, *Das Johannesevangelium*.

18   Cf. on this point Ruben Zimmermann, "The Narrative Hermeneutics of John 11. Learning with Lazarus How to Understand Death, Life, and Resurrection," in *The Resurrection of Jesus in the Gospel of John*, WUNT 222, ed. Craig R. Koester and Reimund Bieringer (Tübingen: Mohr, 2008), 75–101.

19   On the story of Lazarus, cf. Thyen, *Das Johannesevangelium*.

20   Cf. on this point Thyen, *Das Johannesevangelium*.

21   Cf. Jean Zumstein, "Die johanneische Ostergeschichte als Erzählung gelesen," *ZNT* 3 (1999): 13: "Although she loves Jesus, she is not in any position to find the way to faith from her own power. She reacts to the empty tomb according to the measure of this world and explains it with a plausible argument: the robbery or relocation of the corpse."

22   Zumstein, "Die johanneische Ostergeschichte," 13.

23   Cf. Thyen, *Das Johannesevangelium*.

24   Cf. F. François Vouga, *Die Johannesbriefe* (HNT 15:3; Tübingen: Mohr, 1990), 11–20.

25   Depending on how one understands these threats evoked through prison and sword, the Revelation to John is dated to the time of Nero, Domitian, or Hadrian. Although Thomas Witulski has assembled some interesting indications that point to the reign of Hadrian, his poor and hypothetical argumentation is not able to convince. Otto Böcher, in *Die Johannesapokalypse* (EdF 41; 2nd rev. ed.; Darmstadt: Wissenschaftliche Buchgesellschaft, 1975), brings stronger arguments. With the majority of scholarship, he assumes a dating around the end of the reign of Domitian, thus about A.D. 95. A possible alternative dates the document to the reign of Trajan.

26   Jörg Frey, "Erwägungen zum Verhältnis der Johannesapokalypse zu den übrigen Schriften des Corpus Johanneum," in *Die johanneische Frage. Ein Lösungsversuch, mit einem Beitrag zur Apokalypse von Jörg Frey*, WUNT 67, ed. Martin Hengel (Tübingen: Mohr, 1993), writes, "First of all, it must be noted that the arguments from style, especially the impressive stylistic peculiarities of the Gospel and Letters, speak against the common authorship of the two works (and indeed all five

Johannine writings) with even greater clarity than the data on vocabulary. . . . That result nevertheless does not decide the question of the relationship of the Apocalypse to the other writings of the Corpus Johanneum is clear on the basis of the observed phraseological agreements, which are to be observed precisely in view of the distinct syntactic-stylistic contradictions. A not inconsiderable number of motivic and theological points of contact yield to them" (382).

27   Böcher, "Johannesapokalypse," *RAC* 19 (2001): 596. The interest of the Enlightenment in propositional, rational truths contributed mightily to the increasing sidelining of the Revelation to John in academic theology. Two other factors also played a decisive role. On one hand, it was precisely with the images of the Revelation to John that the Church spread fear and fright again and again and thus maintained its social power. On the other hand, many opposition movements likewise legitimated their own violent rebellions with Revelation. Up into the present time the Revelation to John becomes again and again a football for different political options in the struggle for social power, an ever-increasing tendency that has been observed in the United States for a good two decades. In spite of the outstanding works of Wilhelm Bousset, *Die Offenbarung Johannis* (KEK 16; repr. of the rev. ed. 1906; Göttingen: Vandenhoeck & Ruprecht, 1966); and Adolf von Harnack, *Geschichte der altchristlichen Literatur bis Eusebius II/1* (Leipzig, 1897), the Enlightenment tendency to marginalize the Revelation to John through the Bultmannian school's demythologizing endeavors strengthened after the Second World War. The cosmological visions of the Revelation to John did not well fit with the individualizing existential theology of the Bultmannian school, which probably is also to be regarded as a reaction to the horrors of Nazi ideology, pervaded as it was with numerous mythologems. That may also have contributed to the separation of the Revelation to John from the other Johannine writings on the part of the majority of exegetes. Indeed, Rudolf Bultmann and many of his students regarded the gospel of John, along with the First Letter of John, as a singular theological approach among the writings of the New Testament, which next to the letters of the Apostle Paul correctly drove theology. On this point see Rudolf Bultmann, *Theologie des Neuen Testaments* (9th ed.; rev. and enl. by O. Merk; Tübingen: Mohr, 1984).

28   On this point, see Martin Karrer, *Die Johannesoffenbarung als Brief. Studien zu ihrem literarischen, historischen und theologischen Ort* (FRLANT 140; Göttingen: Vandenhoeck & Ruprecht, 1986).

29   Marco Frenschkowski, "Die Johannesoffenbarung zwischen Vision, astralmythologischer Imagination und Literatur," in *Studien zur Johannesoffenbarung und ihrer Auslegung*, ed. Friedrich Wilhelm Horn (Neukirchen-Vluyn: Neukirchener Verlag, 2005), rightly points to the fact that the recognizable literary composition represents no argument against the experiential quality of the visions in the form they themselves take.

30   It is hardly an accident that John the Baptist is also introduced with the same semantics in the prologue of the gospel of John (1:7), and likewise pays for his witness with his death.

31   See Traugott Holtz, "Sprache als Metapher. Erwägungen zur Sprache der Johannesapokalypse," in Horn, *Studien zur Johannesoffenbarung und ihrer Auslegung*, 17.

32   See Böcher, "Johannesapokalypse," 611–12.

33   Ferdinand Hahn, "Das Geistverständnis in der Johannesoffenbarung," in Horn, *Studien zur Johannesoffenbarung und ihrer Auslegung*, 9.

34   Wolfgang Weiß, "Aufbruch und Bewährung. Hebräerbrief und Apokalypse im
      Vergleich," in Horn, *Studien zur Johannesoffenbarung und ihrer Auslegung*, 257.
      "According to Rev 1:5, Christ is regarded as 'the firstborn of the dead.' This predi-
      cation certainly stands rather close to the Pauline tradition (cf. Rom 8:29; Col
      1:18)."

35   Daria Pezzoli-Olgiati, *Täuschung und Klarheit. Zur Wechselwirkung zwischen Vision
      und Geschichte in der Johannesoffenbarung* (FRLANT 175; Göttingen: Vanden-
      hoeck & Ruprecht, 1997), 22.

36   When I wrote the German version of this book, I used the translation "Lamm," in
      English "lamb." But since I prepared my paper for the conference about Revelation
      that Richard B. Hays and I organized at Duke Divinity School, Durham, N.C.,
      in 2010, I am convinced that "Widderlein" or in English "ram" is the better trans-
      lation here. I quote note 15 of my paper, "Witness or Warrior. How the Book of
      Revelation Helps Christians Live Their Political Lives," in *Revelation and the Poli-
      tics of Apocalyptic Interpretation*, ed. R. B. Hays and S. Alkier (Waco, Tex.: Baylor
      University Press, 2012), 125–41: "My decision to translate the Greek term *arnion*
      with *ram* and not with *lamb* depends on the code instruction of the text in 13:11 (cf.
      5:6). A ram has horns, a lamb has no horns. The textual code instruction has more
      authority than any hypothetical history of terms or traditions, interesting as they
      might be (see, e.g., Loren L. Johns, *The Lamb Christology of the Apocalypse of John.
      An Investigation into its Origins and Rhethorical Force* (WUNT II 167; Tübingen:
      Mohr Siebeck, 2003), 22–39). The reality of the signals in the text should be the
      first criterion of any translation, exegesis, and interpretation." (This note is found
      on p. 197.)

37   See Otto Böcher, "Chiliasmus I," *TRE* 7 (1981): 723–29.

Chapter 5

1   Cf. Broer, *Einleitung in das Neue Testament*, 593.

2   Cf. Schnelle, *Einleitung in das Neue Testament*.

3   Moreover, for the most ancient New Testament writings—and, as we can read in
      an exemplary fashion in 1 Cor 15:3b-7, probably the oldest received tradition in
      early Christianity—the resurrection of the Crucified One played such a central
      role already in the very beginnings of Christianity that its rejection could probably
      hardly have come about through ignorance, as opposed to a thematic misconstrual
      of resurrection theology.

4   This is the plausible genre of the letter as determined by Christoph Burchard,
      Der Jakobusbrief (HNT 15/1; Tübingen: Mohr, 2000), 9. Richard Bauckham also
      explores this extensively in his commentary on James.

5   Cf. Hermann von Lips, *Weisheitliche Traditionen im Neuen Testament* (WMANT
      64; Neukirchen-Vluyn: Neukirchener Verlag, 1990), 434.

6   Matthias Konradt, "Der Jakobusbrief," in *Einleitung in das Neue Testament*,
      KStBTH 6, edited by Martin Ebner and Stefan Schreiber (Stuttgart: Kohlham-
      mer, 2008), 503.

7   Cf. *WA* DB 6:10; *WA* DB 7:384.

8   On the Paulinism of 1 Peter cf. Norbert Brox, *Der erste Petrusbrief* (EKK XXI; 4th
      rev. and enl. ed.; Neukirchen-Vluyn: Neukirchener, 1993), 47–51.

9   Cf. 1 Pet 1:6-7 and James 1:2-3; 1 Pet 1:22–2:2 and James 1:18, 21; 1 Pet 5:5-9 and
      James 4:6-10.

10 For more detailed reasoning, cf. Brox, *Der erste Petrusbrief*, 43–47.

11 Reinhard Feldmeier, *Die Christen als Fremde. Die Metapher der Fremde in der antiken Welt, im Urchristentum und im 1. Petrusbrief* (WUNT 64; Tübingen: Mohr, 1992), 169.

12 Brox, *Der erste Petrusbrief*, 84.

13 On the problems with these most difficult verses, cf. Brox, *Der erste Petrusbrief.*

14 Brox, *Der erste Petrusbrief*, 51.

15 Brox, *Der erste Petrusbrief*, 89.

16 Henning Paulsen, *Der zweite Petrusbrief und der Judasbrief* (KEK XII/2; Göttingen: Vandenhoeck & Ruprecht, 1992), 99.

17 Paulsen, *Der zweite Petrusbrief und der Judasbrief*, 48.

18 Paulsen, *Der zweite Petrusbrief und der Judasbrief*, 100.

19 For moderate yet appropriate criticism of Jude and 2 Peter, cf. Paulsen, *Der zweite Petrusbrief und der Judasbrief*, 101ff. Paulsen also deals with Käsemann's substantive accusations in a clarifying way.

Chapter 6

1 The conviction that God, the creator of everything, can raise the dead, is already found at least in a rudimentary fashion in certain passages in Israel's scriptures, and was certainly shared by the Pharisees and most Jews at the time of Jesus and at the time of the composition of the New Testament writings, but not by all Jews especially the Sadducees; cf. Paul Hoffmann, *Die Toten in Christus. Eine religionsgeschichtliche und exegetische Untersuchung zur paulinischen Eschatologie* (NTA N.F. 2; Münster: Aschendorff, 1978); Günter Stemberger, *Der Leib der Auferstehung. Studien zur Anthropologie und Eschatologie des palästinensischen Juedentums im neutestamentlichen Zeitalter (ca.170 v.Chr.–100n.Chr.)* (Rome: Pontificio Istituto Biblico, 1972); Hans C. Cavallin, "Leben nach dem Tode im Spätjudentum und frühen Christentum," *ANRW II* 19, no. 1 (1979): 240–345.

2 Cf. on this point Stefan Alkier, Hermann Deuser, and Gesche Linde, eds., *Religiöser Fundamentalismus: Analysen und Kritiken* (Tübingen: Francke, 2005); Martin E. Marty and R. Scott Appleby, eds., *The Fundamentalism Project* (5 vols.; Chicago: University of Chicago Press, 1991–1995).

3 Cf. on this point Wilfried Härle, "Die Wirklichkeit—Unser Konstrukt oder widerständige Realität," in *Theologie zwischen Pragmatismus und Existenzdenken*, ed. G. Linde et al. (MTHS 90; Marburg: Elwert, 2006), 163–73. In any event, the exegetical work of Peter Lampe, who expresses a reality concept of radical constructivism, has forced the question of reality and conceptions of reality employed in German-speaking exegesis to be given a hearing. Cf. Peter Lampe, "Die urchristliche Rede von der 'Neuschöpfung des Menschen' im Lichte konstruktivistischer Wissenssoziologie," in *Exegese und Methodendiskussion*, ed. Stefan Alkier und Ralph Brucker (TANZ 23; Tübingen: Francke, 1998), 21–32.

Chapter 7

1 Charles Sanders Peirce, *Semiotische Schriften 2 (1903–1906)*, trans. Leroy Huizenga (Frankfurt: Suhrkamp, 1990), 193. Cf. also Peirce, *Semiotische Schriften 3 (1906–1913)* (Frankfurt: Suhrkamp, 1993), 317–18. Robert C. Neville has developed this corrective function of reality further in detail in his work *Recovery of the Measure.*

Interpretation and Nature (Axiology of Thinking 2; Albany: State University of New York Press, 1989).

2   Härle, "Die Wirklichkeit," 169–70, emphasis in original.

3   Cf. also Charles Sanders Peirce, "On a New List of Categories," in *The Essential Peirce: Selected Philosophical Writings Volume 1 (1867–1893)*, ed. N. Houser and C. Kloesel (Bloomington: Indiana University Press, 1992), 1–10. Cf. also Max H. Fisch, "Peirce's General Theory of Signs," in *Peirce, Semeiotic and Pragmatism*, ed. Max H. Fisch, Kenneth Laine Ketner, and Christian J. W. Kloesel (Bloomington: Indiana University Press, 1986), 322–26. On the history of the doctrine of categorical semiotics from Aristotle through Kant to Peirce, see the outstanding treatment by Klaus Oehler, "Zur Geschichte der Kategorienlehre," in Aristotle, *Kategorien*, ed. K. Flashar, trans. K. Oehler (Aristoteles Werke in deutscher Übersetzung 1/I; Berlin: Akademie Verlag, 1984), 7–56. For an introduction of Peirce's semiotics, see James Jakób Liszka, *A General Introduction to the Semeiotic of Charles Sanders Peirce* (Bloomington: Indiana University Press, 1996).

4   Peirce, *Semiotische Schriften 2*, 269.

5   Peirce, *Semiotische Schriften 3*, 372.

6   Charles Sanders Peirce, "Logic Notebook," sequence 227, accessed November 9, 2012, http://nrs.harvard.edu/urn-3:FHCL.Hough:3686182?n=227.

7   Hermann Deuser, "Einleitung: American Philosophy," in *Gottesinstinkt: Semiotische Religionstheorie und Pragmatismus* (Religion in Philosophy and Theology 12; Tübingen: Francke, 2004), 16. Cf. also Deuser, "Kategoriale Semiotik und Pragmatismus," in Deuser, *Gottesinstinkt*, 32: "The inherent nature of logical final forms and categorical sign structures in the development in the community of the human race is all that human experience can rest on. What is represented under these conditions, what is represented in sign events, that is reality."

8   Deuser, "Die phänomenologischen Grundlagen der Trinität," in Deuser, *Gottesinstinkt*, 41.

9   Charles Sanders Peirce, *Phänomen und Logik der Zeichen* (ed. and trans. H. Pape; Frankfurt: Suhrkamp, 1983) [translated by Leroy Huizenga], 64.

10   We must here distinguish among three types of semiotics: (1) Structuralist semiotics: In the tradition of Ferdinand de Saussure's linguistics with its binary sign model and its reception of A. J. Greimas' structural semantics, structuralist semiotics asks primarily intratextual questions about observable syntagmatic and semantic textual structures. (2) Poststructuralist semiotics: In the reception of the criticism of structuralist sign conceptions put forth by Julia Kristeva, Jacques Derrida, and others, the structuralist understanding of a text as closed structures is opened up in ideological-critical directions above all by Kristeva's theory of intertextuality. (3) Categorical semiotics: While structuralist and poststructuralist semiotics remain indebted to Saussure's binary sign model, categorical semiotics works with the triadic sign model of Charles Sanders Peirce, which he worked out on the basis of his doctrine of categories, combined with the idesa of Umberto Eco and Charles Morris. Cf. on this point the following literature: For (1): Erhard Güttgemanns, "Einleitende Bemerkungen zur strukturalen Erzählforschung," *LingBib* 23/24 (1973): 2–47; Louis Marin, *Semiotik der Passionsgeschichte. Die Zeichensprache der Ortsangaben und Personennamen* (BeTh 70; München: Kaiser, 1976); Jean Delorme, ed., *Zeichen und Gleichnisse. Evangelientext und semiotische Forschung*

(Düsseldorf: Patmos, 1979). For (2): Erhardt Güttgemanns, *Fragmenta semiotico-hermeneutica. Eine Texthermeneutik für den Umgang mit der Heiligen Schrift* (FThL 9; Bonn: Linguistica Biblica, 1983); George Aichele, *Sign, Text, Scripture. Semiotics and the Bible* (Interventions 1; Sheffield: Academic Press, 1997). For (3): Martin Pöttner, *Realität als Kommunikation. Ansätze zur Beschreibung der Grammatik des paulinischen Sprechens in 1Kor 1,4–4,21 im Blick auf literarische Problematik und Situationsbezug des 1. Korintherbriefes* (Theologie 2; Münster: Lit, 1995); Alkier, *Wunder und Wirklichkeit*, 343–60.

11 Cf. Deuser, "Kategoriale Semiotik und Pragmatismus," 20–37. "Signs are therefore not simply the material vehicle that stands for something else. Rather, on the basis of sign communications categorical semiotics describes the comprehensive, logically consistent process of acts of representation ordered in accord with the sign structure. In these alone is the so-called outside world humanly approachable. That our conclusions with respect to the evolution of all reality itself remain hypothetical shows only that human thinking does not generate the world of objects . . . , but probably plays a part in their development" (32).

12 On both concepts and their derivation, cf. Alkier, *Wunder und Wirklichkeit*, 72–79.

13 There is yet another whole series of terms with reference to the concept of the Interpretant of which Liszka has provided an overview in his *General Introduction*, 122–23. Peirce research is therefore busy with clarifying the important questions concerning which of these terms are simply variants of the designation and which actually introduce different conceptions of the Interpretant. For the approach of the present investigation, the differentiation presented in the text suffices. Cf. on this point the further differentiation of Gesche Linde, *Zeichen und Gewissheit. Semiotische Entfaltung eines protestantisch-theologischen Begriffs* (Religion in Philosophy and Theology; Tübingen: Mohr, forthcoming).

14 Charles Sanders Peirce, "Logic Notebook," sequence 538, accessed November 9, 2012, http://nrs.harvard.edu/urn-3:FHCL.Hough:3686182?n=538: "The immediate Interpretant is that which is necessarily generated when the Sign as such should be. It is a vague, potential determination of consciousness, a vague abstraction."

15 Charles Sanders Peirce, "Logic Notebook," sequence 522, accessed November 9, 2012, http://nrs.harvard.edu/urn-3:FHCL.Hough:3686182?n=522.

16 Charles Sanders Peirce, "Logic Notebook," sequence 542, accessed November 9, 2012, http://nrs.harvard.edu/urn-3:FHCL.Hough:3686182?n=542.

17 Cf. Stefan Alkier, "Ethik der Interpretation," in *Der eine Gott und die Welt der Religionen. Beiträge zu einer Theologie der Religionen und zum interreligiösen Dialog*, ed. M. Witte (Würzburg: Religion und Kultur, 2003), 21–41.

18 Helmut Pape, introduction to Peirce, *Phänomen und Logik der Zeichen*, 25.

19 Deuser, "Die phänomenologischen Grundlagen der Trinität," 50.

20 Cited according to Umberto Eco, *Semiotik. Entwurf einer Theorie der Zeichen* (Supplemente 5; München: Fink, 1987), 186. On the semiotic logic of abduction, induction, and deduction, cf. Liszka, *General Introduction*, 53–77.

21 Eco, *Semiotik*, 186–87n24.

Chapter 8

1 Charles Sanders Peirce, "Questions Concerning Certain Faculties Claimed for Man," *Journal of Speculative Philosophy* 2 (1868): 103–14.

2   Gudrun Guttenberger points to this in her instructive essay, "῎Ωφθη. Der visuelle Gehalt der frühchristlichen Erscheinungstradition und mögliche Folgerungen für die Entstehung und Entwicklung des frühchristlichen Glaubens an die Auferstehung Jesu (Teil 1)." *BZ NF* 52, no. 1 (2008): 40–63.

3   This thought is of further relevance below with reference to the theology of creation.

4   Contra Gerd Theissen, *Die Religion der ersten Christen. Eine Theorie des Urchristentums* (Gütersloh: Kaiser, 2001), 72.

5   Cf. on this point the study of Guttenberger, "῎Ωφθη," which advances historical knowledge due to its methodological limiting to the historical.

6   On the reconstruction and criticism of both hypotheses along the lines of intellectual history and the theory of knowledge, see the clarifying study by Georg Essen, *Historische Vernunft und Auferweckung Jesu. Theologie und Historik im Streit um den Begriff geschichtlicher Wirklichkeit* (TSTP 9; Mainz: Matthias-Grünewald, 1995), 295–314.

7   Guttenberger, "῎Ωφθη," 47. In my opinion it stands to reason that Luke knew both 1 Corinthians and Galatians and shaped the depictions of the visions therein in a narrative manner.

8   Guttenberger, "Ωφθη," 51.

9   Cf. Dalferth, *Der auferweckte Gekreuzigte*, 66–67: "It is not the resurrection of Jesus but rather the Easter experience of the disciples that is the decisive historical fact upon which the resurrection message is based. This experience testifies that the crucified one appeared to them. With the resurrection of Jesus they name that which is for them the ground of this experience of his appearance, and that with which they ground their witness for themselves and others. For this witness is shaped through the fundamental tension between two facts, which for the witnesses of the appearances were uncontroversial, since they were certain they experienced both: That Jesus died on the cross and that he appeared powerfully as the living Lord. Together these experiences constitute a fundamental cognitive dissonance and in view of Jesus's role in both of them, taken in and of themselves, necessitate the irreconcilable expressions 'He is dead' and 'He is alive.' . . . Precisely because this death was not in any way in question for them, the experience of the appearance of the living crucified one shattered the unity of their expectations of coherent experiences and thus their identity as subjects of experience in this world, and thus the experience of the appearance of the living crucified one set a fundamental problem of consistency before them."

10   Hans von Campenhausen, *Der Ablauf der Osterereignisse und das leere Grab* (SHAW. PH 4/1952; Heidelberg: Winter, 1977), 50. Cf. Jens Adam, "Das leere Grab als Unterpfand der Auferstehung Jesu Christi," in *Die Wirklichkeit der Auferstehung*, ed. Hans-Joachim Eckstein and Michael Welcker (Neukirchen-Vluyn: Neukirchener, 2004), 59–75.

11   Dale C. Allison, "An Opened Tomb and a Missing Body," in D. C. Allison, *Resurrecting Jesus: The Earliest Christian Tradition and its Interpreters* (London: T&T Clark, 2005), 299–337.

12   Cf. Allison, "An Opened Tomb and a Missing Body," 332.

13   Allison, "An Opened Tomb and a Missing Body," 334.

14   Cf. John Dominic Crossan, *Der Historische Jesus*, trans. P. Hahlbrock (München: Beck, 1995), 516ff.

15 Cf. on this point also Andreas Lindemann, *Auferstehung—unsere Hoffnung* (Kleine Schriften aus dem Reformierten Bund 8; Wuppertal: Foedus, 1997), 18ff.

16 Dalferth, *Der auferweckte Gekreuzigte*, 44.

17 Lindemann, *Auferstehung*, 23.

18 Lindemann, *Auferstehung*, 19.

19 This thesis means no less than this: Jews and Christians indeed have many texts in common, but they belong to different grand narratives and therefore also respectively signify something other, even if the texts' wording is not different. Within the framework of the grand story that the sacred Scriptures of Israel relate, the book of Isaiah signifies something other than what it does within the framework of the grand story that Christian Bibles narrate.

20 Guttenberger, "ὥφθε," 42.

21 Essen, *Historische Vernunft und Auferweckung Jesu*, 23.

Chapter 9

1 On contemporary historical Jesus research, cf. *ZNT* 1 on the subject *Jesus Christus* and *ZNT* 20 on the subject *Der erinnerte Jesus*.

2 On this point cf. Roman Heiligenthal, *Der verfälschte Jesus. Eine Kritik moderner Jesusbilder* (Darmstadt: Wissenschaftliche Buchgesellschaft, 1997).

3 Raymond A. Moody, *Life After Life: The Investigation of Phenomenon—Survival of Bodily Death* (San Francisco: Harper, 2001).

4 Cf. Elisabeth Kübler-Ross, *On Children and Death: How Children and Their Parents Can and Do Cope with Death* (New York: Touchstone, 1997).

5 Werner Thiede, "Sterben, Tod und Auferstehung als Themen für Kinder und Jugendliche," *PTh* 83 (1994): 225.

6 Dale C. Allison, *Resurrecting Jesus: The Earliest Christian Tradition and Its Interpreters* (New York: Clark, 2005), 239–69.

7 Allison, *Resurrecting Jesus*, 268.

8 Allison, *Resurrecting Jesus*, 269.

9 Allison, *Resurrecting Jesus*, 269–99.

10 Cf. Allison, *Resurrecting Jesus*, 275ff.

11 Allison, *Resurrecting Jesus*, 271.

12 Cf. Allison, *Resurrecting Jesus*, 288ff.

13 Allison, *Resurrecting Jesus*, 342–43.

14 Cf. Allison, *Resurrecting Jesus*, 342, 347–48.

15 Deuser, *Gottesinstinkt*, 168.

16 Charles Sanders Peirce, "Private Thoughts, Principally on the Conduct of Life" (Number 37, August 1860), in *Writings of Charles S. Peirce: A Chronological Edition, Volume 1, 1857–1866*, ed. Peirce Edition Project (Bloomington: Indiana University Press, 1983), 9.

17 Christian Link, *Schöpfung. Schöpfungstheologie in reformatorischer Tradition* (HST 7/1; Gütersloh: Gütersloher Verlagshaus Mohn, 1991); Link, *Schöpfung. Schöpfungstheologie angesichts der Herausforderungen des 20. Jahrhunderts* (HST 7/2; Gütersloh: Gütersloher Verlagshaus Mohn, 1991).

18 Hermann Deuser, "Religion und Evolution," in *Gegenwart des lebendigen Christus*, ed. Günter Thomas and Andreas Schüle (Leipzig: Evangelische Verlagsanstalt, 2007), 271–94, 282.

19 Deuser, "Religion und Evolution," 272.

20   Deuser, "Religion und Evolution," 288.
21   Deuser, "Religion und Evolution," 289.
22   Deuser, "Religion und Evolution," 295.

Chapter 10

1   Oscar Cullmann has presented this with all desirable clarity in *Unsterblichkeit der Seele oder Auferstehung der Toten? Antwort des Neuen Testaments* (Stuttgart: Kreuz, 1969).
2   *Bestattung. Agende für die Union Evangelischer Kirchen in der EKD 5*, ed. Kirchen-kanzlei der EKU (Bielefeld: Luther Verlag, 2004), 19.
3   Yorick Spiegel, *Der Prozeß des Trauerns. Analyse und Beratung* (München: Kaiser, 1989).

Chapter 11

1   Thiede, "Sterben, Tod und Auferstehung," 215.
2   Heidi Löbsack, *Das Todesbewusstsein des Kindes: Eine heilpädagogische Studie* (Stu-dientexte Heil- und Sonderpädagogik 5; Gießen: Institut für Heil- und Sonderpä-dagogik, 1982), cited by Thiede, "Sterben, Tod und Auferstehung."
3   Hubertus Halbfas, "Nach vorne gedacht. Wie soll der Religionsunterricht in einer nichtchristlichen Gesellschaft aussehen," *RHS* 35 (1992): 372–77, cited from *Arbeitsbuch Religionsunterricht: Überblicke—Impulse—Beispiele*, ed. H. Lenhard (Gütersloh: Gütersloher Verlagshaus Mohn, 1996), 23–26, 25.
4   Leonie Getta et al., eds., *Mitten ins Leben. Religion Band 1 (5./6. Schuljahr)* (Berlin: Cornelsen, 2007), 78–79. I cite the text of the chapter on "Jesus' Death and Resur-rection" in full: "1. Take time with each picture and observe it in peace and quiet. Complete the sentences: I see . . . I feel . . . I wonder . . . 2. The disciples are sad, terrified, and full of fear on Good Friday! They could jump for joy and happiness on Easter. Alfred Manessier has attempted to paint this. Gather words that describe the moods of both pictures. Find titles for the pictures. You can also compose instrumental music as well. 3. For each image, make a page for your portfolio. Use colours similar to those Manessier uses. Write or paste what belongs to it—from the perspective of Jesus' friends—from the perspective of people living today."
5   Dalferth, *Der auferweckte Gekreuzigte*, 44.

Chapter 12

1   Cf. Dirk Frickenschmidt, "Empfänger unbekannt verzogen? Ergebnisse empiri-scher Glaubensforschung als Herausforderung für die neutestamentliche Herme-neutik," *ZNT* 4 (1999): 52–64; Ingrid Schoberth, "Nicht bloß ein 'lieber Gott.' Die Verharmlosung der Gottesrede als Problem der Praktischen Theologie," *ZNT* 9 (2002): 60–66.
2   Cf. my narrative sketch of this great story in part II of this investigation.
3   Jean-François Lyotard, *The Postmodern Condition: A Report on Knowledge* (Min-neapolis: University of Minnesota Press, 1984), 27.
4   Lyotard, *Postmodern Condition*, 31.
5   Lyotard, *Postmodern Condition*, 31.
6   Lyotard, *Postmodern Condition*, 32.
7   Lyotard, *Postmodern Condition*, 33–34.

8   Lyotard, *Postmodern Condition*, 37.
9   Cf. Lyotard, *Postmodern Condition*, 121–22.
10   This has reawakened interest in Paul and his resurrection discourse among some philosophers. But they miss Paul's argumentation, since they are not prepared to confront the ontological question of the reality of the resurrection. They remain wholly trapped by the "wisdom of this world." On this point cf. Alain Gignac, "Neue Wege der Auslegung. Die Paulus-Interpretation von Alain Badiou und Giorgio Agamben," *ZNT* 18 (2006): 15–25.
11   Gignac, "Neue Wege der Auslegung," 123.
12   Gignac, "Neue Wege der Auslegung," 113.
13   Cf. Reinmuth, "Narratio und argumentatio"; Reinmuth, *Paulus*.
14   Dalferth, *Der auferweckte Gekreuzigte*, 44.
15   In the framework of categorical semiotics, by miracles I understand not the breaking of natural laws but rather God's deeds that surpass human possibilities. Miracles—and in this sense also the miracle of the resurrection of Jesus—are creations (better, new creations) of God that cannot at all be located within the natural sciences' framework of cause and effect, but rather point to God's all-encompassing reality. Cf. on this point Alkier, *Wunder und Wirklichkeit*; Deuser, *Gottesinstinkt*; *ZNT* 19 (2007) on the subject "Auferstehung."
16   Cf. CA 7.
17   A similarly theologically complex but comprehensible presentation of the Lord's Supper is offered by Welker, *Was geht vor beim Abendmahl*. This study belongs to the fundamental literature of Protestant theology.
18   Hofius, "Der Gott allen Trostes," 327. Indeed, Hofius brings the later dogma of the Trinity and the even later dogma of the two natures into the New Testament texts in almost too seamless a manner when he writes, "On Golgotha—and it simply cannot be emphasized enough—dies in no way a mere man 'like you and I.' Rather, here dies the Son of God, who according to his origin and being belongs wholly at the side of his Father, but who in the freedom of his love became man for us, in order to make our lost human loves marked by sin and death his own."

Bibliography

Commentaries

Becker, Jürgen. *Die Briefe an die Galater, Epheser, Philipper, Kolosser, Thessalonicher und Philemon.* Übers. und erkl. von Jürgen Becker, Hans Conzelmann, and Gerhard Friedrich, NTD 8, 15., 15th rev. and enl. ed. Aufl. Göttingen: Vandenhoeck & Ruprecht, 1981.

Betz, Hans Dieter. *Der Galaterbrief. Ein Kommentar zum Brief des Apostels Paulus an die Gemeinden in Galatien.* München: Kaiser, 1988.

Bousset, Wilhelm. *Die Offenbarung Johannis.* KEK 16; repr. of the rev. ed. 1906. Göttingen: Vandenhoeck & Ruprecht, 1966.

Bovon, François. *Das Evangelium nach Lukas (1:1–9:50).* EKK III/1. Neukirchen-Vluyn: Neukirchener, 1989.

———. *Das Evangelium nach Lukas (9:51–14:35).* EKK III/2. Neukirchen-Vluyn: Neukirchener, 1996.

———. *Das Evangelium nach Lukas (15:1–19:27).* EKK III/3. Neukirchen-Vluyn: Neukirchener, 2001.

Brox, Norbert. *Der erste Petrusbrief.* EKK XXI; 4th rev. and enl. ed. Neukirchen-Vluyn: Neukirchener, 1993.

Bultmann, Rudolf. *Der zweite Brief an die Korinther, erkl. von Rudolf Bultmann, hrsg. von Erich Dinkler, Kritisch-exegetischer Kommentar über das Neue Testament Sonderband.* Göttingen: Vandenhoeck & Ruprecht, 1976.

Burchard, Christoph. *Der Jakobusbrief.* HNT 15/1. Tübingen: Mohr, 2000.

Cranfield, Charles E. B. *A Critical and Exegetical Commentary on the Epistle to the Romans. Introduction and Commentary on Romans I–VIII.* ICC. Edinburgh: T&T Clark, 1977.

———. *A Critical and Exegetical Commentary on the Epistle to the Romans. Commentary on Romans IX–XVI.* ICC. Edinburgh: T&T Clark, 1981.

Davies, William D., and Dale C. Allison. *A Critical and Exegetical Commentary on the Gospel according to Saint Matthew.* ICC, 3 vols. Edinburgh: T&T Clark, 1988.

————. *A Critical and Exegetical Commentary on the Gospel according to Saint Matthew. Commentary on Matthew VIII–XVIII.* ICC. Edinburgh: T&T Clark, 1991.

————. *A Critical and Exegetical Commentary on the Gospel according to Saint Matthew. Commentary on Matthew XIX–XXVIII.* ICC. Edinburgh: T&T Clark, 1997.

Eckey, Wilfried. *Die Apostelgeschichte. Der Weg des Evangeliums von Jerusalem nach Rom I (1,1–15,35).* Neukirchen-Vluyn: Neukirchener, 2000.

————. *Die Apostelgeschichte. Der Weg des Evangeliums von Jerusalem nach Rom II (15,36–28,31).* Neukirchen-Vluyn: Neukirchener, 2000.

Friedrich, Gerhard. "Der Brief an die Philipper." In *Die Briefe an die Galater, Epheser, Philipper, Kolosser, Thessalonicher und Philemon*, edited by G. Friedrich, H. Conzelmann, and J. Becker. NTD 8,15; 15th rev. and enl. ed. Göttingen: Vandenhoeck & Ruprecht, 1981.

Furnish, Victor Paul. *II Corinthians.* Translated with introduction, notes, and commentary. AB 32A. Garden City, N.Y.: Doubleday, 1984.

Gnilka, Joachim. *Der Philipperbrief.* hTkNT 10. Freiburg: Herder, 1980.

————. *Das Evangelium nach Markus (Mk 8,27–16,20).* EKK II/2, 4. Aufl. Neukirchen-Vluyn: Neukirchener, 1994.

————. *Das Evangelium nach Markus (Mk 1–8,26).* EKK II/1, 5. Aufl. Neukirchen-Vluyn: Neukirchener, 1998.

Gould, Ezra P. *A Critical and Exegetical Commentary on the Gospel according to St. Mark.* ICC, reimpr. of the 1. impr. Edinburgh: T&T Clark, 1969.

Gräßer, Erich. *An die Hebräer (Hebr 1–6).* EKK XVII/1. Neukirchen-Vluyn: Neukirchener, 1990.

————. *An die Hebräer (Hebr 7,1–10,18).* EKK XVII/2. Neukirchen-Vluyn: Neukirchener, 1993.

————. *An die Hebräer (Hebr 10,19–13,25).* EKK XVII/3. Neukirchen-Vluyn: Neukirchener, 1997.

Haenchen, Ernst. *Die Apostelgeschichte.* KEK 3, 12th rev. ed. Göttingen: Vandenhoeck & Ruprecht, 1959.

Hays, Richard B. *Interpretation: A Bible Commentary for Teaching and Preaching.* Louisville, Ky.: Westminster John Knox, 1997.

Holtz, Traugott. *Der erste Brief an die Thessalonicher.* EKK XIII. Neukirchen-Vluyn: Neukirchener, 1986.

Jervell, Jacob. *Die Apostelgeschichte.* KEK 3, 17th ed., 1st rev. ed. Göttingen: Vandenhoeck & Ruprecht, 1998.

Käsemann, Ernst. *An die Römer.* HNT 3a; 3rd rev. ed. Tübingen: Mohr, 1974.

Kessler, Hans H. *Sucht den Lebenden nicht bei den Toten. Die Auferstehung Jesu Christi in biblischer, fundamentaltheologischer und systematischer Sicht.* Topos plus Taschenbücher 419. Würzburg: Echter Verlag, 2002.

————. *Wie Auferstehung der Toten denken?* ZNT 19 (2007): 50–56.

Klauck, Hans-Josef. *Der Erste Johannesbrief.* EKK XXIII/1. Neukirchen-Vluyn: Neukirchener, 1991.

————. *Der Zweite und Dritte Johannesbrief.* EKK XXIII/2. Neukirchen-Vluyn: Neukirchener, 1992.

Kremer, Jakob. *Lukasevangelium.* Neue Echter Bibel 3. Würzburg: Echter Verlag, 1988.

————. *Der Erste Brief an die Korinther.* RNT. Regensburg: Pustet, 1997.

Lang, Friedrich. *Die Briefe an die Korinther.* NTD 7. Göttingen: Vandenhoeck & Ruprecht, 1986.

Lindemann, Andreas. *Der Kolosserbrief.* ZBk 10. Zürich: Theologischer Verlag, 1983.

Lohmeyer, Ernst. *Der Brief an die Philipper, and die Kolosser und an Philemon.* KEK 9, 13th ed. Göttingen: Vandenhoeck & Ruprecht, 1964.

Lohse, Eduard. *Die Offenbarung des Johannes.* NTD 11. Göttingen, 1979.

Luz, Ulrich. *Das Evangelium nach Matthäus (Mt 8-17).* EKK I/2. Neukirchen-Vluyn: Neukirchener, 1990.

————. *Das Evangelium nach Matthäus (Mt 18-25).* EKK I/3. Neukirchen-Vluyn: Neukirchener, 1997.

————. *Das Evangelium nach Matthäus (Mt 1-7).* EKK I/1. Neukirchen-Vluyn: Neukirchener, 2002.

————. *Das Evangelium nach Matthäus (Mt 26-28).* EKK I/4. Neukirchen-Vluyn: Neukirchener, 2002.

Malina, Bruce, and John Pilch. *Social-Science Commentary on the Book of Revelation.* Minneapolis: Fortress, 2000.

Marcus, Joel. *Mark 1–8. A New Translation with Introduction and Commentary.* AncB 27. New Haven, Conn.: Yale University Press, 2002.

Marxsen, Willi. *Der Evangelist Markus. Studien zur Redaktionsgeschichte des Evangeliums.* FRLANT 67, 2nd ed. Göttingen: Vandenhoeck & Ruprecht, 1959.

————. *Der erste Brief an die Thessalonicher.* ZBK.NT 11.1. Zürich: Theologischer Verlag Zürich, 1979.

Michel, Otto. *Der Brief an die Römer.* KEK 4; 14th ed.; 5th rev. ed. Göttingen: Vandenhoeck & Ruprecht, 1978.

Paulsen, Henning. *Der zweite Petrusbrief und der Judasbrief.* KEK 12.2. Göttingen: Vandenhoeck & Ruprecht, 1992.

Pesch, Rudolf. *Die Apostelgeschichte (1–12).* EKK V/1. Neukirchen-Vluyn: Neukirchener, 1986.

————. *Die Apostelgeschichte (13–28).* EKK V/2. Neukirchen-Vluyn: Neukirchener, 1986.

Reinmuth, Eckart. "Der zweite Brief an die Thessalonicher." In Walter, Reinmuth, and Lampe, *Die Briefe an die Philipper, Thessalonicher und an Philemon,* 158–202.

Roloff, Jürgen. *Der erste Brief an Timotheus.* EKK XV. Neukirchen-Vluyn: Neukirchener, 1988.

Schmithals, Walter. *Der Römerbrief. Ein Kommentar.* Gütersloh: Gütersloher Verlagshaus, 1988.

Schnackenburg, Rudolf. *Der Brief an die Epheser.* EKK X. Neukirchen-Vluyn: Neukirchener, 1982.

Schrage, Wolfgang. *Der erste Brief an die Korinther (1Kor 1,1–6,11).* EKK VII/1. Neukirchen-Vluyn: Neukirchener, 1991.

―――. *Der erste Brief an die Korinther (1Kor 6,12–11,16).* EKK VII/2. Neukirchen-Vluyn: Neukirchener, 1995.

―――. *Der erste Brief an die Korinther (1Kor 11,17–14,40).* EKK VII/3. Neukirchen-Vluyn: Neukirchener, 1999.

―――. *Der erste Brief an die Korinther (1Kor 15,1–16,24).* EKK VII/4. Neukirchen-Vluyn: Neukirchener, 2001.

Schweizer, Eduard. *Das Evangelium nach Lukas.* NTD 3, 18th ed., 1st rev. ed. Göttingen: Vandenhoeck & Ruprecht, 1982.

―――. *Der Brief an die Kolosser.* EKK XII; 3rd rev. ed. Neukirchen-Vluyn: Neukirchener, 1989.

Sellin, Gerhard. *Der Brief an die Epheser.* KEK 9. Göttingen: Vandenhoeck & Ruprecht, 2008.

Stuhlmacher, Peter. *Der Brief an Philemon.* EKK XVIII, 2., durchges. und verb. Aufl. Neukirchen-Vluyn: Neukirchener, 1981.

―――. *Der Brief an die Römer.* NTD 6.; 15th ed.; 2nd rev. ed. Göttingen: Vandenhoeck & Ruprecht, 1998.

Thrall, Margaret E. *A Critical and Exegetical Commentary on the Second Epistle to the Corinthians. Introduction and Commentary on II Corinthians I–VII.* ICC. Edinburgh: T&T Clark, 1994.

―――. *A Critical and Exegetical Commentary on the Second Epistle to the Corinthians. Commentary on II Corinthians VIII–XIII.* ICC. Edinburgh: T&T Clark, 2004.

Thyen, Hartwig. *Das Johannesevangelium.* HNT 6. Tübingen: Mohr, 2005.

Trilling, Wolfgang. *Der zweite Brief an die Thessalonicher.* EKK XIV. Neukirchen-Vluyn: Neukirchener, 1980.

Vögtle, Anton. *Der Judasbrief. Der zweite Petrusbrief.* EKK XXII. Neukirchen-Vluyn: Neukirchener, 1994.

Vouga, François. *Die Johannesbriefe.* HNT 15:3. Tübingen: Mohr, 1990.

―――. *An die Galater.* HNT 10. Tübingen: Mohr, 1998.

Walter, Nikolaus, Eckart Reinmuth, and Peter Lampe, eds. *Die Briefe an die Philipper, Thessalonicher und an Philemon.* NTD 8/2; 18th ed.; 1st rev. ed. Göttingen: Vandenhoeck & Ruprecht, 1998.

Weiser, Alfons. *Der zweite Brief an Timotheus.* EKK XVI/1. Neukirchen-Vluyn: Neukirchener, 2003.

Weiß, Hans-Friedrich. *Der Brief an die Hebräer.* KEK 13; 15th ed.; 1st rev. ed. Göttingen: Vandenhoeck & Ruprecht, 1991.

Wilckens, Ulrich. *Der Brief an die Römer (Röm 6–11)*. EKK VI/2. Neukirchen-Vluyn: Neukirchener, 1980.

———. *Der Brief an die Römer (Röm 12–16)*. EKK VI/3. Neukirchen-Vluyn: Neukirchener, 1982.

———. *Der Brief an die Römer (Röm 1–5)*. EKK VI/1; 2nd rev. ed. Neukirchen-Vluyn: Neukirchener, 1987.

Windisch, Hans. *Der zweite Korintherbrief.* Göttingen: Vandenhoeck & Ruprecht, 1970.

Wolff, Christian. *Der zweite Brief des Paulus an die Korinther.* ThkNT 8. Berlin: Evangelische Verlagsanstalt, 1989.

Zeller, Dieter. *Der Brief an die Römer.* Regensburger NT. Regensburg: Pustet, 1985.

Monographs and Articles

Adam, Jens. "Das leere Grab als Unterpfand der Auferstehung Jesu Christi." In *Die Wirklichkeit der Auferstehung*, edited by Hans-Joachim Eckstein and Michael Welcker, 59–75. Neukirchen-Vluyn: Neukirchener, 2004.

Aichele, George. *Sign, Text, Scripture. Semiotics and the Bible.* Interventions 1. Sheffield: Sheffield Academic, 1997.

Aland, Kurt. "Der wiedergefundene Markusschluss? Eine methodologische Bemerkung zur textkritischen Arbeit." *ZTK* 67 (1970): 3–13.

———. "Der Schluss des Markusevangeliums."In *Neutestamentliche Entwürfe*, edited by Kurt Aland, 246–83. TB 63. München: Kaiser, 1979.

Albert-Zerlik. *Liturgie als Sterbebegleitung und Trauerhilfe. Spätmittelalterliches Erbe und pastorale Gegenwart unter besonderer Berücksichtigung der Ordines von Castellani (1523) und Sanctorius (1602).* Pietas Liturgica 13. Tübingen: Francke, 2003.

Alkier, Stefan. *Wunder und Wirklichkeit in den Briefen des Apostel Paulus: Ein Beitrag zu einem Wunderverständnis jenseits von Entmythologisierung und Rehistorisierung.* WUNT 134. Tübingen: Mohr, 2001.

———. "Ethik der Interpretation." In *Der eine Gott und die Welt der Religionen. Beiträge zu einer Theologie der Religionen und zum interreligiösen Dialog*, edited by Markus Witte, 21–41. Würzburg: Religion & Kultur, 2003.

———. "Semiotik—III. Bibelwissenschaftlich." *RGG* 7 (2004): 4. Aufl, 1194f.

———. "Zeichen der Erinnerung—Die Genealogie in Mt 1 als intertextuelle Disposition." In *Bekenntnis und Erinnerung*, edited by Klaus-Michael Bull and Eckart Reinmuth, 108–28. RTS 16. Münster: Lit, 2004.

———. "Die Bibel im Dialog der Schriften und das Problem der Verstockung in Mk 4. Intertextualität im Rahmen einer kategorialen Semiotik biblischer Texte." In *Die Bibel im Dialog der Schriften. Konzepte intertextueller Bibellektüre*, edited by Stefan Alkier, Richard B. Hays, et al., 1–22. NET 10. Tübingen: Francke, 2005.

———. "From Text to Intertext: Intertextuality as a Paradigm for Reading Matthew." *HTS* 61, nos. 1–2 (2005): 1–18.

————. "Neutestamentliche Wissenschaft—Ein semiotisches Konzept." In *Kontexte der Schrift II. Kultur, Politik, Religion, Sprache*, edited by Christian Strecker, 343–60. Stuttgart: Kohlhammer, 2005.

————. "Implicit Epistemology in the Letters of Paul. Story, Experience and the Spirit." WUNT II 205, Tübingen: Mohr-Siebeck, 2006. *ThLZ* 5 (2007): 945–46.

————. "Himmel und Hölle. Zur Kontextualität und Referenz gleichnishafter Rede unter besonderer Berücksichtigung des Gleichnisses vom Fischnetz (Mk 13,47-50)." In *Unter der Mitarb. v. Gabi Kern, Hermeneutik der Gleichnisse Jesu. Methodische Neuansätze zum Verstehen urchristlicher Parabeltexte*, edited by Ruben Zimmermann, 588–603. WUNT 231. Tübingen: Mohr, 2008.

————. "Leben in qualifizierter Zeit: Die präsentische Eschatologie des Evangeliums vom römischen Novum Saeculum und die apokalyptische Eschatologie des Evangeliums vom auferweckten Gekreuzigten." *ZNT* 22 (2008): Themenheft Apokalypse, 20–34.

————. "Intertextuality and the Semiotics of Biblical Texts." In *Reading the Bible Intertextually*, edited by R. B. Hays, S. Alkier, and L. A. Huizenga, 3–22. Waco, Tex.: Baylor University Press, 2009.

————. "Witness or Warrior. How the Book of Revelation Helps Christians Live Their Political Lives. In *Revelation and the Politics of Apocalyptic Interpretation*, edited by R. B. Hays and S. Alkier, 125–41. Waco, Tex.: Baylor University Press, 2012.

Alkier, Stefan and Ralph Brucker, eds. *Exegese und Methodendiskussion*. TANZ 23. Tübingen: Francke, 1998.

Alkier, Stefan, Hermann Deuser, and Gesche Linde, eds. *Religiöser Fundamentalismus. Analysen und Kritiken*. Tübingen: Francke, 2005.

Alkier, Stefan, and Stefanie Karweick. "'So hab' ich Jesus ja noch nie erlebt!' Die sogenannte 'Tempelreinigung' in der sechsten Klasse einer Realschule." In *"Man hat immer ein Stück Gott in sich." Mit Kindern biblische Geschichten deuten*. Jahrbuch für Kindertheologie Sonderband, vol. 2, edited by Gerhard Büttner, 150–67. Stuttgart: Calwer, 2006.

Allison, Dale C. "An Opened Tomb and a Missing Body." In Allison, *Resurrecting Jesus*, 299–337.

————. *Resurrecting Jesus: The Earliest Christian Tradition and Its Interpreters*. New York: T&T Clark, 2005.

Aristotle. *Kategorien*. Aristoteles Werke in deutscher Übersetzung 1/I. Berlin: Akademie Verlag, 1984.

Arnold, Clinton E. *Ephesians. Power and Magic: The Concept of Power in Ephesians in Light of Its Historical Setting*. SNTSMS 63. Cambridge: Cambridge University Press, 1989.

Avemarie, Friedrich and Hermann Lichtenberger, eds. *Auferstehung—Resurrection: The Fourth Durham–Tübingen Research Symposium: Resurrection, Transfiguration and Exaltation in Old Testament, Ancient Judaism and Early*

Christianity (Tübingen, September 1999). WUNT 135. Tübingen: Mohr, 2001.

Becker, Eve-Marie. *Das Markus-Evangelium im Rahmen antiker Historiographie.* WUNT 194. Tübingen: Mohr, 2006.

Becker, Jürgen. *Auferstehung der Toten im Urchristentum.* SBS 82. Stuttgart: Katholisches Bibelwerk, 1976.

———. *Paulus. Der Apostel der Völker.* Stuttgart: UTB, 1989.

———. "Die Erwählung der Völker durch das Evangelium. Theologiegeschichtliche Erwägungen zum 1Thess." In *Annäherungen zur Urchristlichen Theologiegeschichte und zum Umfang mit ihren Quellen*, edited by Ulrich Mell, 81–102. BZNW 76. Berlin: de Gruyter, 1995.

———. *Johanneisches Christentum. Seine Geschichte und Theologie im Überblick.* Tübingen: Mohr-Siebeck, 2004.

———. *Die Auferstehung Jesu Christi nach dem Neuen Testament. Ostererfahrung und Osterverständnis im Urchristentum.* Tübingen: Mohr, 2007.

Bestattung. Agende für die Union Evanelischer Kirchen in der EKD 5. Edited by Kirchenkanzlei der EKU. Bielefeld: Luther Verlag, 2004.

Betz, Hans Dieter. *Der Apostel Paulus und die sokratische Tradition. Eine exegetische Untersuchung zu seiner "Apologie" 2. Korinther 10–13.* BhT 45. Tübingen: Mohr, 1972.

Böcher, Otto. *Die Johannesapokalypse.* EdF 41, 2nd rev. ed. Darmstadt: Wissenschaftliche Buchgesellschaft, 1975.

———. "Chiliasmus I." *TRE* 7 (1981): 723–29.

———. "Johannesapokalypse." *RAC* 19 (2001): 595–646.

Böttrich, Christfried. "Proexistenz im Leben und Sterben. Jesu Tod bei Lukas." In Frey and Schröter, *Deutungen des Todes Jesu im Neuen Testament*, 413–36.

Boyarin, Daniel. *A Radical Jew: Paul and the Politics of Identity.* Berkeley: University of California Press, 1994.

Brockhaus, Ulrich. *Charisma und Amt. Die paulinische Charismenlehre auf dem Hintergrund der frühchristlichen Gemeindefunktionen.* Wuppertal: Brockhaus, 1987.

Broer, Ingo. *Einleitung in das Neue Testament 2. Die Briefliteratur, die Offenbarung des Johannes und die Bildung des Kanons.* NEchtB; 2 vols. Würzburg: Echter Verlag, 2001.

Brucker, Ralph. *"Christushymnen" oder "epideiktische Passagen"? Studien zum Stilwechsel im Neuen Testament und seiner Umwelt.* FRLANT 176. Göttingen: Vandenhoeck & Ruprecht, 1997.

Bühler, Pierre. "Kreuzestheologie und die Frage nach dem Kanon. Einige hermeneutische Thesen—im Gespräch mit Francois Vouga." In Dettwiler and Zumstein, *Kreuzestheologie im Neuen Testament*, 327–32.

Bultmann, Rudolf. *Theologie des Neuen Testaments.* 9th ed.; rev. and enl. by O. Merk. Tübingen: Mohr, 1984.

Burkett, Delbert. *The Son of Man Debate. A History and Evaluation.* SNTSMS 105. Cambridge: Cambridge University Press, 1999.

Campenhausen, Hans von. *Der Ablauf der Osterereignisse und das leere Grab.* SHAW.PH 4/1952. Heidelberg: Winter, 1977.

Carter, Warren. *Matthew and Empire. Initial Explorations.* Harrisburg, Pa.: Trinity Press, 2001.

Cavallin, Hans C. "Leben nach dem Tode im Spätjudentum und frühen Christentum." *ANRW II* 19, no. 1 (1979): 240–345.

Chester, Andrew. "Resurrection and Transformation." In Avemarie and Lichtenberger, *Auferstehung/Resurrection,* 44–77.

Crossan, John Dominic. *Der historische Jesus.* Translated by P. Hahlbrock. München: Beck, 1995.

Cullmann, Oscar. *Unsterblichkeit der Seele oder Auferstehung der Toten? Antwort des Neuen Testaments.* Stuttgart: Kreuz, 1969.

Dalferth, Ingolf U. *Der Auferweckte Gekreuzigte. Zur Grammatik der Christologie.* Tübingen: Mohr, 1994.

———, ed. *The Presence and Absence of God.* Claremont Studies in the Philosophy of Religion, Conference 2008. Religion in Philosophy and Theology 42. Tübingen: Mohr, 2009.

Delorme, Jean, ed. *Zeichen und Gleichnisse. Evangelientext und semiotische Forschung.* Düsseldorf: Patmos, 1979.

Dettwiler, Andreas, and Jean Zumstein, eds. *Kreuzestheologie im Neuen Testament.* WUNT 151. Tübingen: Mohr, 2002.

Deuser, Hermann. "Einleitung: American Philosophy." In Deuser, *Gottesinstinkt,* 1–18.

———. *Gott: Geist und Natur.* Berlin: de Gruyter, 1998.

———. *Gottesinstinkt. Semiotische Religionstheorie und Pragmatismus.* Religion in Philosophy and Theology 12. Tübingen: Mohr, 2004.

———. "Kategoriale Semiotik und Pragmatismus." In Deuser, *Gottesinstinkt,* 20–37.

———. "Die phänomenologischen Grundlagen der Trinität." In Deuser, *Gottesinstinkt,* 38–54.

———. "Semiotik—VII. Ethisch." *RGG* 7 (2004): 4. Aufl., 1196f.

———. "Religion und Evolution." In *Gegenwart des lebendigen Christus,* edited by Günter Thomas and Andreas Schüle, 271–94. Leipzig: Evangelische Verlagsanstalt, 2007.

Dronsch, Kristina. *Bedeutung als Grundbegriff Neutestamentlicher Wissenschaft. Texttheoretische und semiotische Entwürfe zur Kritik der Semantik dargelegt anhand einer Analyse zu avkou,w in Mk 4, Dissertationsschrift.* Frankfurt, 2006.

———. "Text-Ma(h)le. Die skripturale Funktion des Abendmahls in Mk 14." In *Eine gewöhnliche und harmlose Speise? Von den Entwicklungen frühchristlicher Abendmahlstraditionen,* edited by Angelika Standhartinger, 157–79. Gütersloh: Gütersloher Verlagshaus, 2008.

———. *Bedeutung als Grundbegriff neutestamentlicher Wissenschaft. Texttheoretische und semiotische Entwürfe zur Kritik der Semantik dargelegt anhand einer Analyse zu* ἀκούω in Mk 4. NET 15. Tübingen: Francke, 2010.

Dunn, James D. G. "The New Perspective on Paul." *BJRL* 65 (1983): 95–122.

Ebner, Martin and Stefan Schreiber, eds. *Einleitung in das Neue Testament.* KSt-BTH 6. Stuttgart: Kohlhammer, 2008.

Eckstein, Hans-Joachim. "Denn Gottes Zorn wird vom Himmel her offenbar werden. Exegetische Erwägungen zu Röm 1,18." *ZNW* 78 (1987): 74–89.

Eckstein, Hans-Joachim, and Michael Welker, eds. *Die Wirklichkeit der Auferstehung, 2. Aufl.* Neukirchen-Vluyn: Neukirchener, 2004.

Eco, Umberto. *Lector in fabula. Die Mitarbeit der Interpretation in erzählenden Texten.* Translated by H. G. Held. München: Hanser, 1987.

———. *Semiotik. Entwurf einer Theorie der Zeichen.* Supplemente 5. München: Fink, 1987.

Ego, Beate. "Abraham als Urbild der Treue Israels. Traditionsgeschichtliche Überlegungen zu einem Aspekt des biblischen Abrahambildes." In *Bund und Tora. Zur theologischen Begriffsgeschichte in alttestamentlicher, frühjüdischer und urchristlicher Tradition*, edited by Friedrich Avemarie and Hermann Lichtenberger, 25–40. WUNT 98. Tübingen: Mohr, 1996.

Eisen, Ute E. *Die Poetik der Apostelgeschichte. Eine narratologische Studie.* NTOA/SUNT 58. Göttingen: Vandenhoeck & Ruprecht, 2006.

Engberg-Pedersen, Troels. "A Stoic Understanding of *Pneuma* in Paul." In *Philosophy at the Roots of Christianity*, edited by Troels Engberg-Pedersen and Henrik Tronier, 101–23. Biblical Studies Section. Copenhagen: University of Copenhagen, Faculty of Theology, 2006.

Essen, Georg. *Historische Vernunft und Auferweckung Jesu. Theologie und Historik im Streit um den Begriff geschichtlicher Wirklichkeit.* TSTP 9. Mainz: Matthias-Grünewald, 1995.

Feldmeier, Reinhard. *Die Christen als Fremde. Die Metapher der Fremde der antiken Welt, im Urchristentum und im 1. Petrusbrief.* WUNT 64. Tübingen: Mohr, 1992.

Fisch, Max H. "Peirce's General Theory of Signs." In *Peirce, Semeiotic and Pragmatism*, edited by Max H. Fisch, Kenneth Laine Ketner, and Christian J. W. Kloesel, 322–26. Bloomington: Indiana University Press, 1986.

Frenschkowski, Marco. "Die Johannesoffenbarung zwischen Vision, astralmythologischer Imagination und Literatur." In Horn, *Studien zur Johannesoffenbarung*, 20–45.

Frey, Jörg. "Erwägungen zum Verhältnis der Johannesapokalypse zu den übrigen Schriften des Corpus Johanneum." In *Die johanneische Frage. Ein Lösungsversuch, mit einem Beitrag zur Apokalypse von Jörg Frey*, edited by Martin Hengel, 326–429. WUNT 67. Tübingen: Mohr, 1993.

———. *Die johanneische Eschatologie II. Das johanneische Zeitverständnis.* WUNT 110. Tübingen: Mohr, 1998.

———. *Die eschatologische Verkündigung in den johanneischen Texten.* WUNT 117. Tübingen, 2000.

————. "Das Judentum des Paulus." In *Paulus. Leben—Umwelt—Werk—Briefe*, edited by Oda Wischmeyer, 5–43. Tübingen: Mohr, 2006.

Frey, Jörg and Jens Schröter, eds. *Deutungen des Todes Jesu im Neuen Testament.* WUNT 181. Tübingen: Mohr, 2005.

Frickenschmidt, Dirk. "Empfänger unbekannt verzogen? Ergebnisse empirischer Glaubensforschung als Herausforderung für die neutestamentliche Hermeneutik." *ZNT* 4 (1999): 52–64.

Getta, Leonie, et al., eds. *Mitten ins Leben. Religion Band 1 (5./6. Schuljahr).* Berlin: Cornelsen, 2007.

Gignac, Alain. "Neue Wege der Auslegung. Die Paulus-Interpretation von Alain Badiou und Giorgio Agamben." *ZNT* 18 (2006): Themenheft "Apostelgeschichten," 15–25.

Guttenberger, Gudrun. "Ὤφθη. Der visuelle Gehalt der frühchristlichen Erscheinungstradition und mögliche Folgerungen für die Entstehung und Entwicklung des frühchristlichen Glaubens an die Auferstehung Jesu (Teil 1)." *BZ NF* 52, no. 1 (2008): 40–63.

Güttgemanns, Erhardt. *Der leidende Apostel und sein Herr. Studien zur paulinischen Christologie.* FRLANT 90. Göttingen, 1966.

————. *Offene Fragen zur Formgeschichte des Evangeliums. Eine methodologische Skizze der Grundlagenproblematik der Form- und Redaktionsgeschichte, 2. Aufl.* BEvTh 54. München: C. Kaiser, 1971.

————. *Studia linguistica neotestamentica. Gesammelte Aufsätze zur linguistischen Grundlage einer Neutestamentlichen Theologie, 2. Aufl.* München: C. Kaiser, 1971.

————. "'Text' und 'Geschichte' als Grundkategorien der Generativen Poetik. Thesen zur aktuellen Diskussion um die 'Wirklichkeit' der Auferstehungstexte." *LingBib* 11 (1972): 1–12.

————. "Einleitende Bemerkungen zur strukturalen Erzählforschung." *LingBib* 23/24 (1973): 2–47.

————. *Fragmenta semiotico-hermeneutica. Eine Texthermeneutik für den Umgang mit der Heiligen Schrift.* FThL 9. Bonn: Linguistica Biblica, 1983.

————. "Der Mythos als Ort des Paradigmenwechsels. Zur neueren Diskussion um den Mythos." *LingBib* 62 (1989): 49–96.

————. "Die Darstellung einer Theologie des Neuen Testaments als semiotisches Problem." *LingBib* 68 (1993): 5–94.

Häfner, Gerd. "Die Pastoralbriefe (1Tim/2Tim/Tit)." In Ebner and Schreiber, *Einleitung in das Neue Testament*, 450–73.

Hahn, Ferdinand. "Das Geistverständnis in der Johannesoffenbarung." In Horn, *Studien zur Johannesoffenbarung*, 3–9.

Halbfas, Hubertus. "Nach vorne gedacht. Wie soll der Religionsunterricht in einer nichtchristlichen Gesellschaft aussehen?" *RHS* 35 (1992): 372–77, cited from *Arbeitsbuch Religionsunterricht: Überblicke—Impulse—Beispiele*, edited by H. Lenhard, 23–26. Gütersloh: Gütersloher Verlagshaus Mohn, 1996.

Härle, Wilfried. "Die Wirklichkeit—Unser Konstrukt oder widerständige Realität." In *Theologie zwischen Pragmatismus und Existenzdenken*, edited by Gesche Linde, et al., 163–73. MTHS 90. Marburg: Elwert, 2006.

Harnack, Adolf von. *Geschichte der altchristlichen Literatur bis Eusebius II/1.* Leipzig, 1897.

Hays, Richard B. *The Faith of Jesus Christ. An Investigation of the Narrative Substructure of Galatians 3:1–4:11.* SBLDS 56. Chico, Calif.: Scholars Press, 1983.

———. *Echoes of Scripture in the Letters of Paul.* New Haven, Conn: Yale University Press, 1989.

———. "Reading Scripture in Light of the Resurrection." In *The Art of Reading Scripture*, edited by Ellen F. Davis and Richard B. Hays, 216–38. Grand Rapids: Eerdmans, 2003.

Hays, Richard B., Stefan Alkier, and Leroy A. Huizenga, *Reading the Bible Intertextually.* Waco, Tex.: Baylor University Press, 2009.

Heckel, Ulrich. *Kraft in Schwachheit. Untersuchungen zu 2 Kor 10–13.* WUNT 2/52. Tübingen: Mohr, 1993.

Heiligenthal, Roman. *Der verfälschte Jesus. Eine Kritik moderner Jesusbilder.* Darmstadt: Wissenschaftliche Buchgesellschaft, 1997.

Hieke, Thomas. *Habilitation, Die Genealogien der Genesis.* Herders biblische Studien 39. Freiburg: Herder, 2003.

———. "Neue Horizonte. Biblische Auslegung als Weg zu ungewöhnlichen Perspektiven." *ZNT* 12 (2003): Themenheft Kanon, 65–76.

Hieke, Thomas, and Tobias Nicklas. *"Die Worte der Prophetie dieses Buches." Offenbarung 22,6–21 als Schlussstein der christlichen Bibel Alten und Neuen Testaments gelesen.* BThS 62. Neukirchen-Vluyn: Neukirchener, 2003.

Hoffmann, Paul. *Die Toten in Christus. Eine religionsgeschichtliche und exegetische Untersuchung zur paulinischen Eschatologie.* NTA N.F. 2. Münster: Aschendorff, 1978.

Hofius, Otfried. "Der Gott allen Trostes. Paraklesis und parakalein in 2 Kor 1, 3–7." In *Paulusstudien*, edited by Otfried Hofius, 244–54. WUNT 51. Tübingen: Mohr, 1989.

———. *Der Christushymnus Philipper 2,6-11. Untersuchungen zu Gestalt und Aussage eines urchristlichen Psalms.* Tübingen: Mohr, 1991.

Holtz, Traugott. "Sprache als Metapher. Erwägungen zur Sprache der Johannesapokalypse." In Horn, *Studien zur Johannesoffenbarung*, 10–19.

Horn, Friedrich Wilhelm, ed. *Studien zur Johannesoffenbarung und ihrer Auslegung.* Neukirchen-Vluyn: Neukirchener, 2005.

Janowski, Bernd. *Sühne als Heilsgeschehen. Studien zur Sühnetheologie der Priesterschrift und zur Wurzel KPR im Alten Orient und im Alten Testament.* WMANT 55. Neukirchen-Vluyn: Neukirchener, 1982.

———. "Die Toten loben JHWH nicht. Psalm 88 und das alttestamentliche Todesverständnis." In Avemarie and Lichtenberger, *Auferstehung/Resurrection*, 3–45.

———. "Das Leben für andere hingeben. Alttestamentliche Voraussetzungen für die Deutung des Todes Jesu." In Frey and Schröter, *Deutungen des Todes Jesu im Neuen Testament*, 97–118.

Johanson, Bruce C. *To All the Brethren. A Text-Linguistic and Rhetorical Approach to I Thessalonians.* CB.NT 16. Stockholm: Almquist & Wiksell, 1987.

Johns, Loren L. *The Lamb Christology of the Apocalypse of John: An Investigation into Its Origins and Rhetorical Force.* WUNT II 167. Tübingen: Mohr, 2003.

Jörns, Klaus-Peter. *Notwendige Abschied. Auf dem Weg zu einem glaubwürdigen Christentum, 1. Aufl.* Gütersloh: Gütersloher Verlagshaus, 2004.

Kahl, Werner. *New Testament Miracle Stories in Their Religious-Historical Setting. A Religionsgeschichtliche Comparison from a Structural Perspective.* FRLANT 163. Göttingen: Vandenhoeck & Ruprecht, 1994.

————. "Zur Interpretation des Neuen Testaments im sozio-kulturellen Kontext Westafrikas." *ZNT* 5 (2000): Themenheft Interreligiöser Dialog, 27–35.

————. "Erhebliche matthäisch-lukanische *Übereinstimmungen* gegen das Markusevangelium der Triple-Tradition. Ein Beitrag zur Klärung der synoptischen Abhängigkeitsverhältnisse." *ZNW* 103 (2012): 20–46.

Kähler, Martin. *Der sogenannte historische Jesus und der geschichtliche, biblische Christus.* TB 2, 3rd vol. München: Kaiser, 1961.

Karrer, Martin. *Die Johannesoffenbarung als Brief. Studien zu ihrem literarischen, historischen und theologischen Ort.* FRLANT 140. Göttingen: Vandenhoeck & Ruprecht, 1986.

Käsemann, Ernst. *Die Legitimität des Apostels. Eine Untersuchung zu 2. Korinther 10–13.* Libelli 33. Darmstadt: Wissenschaftliche Buchgesellschaft, 1956.

————. *Paulinische Persepktiven.* Tübingen: Mohr, 1969.

————. "Kritische Analyse von Phil 2:5-11." In *Exegetische Versuche und Besinnungen I*, 6th ed., vol. 1; 3rd ed., vol. 2, edited by Ernst Käsemann, 51–95. Göttingen: Vandenhoeck & Ruprecht, 1970.

————. *Jesu letzter Wille nach Johannes 17, 4.* Auflage. Tübingen: Mohr, 1980.

Konradt, Matthias. "Der Jakobusbrief." In Ebner and Schreiber, *Einleitung in das Neue Testament*, 496–510.

Kraus, Wolfgang. "Der Tod als Sühnetod bei Paulus. Überlegungen zur neueren Diskussion." *ZNT* 3 (1999): 20–30.

Kremer, Jakob. *Lukasevangelium.* Neue Echter Bibel 3. Würzburg: Echter Verlag, 1988.

————. "Art. ἀνάστασιξ, κτλ." In *EWNT I, 2., verb. Auflage.*, edited by Horst Balz and Gerhard Schneider, 210–21. Stuttgart: Francke, 1992.

————. "Art. ἐγείρω." In *EWNT I, 2.*

Kübler-Ross, Elisabeth. *On Children and Death: How Children and Their Parents Can and Do Cope with Death.* New York: Touchstone, 1997.

Laato, Timo. *Paul and Judaism: An Anthropological Approach.* Atlanta: Scholars Press, 1995.

Lampe, Peter. "Die urchristliche Rede von der 'Neuschöpfung des Menschen' im Lichte konstruktivistischer Wissenssoziologie." In Alkier and Brucker *Exegese und Methodendiskussion*, 21–32. TANZ 23.

———. *Die Wirklichkeit als Bild. Das Neue Testament als ein Grunddokument abendländischer Kultur im Lichte konstruktivistischer Epistemologie und Wissenssoziologie.* Neukirchen-Vluyn: Neukirchener, 2006.

Linde, Gesche. *Zeichen und Gewissheit. Semiotische Entfaltung eines protestantisch-theologischen Begriffs.* Religion in Philosophy and Theology. Tübingen: Mohr, forthcoming.

Lindemann, Andreas. "Zum Abfassungszweck des zweiten Thessalonicherbriefes." *ZNW* 68 (1977): 35–47.

———. "Die Gemeinde von 'Kolossä.' Erwägungen zum 'Sitz im Leben' eines pseudopaulinischen Briefes." *WD* 16 (1981): 111–34.

———. *Auferstehung—unsere Hoffnung.* Kleine Schriften aus dem Reformierten Bund 8. Wuppertal: Foedus, 1997.

Link, Christian. *Schöpfung. Schöpfungstheologie angesichts der Herausforderungen des 20. Jahrhunderts.* HST 7/2. Gütersloh: Gütersloher Verlagshaus Mohn, 1991.

———. *Schöpfung. Schöpfungstheologie in reformatorischer Tradition.* HST 7/1. Gütersloh: Gütersloher Verlagshaus, 1991.

Linnemann, Eta. "Der (wiedergefundene) Markusschluss." *ZTK* 66 (1969): 255–87.

Lips, Hermann von. *Weisheitliche Traditionen im Neuen Testament.* WMANT 64. Neukirchen-Vluyn: Neukirchener, 1990.

Liszka, James Jakób. *A General Introduction to the Semeiotic of Charles Sanders Peirce.* Bloomington: Indiana University Press, 1996.

Lohmeyer, Ernst. *Kyrios Jesus. Eine Untersuchung zu Phil 2,5–11.* Darmstadt: Wissenschaftliche Buchgesellschaft, 1961.

Luck, Ulrich. "Die Bekehrung des Paulus und das paulinische Evangelium. Zur Frage der Evidenz in Botschaft und Theologie des Apostels." *ZNW* 76 (1985): 187–208.

Lyotard, Jean-François. *La condition postmoderne. Rapport sur le savoir.* Paris: Éditions de Minuit, 1979.

———. *Das postmoderne Wissen. Ein Bericht, Theatro Machinarum ¾.* Bremen: Passagen Verlag, 1982.

———. *The Postmodern Condition: A Report on Knowledge.* Minneapolis: University of Minnesota Press, 1984.

Mädler, I. "Transfigurationen. Materielle Kultur in praktisch-theologischer Perspektive." *THLZ* 132, no. 9 (2007): 368–70.

Marin, Louis. *Semiotik der Passionsgeschichte. Die Zeichensprache der Ortsangaben und Personennamen.* BeTh 70. München: Kaiser, 1976.

Martin, Dale B. *The Corinthian Body.* New Haven, Conn.: Yale University Press, 1995.

Marty, Martin E., and R. Scott Appleby, eds. *The Fundamentalism Project.* 5 vols. Chicago: University of Chicago Press, 1991–1995.

Meeks, Wayne A. "The Man from Heaven in Paul's Letter to the Philippians."

In *The Future of Early Christianity*, edited by B. A. Pearson et al., 329–36. Minneapolis: Fortress, 1991.

Merz, Annette. *Die fiktive Selbstauslegung des Paulus. Intertextuelle Studien zur Intention und Rezeption der Pastoralbriefe.* NTOA 52. Göttingen: Vandenhoeck & Ruprecht, 2003.

Meyer, Heinrich August Wilhelm, and Georg Heinrici. *Kritisch exegetisches Handbuch über den zweiten Brief an die Korinther.* KEK 6. Göttingen: Vandenhoeck & Ruprecht, 1883.

Mitchell, Margaret M. *Paul and the Rhetoric of Reconciliation. An Exegetical Investigation of the Language and Composition of 1 Corinthians.* HUTh 28. Tübingen: Mohr, 1991.

Mittelstaedt, Alexander. *Lukas als Historiker. Zur Datierung des lukanischen Doppelwerkes.* TANZ 43. Tübingen: Francke, 2006.

Moffitt, David M. "Affirming the 'Creed': The Extent of an Early Christian Formula in 1 Cor 15,3b-7." *ZNW* 99 (2008): 49–73.

———. *Atonement and the Logic of Resurrection in the Epistle to the Hebrews.* SNT 141. Leiden: Brill, 2011.

———. "Der Hebräerbrief im Kontext der neueren englischen Forschung. Ein kurzer Überblick über die wichtigsten Forschungsprobleme." *ZNT* 29 (2012): 2–13.

Moody, Raymond A. *Das Licht von drüben. Neue Fragen und Antworten.* Reinbek, 1989.

———. *Life After Life: The Investigation of Phenomenon—Survival of Bodily Death.* San Francisco: Harper, 2001.

Mußner, Fraunz. "Zur stilistischen und semantischen Struktur der Formel von 1Kor 15:3b-5." In *Die Kirche des Anfangs*, edited by R. Schnackenburg, 405–15. Freiburg: Herder, 1978.

Neville, Robert C. *Recovery of the Measure. Interpretation and Nature.* Axiology of Thinking 2. Albany: State University of New York Press, 1989.

Niebuhr, Karl-Wilhelm. *Heidenapostel aus Israel. Die jüdische Identität des Paulus nach ihrer Darstellung in seinen Briefen.* WUNT 62. Tübingen: Mohr, 1992.

Paulsen, Henning. *Überlieferung und Auslegung in Römer 8.* WMANT 43. Neukirchen-Vluyn: Neukirchener, 1974.

———. *Zur Literatur und Geschichte des frühen Christentums.* WUNT 99. Tübingen: Mohr, 1997.

Peirce, Charles Sanders. "Questions Concerning Certain Faculties Claimed for Man." *Journal of Speculative Philosophy* 2 (1868): 103–14.

———. *Phänomen und Logik der Zeichen.* Edited and translated by Helmut Pape. Frankfurt: Suhrkamp, 1983.

———. "Private Thoughts, Principally on the Conduct of Life" (Number 37, August 1860). In *Writings of Charles S. Peirce: A Chronological Edition, Volume 1, 1857–1866*, edited by Peirce Edition Project, 9. Bloomington: Indiana University Press, 1983.

————. "On a New List of Categories (1867), dt.: Eine neue Liste der Kategorien." In *Semiotische Schriften 1 (1865–1903)*, edited by Charles Sanders Peirce, 147–59. Frankfurt: Suhrkamp, 1986.

————. *Semiotische Schriften 2 (1903–1906)*. Translated by Leroy Huizenga. Frankfurt: Suhrkamp, 1990.

————. *The Essential Peirce. Selected Philosophical Writings Vol. 1 (1867–1893)*, edited by N. Houser and C. Kloesel. Bloomington: Indiana University Press, 1992.

————. *Semiotische Schriften 3 (1906–1913)*. Frankfurt: Suhrkamp, 1993.

————. "Private Gedanken zur Lebensführung." In Charles Sanders Peirce, *Religionsphilosophische Schriften*, übers., eingel., kommen. und hrsg. Hermann Deuser, 10–26. PhB 478. Hamburg: Meiner, 1995.

————. *The Essential Peirce. Selected Philosophical Writings Vol. 2 (1893–1913)*, edited by Peirce Edition Project. Bloomington: Indiana University Press, 1998.

Pezzoli-Olgiati, Daria. *Täuschung und Klarheit. Zur Wechselwirkung zwischen Vision und Geschichte in der Johannesoffenbarung*. FRLANT 175. Göttingen: Vandenhoeck & Ruprecht, 1997.

Pilhofer, Peter. *Philippi I*. WUNT 87. Tübingen: Mohr, 1995.

————. *Philippi II*. WUNT 119. Tübingen: Mohr, 2009.

Plümacher, Eckhard. *Lukas als hellenistischer Schriftsteller. Studien zur Apostelgeschichte*. SNT 9. Göttingen: Vandenhoeck & Ruprecht, 1972.

————. "Stichwort: Lukas, Historiker." *ZNT* 18 (2006): Themenheft Apostelgeschichte, 2–8.

Porter, Stanley. *The Paul of Acts. Essays in Literary Criticism, Rhetoric and Theology*. WUNT 115. Tübingen: Mohr, 1999.

Pöttner, Martin. *Realität als Kommunikation. Ansätze zur Beschreibung der Grammatik des paulinischen Sprechens in 1Kor 1,4–4,21 im Blick auf literarische Problematik und Situationsbezug des 1. Korintherbriefes*. Theologie 2. Münster: Lit, 1995.

Preuß, Horst Dietrich. "'Auferstehung' in Texten alttestamentlicher Apokalyptik (Jes 26,7-19, Dan 12,1-4)." In *"Linguistische" Theologie. Biblische Texte, christliche Verkündigung und theologische Sprachtheorie*, edited by Uwe Gerber and Erhardt Güttgemanns, 101–33. FThL 3. Bonn: Linguistica Biblica, 1972.

Reinmuth, Eckart. "Narratio und argumentatio—zur Auslegung der Jesus-Christus-Geschichte im Ersten Korintherbrief. Ein Beitrag zur mimetischen Kompetenz des Paulus." *ZTK* 92 (1995): 3–27.

————. "Historik und Exegese—zum Streit um die Auferstehung Jesu nach der Moderne." In Alkier and Brucker *Exegese und Methodendiskussion*, 1–20.

————. "Erzählen und Begreifen. Ein Beitrag zum neutestamentlichen Verständnis eines theologischen Missverständnisses." In *Die Gleichnisreden Jesu 1899–1999. Beiträge zum Dialog mit Adolf Jülicher*, edited by Ulrich Mell, 237–56. BZNW 103. Berlin: de Gruyter, 1999.

————. *Hermeneutik des Neuen Testaments. Eine Einführung in die Lektüre des Neuen Testaments.* UTB 2310. Göttingen: Vandenhoeck & Ruprecht, 2002.

————. *Neutestamentliche Historik. Probleme und Perspektiven.* TLZ.F 8. Leipzig: Evangelische Verlagsanstalt, 2003.

————. *Paulus. Gott neu denken.* BG 9. Leipzig: Evangelische Verlagsanstalt, 2004.

————. "Ostern—Ereignis und Erzählung. Die jüngste Diskussion und das Matthäusevangelium." *ZNT* 19 (2007): Themenheft Auferstehung, 3–14.

Roh, Tae-Seong. *Der zweite Thessanicherbrief als Erneuerung apokalyptischer Zeitdeutung.* NTOA 62. Göttingen: Vandenhoeck & Ruprecht, 2007.

Sanders, Ed Parish. *Paul and Palestinian Judaism.* Philadelphia: Fortress, 1977.

Schlund, Christine. "Deutungen des Todes Jesu im Rahmen der Pesach-Tradition." In Frey and Schröter, *Deutungen des Todes Jesu im Neuen Testament,* 397–411.

Schneemelcher, Wilhelm. *Neutestamentliche Apokryphen, I.* Evangelien, 6. Aufl. Tübingen: Mohr, 1990.

Schnelle, Udo. *Wandlungen im paulinischen Denken.* SBS 137. Stuttgart: Verlag Katholisches Bibelwerk, 1989.

————. *Einleitung in das Neue Testament.* UTB 1830. Göttingen: Mohr, 1999.

Schoberth, Ingrid. "Nicht bloß ein 'lieber Gott.' Die Verharmlosung der Gottesrede als Problem der Praktischen Theologie." *ZNT* 9 (2002): Themenheft "Gericht und Zorn Gottes," 60–66.

Schulz, Heiko. *Theorie des Glaubens.* RPTh 2. Tübingen: Mohr, 2001.

Schürmann, Heinz. "'Pro-Existenz' als christologischer Grundbegriff." In *Jesus—Gestalt und Geheimnis. Gesammelte Beiträge,* edited by Heinz Schürmann and K. Scholtissek, 286–315. Paderborn: Bonifatius, 1994.

Schwindt, Rainer. *Das Weltbild des Epheserbriefes. Eine religionsgeschichtlich-exegetische Studie.* WUNT 148. Tübingen: Mohr, 2002.

Scott, Ian W. *Implicit Epistemology in the Letters of Paul. Story, Experience and the Spirit.* WUNT 2. Reihe 105. Tübingen: Mohr, 2006.

Sellin, Gerhard. *Der Streit um die Auferstehung der Toten. Eine religionsgeschichtliche und exegetische Untersuchung von 1. Korinther 15.* FRLANT 138. Göttingen: Vandenhoeck & Ruprecht, 1986.

Smit, Joop. "The Letter of Paul to the Galatians: A Deliberative Speech." *NTS* 35 (1989): 1–26.

Spiegel, Yorick. *Der Prozeß des Trauerns. Analyse und Beratung.* München: Kaiser, 1989.

Stegemann, Hartmut. "'Die des Uria.'" In *Tradition und Glaube. Das frühe Christentum in seiner Umwelt,* edited by Gert Jeremias, 246–76. Göttingen: Vandenhoeck & Ruprecht, 1971.

Stemberger, Günter. "Das Problem der Auferstehung im Alten Testament." *Kairos* 14 (1972): 273–90.

————. *Der Leib der Auferstehung. Studien zur Anthropologie und Eschatologie des palästinensischen Judentums im neutestamentlichen Zeitalter Juedentums im neutestamentlichen Zeitalter (ca.170 v.Chr.–100n.Chr.)*. Rome: Pontificio Istituto Biblico, 1972.

Svenbro, Jesper. *Phrasikleia. Anthropologie de la lecture en Grèce ancienne*. Textes à l'appui 188. Paris: Éditions la Découverte, 1988.

Talbert, Charles H. *Literary Patterns, Theological Themes and the Genre of Luke–Acts*. SBL MS 20. Missoula, Mont.: Society of Biblical Literature, 1974.

Tannehill, Robert C. "The Disciples in Mark: The Function of a Narrative Role." *JR* 57 (1977): 386–405.

Theissen, Gerd. *Die Religion der ersten Christen. Eine Theorie des Urchristentums*. Gütersloh: Gütersloher Verlagshaus, 2001.

Theobald, Michael. "Der Epheserbrief." In Ebner and Schreiber, *Einleitung in das Neue Testament*, 408–24.

———. "Der Kolosserbrief." In Ebner and Schreiber, *Einleitung in das Neue Testament*, 425–39.

Thiede, Werner. "Sterben, Tod und Auferstehung als Themen für Kinder und Jugendliche." *PTh* 83 (1994): 210–28.

Ulland, Harald. *Die Vision als Radikalisierung der Wirklichkeit in der Apokalypse des Johannes*. TANZ 21. Tübingen: Francke, 1997.

Vanhoye, Albert. *La structure littéraire de l'épître aux Hébreux*. StudNeot 1. Paris: Desclée de Brouwer, 1963.

———. "Literarische Struktur und theologische Botschaft des Hebräerbriefs." *SNTSU* 4 (1979): 119–47.

———. "Hebräerbrief." *TRE* 14 (1985): 494–510.

Vouga, François. "Zur rhetorischen Gattung des Galaterbriefes." *ZNW* 79 (1988): 291–92.

———. "Crux probat omnia: Der oder ein Prüfstein der neutestamentlichen Hermeneutik? Dialog und Konsens mit Pierre Bühler." In Dettwiler and Zumstein, *Kreuzestheologie im Neuen Testament*, 333–39.

———. "Ist die Kreuzestheologie das hermeneutische Zentrum des Neuen Testaments?" In Dettwiler and Zumstein, *Kreuzestheologie im Neuen Testament*, 283–326.

Walter, Nikolaus. "Geschichte und Mythos in der urchristlichen Präexistenzchristologie." In *Praeparatio Evangelica. Studien zur Umwelt, Exegese und Hermeneutik des Neuen Testaments*, edited by Nikolaus Walter, 281–92. WUNT 98. Tübingen: Mohr, 2002.

Waschke, Ernst-Joachim. "Auferstehung I. Auferstehung der Toten 2. Altes Testament." *RGG* 1, no. 4. (1998): 915–16.

Wedderburn, Alexander J. M. "Paul and the Story of Jesus." In *Paul and Jesus*, edited by Alexander J. M. Wedderburn, 161–91. JSNT.S 37. Sheffield: JSOT Press, 1989.

Weiser, Alfons. "Freundschaftsbrief und Testament. Zur literarischen Gattung des Zweiten Briefes an Timotheus." In *Zeit-Geschichte und Begegnungen*, edited by Günther Riße, 158–70. Paderborn: Bonifatius, 1998.

Weiß, Wolfgang. "Aufbruch und Bewährung. Hebräerbrief und Apokalypse im Vergleich." In Horn, *Studien zur Johannesoffenbarung und ihrer Auslegung*, 248–62.

Welker, Michael. *Was geht vor beim Abendmahl?* 3rd ed. Gütersloh: Gütersloher Verlagshaus, 2005.

Wiefel, Wolfgang. "Die Hauptrichtung des Wandels im eschatologischen Denken des Paulus." *ThZ* 30 (1974): 65–84.

Wilckens, Ulrich. *Theologie des Neuen Testaments, Bd. ½: Jesu Tod und Auferstehung und die Entstehung der Kirche aus Juden und Heiden.* Neukirchen-Vluyn: Neukirchener, 2003.

Wischmeyer, Oda, ed. *Paulus. Leben, Umwelt, Werk, Briefe.* Tübingen: UTB, 2006.

Witherington, Ben, III. *Paul's Narrative Thought World: The Tapestry of Tragedy and Triumph.* Louisville, Ky.: Westminster John Knox, 1994.

Wolter, Michael. *Die Pastoralbreife als Paulustradition.* FRLANT 146. Göttingen: Vandenhoeck & Ruprecht, 1988.

Wrede, William. *Das Messiasgeheimnis in den Evangelien. Zugleich ein Beitrag zum Verständnis des Markusevangeliums.* 4th ed. Göttingen: Vandenhoeck & Ruprecht, 1969.

Wright, N. T. *The Resurrection of the Son of God, Christian Origins and the Question of God III.* London: Fortress, 2003.

Zeller, Dieter. "Religionsgeschichtliche Erwägungen zur Auferstehung." *ZNT* 19 (2007): Themenheft Auferstehung, 15–23.

Zimmermann, Ruben. *Christologie der Bilder im Johannesevangelium. Die Christopoetik des vierten Evangeliums unter besonderer Berücksichtigung von Joh 10.* WUNT 171. Tübingen: Mohr, 2004.

———. "Das Leben aus dem Tod. Vom sterbenden Weizenkorn—Joh 12,24." In *Kompendium der Gleichnisse Jesu*, edited by Ruben Zimmermann, 804–16. Gütersloh: Gütersloher Verlagshaus, 2007.

———. "The Narrative Hermeneutics of John 11. Learning with Lazarus How to Understand Death, Life, and Resurrection." In *The Resurrection of Jesus in the Gospel of John*, edited by Craig R. Koester and Reimund Bieringer, 75–101. WUNT 222. Tübingen: Mohr, 2008.

Zumstein, Jean. "Das Johannesevangelium: Eine Strategie des Glaubens." In *Kreative Erinnerung. Relecture und Auslegung im Johannesevangelium*, edited by Jean Zumstein, 31–45. Zürich: Pano, 1999.

———. "Die johanneische Ostergeschichte als Erzählung gelesen." *ZNT* 3 (1999): 11–19.

Scripture Index

Index of Names

Subject Index